Final Wicket

Dedicated to my extraordinary children without whom there would be no point

Luke, Emily and Rebecca
With all my love

Final Wicket

Test and First-Class Cricketers Killed in the Great War

Nigel McCrery

Pen & Sword
MILITARY

First published in Great Britain in 2015 by
Pen & Sword Military
An imprint of
Pen & Sword Books Ltd
47 Church Street
Barnsley
South Yorkshire
S70 2AS

ISBN 978 1 47382 714 1

Typeset in 10pt Dante by
Mac Style Ltd, Bridlington, East Yorkshire

Printed and bound in the UK by CPI Group (UK) Ltd, Croydon, CRO 4YY

Pen & Sword Books Ltd incorporates the imprints of Pen & Sword Archaeology, Atlas, Aviation, Battleground, Discovery, Family History, History, Maritime, Military, Naval, Politics, Railways, Select, Transport, True Crime, and Fiction, Frontline Books, Leo Cooper, Praetorian Press, Seaforth Publishing and Wharncliffe.

For a complete list of Pen & Sword titles please contact
PEN & SWORD BOOKS LIMITED
47 Church Street, Barnsley, South Yorkshire, S70 2AS, England
E-mail: enquiries@pen-and-sword.co.uk
Website: www.pen-and-sword.co.uk

Contents

Contents

Contents

1918

Contents

Although Second Lieutenant Frederick Bertram Key of the Royal Warwickshire Regiment was not a first-class cricketer, playing his cricket for Lichfield, he wrote the following lines to his parents before going into action on 1 July 1916 (First Day of the Battle of the Somme), where he was killed.

'If you receive this you will know that I have unfortunately been bowled out middle peg, but you may be sure that I batted well.'

Acknowledgments

The author wishes to thank the following for helping throughout the researching and writing of this book:

Mike Askham and **Wellingborough School** for their time and effort; **Trevor Bailey** and **Bill Hazley**, Northamptonshire CCC, for their time, trouble and expertise; **Jill Barlow**, Cheltenham College Archives; **Jamie Bell**, New Zealand Cricket Museum, for his time trouble and advice; **Richard Black**, London Medal Company, London, for his help, advice and loan of books and Cecilia; **Mat Blurton** and **Katie Noble**, who did an amazing job of putting this book together; **Charles Bradshaw**, Oratory School; **Brian Butchers** of Beddington CC, for taking the time to help; **Graeme Clarke**, Great War Forum, for his help and research; **Alan Clay**, collector and researcher who, as ever, has done all he could to help and that was a lot; **Cecilia Cooper-Colby,** photographer, for her brilliant copies of photographs from some very aged books; **Eleanor Cracknell**, College Archivist, Eton College, for her time and trouble; **Ed Dawes**, BBC Radio Derby Sport; **Richard Doherty**, my editor; **David Duffieldbank**, Derbyshire CCC, for his help and advice; **Leigh Duncan**, for her help, assistance and a few laughs; **Hiram Dunn**, Great War Forum; **Mark Eklid**, *Derby Telegraph*, for his help and advice in searching for the last few Derbyshire cricketers; **Brian Ellis**, for his help with Lt.-Col. Mosse; **John Fidler** and **Jenny Cornell**, researchers at Bedford School, for once again giving up their time and taking the trouble to search for information on old boys of the school; **Roddy Fisher**, keeper, Eton College Photographic Archive; **Roger Gibbons**, researcher; the late **Hal Giblin**, gentleman, historian, writer, my inspiration; **Rolland Hackney**, for his continual help and advice; **Jake Haddow,** Lancaster Royal Grammar School; **Peter Henderson**, Archivist, The King's School, Canterbury, Kent, for his time and trouble; **Chris Highton**, who gave up a lot of time and made a lot of effort to locate several photographs; **Clive Holden**, Lancaster Royal Grammar School; **Jonathan Holmes**, Queens' College, Cambridge; **Dave Horne**, Bromleigh Pool CC; the late and much missed **Dennis Ingle**, researcher and medal dealer; **Robin Isherwood**, for general research on South African cricketers; **William Ivory** and **Phil Nodding**, for keeping me going; **Alastair Jack,** historian/researcher; **Dean Johnson**, for his time and research; **Jane Jones**, WWI photos, obituaries and service records database, for providing many of the photographs and obituaries; **Matt Jones**, Pen & Sword; **Anziske Kayster**, Graaff-Reinet Museum, South Africa; **Maurice Kent**, Archivist, Northamptonshire CCC; **Jack Langley**, for taking the time to help out; **The Roger Mann Cricket Photograph Collection**, charming man and an extraordinary life long collection. He took the time and trouble to find some of the missing photographs and has a large wealth of knowledge; **Paul McCormick**, for his help without complaint; **Ashley McCrery**, for his help and advice; **Sam McIntyre**, Somerset Cricket Club, for his time and effort; **Liz Moloney**, researcher and historian who gave her time and trouble and found one of the missing photographs; **Pearce Noonan**, Nimrod Dix medals, for his continual help and advice; **Paul Paton**, Auckland Grammar School AGS Archives; **Ian Quickfall** and **Denise Goodrum** from Malvern College for their time, effort, information and photographs; **Andrew Renshaw** (**Wisden**), for his time, trouble, excellent advice and information. Generous man and first-class researcher; **Sue**

Final Wicket

Ryder (Mosse), for her research and time; **Jill Shepherd** BA MCLIP, Archives Librarian, Wellington College, for her time, trouble, information and photographs; The **Rick Smith Collection** (cricket photographs) for his time, trouble and keenness to see this book written. Many thanks; **Robert Smith**, collector and researcher, without whose generous help some of the information would have been wrong and photographs not discovered; **The Staunton Family** of Staunton Hall; **Richard Steel**, for his help and advice and for the Odell medals, which I treasure; **Clare Taylor**, cricketer and historian, for her brilliant work on OTAGO cricket players; **Peter Wynne-Thomas**, Nottingham CCC; **Brian Turner,** historian and collector who gave up much time and made much effort helping in the writing of this book; **John Watson**, supporter and collector, Northamptonshire CCC; **Jon Wilkinson**, Pen & Sword, who did an excellent job yet again of the jacket design; **Tony Williams**, for his superb proofreading skills; **Henry Wilson**, Pen & Sword; **Gina Worboys**, Bedford School, for all her help and time; **Jonathan Wright**, Pen & Sword, for his tireless work behind the scenes.

Forums:
Great War Forum, a superb research tool, which everyone interested in the subject should be a member of; **Medals Forum,** a first-class online research tool, well worth joining.

Cricket Clubs:
Border Cricket; **Cambridge CCC**; **Eastern Province Cricket**; **Essex CC**; **Gloucestershire CC**; **Griqualand West Cricket**; **Hampshire CCC**; **Kent CCC**; **Lancashire CCC**, for help and assistance with photographs and information; **Leicestershire CCC**; **Marylebone CC**, for their advice and direction; **Middlesex CCC**; **Natal Cricket**; **Northamptonshire CC**; **Nottinghamshire CCC**; **Otago CC**; **Somerset CC**; **Suffolk CCC**; **Transvaal CC**; **Wellington CC**; **West Province Cricket**; **Worcestershire CCC**; **Yorkshire CCC**.

Schools, Colleges and Museums/Archives:
Cambridge University; **Clifton College**, who greatly assisted in searching for information and photographs of old boys; **Cheltenham College Archives**; **Dublin University**; **Eton School**, who provided much information and many photographs of old boys; **Guards Museum**, London; **Kent County Council Libraries and Archives**; **Malvern College**; **Repton School**, who greatly assisted with information on their old boys; **Orange Free State Cricket**; **Oxford University**; **The Royal Military College**, Sandhurst; **Rugby School**, who helped in the finding of several photographs and information on their old boys; **Trinity College**, Cambridge; **Wellingborough School**; **Winchester College,** who provided a number of photographs and a lot of information on their old boys.

To anyone who I may have forgotten a big apology, and I will try to put it right in the next edition.

Nigel McCrery, June 2015

Preface

I always find these books hard to research and hard to write. It's the emotion of having to learn that these people were not just numbers or statistics on some general's battle plan but real characters who loved and were loved. Who had extraordinary lives and talents, had achieved great things and would – had they been given the chance – have achieved every kind of greatness. All their hopes and dreams, however, ended on bloody battlefields around the world in five short years. Within this book I have written brief biographies of the 275 first-class cricketers (men who played in at least one first-class game of cricket) who died between August 1914 and December 1918. So far, I have left out those who died of wounds after 1918. There are two reasons for this: firstly, I am still researching those who actually died as a result of wounds received in battle after the war; secondly, the size of the book. I could have written so much more about most of the cricketers and, before you ask why I didn't, it's because of the sheer size of the book as it's presented now. Pen & Sword were already very generous in their word allowance, which I seemed to continually breach, but there is only so far you can push it. I hope to resolve this problem in later editions. I have managed to locate 266 photographs of the 275 cricketers I have written about. Alas, search as I might, I have been unable to find the final nine. However, the search goes on and I hope to have found at least a few more by the time of the next edition. Anyone who might have a photograph of any of the nine, please contact me; I'd be glad to hear from you. The photos vary in condition. I have done my best to get quality copies but this hasn't always been possible. My attitude in such cases is better a poor photograph than no photograph at all. Once again, if anyone is able to improve on any of the photographs I would be glad to hear from them. I am sure that when writing so many biographies and absorbing so many facts and statistics I will have made mistakes. If you spot any, as long as you're not rude, please let me know and I will change the information in the following editions. Also, if you feel I have missed someone, please come forward and present your case and I will include them in the next edition.

My biggest thanks have to go to all the people who have helped and supported me in writing these books. To all of them a very big 'thank you' for taking the time and trouble to make the book as good as I can make it. Books like this are a labour of love; any money you are paid is quickly spent buying photographs, travelling to various sites, telephone bills, ink and, most of all, time. However, despite all this, it's worth it. As the poem says, 'At the going down of the sun and in the morning, we will remember them.' That is what this book is all about, remembrance, remembering those sporting greats of yesteryear, people who, in their day, were as famous as Lewis Hamilton, Andy Murray, Sebastian Coe, Lennox Lewis and Chris Hoy. Imagine waking up each morning to find one of your sporting idols had been killed in action or died of wounds. Imagine the shock of these immortals dying in their hundreds and thousands.

Most of all, I hope you enjoy the book and it helps you remember some of the men who played a 'gentlemen's' game during cricket's golden age.

Nigel McCrery

A.E.J. Collins

A.E.J. Collins (left) and R.P. Keigwin, who survived the war and played 74 first-class matches for Cambridge, Essex and the MCC.

I feel I can't write this book without including one cricketer who, although he made the supreme sacrifice, failed to play in a first-class match. He did, however, make an extraordinary contribution to the game. His name was Arthur Edward Jeune 'James' Collins (although normally referred to as A.E.J. Collins), born on 18 August 1885 at Hazaribagh in India, the son of Arthur Herbert Collins, a judge in the Indian Civil Service, and Mrs Esther Ida Collins. He went to Clifton College Bristol in 1897, becoming a member of Clark's House and later North Town House. Clifton had an excellent reputation for sport. The legendary W. G. Grace scored thirteen first-class centuries on the Close (Clifton's first XI ground) and was so impressed by the school that he sent his sons there. As well as playing in the first XI, he also represented the school at rugby and boxing, winning the bronze medal at the public schools' tournament held at Aldershot in 1901. In June 1899, as a 13-year-old schoolboy, Collins made the highest-ever recorded cricket score of 628 not out. This feat took place during a junior schoolhouse cricket match between Clarke's House and North Town House. These matches were timeless, played to a finish, however long it took. The match was played on an outfield off Guthrie Road, Bristol, now named *Collin's Piece*. Although many cricketers have scored into the 500s, no one has ever bettered his score. Tim Rice wrote of him in an article for the *Daily Telegraph* on 9 June 1999 to celebrate the centenary of the score, entitled 'On the seventh day A.E.J. Collins rested'.

He was an orphan whose guardians lived in Tavistock, Devon. He was a reserved boy, short and stockily built, fair-haired and pale. He was remembered by contemporaries as one who led by example, rather than by inspiration, although paradoxically he was regarded as likely to fall short of the highest standards as a cricketer because of his recklessness at the crease.

Upon this ground
A.E.J. COLLINS
in a junior House Match
in June 1899 scored
628 NOT OUT
THIS INNINGS IS THE HIGHEST
RECORDED IN THE HISTORY
OF CRICKET

After leaving school in 1902 he joined the British Army, being trained at the Royal Military Academy Woolwich and commissioned in the Royal Engineers. He was sent to France where, on 11 November 1914 at the First Battle of Ypres, while serving as a captain with 5 Field Company Royal Engineers, he was killed in action. He was 29 years old. He was signaling for more men to protect the flank of his trench when he was wounded; he was dragged back into the trench but died shortly after. Although he was buried with military ceremony, due to the continual fighting over this area for the next four years, his grave was lost and his name is recorded at the Menin Gate Memorial in Belgium, panel 9. He was also Mentioned in Despatches for his bravery. His younger brother, Herbert, a lieutenant in the 24th Battalion Manchester Regiment, also an old Cliftonian, was killed in action on 11 February 1917, aged 27.

1914

Lieutenant The Hon. Archer Windsor-Clive
Cambridge University
3rd Bn Coldstream Guards
Died 25 August 1914
Aged 23
Left-handed Bat/Left-arm Medium Bowler

'A man of so much promise'
'The first of the first-class cricketers to die'

Archer Windsor-Clive was born on 6 November 1890, at Hewell Grange, Redditch, Worcestershire, the third son of the 1st Earl and Countess of Plymouth. Educated at Eton he was in the first XI between 1907–09. In the former season he scored 10 and 38 against Harrow and a solid 105 against Winchester. Going up to Trinity College, Cambridge, he scored 12 and took seven wickets for 49 during the Freshmen's match in 1910.

Clive-Wilson made seven first class appearances for Cambridge University between May 1910 and June 1912. His first match was against Essex on 9 May 1910 at the Fenner's Ground, Cambridge (Fenner's has hosted first-class cricket matches since 1848 and many a great player has cut his cricketing teeth there. The ground was established on land leased for the purpose by Francis Fenner after whom the ground is named). He scored 13 and 15 and took three wickets for 56 runs off 23 overs. Essex won by an innings and 89 runs. He also played against Surrey, Kent, Free Foresters, Sussex and Hampshire. His final first class match was played on 27 June 1912 against H. D. G. Leveson-Gower's XI, played at the Saffrons, Eastbourne, Windsor-Clive scoring 2 and 22 and taking no wickets. The match was drawn. During his first-class career he made 108 runs, his highest score being 22 against Leveson-Gower's XI on 27 June 1912. He also took three wickets for 217 runs, his best figures being 3 for 56 against Essex on 9 May 1910. He took one catch. Between 1908 and 1912 he turned out for Glamorganshire, then a minor county side. He also represented the Perambulators (1910), B. H. Holloway's XI (1911) and the Household Brigade in 1914.

Commissioned as second lieutenant into the Coldstream Guards, with effect from 8 September,1911, on 12 August 1914, shortly after the outbreak of the war, he left Chelsea Barracks, London, for France with No. 2 Company, 3rd Battalion. Promoted to lieutenant, he moved with his battalion to Southampton, where he crossed to France with his company on the SS *Cawdor Castle*. On arrival in France the Guards moved forward to Harveng, and on the 23rd formed a defensive position.

The Retreat from Mons began the following day. The 3rd Battalion Coldstream fell back via Malgarni to Landrecies, arriving there during the late afternoon, being positioned to defend the north-west section of the town. Lieutenant Colonel Sir John Ross-of-Blandensburg, records that No. 2 Company fired on advancing enemy patrols, driving them back from the le Quesnoy road. Around dusk, a column was seen moving up the road. The men were singing French songs and, when challenged, an officer replied that they were friends. However, although the troops at the front were wearing French and Belgian uniforms, it was noticed that those at the back were German. The order to open fire was given, but not quickly enough and the Germans managed to rush the Coldstream position, killing one man.

The battle continued along the streets into Landrecies. During the night, the Germans launched repeated attacks down the two roads from the north-west, all of which were held and driven back by 3rd Coldstream. The position of a farm building at the right end of the British line enabled the Germans to enfilade the Coldstream with a machine gun. The Germans were supported by a field gun, firing up the road. This gunfire set a haystack on fire close to the Coldstream positions. The sudden blaze illuminated the British troops, and made them easy targets for the German Infantry. Private 5854 G. H. Wyatt rushed forward and put out the blaze, under fire from the Germans, who were within twenty-five yards of the Coldstream position. Once again the stack was ignited, and again Wyatt put the flames out. For his actions on this day Wyatt was awarded the Victoria Cross.

One of the German attacks, infiltrating round the left flank of 3rd Coldstream, reached as far as the railway station, where it was repelled by the Grenadiers of Number 2 Company, commanded by Major Lord Bernard Gordon-Lennox.

The Grenadiers' machine-gun section, commanded by Lieutenant Cecil, moved forward and provided additional support to the 3rd Coldstream, who were suffering from the fire of the single German field gun, directed down the street.

Lieutenant Colonel Fielding, Commanding Officer of 3rd Coldstream, brought up a howitzer from the supporting RFA battery. The howitzer was manhandled up to the level-crossing and opened fire on the German gun. The third round put the German gun out of action. Unfortunately, sometime between 7.00 and 8.00pm, Archer Windsor-Clive, together with his batman Frank Lethbridge, were killed by a shell.

Relieved the following morning, 26 August, 3rd Coldstream withdrew to Etreux. Their casualties amounted to two officers (including Archer's close friend and another member of the British aristocracy Lieutenant The Viscount Hawarden) and ten other ranks killed, 108 wounded and seven missing.

Archer is buried in Landrecies Communal Cemetery B. 1, close to the grave of his servant Frank Lethbridge.

Batting and fielding averages

	Mat	Inns	NO	Runs	HS	Ave	100	50	Ct	St
First-class	7	14	1	108	22	8.30	0	0	1	0

Bowling averages

	Mat	Balls	Runs	Wkts	BBI	Ave	Econ	SR	5w	10
First-class	7	437	217	3	3/56	72.33	2.97	145.6	0	0

Lieutenant Colonel Sir Evelyn Ridley Bradford Bart
Hampshire
Commanding Officer 2nd Bn Seaforth Highlanders
(Ross-Shire Buffs, The Duke of Albany's)
Died 14 September 1914
Aged 47
Right-handed Bat/Right-arm Fast Bowler

'He led in everything'

Evelyn Ridley Bradford was born in Goonah, India on 16 April 1869. He was the son of Sir Edward Ridley Colborne Bradford, 1st Baronet, former Commissioner of the London Metropolitan Police and extra Equerry to His Majesty the King, and Lady Bradford (nee Knight). Educated at Eton College and the Royal Military College, Sandhurst, Bradford was commissioned into the Seaforth Highlanders on 22 August 1888.

Promoted to lieutenant on 11 June 1890, five years later, on 3 July 1895, he became a captain and received his majority on 26 June 1902. He was appointed brevet lieutenant colonel on 10 May 1913 and confirmed in that rank on 10 June. Bradford served in the Sudan Expedition of 1898 being present at the actions of Atbara and Khartoum. During the Second Boer War, 1899–1902, he served on the staff, taking part in operations in the Orange Free State including the actions at Poplar Grove, Driefontein and Witteberier. During this time he was Mentioned in Despatches twice.

Upon his father's death in 1911, Bradford assumed the title of 2nd Baronet. In 1909 he married Elsie Surrey, third daughter of Colonel James Clifton Brown of Medstead Manor, Alton, Hampshire. They had three children: Sir Edward Montagu Andrew, was born on 30 November 1910 and, aged only 4 years, became the 3rd Baronet on his father's death in 1914; Ridley Lewkenor, born 11 April 1912, and Donald Clifton, born 22 May 1914. Bradford's father had married twice, his first wife being a daughter of Edward Knight, of Hampshire and Kent, and his second a daughter of William Nicholson, of Harrow and the MCC. Through his grandfather, Colonel Bradford was thus related to a host of famous cricketers, including the Jenners, Normans, Nepeans, Barnards, Bonham-Carters, Wathens, and Dykes.

Bradford made eight first-class appearances for Hampshire between July 1895 and May 1905, all but one in the County Championship. His first-class debut came for Hampshire in the County Championship against Somerset on 1 July 1895 at the County Ground, Southampton. He scored 12 and 9 and failed to take a wicket, Somerset winning by 183 runs. Bradford also played against Surrey, Essex, Australia, Derbyshire and Leicestershire. His final first-class appearance came on 25 May 1905 against Surrey played at the Officers' Club Service Ground, Aldershot, in which he scored 60 and 2 and caught Walter Scott Lee off the bowling of Henry Persse (KIA 28 June 1918) for 130. Surrey won by seven wickets. During his first-class career Bradford made 311 runs, his highest score being 102 against Leicestershire on 10 August 1899. He also took 20 for 328 runs, his best figures being 6 for 28 against Essex in August 1896. He made five catches.

During his brief career, Bradford's bowling action was not approved of by several first-class umpires and he was no-balled on numerous occasions. While playing for Hampshire in 1899, he was no-balled by White and Pickett in the match with the Australians at Southampton, and by A. F. Smith at Leicester. In military matches he was a heavy run-getter, and as recently as May 1913, had played an innings of 251 for Shorncliffe Garrison against Folkestone. For Aldershot Command versus Incogniti in May 1895 he scored 248.

At the outbreak of the First World War Bradford was in command of the 2nd Battalion Seaforth Highlanders which went to France as part of 10 Infantry Brigade. His battalion covered the retirement of the Expeditionary Force on Cambrai. Positioned in the middle of the line 2nd Seaforth helped break up the front of the German pursuit suffering heavy casualties as I and II Corps fell back. Bradford was killed at the Battle of Aisne by a shell on 14 September 1914. He was Mentioned in Despatches by Sir John French for his services in the earlier part of the war (*London Gazette*, 8 October, 1914).

He was buried in Crouy-Vauxrot French National Cemetery, Crouy, Grave B. 11.

Batting and fielding averages

	Mat	Inns	NO	Runs	HS	Ave	100	50	Ct	St
First-class	8	14	2	311	102	25.91	1	1	5	0

Bowling averages

	Mat	Balls	Runs	Wkts	BBI	Ave	Econ	SR	5w	10
First-class	8	743	328	20	6/28	16.40	2.64	37.1	2	1

Captain Arthur Maitland Byng
Hampshire and Jamaica
4th Bn Royal Fusiliers
Died 14 September 1914
Aged 41
Right-handed Bat

'No man could have done more'

Born in Southsea on 26 September 1872, Arthur Maitland Byng was the son of Major A. H. Byng, late of the Prince of Wales's Leinster Regiment (Royal Canadians) and formerly lieutenant Royal Navy. He was also related to the Viscount Torrington. Byng was educated at The Grange, Cowes, and by an Army tutor at Caen. In September 1895 he was gazetted into the West Indian Regiment. Promoted captain in June 1900 he continued to serve with the regiment until March 1901 when he transferred to the 4th Battalion Royal Fusiliers (City of London Regiment). He served in the South African (Boer) War in 1901 and 1902 with the mounted infantry, taking part in operations in the Transvaal, Orange Free State and Cape Colony. Between 1903 and 1905 he was employed by the Egyptian Army and was adjutant in the Special Reserve from 1908 to 1912.

Byng played in eight first-class matches between September 1896 and July 1905, five for Jamaica and three for Hampshire. His debut first-class match took place on 10 September 1896 against British Guiana at Bourda, Georgetown, Jamaica. He scored 13 and 32, took 3 wickets for 53 off 19 overs and caught Charles Chandler off the bowling of George Garnett for 11. British Guiana won by an innings and 45 runs. In addition, he played against Barbados and A. Priestley's XI. On returning to England Byng joined Hampshire, playing for them in three first-class matches, the first against Kent and the others against Warwickshire and Northamptonshire. His final first-class match for Hampshire was played against Northampton at the County Ground, Northampton, on 10 July 1905 in the County Championship. Byng scored 6 and 4 and failed to take a wicket; Northampton won by 231 runs. During his first-class career Byng made 252 runs, his highest score being 70 against British Guiana on 12 September 1896. He also took 7 wickets for 168 runs, his best bowling figures being 3 for 53, once again against British Guiana, on 10 September 1896.

Arthur Byng also played for the Hampshire Hogs against the Royal Navy at Portsmouth in July 1905, when he scored 204 runs in a partnership with D. A. Steel; the two actually put on 335 runs for the first wicket. An established batsman for the Army, he made hundreds of runs for the Royal Fusiliers.

Byng travelled to France with his battalion, landing in le Havre on 13 August 1914. The battalion was soon in the thick of the fighting, winning the war's first two Victoria Crosses (Lieutenant Maurice Dease and Private Sidney Frank Godley) on 23 August 1914.

Captain Byng was killed at Vailly, at the Battle of the Aisne, on 14 September 1914 while looking through his field-glasses; shot in the throat he was killed instantaneously.

A brother officer gave the following account of him and his work during the early part of the war: 'He has done very well with his Company; no man could have done more … He was our great interpreter, being very good at French' and 'He was always taking risks and leaving the trenches with a rifle to walk about in front.'

Byng has no known grave and is commemorated on the la Ferté-sous-Jouarre Memorial, Seine-et-Marne, France.

Batting and fielding averages

	Mat	Inns	NO	Runs	HS	Ave	100	50	Ct	St
First-class	8	15	0	252	70	16.80	0	1	8	0

Bowling averages

	Mat	Runs	Wkts	BBI	Ave	5w	10
First-class	8	168	7	3/53	24.00	0	0

Captain Leonard Slater
Gentlemen of the South
2nd Bn Royal Sussex Regiment
Died 14 September 1914
Aged 38
Right-handed Bat

'Never gave up until the last ball was bowled'

Leonard Slater was born at Instow, North Devon, on 11 October 1875, the son of the Reverend Francis and Mrs Harriet Slater. Educated at Marlborough College and the Royal Military College, Sandhurst, he was gazetted to an unattached second lieutenancy in August 1895 and joined the Indian Staff Corps in 1896. Promoted to lieutenant in November 1897 and then captain in August 1904, he served with the 22nd Cavalry, Punjab Frontier Force, for eight years in Waziristan (North-West Frontier) before returning home in 1904 and joining the Royal Sussex Regiment and being appointed adjutant of the 5th Battalion (Cinque Ports) from 1909. He married Constance Dorothy daughter of Colonel F. Pridham of Instow, Devon, in 1901. They had three children, Francis, born in 1902, Helen Elizabeth, born 1903, and finally John Frederick, born 1909, who would have a very distinguished military career, winning a DSO and Bar and being credited with forming the Army's first commando unit during the Second World War.

While serving in India, Leonard played for Peshawar and Northern Punjab at a time when neither team had first-class status. He played for both teams in the 1902–03 season. Returning to England, he played a single Minor Counties Championship match for Devon against Glamorgan and, five years later on 9 September 1909, played his only first-class match when he represented the Gentlemen of the South against the Players of the South at the Central Recreation Ground, Hastings. He scored 15 and 0; the Players of the South won by 228 runs.

Slater crossed to France with the 2nd Bn Royal Sussex in August 1914. He was involved in heavy fighting before being killed on 14 September 1914, together with six other officers of his battalion during the early part of the Battle of the Aisne. His commanding officer had a very high opinion of Captain Slater's capacity as a company commander and leader of men. 'Slater was full of energy and fond of games and sport of all kinds. He was a very keen cricketer, and played for the MCC, the Gentlemen of Sussex, and other good teams.'

His body was laid to rest at the Vendresse British Cemetery, grave I.C. 12, and his name was engraved on several memorials following his death, including the War Memorial at Instow. The south side of the nave of St John the Baptist Church in Instow is also dedicated to him while his name is included on the Godalming War Memorial in Godalming, Surrey.

Batting and fielding averages

	Mat	Inns	NO	Runs	HS	Ave	100	50	Ct	St
First-class	1	2	0	15	15	7.50	0	0	0	0

Bowling averages

	Mat	Balls	Runs	Wkts	BBI	BBM	Ave	Econ	SR	4w	5w	10
First-class	1	-	-	-	-	-	-	-	-	-	-	-

Captain William Thomas Payne-Gallwey MVO
Army/Marylebone Cricket Club (MCC)
2nd Bn Grenadier Guards
Died 14 September 1914
Aged 33
Right-arm fast

'The old son of a distinguished family, he laid down his life for his country'

William Thomas Payne-Gallwey was born on 25 March 1881 at Blackrock, County Dublin, the only son (although he did have four sisters) of Sir Ralph William Frankland Payne-Gallwey 3rd Baronet (who wrote several books on military and sporting history, the best known being *The Crossbow* (1903), which was re-published in 2007, by Skyhorse Publishing) and Edith Alice Usborne. He was educated at Eton College where he was in the XI. As a right-arm fast bowler, was second in the bowling averages in 1900 with 27 wickets for 18.37. In the same year he played for the Yorkshire Second XI against Surrey at the Oval in the Minor Counties Championship. He was a regular with the Household Brigade.

He played in two first-class matches in 1912. The first took place on 6 May 1912 when he turned out for the MCC against Yorkshire at Lords, he scored 16 and 9 and took one wicket for 20. He also caught David Denton off the bowling of Hesketh Vernon Hesketh-Prichard for 21. Yorkshire won by 2 wickets. His next first-class match also took place at Lords, for the Army against the Navy, on 30 May 1912, he scored 0 and 12 and took one wicket for 35. The Army won by 161 runs.

A career soldier, he served with the Grenadier Guards during the South African (Boer War) of 1899 to 1902. In 1908 he was awarded the MVO (5th Class). He travelled with 2nd Grenadier Guards to France on 15 August 1914 and was reported missing in action only a month later on 14 September. In January 1915 his parents were given some hope when it was reported that he was a prisoner of the Germans. However, this proved to be untrue and his death was assumed to have taken place on the 14th.

His body was never recovered and he is commemorated on the la Ferté- sous-Jouarre Memorial in France.

Batting and fielding averages

	Mat	Inns	NO	Runs	HS	Ave	100	50	Ct	St
First-class	2	4	2	37	16	18.50	0	0	1	0

Bowling averages

	Mat	Balls	Runs	Wkts	BBI	Ave	Econ	SR	5w	10
First-class	2	90	55	2	1/10	27.50	3.66	45.0	0	0

Lieutenant Mark Kincaid Mackenzie
Oxford University
King's Royal Rifle Corps
Died 25 September 1914
Aged 26
Left-arm-fast-medium

'Forward, Come, come'

Mark Kincaid Mackenzie was born on 22 August 1888 in New Town, Edinburgh, Scotland. The son of the Honourable Charles Kincaid Mackenzie LLD and Lady Mackenzie (née Young) of Wester Shian, Gullane, East Lothian, he was educated at Horris Hill, Winchester College and Magdalen College, Oxford. Whilst at Winchester he was a house prefect and second captain of Lords in his last year. He was gazetted to The King's Royal Rifle Corps in July 1911, joining the 4th Battalion in India. When war broke out, Mackenzie was on home leave and was seconded to the 3rd Bn Rifle Brigade.

He played for the Winchester XI in 1905, 1906 and 1907 and was a Harlequin while at Oxford. In 1910 Mackenzie played three first-class matches, all for Oxford University. His debut came against Kent on 12 May 1910 at The University Parks, Oxford. He scored 15 in his one innings and took a wicket for 8 off 4 overs; Oxford won by 8 wickets. His second appearance was on 26 May 1910 against Surrey, once again at the University Parks, Oxford when he scored 0 and 1, taking one wicket for 28 off 12 overs in the first innings and 1 for 21 off 6 overs in the second. He also managed to catch George Platt off the bowling of John Lowe for 0; Surrey won by 116 runs. Mackenzie's final first-class appearance was on 30 June 1910 against the Gentlemen of England at The Saffrons, Eastbourne. He scored 48 not out and 1, taking one wicket for 36 off 13 overs during the first innings and 2 for 65 off 18 overs in the second. The Gentlemen of England won by 113 runs. In 1914 he played for Marylebone Cricket Club, as well as the Rifle Brigade.

On 25 September 1914, during the battle of Aisne, Mackenzie was involved in a dawn attack on a line of German trenches near Soupir, north-east of Soissons. During this attack he was seen to fall, badly wounded. Pulling himself to his feet he continued to lead his platoon in the attack. The fire was withering from German machine-gun and infantry positions and Mackenzie was wounded for a second time, this time close to the enemy trenches. Despite being mortally wounded, he still called out to his men and was heard to shout, 'Forward, Come on, come on!' He was never seen alive again.

Mackenzie played cricket for and was a member of the MCC and I Zingari and he was also a keen hunter, hunting with the Duke of Buccleuch's Hounds. An outstanding golfer, he was also a member of the Honourable Company of Edinburgh Golfers.

He is buried in Montcornet Military Cemetery, grave H.6.

Batting and fielding averages

	Mat	Inns	NO	Runs	HS	Ave	100	50	Ct	St
First-class	3	5	1	65	48*	16.25	0	0	3	0

Bowling averages

	Mat	Balls	Runs	Wkts	BBI	Ave	Econ	SR	5w	10
First-class	3	390	185	6	2/65	30.83	2.84	65.0	0	0

Second Lieutenant Wilfred Methven Brownlee
Gloucestershire
3rd Bn Dorsetshire Regiment
Died 12 October 1914
Aged 24
Right-handed Bat/Right-arm Fast Medium

'A great loss to the game of cricket,
died before he could serve'

Wilfred Methven Brownlee was born on 18 April 1890 at Cotham, Redland, Bristol, Gloucestershire. Steeped in cricket from an early age, his father was William Methven Brownlee, who played cricket for Gloucestershire and wrote a biography of W. G. Grace.

Brownlee was educated at Clifton College, Bristol, where he was in the XI between 1906 and 1909, being head of the batting averages with 23.57 in 1908, in which season he also took 49 wickets. In 1909 he was made captain and during that season took 34 wickets. He was selected for the Public Schools XI to play against the MCC at Lord's and took 8 wickets for 61. A free-hitting batsman and fast-medium bowler, he was also quick in the field and went on to play, like his father before him, for Gloucestershire.

He made thirty-three first-class appearances between July 1909 and June 1914, all but one for Gloucestershire and the other for The Players of the South. He made his debut for Gloucestershire on 29 July 1909 in the County Championship against Worcestershire at the County Ground, New Road, Worcestershire. He made 1 and 64 and took a wicket for 20 off 4 overs. Worcestershire won by a wicket. His final match came on 4 June 1914 against Hampshire, again in the County Championship, this time played at the United Services Ground, Portsmouth, Brownlee scoring 11 and 4 and failing to take a wicket. The match was eventually drawn.

During his first-class career Brownlee made 773 runs including three fifties, his highest score being 68 against Northamptonshire on 22 August 1910. He also took 46 wickets for 1251 runs, his best figures being 6 for 61. He made 26 catches.

The Times said of him:

all the gifts of the gods were his, among them tireless energy, intellect, Grecian good looks, a fundamental kindness and charity, (and) a Christian soul beyond his years.

It was said of Brownlee that his greatest challenges in life were to be his future direction: should he be captain of the England cricket team or, perhaps, prime minister. A brother officer later said 'he might equally have played either role, or possibly both, with distinction'.

During the war he was commissioned as a second lieutenant in the Dorsetshire Regiment but, before he had chance to serve abroad, he died of meningitis on 12 October 1914.

He is buried in Bristol (Arnos Vale) Cemetery, grave reference G 437. Always worth a visit and a few flowers.

Batting and fielding averages

	Mat	Inns	NO	Runs	HS	Ave	100	50	Ct	St
First-class	33	53	4	773	68	15.77	0	3	26	0

Bowling averages

	Mat	Runs	Wkts	BBI	Ave	5w	10
First-class	33	1251	46	6/61	27.19	3	0

Lieutenant Walter Evelyn Parke
Army
2nd Bn Durham Light Infantry
Died 13 October 1914
Aged 23
Left-handed Bat

'Small in size but a giant in his heart'

Walter Evelyn Parke was born on 27 August 1891, the second son of Lieutenant Colonel Lawrence Parke and Mrs L. Parke, of Moreton Heath, Moreton, Dorset. Educated at Mr Pellat's school at Langton Matravers and Winchester College (1905–09), his obituary in *Wisden* described him as 'very short, but one of the best batsmen turned out by the College for many years'.

Parke played in the Winchester XI between 1907 and 1909, becoming captain in his last year. He played at Lord's in his second year and was largely responsible for the victory over Eton that same year, scoring 49 and 46 not out and striking the winning hit. In 1909 he batted for four and a half hours on a difficult wicket, scoring 33 and 30 not out and almost carrying his bat through both innings, certainly saving his side from defeat. He played golf for the school in 1908 and 1909 and in his last year was appointed a commoner prefect.

Deciding on a career in the Army he continued to play cricket and became a prolific scorer. In 1913, playing for Dorset at Lord's against the MCC, he knocked up an impressive 111 and 103. He played in one first-class match for the Army against Cambridge University on 11 June 1914 at Fenner's Ground, Cambridge, scoring a not very impressive 11 and 7, although he did manage to catch R. B. Lagden off the bowling of Yates. Despite Parke being under par, Cambridge still managed to come out on top by an innings and 80 runs.

At the outbreak of war he was serving with the 2nd Bn Durham Light Infantry and proceeded to France in September 1914. He died while trying to lift a machine gun over a hedge near les Fermes at approximately 2.00pm on 13 September whilst in command of the machine-gun section. In January 1915 he received a posthumous mention in Sir John French's Despatches for his bravery in the field.

Parke was buried initially at the Vieux Berquin crossroads (there is a famous photograph of two very young French girls tending his original grave, see attached). After the war his remains were moved and he now lies in grave I.E.10 of Outtersteene Communal Cemetery Extension, Bailleul.

His elder brother, Lieutenant John Aubrey Parke, Durham Light Infantry, was also killed in action on 25 September 1915.

13

Batting and fielding averages

	Mat	Inns	NO	Runs	HS	Ave	100	50	Ct	St
First-class	1	2	0	18	11	9.00	0	0	1	0

Bowling averages

	Mat	Balls	Runs	Wkts	BBI	BBM	Ave	Econ	SR	4w	5w	10
First-class	1	-	-	-	-	-	-	-	-	-	-	-

Captain William Miles Kington
Europeans (India)
1st Bn Royal Welsh Fusiliers
Died 20 October 1914
Aged 38
Not Known

'Always made people laugh, even in the most trying circumstances'

William Miles Kington was born on 25 April 1876 at Cheltenham, Gloucestershire, England, the eldest son of Colonel Kington, formerly of the 4th Hussars. He was educated at Glenalmond College and the RMC Sandhurst before taking a commission in the Royal Welsh Fusiliers in September 1896.

He was promoted lieutenant in January 1899 and took part in the Second Boer War, being on the staff as a brigade signalling officer from November 1899 to December 1900. He was Mentioned in Despatches on four occasions, and was present at the relief of Ladysmith and the Battle of Colenso, as well as operations in Val Krans, on the Tugela Heights and in the action at Pieter's Hill. In 1902 he was awarded the DSO for his actions. Between February 1902 and May 1904 he served with the South African Constabulary before serving as an adjutant to Volunteer and Territorial battalions.

He played one first-class match for the Europeans (Indians) during the Bombay Presidency match, which was played on 14 September 1911 at the Deccan Gymkhana Ground, Poona. Kington scored 3 and 1 but, despite his poor showing, the Europeans went on to win by 140 runs. He was also a member of the MCC, I Zingari and the Free Foresters. As well as being a first-class shot, he was able to play any musical instrument.

At the outbreak of war Kington rejoined the Royal Welsh Fusiliers, travelling to France with them in August 1914. At 8.00am on 20 October, while attacking a German position near Zonnebeke, which was found to be stronger than they had realized, Captain Kington was hit by a shell and killed instantly.

A brother officer later wrote to his wife:

> For three days we remained in the trenches firing and being fired at without food or water. Lieutenant Hoskyns, who commanded my platoon, was killed by a sniper, and about three hours later Captain Kington DSO was killed. He was a fine officer, and would crack a joke in the trenches, which would set us all laughing our sides out. It made us mad to avenge his death.

Captain Kington was married to Edith, daughter of Mr F. Soames, Bryn-Estyn, Wrexham. They had one son.

His body was never recovered or identified and he is commemorated on the Ypres (Menin Gate) Memorial, Panel 22.

Batting and fielding averages

	Mat	Inns	NO	Runs	HS	Ave	100	50	Ct	St
First-class	1	2	0	4	3	2.00	0	0	1	0

Bowling averages

	Mat	Balls	Runs	Wkts	BBI	BBM	Ave	Econ	SR	4w	5w	10
First-class	1	-	-	-	-	-	-	-	-	-	-	-

Lieutenant Harold Edwin Hippisley
Somerset
1st Bn Gloucestershire Regiment
Died 23 October 1914
Aged 24
Right-handed Bat

'Without his bravery the situation would have been hopeless'

Harold Edwin Hippisley was born on 3 September 1890 at Wells in Somerset, the youngest son of William John and Mary Hippisley of Northam House, New Street, Wells. Educated at King's School, Bruton, in Somerset, where he was captain of cricket, in 1909 he headed the batting averages at 62.90, his highest score being 113. He also shone at both hockey and football. After leaving school, Hippisley continued with his hockey and cricket careers, playing hockey for Somerset and the West of England, and in 1913 he tried out for England, although he never won a cap.

Hippisley played in seven first-class matches, all for Somerset, between August 1909 and July 1913. He made his debut on 23 August 1909 in the County Championship against Worcestershire at the County Ground, New Road, Worcester, scoring 40 in his only innings, a score that turned out to be the highest of his first-class career. He also caught Henry Knollys Foster off the bowling of Albert Lewis for 7. The match was drawn. His longtime friend Leonard Sutton was also selected to play for Somerset at the same time. He was to lose his life in 1916; Oswald Samson who also played for Somerset that day was killed in action in 1918. Hippisley's final first-class match for Somerset came on 14 July 1913 against Derbyshire once again in the County Championship and played at the County Ground, Derby. He scored 0 and 2, but, despite this poor showing, Somerset still managed to win the match by 59 runs. During his first-class career Hippisley scored 114 runs, his highest score being 40 against Worcestershire on 23 August 1909. He never bowled in a first-class match but did take two catches

Harold attended the Royal Agricultural College at Cirencester in 1911 to study Estate Management and Forestry, gaining the National Diploma of Agriculture; he was also a Professional Associate of the Surveyors Institution, playing both cricket and hockey for them. While there he was also a member of the Officers' Training Corps and was appointed to the Special Reserve and commissioned as a second lieutenant in the Gloucestershire Regiment on 10 August 1912. Over the next two years he continued with his military training and was called up at the beginning of the war on 5 August 1914, being posted to the 1st Bn Gloucestershire Regiment, based at Bordon Camp.

Posted to No.4 Platoon A Company he travelled with his battalion to land in le Havre on 13 August as part of 3 Brigade in 1st Division. The day before he went overseas, however, he found time to marry his longtime girlfriend, Ivy Gwendoline Cooper, at Portsmouth.

After taking part in much of the heavy fighting during August and September 1914, including the Retreat from Mons, the regiment marching 200 miles in thirteen days they travelled by train to Poperinghe. On 21 October they marched to Langemarck. On arriving, 3 Brigade was immediately ordered to attack in the area of Poelcapelle. The battalion's objective was the farm at Koekuit, which was taken later that day after much fighting. The battalion was then withdrawn to billets near Pilckem for rest, but at 9.00am on 22 October it received an immediate message to stand to after a major German breakthrough in the Langemarck area. At 7.30am the battalion spotted masses of German infantry advancing down the Koekuit-Langemarck road. An artillery barrage then bombarded the front-line trenches, along with sustained rifle fire as the Germans advanced on Langemarck. Some of the enemy managed to get within fifty yards of A Company's trenches but were eventually beaten back. Lieutenant Hippisley was killed on the 23rd whilst gallantly holding his trench, along with many of his platoon. Although the Glosters lost 60 per cent of their number, the Germans were still forced to retreat, largely due to the vigorous actions of elements of A and C Companies. Without their bravery the situation would have become impossible. Hippisley was shot in the middle of the forehead at about 10.30am. A fellow officer wrote back to his family:

> He was attended by his servant, Private Brown, who was under the impression that if he kept the brain from oozing out of the hole he would be alright. After a time he was convinced that the wound was fatal.

Hippisley's body was never recovered and he is commemorated on the Ypres (Menin Gate) Memorial, Panels 22 and 34. After his death Ivy moved to Wells, 'to feel closer to him'.

Batting and fielding averages

	Mat	Inns	NO	Runs	HS	Ave	100	50	Ct	St
First-class	7	13	1	114	40*	9.50	0	0	2	0

Bowling averages

	Mat	Balls	Runs	Wkts	BBI	BBM	Ave	Econ	SR	4w	5w	10
First-class	7	-	-	-	-	-	-	-	-	-	-	-

Lieutenant William Stanley Yalland
Gloucestershire
1st Bn Gloucestershire Regiment
Died 23 October 1914
Aged 25
Right-handed Bat

'Not one step back'

William Stanley Yalland was born on 27 June 1889 at Fishponds, Bristol, the youngest child of Thomas King and Mary E. Yalland of The Manor House, Manor Road, Fishponds, Bristol. He had an older sister, Mary, and a brother, Robert. At first he was educated privately before going up to Clifton College, Bristol in 1903. A good all-round sportsman he played rugby for Clifton RFC and later for his regiment. He made one first-class appearance for Gloucestershire against Somerset on 1 August 1910 at the Ashley Down Ground, Bristol, in the County Championship. Playing in the lower order he scored a single run. The match was drawn. It was to be his only appearance in first-class cricket.

On 24 December 1910 he was commissioned as a second lieutenant in the 3rd (Reserve) Bn Leicestershire Regiment, being promoted to lieutenant on 16 February 1912. He requested a transfer to the Gloucestershire Regiment, which was granted and on 16 December 1912 he made the move to become a second lieutenant, in the 3rd (Reserve) Bn (having lost his rank as lieutenant due to the transfer). The next two years were spent in military and officer training. On 5 August 1914 at the outbreak of the First World War he was called up and posted to the 1st Bn Gloucestershire Regiment based at Bordon Camp.

The battalion was part of 3 Brigade in 1st Division. On landing at le Havre on 14 August 1914 Yalland was given command of No. 15 Platoon of D Company. He was promoted back to lieutenant on 18 August and moved with the Glosters to battle positions at Mons. The Glosters were not heavily engaged at Mons and on the 24th withdrew with the rest of the Expeditionary Force. The division moved south-west, crossing the river Aisne at Soissons before crossing the Marne a few days later. The Glosters reached Mouroux on 6 September, having marched 200 miles in thirteen days. On 9 September they re-crossed the Marne at Nogent during an Allied counter-offensive. They also re-crossed the Aisne to the east of Soissons before reaching the Chemin des Dames ridge on 14 September. The battalion remained in the area of Troyon, Bourg, Moulins and Pargnan until relieved on 15 October.

On 21 October 1st Division moved by train to Poperinghe before marching to the Langemarck sector. As soon as they arrived they were ordered to attack in the area of Poelcapelle. The battalion's objective was the farm at Koekuit, which they eventually took after much heavy fighting. The battalion was sent to get some rest at a camp near Pilckem, but their 'rest' didn't last long and at 9.00am on the 22nd they received information that the Germans had broken through in the Langemarck area. The battalion stood to. At 7.30am the following day a large formation of German infantry was spotted advancing down the Koekuit-Langemarck road towards them. The battalion then came under fire from German artillery as well as accurate rifle fire as the Germans stormed forward towards Langemarck. Such was the power of the assault that the enemy managed to get within fifty yards of the battalion's forward trenches before being beaten back. Lieutenant Stanley Yalland was shot through the head and killed whilst defending his trench, along with many members of his platoon. Eventually the Germans were pushed back and forced to retreat.

William Yalland's body was never discovered or identified and he is commemorated on the Ypres (Menin Gate) Memorial, Panels 22 and 34.

Batting and fielding averages

	Mat	Inns	NO	Runs	HS	Ave	100	50	4s	6s	Ct	St
First-class	1	1	0	1	1	1.00	0	0	0	0	0	0

Bowling averages

	Mat	Balls	Runs	Wkts	BBI	BBM	Ave	Econ	SR	4w	5w	10
First-class	1	-	-	-	-	-	-	-	-	-	-	-

9576 Rifleman John Thomas Gregory
Hampshire
1st Bn King's Royal Rifle Corps
Died 27 October 1914
Aged 27
Left-handed Bat/Slow-left-arm Orthodox

'Always cheerful' The first 'other rank'
first-class cricketer to be killed in the war

John Thomas Gregory was born on 13 July 1887 at Forest Lane, Sutton-in-Ashfield, the son of Thomas and Eliza Gregory of Station Road, Sutton. Thomas started his life as an errand boy before becoming a miner. He played cricket for St Modwen's, where he was a choirboy, and Sutton Town Cricket Club. Between 1905 and 1907 he was on the ground staff at Trent Bridge Cricket Ground, although he never played for Nottinghamshire. He also played cricket for Hucknall Colliery. In February 1876 he married Eliza Kendall at St Mary's, Sutton-in-Ashfield.

During the war he served as Private 9576 in the ranks of the King's Royal Rifle Corps, a regiment that recruited strongly in the East Midlands. While serving in the Army his talent for cricket was quickly recognized. Gregory, a slow left-arm bowler took many wickets in military matches and came to Hampshire's notice when playing for his regiment at Aldershot. He took all 10 wickets of the 2nd Worcestershire Regiment for only 15 runs, an impressive display. On the strength of this he was selected to play for Hampshire against Oxford University at the County Ground Southampton on 30 June 1913. He scored a duck in his first innings and failed to bat in his second. He also took no wickets for 87. It was his only first-class match.

He also played football at inside right for his regiment and represented the Army against the Amateur Internationals.

Rifleman John Thomas Gregory was killed in action on 27 November 1914 near Zonnebeke, Belgium, the same day that Prince Maurice Victor Donald Battenberg KCVO, grandson of Queen Victoria, serving with the same battalion, also fell.

Ray Westlake's book *British Battalions in France and Belgium 1914* gives an idea of the circumstances surrounding Gregory's death.

OCTOBER – To Polygon Wood during the afternoon (25th). Advanced early morning (26th) – D Company followed by C and with A and B in support … . The attack was held up, the Battalion holding its positions until relieved by 1st Irish Guards about 5am (27th)… . Withdrew to a farm in valley south of Zonnebeke. Advanced again about 9am – A Company followed by B Company. Lieutenant Colonel Northey records that the Battalion, having crossed the Paschendale-Becelaere, road came under terrific shell and rifle fire. Casualties – Captain W. Wells (3rd Buffs attached), Lieutenant H. H. Prince Maurice VD of Battenburg, and 24 other ranks killed, Second Lieutenants T. N. Horne, H. Sweeting and 130 other ranks wounded, 19 missing. Dug-in about 800 yards east of the road and held positions under heavy shell fire…

His body was never recovered or identified and he is commemorated on the Ypres (Menin Gate) Memorial, Panel 51 and 53.

Batting and fielding averages

	Mat	Inns	NO	Runs	HS	Ave	100	50	4s	6s	Ct	St
First-class	1	1	0	0	0	0.00	0	0	0	0	0	0

Bowling averages

	Mat	Balls	Runs	Wkts	BBI	BBM	Ave	Econ	SR	4w	5w	10
First-class	1	144	87	0	-	-	-	3.62	-	0	0	0

Lieutenant Colonel Henry Lawrence Anderson
Europeans (India)
9th Bhopal Infantry (Indian States Forces)
Died 29 October 1914
Aged 47
Right-handed Bat

'Would do anything for his men'

Henry Lawrence Anderson was born on 2 June 1867 in Lucknow, Uttar Pradesh and was probably named after the famous leader of the defence of Lucknow during the Indian Mutiny of 1857. He was the son of General R. P. and Mrs Anderson of Holland Road, Kensington.

Educated at Dulwich and gazetted to the Yorkshire Light Infantry in August 1888, he was promoted to lieutenant in March 1890 and the following month transferred to the Indian Staff Corps. Promoted to captain, Indian Army, in August 1899, in 1903–04 he saw active service in Tibet. In August 1914, he was promoted to lieutenant colonel and became second in command of the 9th Bhopal Infantry (Indian States Forces).

Anderson made two first-class appearances for the Europeans (India) in 1892 and 1893. He made his debut on 19 September 1892 in a Bombay Presidency Match at the Poona Gymkhana Ground, Poona, against the Parsees. He scored 10 and 1 and failed to take a wicket. Parsees won by three wickets. His second first-class match was played on 23 August 1895 at the Gymkhana Ground, Bombay, Anderson failed to bat in either innings but took a wicket for 13 off 7 overs in the first innings. He also managed to catch D. E. Modi off the bowling of R. M. Poore, the Europeans finally winning by 9 wickets.

During the First World War, the 9th Bhopal Infantry were despatched to France in 1914 as part of the Ferozepore Brigade, Lahore Division. The regiment suffered heavy losses at the Battles of Neuve Chapelle, Festubert, Givenchy and Second Ypres. It was during the chaotic fighting of 1914 that Lieutenant Colonel Anderson was killed by a shell near la Gorgue while the battalion was entrenching under heavy fire.

He left a widow, Ethel A. A. Anderson. Anderson is buried in Pont-Du-Hem Military Cemetery, la Gorgue, VI. F. 2.

Batting and fielding averages

	Mat	Inns	NO	Runs	HS	Ave	100	50	Ct	St
First-class	2	2	0	11	10	5.50	0	0	2	0

Bowling averages

	Mat	Runs	Wkts	BBI	Ave	5w	10
First-class	2	40	1	1/13	40.00	0	0

Captain Stuart Ronald Gordon
Europeans (India)
57th Wilde's Rifles (Frontier Force) Indian Army
Died Between 29 and 31 October 1914
Aged 37
Right-handed Bat

'He did the most gallant thing I have ever seen'

Ronald Stuart Gordon was born on 24 November 1876, the fifth son of the late John Lewis Gordon, of West Park, Elgin, Scotland and Colombo, Ceylon. He was educated at Trinity College, Glenalmond, Perthshire before attending RMC Sandhurst in July 1895. Whilst at Sandhurst he won the bronze medals for cricket, rugby and association football. He was also a fine shot and keen fisherman as well as being a member of the Caledonian Club, London.

In January 1897 he became a second lieutenant in the Indian Army, at first attached to the 61st Pioneers before being transferred to the 57th Wilde's Rifles. He served as the regimental adjutant and was promoted captain in 1906. While in India he helped to win many cups for polo, football, golf and cricket. He played his one and only first-class match on 11 August 1899 when he played in the Bombay Presidency Match 1899–1900 for the Europeans against the Parsees at the Gymkhana Ground, Bombay. Gordon scored 8 in his only innings and caught Hormasji Kanga off Lionel Deas for 48. The match was drawn.

Gordon served in the Boxer Rebellion in China in 1900 and also on the North-West Frontier of India in 1908, taking part in operations in the Mohmand country, and engagements at Kargha and Malta. For these actions he was Mentioned in Despatches (*London Gazette*, 14 August 1908). On 6 August 1914 Captain Gordon married Ruby Mary, eldest daughter of Henry Byron Moore, Melbourne, Australia, at St Peter's, Melbourne. The following day Gordon and his wife returned to India.

In 1914 the 57th Rifles, a one-battalion regiment, sailed with the Lahore Division to France where it fought until December 1915 when it was despatched to Egypt. On the voyage to France the regiment had converted from an eight- to a four-company unit but retained the class composition of one rifle company each of Sikhs, Dogras, Pathans and Punjabi Mussulmans. Gordon was killed in action at Messines on 31 October 1914. A brother officer sent the following account of his death to his wife:

> He did the most gallant thing I have ever seen, he took a platoon and went forward to check the advance of the Germans to cover the retirement of the rest of his company, though he must have known it was certain death. While advancing he was shot through the head and died instantaneously.

Another officer also wrote to his family:

> He was the best officer I have ever known. He was extraordinarily popular with the men, and I have never seen them so cut up about anything as they were when they came in.

His body was never recovered or identified and he is commemorated on the Menin Gate Memorial, Ypres, West-Vlaanderen, Panels 1A and 2.

Batting and fielding averages

	Mat	Inns	NO	Runs	HS	Ave	100	50	Ct	St
First-class	1	1	0	8	8	8.00	0	0	1	0

Bowling averages

	Mat	Balls	Runs	Wkts	BBI	BBM	Ave	Econ	SR	4w	5w	10
First-class	1	-	-	-	-	-	-	-	-	-	-	-

Lieutenant Ralph Escott Hancock DSO
Somerset
2nd, attd 1st Bn Devonshire Regiment
Died 29 October 1914
Aged 26
Right-handed Bat

'Non braver or more selfless'

Ralph Escott Hancock was born on 20 December 1887 at Llandaff, South Wales, the son of Mr and Mrs Frank Hancock of Ford, Wiveliscombe, Somerset. His father was Frank Hancock, the managing director of the Cardiff Brewing Company and a pioneering rugby union international for Wales. His uncles were Froude Hancock and William Hancock, both of whom played rugby union for England, William also playing cricket for Somerset in 1892.

Ralph was educated at Connaught House Preparatory School Portmore, Weymouth, and Rugby School. At Rugby he played for the Cricket XI in 1905 and 1906 and from Rugby went to the RMC Sandhurst in August 1906. In January 1908 he was gazetted to the 2nd Bn Devonshire Regiment, becoming a lieutenant in February 1911. Between 1909 and 1912 he served in Crete, Malta and Alexandria. In September 1913 Ralph married Mary Hamilton Broadmead, younger daughter of the Reverend P. P. Broadmead, of Olands, Milverton, Somerset.

A good all-round sportsman, Hancock played polo, won the regimental cup whilst stationed in Malta and captained the Army polo team versus the Navy. He also won several prices for shooting. An excellent horseman, he won the East Devon Hunt heavyweight Point to Point in 1913 and 1914.

Ralph Hancock was a right-handed middle-order batsman and a sometime bowler. He made nine first-class appearances for Somerset between August 1907 and May 1914. He made his debut against the visiting South Africans on 29 August 1907 at the Recreation Ground, Bath. Hancock scored 15 and 6, the South Africans winning comfortably by 358 runs. He played two further first-class matches in May and July 1908 against Lancashire and Kent, losing both. Hancock then disappeared from first-class cricket for four seasons but reappeared in four games during the 1913 season playing against Worcestershire, Derbyshire, Sussex and Kent. He made two further appearances in May 1914 against Surrey on 21st and Sussex on 25th which was to prove to be his final first class appearance. Hancock scored 25 and 0 Sussex winning by 85 runs. Hancock scored a total of 206 first-class runs, his highest score was 34 against Sussex on 11 August 1913.

After two years stationed at the depot in Exeter, he left for France on 30 August 1914 as part of the reinforcement for the 1st Battalion. He was awarded the DSO (*London Gazette*, 1 December 1914), a very high award for a junior officer. His citation read:

On October 23rd displayed conspicuous gallantry in leaving his trench under very heavy fire and going back some sixty yards over absolutely bare ground to pick up Corporal Warwick, who had fallen whilst coming up with a party of reinforcements. Lieutenant Hancock conveyed this non-commissioned officer to the cover of a haystack, and then returned to his trench. (since Killed in Action).

Ralph was killed on 29 October 1914 and was subsequently mentioned in Sir John French's Despatches on 11 January 1915.

His body was never recovered or identified and he is commemorated on the le Touret Memorial, Panels 8 and 9.

Batting and fielding averages

	Mat	Inns	NO	Runs	HS	Ave	100	50	Ct	St
First-class	9	17	0	206	34	12.11	0	0	0	0

Bowling averages

	Mat	Balls	Runs	Wkts	BBI	BBM	Ave	Econ	SR	4w	5w	10
First-class	9	42	29	0	-	-	-	4.14	-	0	0	0

Lieutenant The Hon. Gerald Ernest Francis Ward MVO
Marylebone Cricket Club (MCC)
1st Life Guards
30 October 1914
Aged 36
Right-handed Bat/Right-arm Fast Bowler

'Could mix with officers and men alike'

Gerald Ernest Francis Ward was born on 9 November 1877 at Himley Hall, Staffordshire, the son of the 1st Earl of Dudley, and Lady Evelyn Ward, of 52 Danes Street, London. Educated at Eton, where he played in the First XI, he was the most successful bowler of the 1896 season, taking 35 wickets for just over 11 runs each. However, despite this, he failed to impress against Harrow at Lord's. As well as Eton, he played cricket for the Gloucestershire XI, the Marylebone Cricket Club (MCC) and the Household Brigade. He made one first-class appearance for the MCC against Oxford University on 29 June 1903 at Lord's, scoring 8 in his first innings and failing to bat in the second. The match was eventually drawn.

He took a commission as a second lieutenant in the Gloucestershire Regiment before transferring into the 1st Life Guards. Promoted to lieutenant, he saw service during the Second Boer War between 1899 and 1902. He was also invested as a Member of the Royal Victorian Order (MVO). Ward married Lady Evelyn Selina Louisa Crichton, daughter of John Henry Crichton, 4th Earl of Erne, of Crom Castle, County Fermanagh.

At the outbreak of war the Life Guards were based at their barracks in Hyde Park. On 8 October 1914 Ward crossed to Belgium with his regiment. Apart from the first two weeks when the Life Guards were used in the traditional cavalry role for mobile reconnaissance, it fought most of the war as a dismounted force.

The regiment was heavily involved at the First Battle of Ypres (October–November 1914), during which, on 30 October, Lieutenant Gerald Ernest Francis Ward was killed at Zandvoorde, Belgium. The book *Troop Horse and Trench* describes Ward's loss in more detail.

> Both A and D Sqns had sustained losses but C Sqn had with the exception of Charlie Wright and six or seven men been absolutely wiped out. Charlie and his little bunch were not in the same section of line with their Sqn, but in close touch with D Sqn. When the order to retire was given, it did not reach the main body of C Sqn owing to its position being slightly detached from, and in front on the left of, the rest of the Regiment. Lord Hugh Grosvenor, C Sqn leader was not the man who would retire without orders, so they just fought it out and died where they stood. No trace of Lord Hugh and his hundred odd men was ever found ... .

Four officers of the Life Guards died that day. In addition to Major Hugh Grosvenor, son of Lord Grosvenor, they were Lieutenant The Hon. Gerald Francis Ward, son of the 1st Earl of Dudley, Captain Edward Denis Festus Kelly and Lieutenant John Charles Closebrooks.

The war diary of the 1st Life Guards also mentions the action.

Zandvoorde-Oct 30 6.00am

Heavy bombardment of position opened. At 7.30am position was attacked by large force of infantry. This attack proved successful owing to greatly superior numbers. Regiment retired in good order about 10.00am except C Squadron on left flank from which only about ten men got back. Remainder of Squadron missing. Also one machine gun put out of action.

Lieutenant Ward's body was never discovered or identified and he is commemorated on the Ypres (Menin Gate) Memorial, Panel 3.

Batting and fielding averages

	Mat	Inns	NO	Runs	HS	Ave	100	50	Ct	St
First-class	1	1	0	8	8	8.00	0	0	0	0

Bowling averages

	Mat	Balls	Runs	Wkts	BBI	BBM	Ave	Econ	SR	4w	5w	10
First-class	1	-	-	-	-	-	-	-	-	-	-	-

Lieutenant William Hugh Holbech
MCC/Warwickshire
2nd Bn Scots Guards
Died 1 November 1914
Aged 32
Right-handed Bat

'In him we have lost a gallant soldier and a great friend'

William Hugh Holbech was born on 18 August 1882 at Murray Bay, Quebec, Canada, the son of Mary Holbech, of The Cottage, Farnborough, Banbury, Oxfordshire and Lieutenant Colonel W. H. Holbech, formerly of the King's Royal Rifle Corps; his father, who died on 6 March 1901, was also one of HM's Hon. Corps of Gentlemen at Arms and served in the Red River Expedition, 1870; was a brigade major in the Egyptian Campaign of 1882, and was Mentioned in Despatches).

Educated at Eton, he failed to get into the XI. On leaving Eton he decided to make a career in the Army and entered the RMC Sandhurst and was appointed second lieutenant in the 2nd Battalion Scots Guards in 1902, being promoted lieutenant in March 1904. Holbech was in the Sandhurst XI and played on four occasions during the 1901 season, against the Household Brigade, Royal Military Academy, Woolwich, Charterhouse School and the MCC. Between 1902 and 1905 he represented the Household Brigade against the MCC on four occasions. He joined the MCC in 1903. Holbech retired from the Army in 1907, joining the reserve of officers.

Between June 1908 and July 1910 he played in three first-class matches, the first two for the MCC and one for Warwickshire against Hampshire in the County Championship. He made his first-class debut appearance on 25 June 1908 against Cambridge University at Lord's where he made 7 and 0 and caught Kenneth Macleod off the bowling of Charles Llewellyn for 21. Cambridge University won by two wickets. His second first-class appearance for the MCC was against Oxford University on 10 June 1909 at The University Parks, Oxford. Holbech scored 0 and 21 and the match was drawn. He made his final first-class appearance for Warwickshire against Hampshire on 11 July 1910 at Edgbaston, Birmingham, making two ducks; Hampshire won by an innings and 119 runs.

At the outbreak of the war Holbech joined the 3rd Bn Scots Guards, later transferring to his old battalion on 2 October 1914, that unit being based at the Tower of London. In September 1914 the battalion was attached to 20 Brigade in 7th Division. The division assembled in the New Forest and landed in Zeebrugge during the first week of October 1914. Holbech, together with his battalion, arrived at the front line on 18 October during the First Battle of Ypres. Between 19 October and 22 November 1914, the division fought the advancing Germans to a standstill. As a result of this gallant action, 2nd Scots Guards, together with many other regiments, suffered heavy losses.

During this action rapid British rifle fire cut the German advance to pieces and prevented a German breakthrough. After this the division became known as the 'Immortal Seventh'. On 25 October Holbech was severely wounded at Kruseid and was evacuated to England.

Although he arrived back safely, he finally succumbed to his wounds at the Herbert Hospital, Woolwich on 1 November.

On hearing of his death his commanding officer, Colonel Bolton, wrote:

> From the time Willie joined us at Southampton until he was mortally wounded, he was one of the most cheery, unselfish, capable, and keenest of the officers in my battalion. We all deplore his loss more than I can say. I look back on both him and poor young Cottrell Dormer, as two of the best officers in every way.

A brother officer, Major Cator, also wrote to the family:

> He defended his trench all night at Kruseik when the Germans got through our line. He and Capt. Paynter had the Germans all round them and defended their trenches most gallantly – I only wish I could tell you more; in him we have lost a gallant soldier and a great friend.

He is buried against the north side of the tower in St Botolph Churchyard, Farnborough, Warwickshire.

Batting and fielding averages

	Mat	Inns	NO	Runs	HS	Ave	100	50	Ct	St
First-class	3	6	0	28	21	4.66	0	0	1	0

Bowling averages

	Mat	Balls	Runs	Wkts	BBI	BBM	Ave	Econ	SR	4w	5w	10
First-class	3	-	-	-	-	-	-	-	-	-	-	-

Major Eustace Crawley
Cambridge University
12th (The Prince of Wales's Royal) Lancers
Died 2 November 1914
Aged 46
Right-handed Bat

'The finest truest officer I ever met'

Eustace Crawley was born on 16 April 1868 in Highgate, Middlesex, the third son of Baden Crawley. Educated at Harrow, he played for the Harrow XI (1885–86) before going up to Trinity College Cambridge. He made seventeen first-class appearances for Cambridge University between May 1887 and July 1889, his first class debut being on 12 May 1887 for Cambridge against C. I. Thornton's XI at Fenner's. He made 24 in his one innings; Cambridge University won by ten wickets. He went on to play against A. J. Webbe's XI, Yorkshire, Sussex, MCC, Oxford University, Gentlemen of England and Surrey. He made his final first-class appearance on 1 July 1889 against Oxford University at Lords. Crawley scored 54 in his one innings, Cambridge University winning by an innings and 105 runs. During his first-class career Crawley scored 424 runs, his highest score being 103 against Oxford University on 4 July 1887, and made eight catches. He also turned out for Hertfordshire (1885–1889), Worcestershire (1887–1892), the Army (1892), I Zingari (1892–1893) and Marylebone Cricket Club (1893).

Crawley made his career in the Army and joined 12th Lancers in August 1889 as a second lieutenant; he was promoted to lieutenant in 1891 and captain in November 1897. Between 1880 and 1890 he took part in operations in Sierra Leone and in 1899 was in command of the Bula Expedition in Nigeria, for which he was Mentioned in Despatches for his leadership.

Crawley also commanded the Nigeria Company Constabulary. In the years 1900 to 1902 he was a Special Service Officer in the South African War. He was DAAG (Deputy Assistant Adjutant and Quarter Master General) of Ridley's Corps of Mounted Infantry from April to December 1900 and took part in General Ian Hamilton's march. Present at the actions of Diamond Hill, Johannesburg, and Wittebergen, he was on operations in Cape Colony under General French, served as Intelligence Officer to Capper's Column at the end of 1901, and Staff Officer to Doran's Column from December 1901 to May 1902. For his services, Lord Roberts mentioned him in despatches on 4 December 1901.

From May to November 1902 Captain Crawley was DAAG on the staff of Colonel Hickman, commanding the troops at Middelburg, Cape Colony. In 1902 and 1903 he again saw service in Nigeria, being in command of a column in the Kano Expedition. He commanded Mounted Infantry in India in 1903 and obtained the substantive rank of major in July 1905 before, in 1906 and 1907, he became officiating Brigade Major of the Amballa Cavalry Brigade and ADC to the Inspector General of Cavalry in India. Major Crawley married Lady Violet Ella Finch, eldest daughter of the eighth Earl of Aylesford in December 1904, and they resided at 5 Lancaster Gate Terrace, London.

Eustace Crawley was killed by a shell at Wytschaete, Hollebeke, Belgium on 2 November 1914. His body was never recovered or identified and he is commemorated on the Ypres (Menin Gate) Memorial, Panel 5.

Batting and fielding averages

	Mat	Inns	NO	Runs	HS	Ave	100	50	Ct	St
First-class	17	28	2	424	103*	16.30	1	1	8	0

Bowling averages

	Mat	Balls	Runs	Wkts	BBI	BBM	Ave	Econ	SR	4w	5w	10
First-class	17	-	-	-	-	-	-	-	-	-	-	

Captain Bruce Edward Alexander Manson
61st King George's Own Pioneers
Europeans (India)
Died 4 November 1914
Aged 35

'The King spoke very well of him'

Bruce Edward Alexander Manson was born on 7 December 1878, the son of F. B. Manson (Indian Forest Service) and Emily Manson. On passing for the Indian Army he was gazetted to an unattached second lieutenancy in July 1898 before being appointed to the Indian Staff Corps in October 1899.

In 1900 Manson saw service in China during the Boxer Rebellion, for which he was awarded the Military Order of the Dragon. It was also in 1900, in October, that he was promoted lieutenant in the Indian Army, obtaining his company in July 1907. He married Mable Manson and was ADC to HM King George V at the Delhi Durbar in 1911.

Manson played one first-class match for the Europeans against the Parsees on 21 September 1903 during a Bombay Presidency Match. The match was played at the Deccan Gymkhana Ground, Poona. Manson scored 1 and 7 and took three wickets for 54, Parsees eventually winning by an innings and six runs.

At the outbreak of war Manson found himself in Tanga, East Africa. The British resolved to capture German East Africa with an amphibious attack on Tanga but, although the plan looked good on paper, the attack turned into a debacle. On 2 November 1914 Captain Francis W. Caulfeild, commander of the British cruiser HMS *Fox*, gave the German garrison in Tanga one hour to surrender. After three hours the German flag was still flying and *Fox* attacked with a force of fourteen troop transports. Unfortunately, the time given by Caulfeild for the garrison to surrender was used to strengthen their positions and bring up reinforcements, eventually numbering about 1,000 in six companies. It also gave time for one of Germany's most able commanders, Lieutenant Colonel Paul Emil von Lettow-Vorbeck to get back to Tanga.

By evening on 3 November the invasion force was ashore. At noon on 4 November the troops were ordered to march on the city. Well concealed defenders quickly broke up the advance. The fighting then turned to jungle skirmishing and bitter street fighting. The harbour contingent pushed on and entered the town, capturing the customs' house and the Hotel Deutscher Kaiser and running up the Union Jack. Unfortunately, poorly trained and equipped battalions of the Imperial Service Brigade scattered and retreated under an intense German fire and ran from the town. To make things worse the 98th Infantry were attacked by swarms of angry bees and also ran. The battle was a disaster for the British who were forced to evacuate back to the transport. British troops left behind nearly all their equipment. As a result Lettow-Vorbeck re-equipped three Askari companies with the latest rifles, together with 60,000 rounds of ammunition. He also captured sixteen machine guns and several field telephones. The British *Official History of the War* said it was 'one of the most notable failures in British military history'.

Casualties included 360 killed and 487 wounded on the British side; the *Schutztruppe* lost sixteen Germans and fifty-five Askaris killed, and seventy-six in total wounded. Among the British dead was the unfortunate Bruce Edward Alexander Manson.

Bruce Manson is commemorated in the Tanga memorial Cemetery, Tanzania.

Batting and fielding averages

	Mat	Inns	NO	Runs	HS	Ave	100	50	Ct	St
First-class	1	2	0	8	7	4.00	0	0	0	0

Bowling averages

	Mat	Runs	Wkts	BBI	Ave	5w	10
First-class	1	54	3	3/54	18.00	0	0

Captain Arnold Stearns Nesbitt
Worcester
Worcestershire Regiment
Died 7 November 1914
Aged 36
Right-handed Bat/Wicket-keeper

'Refused to retreat even when his life was in danger'

Arnold Stearns Nesbitt was born on 16 November 1878 at Walton-on-Thames. The son of Mr and Mrs William Henry Nesbitt of Oatlands Drive, Weybridge, Surrey, he was educated at Bradfield College, Berkshire where he played for the First XI. On leaving school Arnold decided to make a career in the Army and, leaving the Militia, took a commission in the 3rd Bn Worcestershire Regiment as a second lieutenant. He was promoted lieutenant later that year before being promoted to captain in 1904. As Adjutant of the 6th Battalion from 1911 to 1914 at the depot at Norton Barracks, Worcester, he organized a Military Tournament at the Skating Rink which, owing to his energies and foresight, as well as his tact and courtesy, was a great success. He also played for his regiment in 1900. He was employed with the Egyptian Army between 1907 and 1908.

Nesbitt made one first-class appearance for Worcestershire against Middlesex on 27 May 1914 at Lord's, making 2 not out and 3. He also caught John Hearne off the bowling of Robert Burrows for 104. Middlesex won by an innings and 56 runs. He was a member of Incognito, the Worcestershire County, and the Gentlemen of Worcester Cricket Clubs and was also a very keen hunter.

Arnold Nesbitt was killed in action on 7 November 1914. *The Worcestershire Regiment in the Great War* by Captain H. F. Stacke (1928) describes what happened:

> November 6th 1914 saw the low-lying valley of the Lys blanketed by a thick fog. The fog lasted all day, great shells hurtling through the air while the men in the waterlogged trenches stared ahead. In the darkness between 3 and 4 a.m. on 7th November a very heavy shellfire was opened on the British line east of Ploegsteert Wood. Around 5 a.m. masses of German infantry came plunging through the fog. Losses were heavy with over 200 soldiers killed including Captain Nesbit. A brother officer said of Nesbitt, 'He was one of the best officers the regiment had ever had.'

He was also mentioned for his gallant service in Sir John French's Despatches of 14 January 1915.

His body was never recovered or identified and he is commemorated on the Ypres Menin Gate Memorial, Panel 34.

Nesbitt was also a prominent Mason being a member of Lodge of Erin No. 2895, London.

Batting and fielding averages

	Mat	Inns	NO	Runs	HS	Ave	100	50	Ct	St
First-class	1	2	1	5	3	5.00	0	0	1	0

Bowling averages

	Mat	Balls	Runs	Wkts	BBI	BBM	Ave	Econ	SR	4w	5w	10
First-class	1	-	-	-	-	-	-	-	-	-	-	-

Major Lord Bernard Charles Gordon-Lennox
Middlesex
2nd Bn Grenadier Guards
Died 10 November 1914
Aged 36
Right-handed Bat

'As brave as anyone I have ever seen'

Lord Bernard Charles Gordon-Lennox was born on 1 May 1878 in Westminster London, the third son of the seventh Duke of Richmond and Gordon KG by his first wife Amy Mary, daughter of Percy Ricardo, of Bramley Park, Guildford. He was educated at Eton College, but failed to make the College's First XI. However, on entering Sandhurst he did make the First XI and played a memorable innings against Woolwich, scoring 80 runs. He made one first-class appearance on 25 May 1903, for Middlesex against Gloucestershire at Lord's in the County Championship. He scored 0 in his only innings and caught Frederick Roberts off the bowling of John Hearne for 6. Middlesex won by an innings and 118 runs. He later became a member of the MCC and I Zingari. In 1914 he toured Egypt with I Zingari, scoring an impressive 119 against an All-Egyptian side at Alexandria. Gordon-Lennox also turned out for the Household Brigade where he was a prolific scorer.

He was commissioned into the Grenadier Guards in February 1898 as a second lieutenant being promoted to lieutenant in October 1899 and served in the Second Boer War, being present at operations in the Orange Free State, including the actions at Poplar Grove and Driefontein. Between 1904 and 1906 he was seconded for service with the Chinese Regiment at Wei-hai-Wei. Promoted captain in 1909, he was an ADC from November 1907 to July 1909, and Assistant Military Secretary from August 1909 to November 1911 to the General Officer Commanding-in-Chief, Northern Command.

Gordon-Lennox married Evelyn, daughter of Henry Loch, 1st Baron Loch in 1907. They had two sons, George, later Lieutenant General Sir George Gordon-Lennox, and Alexander, later Rear Admiral Sir Alexander Gordon-Lennox. Promoted to major in 1913, he was a member of the Guards and Turf Clubs.

The 2nd Battalion landed at le Havre on 13 August 1914 as part of 4 Guards Brigade in 2nd Division with Major Lord Gordon-Lennox commanding No. 3 Company. Gordon-Lennox served at Mons on 23 August and the subsequent retreat, taking part in the battles of the Marne and Aisne. In October 1914 the battalion moved north, arriving at Hazebrouck on the 14th. The battalion arrived in the Ypres sector, going into trenches at St Jean, north of Ypres on the 20th. Lieutenant Stocks of the Grenadier Guards wrote:

> Marched off at 6 a.m. to Ypres, through which we marched. Crowds of people in the streets to see us march through, and there seemed to be a tremendous lot of priests and nuns. Rather a nice old town with narrow, cobble-stoned streets, and some fine buildings. We marched through to St Jean where we took up a position and entrenched facing north-east.

On 28 October, the 2nd Battalion Grenadier Guards moved to Nonne-Bosschen Wood. Lieutenant Stocks wrote home, describing the action on 10 November 1914:

> After a quiet night terrific shelling started soon after daybreak and lasted practically without intermission throughout the day. Our trenches on the right where the line was thrown back were taken in enfilade and badly knocked about, and as they (German artillery) have now located us pretty well there were a few direct hits and consequent casualties. The trees too were knocked down.

One of those casualties was Lord Bernard Lennox-Gordon, killed by a high explosive shell. He was mentioned in Sir John French's Despatches for his war service (*London Gazette*, 14 January 1915).

He was buried in Zillebeke Churchyard, Commonwealth War Graves Commission Cemetery, Grave reference E. 3.

Lady Bernard Gordon-Lennox remained a widow until her death in June 1944, aged 67, when a V-1 flying bomb hit the Guards Chapel, Wellington Barracks.

Batting and fielding averages

	Mat	Inns	NO	Runs	HS	Ave	100	50	4s	6s	Ct	St
First-class	1	1	0	0	0	0.00	0	0	0	0	1	0

Bowling averages

	Mat	Balls	Runs	Wkts	BBI	BBM	Ave	Econ	SR	4w	5w	10
First-class	1	-	-	-	-	-	-	-	-	-	-	-

Major The Hon. William George Sydney Cadogan MVO
Europeans (India)
10th, The Prince of Wales's Own Royal Hussars
Died 12 November 1914
Aged 35
Unknown

'Always stood his ground'

William George Sydney Cadogan was born on 31 January 1879 at Chelsea, London, the fifth son of the fifth Earl Cadogan and Countess Cadogan, fourth daughter of the second Earl of Craven. Educated at Eton, he turned out for their First XI, scoring 16 and 2 against Winchester in 1897 (Eton lost by 51 runs) and the same year against Harrow when he scored 5 and 10 in a drawn match. A talented player, he turned out for I Zingari, Vice Regal Lodge, Eton Ramblers, and the Lord Chief Justice's XI, all in 1896.

In February 1899 he took a commission in the 10th Hussars as a second lieutenant becoming a lieutenant in January 1900. He served in the Second Boer War, being present at the Relief of Kimberley, operations in the Orange Free State and Paardeberg, including the actions at Driefontein, Poplar Grove, Houtnek (Thoba Mountain) Vet and Zand rivers in the Transvaal, 1900 and 1901, and in Cape Colony in 1901 and 1902.

In 1906 he was invested as a member of the Royal Victorian Order (MVO) and also received the Cross of Honour of the Order of the Crown of Wurtemberg. He was promoted captain in March 1904, major in January 1911 and, between 1912 and 1914, was Equerry to HRH The Prince of Wales. Prior to this he was ADC to His Royal Highness during his Indian Tour in 1905 and 1906. Cadogan also accompanied the Prince of Wales, who travelled as the Earl of Chester on a visit to Germany (see above photograph).

Cadogan made his one and only first-class appearance on 24 August 1904 for the Europeans (India) against the Parsees at the Gymkhana Ground, Bombay. He made two ducks. He did, however, catch D. C. Daruwala off the bowling of Ernest Coombs for zero, Parsees eventually winning by 180 runs. Cadogan was a member of the Turf and Whites Clubs.

Major Cadogan left with his regiment for the front on 5 October 1914, crossing the channel on the SS *Bosnia*. He was officer commanding C Squadron, which comprised of six officers and 150 other ranks, 153 riding horses, fourteen draft horses, three general service wagons, and four bicycles.

Major William Cadogan was killed in action while in command of his regiment on 14 November 1914. He was mentioned in Sir John French's Despatches for his services during the war. An account of his death and the events leading up to it was later published:

> This force under the command of Major Shearman was subjected to heavy enemy artillery fire throughout the following day resulting in the wounding of 4 Other Ranks. To add to the misery of the attentions of artillery fire, on commencement

of relief at 7.00pm heavy rain started to fall. In this rotation 3 Troops of B Squadron of the Hussars with 40 men from the horse lines plus 2 Squadrons of the 1st (Royal) Dragoons attached now proceeded into the trenches whilst A and C Squadrons of the Regiment took their place in support positions.

As the rain continued to fall the trenches became untenable with the position occupied by A Squadron being completely 'washed in'. The prevailing conditions necessitated a movement of fifty yards towards the rear at dawn under constant harassing fire by the enemy. In particular, sniping from close range resulted in several casualties as the firing line assisted in the completion of this manoeuvre by opening a rapid fire on the positions held by the enemy. In addition to being subjected to rifle fire, the German artillery kept up a steady bombardment throughout the day resulting in the mortal wounding of Major The Hon. W. Cadogan who was hit in the groin.

He is buried in Ypres Town Cemetery, E1. 17

Batting and fielding averages

	Mat	Inns	NO	Runs	HS	Ave	100	50	4s	6s	Ct	St
First-class	1	2	0	0	0	0.00	0	0	0	0	1	0

Bowling averages

	Mat	Balls	Runs	Wkts	BBI	BBM	Ave	Econ	SR	4w	5w	10
First-class	1	-	-	-	-	-	-	-	-	-	-	-

Captain Geoffrey Percy Robert Toynbee
Hampshire
1st Bn The Prince Consort's Own (Rifle Brigade)
Died 15 November 1914
Aged 29
Right-handed Bat

'Never dull always fun'

Geoffrey Percy Robert Toynbee was born in Paddington, London on 18 May 1885, the only son of Percy Toynbee of 92 Westbourne Terrace, London and Mrs Francis Raitt of Brookfield Hall, York.

Educated at Winchester College where he played in the First XI in 1902 and 1903, averaging 18.25 in 1902 and 24.30 in 1903, he was also in the Rugby XV and in the Sixes. Moving onto the RMC Sandhurst, he not only became the captain of the Sandhurst XI, but also one of the most prolific batsmen Sandhurst had ever had through their college, averaging 70.71 in 1904 and 42.33 in 1905. In 1911 Geoffrey played for the Rifle Brigade against Aldershot Command and scored a remarkable 115 and 101. He also represented Sandhurst at Golf. Toynbee was a member of the United Service Club, Pall Mall, of I Zingari and the MCC.

Geoffrey Toynbee made three first class appearances in 1912. He made his first-class debut for the Marylebone Cricket Club at Lord's on 9 May 1912 against Kent. He scored 4 and 0, the MCC winning by 73 runs. This was Toynbee's only appearance for the club. He then went on to play for Hampshire in two first-class matches in the County Championship. The first match was against Gloucestershire on 29 July 1912 at the County Ground, Southampton, he made 14 in his only innings, the match being drawn. His final first-class appearance came on 19 August 1912, again in the County Championship, against Sussex at the United Services Ground, Portsmouth. He failed to bat and the match was drawn.

Toynbee joined the Rifle Brigade in August 1905 as a second lieutenant before being promoted to lieutenant in May 1909 and captain in February 1914. He travelled to France with the 1st Battalion, landing in le Havre on 23 August 1914 as part of 11 Brigade in 4th Division in time to provide infantry reinforcements at the Battle of le Cateau. Toynbee saw action at the Battles of the Marne, the Aisne and at Messines in 1914 but was killed on 15 November 1914 at Ploegstraete, Nord-Pas-de-Calais France.

He has no known grave and is commemorated on the Ploegstraete Memorial, Comines-Warneton, Hainaut, Belgium, Panel 10.

Batting and fielding averages

	Mat	Inns	NO	Runs	HS	Ave	100	50	Ct	St
First-class	3	3	0	18	14	6.00	0	0	1	0

Bowling averages

	Mat	Balls	Runs	Wkts	BBI	BBM	Ave	Econ	SR	4w	5w	10
First-class	3	-	-	-	-	-	-	-	-	-	-	-

Captain George Arthur Murray Docker
Marylebone Cricket Club (MCC)
Royal Fusiliers, attd 1st Bn King's Own Royal Regiment
(Lancaster)
Died 17 November 1914
Aged 37
Right-handed Bat/Right-arm Fast

'An Australian who became a perfect English Gentleman'

George Arthur Murray Docker was born on 18 November 1876 in Sydney, New South Wales, Australia, the eldest son of Arthur Robert Docker and Florence Lucy Docker of Sydney. Educated at the Highgate School, he was in the school XI in 1895 when he scored 312 runs with an average of 18.35 and took 44 wickets for 14.43 runs each. He went up to Oriel College Oxford where he read Law.

However, Docker was unable to finish his studies as he volunteered for the 3rd (Militia) Battalion King's Own Royal Regiment (Lancaster) and went to South Africa in 1900 to take part in the Boer War. During the war he commanded a section of mounted infantry at Zand River and fought in the engagement there on 14 June 1900. He also took part in the action at Ladybrand between 2 and 7 September 1900 and was involved in the pursuit of De Wet in the Orange Free State and the action at Balmoral on 19 November 1900. Eventually, in June 1903, he was invalided home, suffering from rheumatic fever. He received a commission in the King's Liverpool Regiment in 1900, becoming a lieutenant the same year. He transferred to the Royal Fusiliers in 1901 as a lieutenant, being promoted to captain in 1908.

Captain Docker married in 1903, Anna Louisa Maud Josephine, daughter of the late Louis Arthur Goodeve, barrister-at-law, and they had four children, Arthur Guy, born November, 1904, Peter Goodeve, born June, 1908, Michael Lee, born November, 1911, and Alison Everilda Josephine, born February, 1914. He became a member of the MCC in 1898.

Docker played in eleven first-class matches between May 1911 and May 1914, all for the MCC, making his debut against Middlesex on 18 May 1911 at Lord's. Docker scored 4 and 3 and caught Edward Mignon off the bowling of Claude Buckenham for 0; Middlesex won by eight wickets. He travelled with the MCC during their visit to the West Indies in 1913, playing on seven occasions against Barbados (twice), Trinidad (twice), West Indies and British Guiana (twice). On his return he played against Kent and Oxford University. His final appearance was against Yorkshire on 13 May 1914 at Lords when he scored 0 and 4, Yorkshire winning by an innings and 119 runs. Docker made a total of 185 first-class runs, his highest score being 29 against Kent on 9 May 1912 at Lord's; took 5 wickets, his best figures being 2 for 66; and made three catches. He also played for the Oxford University Authentics and the Free Foresters. He was also a fine polo player and won many prizes for athletics and golf.

Between 16 April 1907 and 31 July 1911 he was Instructor of Military Law and Administration to F Company at the RMC Sandhurst. He became Adjutant of the 10th Battalion Middlesex Regiment in April 1912 and, in October 1914, shortly after the outbreak of war the 10th Middlesex Regiment was ordered to India. However, at the very last minute,

Captain Docker received orders to take out a draft of the 3rd King's Own Royal Regiment (Lancaster) to France to help reinforce the 1st Battalion.

He left England on 8 November 1914 reaching the King's Own on 15 November, and went into the front line on the 16th. Early the following morning, Captain Docker was killed at le Touquet, near Armentières. He was initially buried close to where he fell.

His remains were later re-interred in le Touquet Railway Crossing Cemetery, grave reference A 11.

Batting and fielding averages

	Mat	Inns	NO	Runs	HS	Ave	100	50	Ct	St
First-class	11	18	2	185	34*	11.56	0	0	3	0

Bowling averages

	Mat	Runs	Wkts	BBI	Ave	5w	10
First-class	11	169	5	2/66	33.80	0	0

Lieutenant Hervey Robert Charles Tudway
Somerset
2nd Bn Grenadier Guards
Died 18 November 1914
Aged 26
Unknown

'His life for his country, his soul to God'

Hervey Robert Charles Tudway was born on 23 September 1888 at 17 Lower Berkeley Street, Westminster, London, the eldest son of Charles Clement Tudway, of Wells by his second marriage with Alice, daughter of the late Sir Frederick Hervey Bathurst, third Baronet. Educated at Evelyns and Eton, where he won the School Fives in 1907, he was captain of his house in the sixth form, and a member of the Eton Society. Commissioned as a second lieutenant in the Grenadier Guards in February, 1910, he became a lieutenant the following September and served with his regiment until summer 1914.

Tudway was appointed ADC to Viscount Buxton, Governor-General of South Africa, and arrived there to discover that war had broken out in Europe. He resigned his post immediately and returned to England, rejoining his regiment at the front on 2 November 1914.

Although a fine cricketer, Tudway made only one first-class appearance, representing Somerset against Hampshire on 9 June 1910 at the Officers' Club Service Ground, Aldershot. Batting number eight, he made 6 runs in both of his innings. Hampshire won by an innings and 36 runs. He also represented Marylebone Cricket Club in 1911 and the Household Brigade between 1908 and 1914.

Tudway was a member of a long-established family from Wells, Somerset. Three family members had served as MP for Wells from 1754 to 1830, with a further member holding the seat from 1852 to 1855.

Lieutenant Tudway died of wounds to the head at Boulogne on 18 November 1914; he had been injured on 9 November at the First Battle of Ypres. He was buried in Boulogne Eastern Cemetery 11. B. 13 and a brass tablet was erected to his memory in the North Choir Aisle of Wells Cathedral, the inscription concluding with 'His life for his country, his soul to God'.

Tudway was a member of the Guards' and Pratt's Clubs. He was also a member of the MCC and I Zingari. His brother, Lieutenant Lionel C. P. Tudway DSO RN, was taken prisoner at Kut.

Batting and fielding averages

	Mat	Inns	NO	Runs	HS	Ave	100	50	Ct	St
First-class	1	2	0	12	6	6.00	0	0	0	0

Bowling averages

	Mat	Balls	Runs	Wkts	BBI	BBM	Ave	Econ	SR	4w	5w	10
First-class	1	-	-	-	-	-	-	-	-	-	-	-

Lieutenant Norman Seraphio Hobson
Eastern Province
Graaff-Reinet Commando
Died 25 November 1914
Aged 29
Not Known

'The first generation to fall for his country'

Norman Seraphio Hobson was born on 7 May 1885 at Graaff-Reinet, Cape Province, and was educated at St Andrew's College, Grahamstown. His family had settled in South Africa in 1829 and introduced cricket to other farmers. They were also founder members of Harefield County Cricket Club in 1881. In 1905, while playing for Harfield Cricket Club, Port Elizabeth, Hobson scored 241 against Cradock. This score remains a club record to this day.

Hobson played one first-class game, on 20 February 1906, for Eastern Province against the MCC at St George's Park, Port Elizabeth. He scored 6 and 5, the MCC winning by 10 wickets.

Hobson was killed in action at Rooidam while serving with the Graaff Reinet Commando in East Africa on 25 November 1914. At the time his next of kin was given as J. E. Hobson, of Shirlands, Kindrew, Graaf Reinet District. He is buried in the Ebenezer Farm Cemetery, Pearston, Eastern Cape, South Africa.

Batting and fielding averages

	Mat	Inns	NO	Runs	HS	Ave	100	50	Ct	St
First-class	1	2	0	11	6	5.50	0	0	0	0

Bowling averages

	Mat	Balls	Runs	Wkts	BBI	BBM	Ave	Econ	SR	4w	5w	10
First-class	1	-	-	-	-	-	-	-	-	-	-	-

2491 Private Charles (Buster) Gerrard Deane
Somerset
5th Bn Devonshire Regiment
Died 14 December 1914
Aged 29
Not Known
Right-handed Bat/Right-arm Medium

'A big strong chap'

Charles Gerrard Deane was born on 8 March 1885 at Oakhill, Somerset, the son of Doctor Edwin Deane LRCP and Annie Mary Elizabeth Deane of Bronshill House, Torquay. He was educated at Taunton School. A right-hand bat and right-arm medium bowler, he normally played in the middle to lower order. He played thirty-six first-class matches for Somerset between May 1907 and June 1913, all but one in the County Championship; the other was against South Africa on 29 August 1907. He made his debut against Sussex on 27 May 1907 at the County Ground, Taunton. Deane scored 12 and 19 and made two catches, Herbert Chaplin off the bowling of Albert Lewis for 1 and George Leach, once again off the bowling of Lewis for 24. Somerset won by 6 wickets. His final first-class appearance was on 30 June 1913 against Yorkshire at the Park Avenue, Cricket Ground, Bradford; he scored two ducks Yorkshire winning by an innings and 25 runs.

Deane made a total of 753 first-class runs, his highest score being 78 against Hampshire at Southampton, on 11 May 1911. He also took 8 wickets for 206 runs, his best figures being 2 for 36. He made 25 catches. As many first-class cricketers seem to be, he was also a good all-round sportsman, playing centre half for Torquay and Devon, rugby for Torquay and was a fine water polo player. He was described, not surprisingly, as a 'Big strong chap'.

He was serving with the 5th Bn Devonshire Regiment at the outbreak of war and was sent with his battalion to Karachi, India (now Pakistan), arriving there on 11 November. He was later deployed to Multan where he died of fever on 14 December, aged 29.

He has no known grave and is commemorated on the Karachi War Memorial, Karachi, Sindh, Pakistan.

Later a local headstone was organized by his friends from the Devon and Somerset Territorials. This was thought to have been placed on his grave the following April.

Batting and fielding averages

	Mat	Inns	NO	Runs	HS	Ave	100	Ct	St
First-class	36	69	6	753	78	11.95	0	25	0

Bowling averages

	Mat	Balls	Runs	Wkts	BBI	Ave	Econ	SR	5w	10
First-class	36	284	206	8	2/36	25.75	4.35	35.5	0	0

Major Edmund Peel Thomson
MCC
2nd Bn Royal Munster Fusiliers
Died 21 December 1914
Aged 40
Right-handed Bat

'Always the First into the Action'

Edmund Peel Thomson was born on 22 April 1874 in Moss Side, Manchester, Lancashire, the son of William Thomson. He was educated at the Reverend E. W. Hobson's private school in Southport before going up to Fettes College (Carrington House) Edinburgh, where he played for the First XI from 1889 to 1892 and was captain of the XI for two years. Deciding to make a career in the Army, he entered the RMC Sandhurst where, once again, he played in the First XI. He was commissioned in the Royal Munster Fusiliers as a second lieutenant in October 1893 before becoming a lieutenant in February 1896. Between May 1899 and May 1903 he was adjutant of his battalion, being promoted to captain in July 1901.

He took part in the Second Boer War, being present during operations in the Transvaal in 1902 and was Mentioned in Despatches (*London Gazette*, 29 July 1902). Between March 1906 and June 1909 he was Staff Captain, Pretoria Sub-District, South Africa, before being promoted major in February 1912. On 18 July 1912 he played for Wiltshire, then a minor county team, against a Surrey Second XI at the Kennington Oval. Between May 1913 and June 1914 he played six first-class matches, his debut being for the MCC against Kent on 15 May 1913 at Lords where he made 25 and 2 and caught Edward Dillon off the bowling of Francis Tarrant for 30. The MCC won by six wickets. He went on to play against Hampshire and Yorkshire and represented the Free Foresters against Oxford University. His final first-class match was for the Army against Cambridge University on 11 June 1914 at F. P. Fenner's Ground. Thomson scored 41 not out and 7, Cambridge University winning by an innings and 80 runs. He made 201 first-class runs including one 50, his highest score being 53 against Hampshire at Lords on 23 May 1914; he also made one catch.

Thomson was appointed Brigade Major, Middlesex Infantry Brigade, Eastern Command in April 1912, an appointment he held until October 1914, when he re-joined his battalion, the 2nd Royal Munster Fusiliers.

Major Thomson was killed in action on 21 December 1914 while gallantly leading an attack on German trenches at Festubert near la Bassée, France. His body was never found or identified and he is commemorated on the le Touret Memorial, Panels 43 and 44.

He was a member of the Army and Navy Club, the Free Foresters and the MCC.

Batting and fielding averages

	Mat	Inns	NO	Runs	HS	Ave	100	50	Ct	St
First-class	6	12	1	201	53	18.27	0	1	1	0

Bowling averages

	Mat	Balls	Runs	Wkts	BBI	BBM	Ave	Econ	SR	4w	5w	10
First-class	6	-	-	-	-	-	-	-	-	-	-	-

1915

Lieutenant Frederick Harding (Tanky) Turner
Oxford University
10th (Liverpool Scottish) Bn King's (Liverpool Regiment)
Died 10 January 1915
Aged 27
Not Known

'Never have I met a truer, straighter man than he, or one braver or more modest'

Frederick Harding Turner, better known as 'Tanky' because of his physical size and robustness, was born on 29 May 1888 at Sefton Park, Liverpool, the son of William and Jessie Turner. Educated first at the local Greenbank School, before going to Sedbergh where he was captain of both football and cricket, he went up to Trinity College Oxford in 1907. While there he was captain of Oxford's First XV.

He made five first-class appearances, all for Oxford University, during the 1909 season. He made his debut on 10 June 1909 against the MCC at the University Parks, Oxford. He scored 7 and 8 not out and took three wickets for 29 off twelve overs. He also played against Worcestershire, Surrey, and Sussex. He made his final first class appearance against H. D. G. Leveson-Gower's XI on 1 July 1909 at Saffrons, Eastbourne. He made 0 and 4 and took 3 wickets for 30 off eight overs

During his first class career Turner scored 67 runs, his highest score being 44 against Sussex on 24 June 1909. He took seventeen wickets for 272 runs. In 1910 Turner turned out for Oxford University's Authentics, scoring 38 and 36 not out. He also played for the Lancashire Second XI scoring an impressive 92 and 28 and took one wicket for 28. To add to his sporting prowess, Turner, also an outstanding rugby player, represented Scotland on fifteen occasions and become captain of their XV (see "Into Touch' Nigel McCrery. Pen and Sword)

On leaving university Turner worked for his father's printing firm, Turner and Dunnett. When the war broke out he was commissioned as a lieutenant in the 10th Battalion The King's Liverpool Regiment (Liverpool Scottish), leaving for the front on 1 November 1914. He later wrote home from the front:

We are yes the finest battalion in the British Army, nor have we absolutely annihilated the Prussian Guard, all we have really done is to take our share in the discomforts and in some of the dangers of the campaign without grousing.

Turner was shot and killed by a sniper in the trenches near Kemmel on 10 January 1915. A fellow officer later outlined the circumstances of his death.

Freddy had been putting some barbed wire out in front of the trench, and after breakfast he went down to have a look at the position. Twice he was shot at when he looked up for a second. He then got to a place where the parapet was rather low, and was talking to a sergeant when a bullet went between their heads. Freddy said, 'By Jove, that has deafened my right ear,' and the sergeant said, 'and my left one too, sir.' He then went a shade lower down and had a look at the wire, and was shot clean through the middle of the forehead, the bullet coming out of the back of his head, killing him instantly. The same man had evidently been following him all the way down the trench, and he ought not to have looked up for a bit, as a man walking along a trench can be seen by the enemy every time he passes a loophole. We got him down to ------- that night with great difficulty and buried him in the local churchyard in the pouring rain. The grave, though bailed out in the evening was 18 inches deep in water. However, it is quite the best cared-for grave in the churchyard, and looks very pretty, with a nice cross put up by one of the other regiments in the brigade, and also a nice wreath.

A private wrote of him:

His first thought was always of his men; when their spirits were inclined to droop he rallied them and joked with them, though he always took upon himself the most dangerous and disagreeable duties. A sniper who had tracked him along the trench picked him off.

Captain Noel Chavasse, Lord Derby and the King were among those who sent letters of condolence to the Turner family.

His older brother William Turner left for the front straight after Fred's memorial service two weeks later. At the request of the men he took over his brother's former command with the Liverpool Scottish. Aged 31, he was killed with them on 16 June 1915, leading an advance.

Lieutenant Frederick Harding Turner is buried in Kemmel Churchyard (special memorial 13). The church is situated at Heuvelland, West-Vlaanderen, Belgium.

Batting and fielding averages

	Mat	Inns	NO	Runs	HS	Ave	100	50	Ct	St
First-class	5	9	2	67	44	9.57	0	0	2	0

Bowling averages

	Mat	Runs	Wkts	BBI	Ave	5w	10
First-class	5	272	17	4/46	16.00	0	0

Captain Esme Fairfax Chinnery
Surrey
Coldstream Guards, No. 4 Squadron Royal Flying Corps
Died 18 January 1915
Aged 28
Right-handed Bat

'The higher he went the closer to God he felt'

Esme Fairfax Chinnery was born on 28 March 1886 at Hatchford Park, Cobham, Surrey, the son of Walter Moresby DL JP and Alice Emily Chinnery. His father worked as a dealer in the Stock Exchange. Esme was educated at Eton where he was in the First XI in 1905. During Eton's matches against Harrow and Winchester he made 74 runs in four innings and took three wickets. In 1910 Chinnery became a member of the Marylebone Cricket Club (MCC).

Chinnery made one first-class appearance on 21 June 1906 in a university match against Oxford at the Kennington Oval. He scored 47 in his one innings, Surrey winning the match by nine wickets. He also turned out for the Household Brigade during the 1909–10 season. As a freemason he belonged to Apollo University Lodge 357, Oxfordshire. A keen amateur flyer, he received his pilot's licence on 30 April 1912.

At the outbreak of war Chinnery saw service with the Coldstream Guards, being Mentioned in Despatches for his bravery. Eventually, however, he took advantage of his pilot's licence, joining No. 4 Squadron Royal Flying Corps. He died as a result of a flying accident at Issy, Paris, France, while a passenger in a French-made Voisin being flown by Monsieur M. Delaporte, a French civilian test pilot.

Unusually for the time his body was brought home and buried in the family plot at St Matthew's Churchyard, Hatchford, Surrey (always worth a visit and a few flowers).

His brother was Harry Brodrick Chinnery, also a member of the MCC who played for Eton and was killed in Action on 28 May 1916. (see later).

Batting and fielding averages

	Mat	Inns	NO	Runs	HS	Ave	100	50	Ct	St
First-class	1	1	0	47	47	47.00	0	0	0	0

Bowling averages

	Mat	Balls	Runs	Wkts	BBI	BBM	Ave	Econ	SR	4w	5w	10
First-class	1	-	-	-	-	-	-	-	-	-	-	-

Second Lieutenant Arthur Horace Lang
Cambridge University/Sussex
2nd Bn Grenadier Guards (attd Scots Guards)
Died 25 January 1915
Aged 24
Right-handed Bat/Wicket-Keeper

'None could know him well without a deep affection for the loyalty of his nature.'

Arthur Horace Lang was born on 25 October 1890 at Malabar Hill, Bombay (now Mumbai), Maharashtra, India. He was the son of Basil and Alice S. Lang of The Royal Oak Hotel, Seven Oaks, Kent and was educated at Harrow School, where he captained the School XI in both 1908 and 1909. He represented the school at both Racquets and Fives, won the Challenge Racquet twice and the Ebrington Racquet Cup once. Had a share in winning the Fives Shield four times and the Torpid Fives twice. Took part in the Cock House Match every summer while at school. Going up to Trinity College Cambridge, he represented the University at Racquets in 1913 and in the same year kept wicket at Lords in the University Match. In 1907 Lang made his county cricket debut for Suffolk against Hertfordshire in a Minor Counties' Championship match. He made two further appearances for his county that season and played for Suffolk on three more occasions in 1908, but only made one appearance in both the 1909 and 1910 seasons before, in 1911, playing three final matches, his last coming against Norfolk. He joined the MCC in 1910.

Lang made twenty-two first class appearances for Cambridge University and Sussex between May 1911 and July 1914. He made his debut first class appearance for Sussex against Cambridge University on 22 May 1911 at F P Fenner's Ground, Cambridge. He scored 0 and 11, not out. Cambridge University won the match by 41 runs. It was to be his only first-class appearance that season. The following year Lang went on to make a further six first-class appearances for Sussex against Kent, Cambridge University, Surrey and Nottinghamshire. He made his debut for Cambridge University against the Marylebone Cricket Club (MCC) on 4 July 1912 at Lords. Lang scored 53 and 0. He also caught John Ireland the MCC opener off the bowling of Edward Baker for 1 before stumping Allan Steel (Killed in action 8 October 1917) for 21. In the second innings Lang took Steels wicket again this time with a catch off the bowling of Edward Baker for 7. Cambridge University took the match by two wickets. In 1913 he finally obtained his blue at Cambridge, replacing the Cambridge University wicket-keeper Walter Franklin. This was more a reflection of Franklin's batting than his wicket-keeping. Lang went on to play seven times for Cambridge University against, Middlesex, Northamptonshire, Yorkshire, Hampshire, MCC, LG Robinson's XI, Oxford University. Lang made his final first-class appearance for L. G. Robinson's XI on 2 July 1914 at Old Buckenham Hall. Attleborough. He scored 0 and 9 and managed to hang onto a catch from Frederick Knott off the bowling of John Crawford for 26. The match was drawn. In total Lang made 830 first class runs his highest score being 141 against Sussex on 11August 1913. He took seventeen catches and made sixteen stumpings while playing as wicket-keeper.

Final Wicket

At the outbreak of the First World War Lang was commissioned into the Grenadier Guards as a second lieutenant, being attached to the 2nd Battalion. He was later attached to the 1st Bn Scots Guards. It was while serving with the Scots Guards that he was killed, defending the front-line trenches just outside the village of Cuinchy in northern France on 25 January 1915. At first he was reported missing, however as the months drew on this initial optimism faded and he was assumed to have been killed on that day. The poet Robert Graves later described conditions at Cuinchy in his book *Goodbye to All That*: 'Cuinchy bred rats. They came up from the canal, fed on the plentiful corpses, and multiplied exceedingly.'

His former school friend Geoffrey Hopley who was also killed a little later in the war on 12 May 1915, described his feelings for Lang,

> None could know him well without a deep affection for the loyalty of his nature, the quite sense of humor (always ready for a joke against himself), and above all for his simple unquestioning obedience to duty whenever duty called.

Arthur Lang is buried in the Canadian Cemetery No. 2, Neuville-St Vaast, Grave Plot 12, Row E, Grave 22.

Batting and fielding averages

	Mat	Inns	NO	Runs	HS	Ave	100	Ct	St
First-class	22	40	3	830	141	22.43	2	17	16

Bowling averages

	Mat	Balls	Runs	Wkts	BBI	BBM	Ave	Econ	SR	4w	5w	10
First-class	22	-	-	-	-	-	-	-	-	-	-	-

Major de Courcy Ireland
Europeans (India)
36th Sikhs (Indian Army)
Died 28 January 1915
Aged 41
Unknown

'He might be lost but he will never be forgotten'

De Courcy Ireland was born on 1 August 1873 in Henzadah, Burma, the eldest son of W. de Courcy Ireland BA LLB, late commissioner of Burma. He was commissioned into the Royal Fusiliers as a second lieutenant in 1892 before joining the Indian Staff Corps in 1897, taking part in the Tirah Expedition of 1897 against the Afridi tribe who had risen up against the British. In 1909 he also took part in the Kiva Expedition.

He played one first-class match for the Europeans (India) against Parsees in a Bombay President's Match on 16 September 1897, at the Deccan Gymkhana Ground, Poona. The Europeans were trounced by 308 runs, de Courcy only managing 8 and 7 and taking no wickets for twelve runs off three overs.

In December 1910 he married Gabrielle Byron and they resided for a time at Cleavehurst, Buckfastleigh, Devon. They had one son, John de Courcy Ireland, who was born in Lucknow India in 1911 and went on to be a noted maritime historian and political activist. Major de Courcy Ireland was posted to China with his wife in June 1914 and died of fever in either in Hong Kong or Peking (the records differ) on 28 January 1915.

He is commemorated on the Sai Wan (China) Memorial in Hong Kong. His wife remained on in China after her husband's death for a few years. She married again in 1917 to a Geoffrey Blair and later resided at 100 George Street, Portman Terrace, London W1. She must have remembered her first husband with kindness as she applied for his medals during the twenties.

Batting and fielding averages

	Mat	Inns	NO	Runs	HS	Ave	100	50	Ct	St
First-class	1	2	1	15	8	15.00	0	0	2	0

Bowling averages

	Mat	Runs	Wkts	BBI	BBM	Ave	SR	4w	5w	10
First-class	1	12	0	-	-	-	-	0	0	0

Captain Ronald Owen Lagden
Oxford University
4th Bn King's Royal Rifle Corps
Died 3 March 1915
Aged 25
Right-handed Bat/Right-arm Fast Bowler

'He behaved with the utmost gallantry'

Ronald Owen Lagden was born on 21 November 1889 in Maseru, Basutoland (modern Lesotho), on the border of present-day South Africa. He was the son of Sir Godfrey Lagden KCMG and Lady Lagden, from Weybridge, Surrey and was educated at Mr Pellat's School, Swanage, before going to Marlborough College. Whilst at Marlborough he played in the XI and in 1908 scored a remarkable 149 not out and 102 in the match with Liverpool. He also made 84 against Rugby School and a further 64, and took six wickets, against Cheltenham. As a result he was selected for the Public Schools' XI to play against the MCC at Lords where he made 33 and took seven wickets for 67.

Lagden also played rugby, hockey and rackets. After Marlborough he went up to Oriel College, Oxford, where he read chemistry and obtained his Blue as a Freshman. Lagden made thirty-one first class appearances between May 1909 and July 1912. He made his debut for Oxford University against Surrey on 13 May 1909 at the University Parks, Oxford. Lagden made 2 and 8 Oxford University winning by 204 runs. He went on to play against HDG Leveson-Gower's XI, Australia, Kent, MCC, Worcestershire, Sussex, Cambridge University, Kent, Gentlemen of England, South Africa and India. One of his two victims in the match against India was captain Bhupinder Singh of Patiala. He made his final first class appearance on 8 July 1912 against Cambridge University at Lords. Lagden scored 2 and 68 and took three wickets for 40 off seventeen overs in the first innings and 1 wicket for 39 off eleven overs in the second. One of his victims was his brother Reginald who became his fifty-sixth and last first-class wicket. Lagden's brother was also a first-class cricketer, playing for both Cambridge and Surrey. Their father, Godfrey, appeared in a first-class match for the Marylebone Cricket Club at the age of 54.

During his first class career Lagden scored a total of 1197 first class runs his highest score being 99 not out, which he made in 1912 against the H. D. G. Leveson-Gower's XI, missing out on a century when Australian Neville Fraser was adjudged leg before wicket to Ernest Smith for a duck. He also took 56 wickets for 1406 runs his best figures being 6 for 57. He made 18 catches. An excellent all round sportsman Lagden won several other blues in rugby, hockey and rackets. Lagden was also a rugby international turning out for England against Scotland on 18 March 1911, Lagden kicked two conversions, Scotland going down 13–8. England retained the Calcutta cup. For reasons that have never become clear it was to be Lagden's only international appearance. Lagden became a member of the MCC in 1913.

After leaving Oxford, Lagden became a master at Harrow School (Headmaster's House). At the outbreak of the war he was commissioned into the King's Royal Rifle Corps and, while attached to the 4th Battalion, was posted to France being based in the St Éloi sector, some fifteen miles north of Neuve Chapelle in the Ypres salient. By 3 March 1915 Lagden was commanding a company. It was on that fateful day that Lagden was to lose his life while leading an attack on the German lines. Major Jack Poole (another fine cricketer) mentioned Lagden's death in his book *Undiscovered Ends*. (1957):

Apart from the sniping and occasional shelling, there was little action in the front line. Very seldom did we or the Germans undertake a trench raid, but I can remember Charles Poe's company doing a local night attack which proved very costly. We lost three officers killed and two wounded, 16 other ranks killed and 62 wounded, and gained very little except a few prisoners. Charles Lagden, who had only been with us for a week, was killed in action (one of the three officers lost).

His Commanding Officer later wrote to his family, 'He behaved with the utmost gallantry … A survivor who saw him fall says he was well away in front and the first man to fall …'

His body was never recovered or identified and he is commemorated on the Ypres (Menin Gate) Memorial (Panels 51 and 53).

His brother, Reginald Bousfield Lagden, was killed in a plane crash in October 1944 at Karachi airport.

Batting and fielding averages

	Mat	Inns	NO	Runs	HS	Ave	100	Ct	St
First-class	31	54	7	1197	99*	25.46	0	18	0

Bowling averages

	Mat	Runs	Wkts	BBI	Ave	5w	10
First-class	31	1406	56	6/57	25.10	1	0

Major Charles Ernest Higginbotham
Army/Army (South Africa)
2nd Bn Northamptonshire Regiment
Died 11 March 1915
Aged 48
Right-handed-Bat

'was a sportsman in every sense of the word'

Charles Ernest Higginbotham was born on 4 July 1866 at Charing Cross, Glasgow, Lanarkshire, Scotland, the second son of Mr and Mrs Higginbotham, of Craigmaddie, Milngavie. Educated at Cargilfield Prep School, Edinburgh, and Rugby School, in 1884 he was selected for the school XI, scoring 7 (not out) and 2 against Marlborough College. At the Royal Military College Sandhurst he was selected for the XI and played against Woolwich in 1886 where he played two useful innings of 24 and 40.

In February 1887 he was commissioned as a second lieutenant in the Northamptonshire Regiment. He was promoted to lieutenant in April 1890, followed by captain in January 1899 and major in 1907. A keen sportsman, he was a good shot, played hockey, golf, rackets, football, lawn tennis, enjoyed running and skated. However, it was at cricket that he excelled. He belonged to the 'Rag' (Army and Navy Club) and the MCC (1886) as well as the 'Butterflies' and 'Incogniti'.

Stationed in the Far East, he played cricket for the Straits Settlements, turning out three times against Hong Kong between 1890 and 1891. He saw action during the Second Boer War and it was while in South Africa on 12 January 1906 that he made his debut first-class appearance for the South African Army against the touring MCC. He scored 1 and 0, the MCC winning by an innings and 218 runs. His second and final first-class match came on 30 May 1912 for the Army against the Royal Navy at Lord's. Higginbotham scored 40, not out and 4. He also caught Gerald Harrison off the bowling of Edward Henslow for 8. The Army won by 161 runs.

In other matches he scored 117 for Aldershot Command against United Services at Portsmouth in June 1910; he and Captain E. L. Challenor (170) made 297 together for the first wicket. He also captained the Aldershot Officers' XI in 1911.

In 1890 he married Florence Hopkins but she died in South Africa. In 1909 he married again, this time Lucy Frances Gray, fourth daughter of the old Eton and Essex cricketer, the Right Honourable James Round.

Shortly after the outbreak of the First World War, on 5 November 1914, he landed with the 2nd Battalion Northampton Regiment at le Havre. He was killed in action while serving as the battalion's second in command at the battle of Neuve Chapelle on 11 March 1915. An account of the battle was later published in 'Northamptonshire & the Great War' by W. H. Holloway.

The object of the onslaught was to relieve Lille, the village of Neuve Chapelle being eleven miles west of that town. The ground we had to advance over was flat and marshy with a ridge behind, one spur of which was Aubers, where both our 1st and 2nd Battalions were wiped out two months later.

So secretly were the preparations made that the Germans were taken unawares at 7.30 on the morning of March 10th, 1915 by the most terrific bombardment hitherto witnessed in the war. From 350 guns of all calibres – French and English – there poured forth a terrific tornado of shot and shell at short range. Our men, crouching under cover, were appalled by the deafening roar and devastating results. The deluge shattered trenches like sand castles and so close were the Germans to our lines that frightful fragments of once living men came back on us amid a welter of earth, dust and green lyddite fumes. Then at 8.00 the gunners lengthened their range and the village of Neuve Chapelle began to leap in the air. The devastation was so appalling that the whole place soon became a rubbish heap, and when the Northamptons (C & D Companies) rushed forward to assist the 25th Brigade, they found this once happy village so shattered that even the churchyard was uprooted and long dead bodies were unearthed to mingle with the mangled corpses of men, who a few hours earlier had been full of vigorous life. At five o'clock the Battalion, though weary with hard fighting, made an attack in a south-easterly direction with the Worcesters on their right. The gallant colonel, map in hand, led the attack, but they were met by such a withering fire that they could not get beyond a thousand yards and had to dig themselves in forty yards beyond the village.

During the night the enemy had recovered from their surprise sufficiently to bring up heavy reinforcements and such a multiplicity of machine guns that just facing one part of our line there were 20 to an area of 300 yards. The result was that at 7 o'clock next morning when we attempted to renew the attack, we were repulsed with heavy loss. At noon D Company attempted to advance but were again beaten back; Lieutenant Gordon being shot in the throat and Lieutenant W. A. A. Coldwell, though hit in the side, back and foot crawled back over a mile across the shell stricken field. The Battalion remained in the trenches until dawn on the 12th, when the enemy vigorously counter-attacked but were repulsed with fearful slaughter. Then Colonel Prichard ordered the Regiment to charge the enemy's third line of trenches. During this attack Captains Stocker and Wood Martin were both killed. We seized the trench but could not hold it. It was enfiladed by the enemy and bombarded by our own guns, for the telephone communications had been smashed and it was difficult to get messages back to our batteries. The plight of the Steelbacks was terrible. Officers and men were falling on all sides until it seemed that none could survive. They could not advance and would not retire, so that they were faced with the awful prospect of being annihilated. From the messages received or issued by the Brigade Headquarters, the Northamptons seemed to be the first to be fully conscious of the chaos – and to send back candid reports of the accountable delay in sending reinforcements, the blunders of our artillery, and the fearful slaughter due to long stretches of the enemy's entanglements remaining intact. Colonel Prichard complained strongly of artillery shells falling short, also that he had very few officers left and the thin remnant of the Battalion was too tired to keep on. His handwriting of the message indicated the severe strain he was enduring at the gradual annihilation of a battalion in which he took such a pardonable pride. Just previously his adjutant, Captain Power had been killed, his right-hand man Major Higginbotham had been shot down, Captain Capell, who the previous day had been saved by a bullet striking a knife in his breast pocket, was killed instantly, and others who fell were Captain L. J. Robinson, Lieutenants A. M. Wallace, E. Belding, P. B. Lees, G. D. Gordon, E. A. Matthews, besides the following wounded: Lieutenants R. E. Lucy (who succumbed), Willoughby, Eldred, Sparrow and Tyler. Only three officers of the Battalion were not hit, viz. Colonel Prichard (who was afterwards wounded in the lungs two and half miles behind the trenches while talking to the Brigadier), Captain Smyth and Lieutenant G. A. Parker, both of whom fell ill from the effects of being 4 days up to their waists in water.

His commanding officer, writing of him from France after his death, commented, 'Had he alone survived I should have been content for the future of the Regiment.'

Major Higginbotham's body was never recovered or identified and he is commemorated on the le Touret Memorial, Pas de Calais, France, Panels 28 to 30.

Batting and fielding averages

	Mat	Inns	NO	Runs	HS	Ave	100	50	Ct	St
First-class	2	4	1	45	40*	15.00	0	0	1	0

Bowling averages

	Mat	Balls	Runs	Wkts	BBI	BBM	Ave	Econ	SR	4w	5w	10
First-class	2	-	-	-	-	-	-	-	-	-	-	-

Lieutenant Frederick Bonham Burr
Worcestershire
3rd Bn The Worcestershire Regiment
Died 12 March 1915
Aged 27
Not known

'A natural Gentleman'

Frederick Bonham Burr was born on 2 August 1887 at Blacklands, Hastings, Sussex, the son of the Reverend George Frederick Burr, of Highfields Park, Halesowen, Birmingham, and Caroline Burr, originally of Selsley Lawn, Hales Road, Cheltenham. The Burr family was established in Halesowen for about 100 years, having moved there from Warwickshire. His paternal ancestors also owned Hayseech Gunbarrel Mill in Rowley Regis. Frederick was educated at Sandroyd, Cobham and at Denstone College before going up to Keble College Oxford where he was a member of the 'Authentics' cricket club.

Burr played one first-class match for Worcester against Oxford University on 25 May 1911 at the University Parks, Oxford. Burr scored 39 and 7, not out. He also caught another first-class cricketer and rugby international, Ronald Lagden, (killed in action 3 March 1915), for 29 off the bowling of William Taylor for 29. He represented the Worcestershire Gentlemen and played football for Keble College as well as winning his oar in the Torpids. A member of the Authors' Club, he wrote several poems published under the title *The Strummings of Lyre*. (Publisher: A. C. Fifield, 1912)

Although he was studying for the church at Cuddesdon, he had previously joined the Reserve of Officers in January 1913 from the Officer Training Corps (OTC). At the outbreak of war he was commissioned into the 3rd Battalion Worcestershire Regiment and travelled with them to France in September 1914 as part of 7 Infantry Brigade of 3rd Division.

He was killed in action on 12 March 1915 at Kemmel, Belgium and is buried in Kemmel Château Military Cemetery, grave L.9.

His brother, 156562 Corporal Alfred Burr MM, 1st Special Company, Royal Engineers, was also killed in action on 24 March 1918. He has no known grave and is commemorated on Pozières Memorial, Somme, France, Panels 10 to 13.

Batting and fielding averages

	Mat	Inns	NO	Runs	HS	Ave	100	50	Ct	St
First-class	1	2	1	46	39	46.00	0	0	1	0

Bowling averages

	Mat	Balls	Runs	Wkts	BBI	BBM	Ave	Econ	SR	4w	5w	10
First-class	1	-	-	-	-	-	-	-	-	-	-	-

Final Wicket

Captain Francis Whitechurch Townend
J.G. Greig's XI
35 Signal Company Royal Engineers
Died 29 March 1915
Aged 29
Unknown

'the extraordinary courage the man showed—
such courage as I've never seen before, I hardly imagined'

Francis Whitechurch Townend was born on 10 July 1885 in Halifax, Nova Scotia, Canada, the third son of the Reverend Alfred John Townend CF, former chaplain to the forces, and Margaret Wiseman Townend, née Stairs. He was sent to England for his education and attended Dulwich College, but failed to make the school cricket XI.

On leaving school he entered the Royal Military Academy Woolwich, after which he spent two years at the School of Military Engineering, Chatham. Gazetted as a second lieutenant in the Royal Engineers on 21 January 1904, he was promoted to lieutenant on 24 September 1906 and captain on 30 October 1914. In 1906 he was posted to India and attached to the 3rd Sappers and Miners.

He played in three first-class matches, all for the Europeans (India). The first was a Bombay Presidency Match played on 10 September 1908 at the Deccan Gymkhana Ground, Poona in which Townend made two ducks, the Parsees winning by 142 runs. His second match was played on 17 September 1908, this time in the Bombay Triangular Tournament. In this match, Townend did much better, scoring 69 and 7. This time the Europeans took the match by 176 runs. His final first-class appearance came in the final of the Bombay Triangular Tournament played on 21 September 1908, once again at the Gymkhana Ground, Bombay. Townend scored 2 and 17. He also caught R V Agaskar off the bowling of Frank Joy for 0. The Europeans won the final by 119 runs.

While at Woolwich he played in the Association Football XI and became a well-known Army cricketer, representing the Royal Engineers against the Royal Artillery at Lord's on a number of occasions. He also played for the Free Foresters and the Indian Army.

At the outbreak of the war he travelled with the Indian Expeditionary Force to France, landing in October 1914.

He died of wounds on 29 March 1915 at Bethune, France, having been wounded the previous day while laying telephone wires. A motor ambulance driver wrote the following account of the incident to his mother, which was published in the Morning Post, on 12 April 1915:

After dinner I commenced a letter, but was interrupted by a shell bursting somewhere in the vicinity and a man yelling for bandages. Of course I rushed to see if I could be of any use, and found that the shell had burst at the side of the road about forty yards away, right in the midst of a party of Indian engineers who were inspecting the telegraph wires. T. and I grabbed stretchers from our rear, and with some others rushed for the Indians. I was late in starting owing to my litter, and all the Indians were being attended to when I arrived on the scene. However, I saw someone in the shell hole which was on the side of the road opposite from where the men had been hit, and so had escaped notice. In it was a man, the white officer of the Indians, who appeared to have his legs half buried in the debris of the hole. He told us to attend to the others first; he was all right. And then as we moved him we saw that he was standing on the stumps of his legs. Both had been shot off at the knee. (I'm telling you this story, horrible as it is, because of the extraordinary courage the man showed—such courage as I've never seen before, I hardly imagined. It's worthwhile bearing the horror of it to realize that we are officered by such men.) He was perfectly conscious and calm, and spoke as though he were a medical officer and someone else the victim. He looked at his legs as we moved him on to the stretcher and asked me quietly (he was not in the least excited, and his handsome face showed no pain) to tie something tight round both thighs to stop the bleeding. I did what I could with my handkerchief, and another I requisitioned, and we took him to our billet. We had to move hurriedly, of course, as a second shell had followed and we wanted cover in case any more arrived. There were two RAMC men with us, and they attended to the subsequent first aid. They discovered another horrible wound in his arm, and while they were dressing it he told them that he thought he would give up football next year. We then took him to the nearest hospital; he was still conscious and perfectly collected, and laughed quietly and talked, apologizing for the trouble he was causing, while on the way to the hospital. And I came back thinking of that tag in some book or other 'I have seen a man'. The poor fellow died in hospital.

Captain Townend was Mentioned in Despatches by Field Marshal Sir John French (*London Gazette*, 22 June 1915) for his brave and outstanding work.

He is buried in Béthune Town Cemetery, Grave reference II, B. 10.

Batting and fielding averages

	Mat	Inns	NO	Runs	HS	Ave	100	50	Ct	St
First-class	3	6	0	95	69	15.83	0	1	1	0

Bowling averages

	Mat	Balls	Runs	Wkts	BBI	BBM	Ave	Econ	SR	4w	5w	10
First-class	3	-	-	-	-	-	-	-	-	-	-	-

Lieutenant Colonel Henry Louis Rosher
Europeans (India)
2nd Bn The Dorsetshire Regiment
Died 14 April 1915
Aged 48
Unknown

'an able and most gallant commanding officer'

Henry Louis Rosher was born on 7 May 1866 in Edmonton, Middlesex, England, the eldest son of Alfred Rosher JP of the Grange Rosherville and Lilian Rosher, née Hill. Educated at Tonbridge School between 1880 and 1882 (School House), he was commissioned as a second lieutenant in the Dorsetshire Regiment in 1897. On being posted to India with his battalion he became Deputy Assistant Adjutant General under Sir George Wolseley in Madras. In 1910 he was promoted to lieutenant colonel and given command of the 2nd Battalion of the Dorsetshire Regiment, then with the Poona Division.

He made one first-class appearance for J. G. Greig's XI against the Hindus on 29 August 1912 at the Deccan Gymkhana Ground, Poona. He scored 13 runs in his only innings and managed to hang onto a catch, taking the wicket of C.V. Mehta off the bowling of Elliot Tillard for 20. The match was eventually drawn. Although only a two-day match it was still considered to be a first-class one.

Colonel Rosher embarked with his regiment from Bombay on 18 October 1915 on the HT *Varela*, a British-India Liner, in a convoy of fifty-four ships as part of 16 Indian Brigade in Poona Division. The battalion landed in Fao, Persian Gulf, on 14 November 1914 to take part in the campaign in Mesopotamia, as part of Indian Expeditionary Force D. He was Mentioned in Despatches twice, once for the surrender of Basra and the second time for the Battle of Shaiba in which he was unfortunately killed on 14 April 1915. A letter was later received by his wife from the regiment's adjutant:

> 'the colonel was an able and most gallant commanding officer whose death is a great loss to the service.'

He is buried in the Basra War Cemetery, grave reference, III. E. 18.

Batting and fielding averages

	Mat	Inns	NO	Runs	HS	Ave	100	50	Ct	St
First-class	1	1	0	13	13	13.00	0	0	1	0

Bowling averages

	Mat	Balls	Runs	Wkts	BBI	BBM	Ave	Econ	SR	4w	5w	10
First-class	1	-	-	-	-	-	-	-	-	-	-	-

Private John Nathaniel Williams
Gloucestershire, Hawke's Bay
6th (Hauraki) Company, Auckland Regiment
New Zealand Expeditionary Force
Died 25 April 1915
Aged 37
Right-handed Bat

'One of the greatest Englishman to die for New Zealand'

John Nathaniel Williams was born on 24 January 1878 in Kensington, London, the eldest son of Colonel Sir Robert Williams, 1st Baronet, MP, and Lady Williams, of Bridehead, Dorchester, England. He was educated at Matfield Kent, Eton and New College, Oxford, and first saw military service with the 4th (Territorial) Bn Dorsetshire Regiment, where he was promoted to captain before resigning his commission and moving to New Zealand 1910 where he took up employment with the Waihi Gold Mining Company Ltd.

Williams played in four first-class matches between December 1903 and June 1908. He made his debut for Hawks Bay against Wellington on 19 December 1903 at the Recreation Ground, Napier. Williams scored 20 and 1, and caught William Mowatt off the bowling of Basil Cotterill for 20. On returning to England he turned out for Gloucestershire on three occasions, against Middlesex on 4 June 1908 at Lords, Middlesex won by three wickets. Essex on 8 June 1908 at the County Ground, Leyton. Essex won by an innings and 275 runs. Somerset 11 June 1908 at the Recreation Ground Bath. The match was drawn.

On the outbreak of war Williams enlisted as a private in the New Zealand Expeditionary Force and left for Egypt in October 1914. He took part in the repulse of the Turkish attack on the Suez Canal in February 1915, and in the landings at the Dardanelles on 25 April 1915. He was killed in action on the same day at Gaba Tepe. Major General Sir A. I. Godley KCMG CB, Commanding New Zealand Forces, wrote:

> He was killed leading and setting a most gallant example to the men in the forefront of the Battalion, and all the officers, NCOs and men of the company speak of him in the highest terms of admiration and affection. He had evidently made himself most popular with them and respected by all, and had he not fallen he would have been given a commission in this force immediately after the first action. I believe the example which he set in enlisting, and dying as he did in the ranks, has done more for this force and perhaps for the Empire than he would have done as a commissioned officer!

John Williams has no known grave and is commemorated on Lone Pine Memorial, Turkey, Panel 73.

Batting and fielding averages

	Mat	Inns	NO	Runs	HS	Ave	100	50	Ct	St
First-class	4	7	0	52	20	7.42	0	0	2	0

Bowling averages

	Mat	Balls	Runs	Wkts	BBI	BBM	Ave	Econ	SR	4w	5w	10
First-class	4	-	-	-	-	-	-	-	-	-	-	-

77 Sergeant Charles James Backman (Rappie)
South Australia
10th Battalion Australian Imperial Force
Died between 25/29 April 1915
Aged 32
Right-hand bat/Right-arm medium bowler

'A Great Australian'

Charles James Backman was born 14 April 1884, the son of Charles Backman of 44 Elizabeth Street, Adelaide, South Australia. He spent most of his youth with his parents in Bowden in South Adelaide and attended Currie Street and Hindmarsh schools before leaving to become a boilermaker's assistant at the Islington workshops. A good all-round cricketer, he played with West Torrens, and with the A-grade Adelaide team.

Backman made one first-class appearance for South Australia on 10 November 1911 against the touring MCC at the Adelaide Oval, Adelaide. He scored 16 and 0 and took three wickets for 53 off 16 overs, including the wickets of Plum Warner (151), Frank Woolley (15), and Joe Vine (5). He also managed to catch George Gunn off the bowling of William Whitty for 106. The MCC won by an Innings and 194 runs. Backman later became captain of the South Australian cricket team.

On 19 August 1914 he enlisted into the ranks of the 10th Australian Infantry in Adelaide, one of the first to do so. After completing basic training he embarked with his battalion for Egypt on Transport A11 the *Ascanius* on 20 October, as a sergeant (No. 77), being part of C Company. On arrival they began further training in preparation for the Western Front, however their destination changed and they began to prepare for their assault on the Dardanelles.

During the landings on 25 April 1915, Backman was seen to reach the beach, one of the first to do so. However, in the confusion C Company became separated and Backman disappeared. One report said that he had been killed on the beach but this was unsubstantiated. There was no roll call for the 10th Battalion until 28 April. Enquiries with the American Embassy in Constantinople were made in an attempt to see if Backman was a prisoner of war but no trace was found. His family, like thousands of other Australian families, didn't give up, however, and his brother, A. Backman, wrote to the Minister of Defence on 5 August 1915:

> I sent yesterday to you about my Brother Sgt. C.J. Backman, trying to find out about news of him. I told you only of letters but today I can tell you of men we have met, returned soldiers that met him there and tell us that my brother was in the hospital in the next bed to one of these men. They tell us that he was wounded in the leg and was crawling to the trenches and his own men called halt and he never stopped and they (the Turks) shot him in the back. Now I think that anything like that we ought to have heard before now and another letter I have just got from the hospital states that he, Backman, is in the hospital with him now. I think it's awful not to know before this as this letter was dated July 4, 1915.

Backman's sister, Mrs A. Kearns, wrote to Base Records on 3 October 1916 continuing the families search for information:

> if we do not get news one way or the other I am sure it will kill my Mother as well, for it is awful waiting for news and none coming.

However, a statement found in Red Cross File No 0171004D from Private 752 J.W. Gillett, of the 10th Battalion, then a patient at Havre Hospital, written on 12 June 1916, four months before Backman's sister's letter shows more light on the fate of the gallant cricketer.

> This man (Backman) was killed on the beach at Anzac on the 1st day of the landing. I was told this by several of my pals who were there and saw Blackman killed.

We can have no idea if the authorities were aware of this letter at the time. Finally, the authorities had to make a decision about the fate of Backman and thousands like him. On 5 June 1916 a court of enquiry was held and Backman's status was changed from missing to killed between the 25–29 April. We can only imagine what his family felt when they were informed.

Backman is commemorated on the Lone Pine Memorial in Gallipoli, Panel 32.

Batting and fielding averages

	Mat	Inns	NO	Runs	HS	Ave	100	50	Ct	St
First-class	1	2	0	16	16	8.00	0	0	1	0

Bowling averages

	Mat	Runs	Wkts	BBI	Ave	5w	10
First-class	1	53	3	3/53	17.66	0	0

Captain Percy d'Aguilar Banks
Somerset
Queen Victoria's Own Corps of Guides (Frontier Force)
(Lumsden's) Indian Army, att'd 57th Wilde's Rifles (Frontier
Force)
Died 26 April 1915
Aged 29
Right-handed Bat

'an able man and a most promising officer'

Percy d'Aguilar Banks was born in Bath, Somerset, on 9 May 1885, the only son of Colonel S. H. O'Brien Banks of 9 Eaton Place, Brighton. He was educated at Cheltenham, where he made his mark in cricket playing for the First XI at the tender age of 15 years. A good all-round sportsman, he also won the school Racquets and Fives. In April 1902 he played in the Public Schools' Racquets at Queen's and in the same year played cricket for Cheltenham against Haileybury at Lord's, making a remarkable 103 runs for his side. Overall during the 1902 season he made 312 runs, making 27 and 103 against Haileybury, 8 and 6 against Marlborough, and 62 and 6 against Clifton. Writing of his batting in *Wisden* of 1903, Mr W. J. Ford said of him,

> Banks played a remarkable innings of 103 v. Haileybury. The pavilion critics were unanimous in calling it equal to any innings ever played by a boy at Lord's, his variety of strokes and his manipulation of the bat being quite Trumperesque. I fancied that he must be exceedingly strong in wrist and elbow.

After leaving school he decided to make his career in the Army and entered the Royal Military College Sandhurst. In 1903 he was third in the Sandhurst averages with 33.00. He also played for the Somerset Colts, making another impressive score of 135.

Banks made seven first class appearances between August 1903 and June 1908 all for Somerset and all in the County Championship. He made his debut on 31 August 1903 against Hampshire at Dean Park, Bournemouth. He made 0 and 27, Somerset won by 109 runs. He went on to play against Lancashire, Sussex, Warwickshire and Worcestershire. He made his final first class appearance against Yorkshire on 29 June 1908 at Dewsbury and Savile Gound, Dewsbury. Banks scored 30 and 2, Yorkshire winning by 8 wickets. During his first class career Banks scored 161 runs his highest score being against Yorkshire. He took one catch.

In 1903 he was gazetted into the Duke of Edinburgh's Wiltshire Regiment. Posted to India in 1904, he played for the Army against the Rest of Lahore. In 1905 he was transferred to the Indian Army, joining Queen Victoria's Own Corps of Guides and quickly earned a reputation as a first-class polo player, competing for his regiment and playing for the German Frankfurt Team, which won the Challenge, Champion and Ladies Cups in January 1914. He also played at Peshawar as captain of his regimental team, the Guides winning two major tournaments.

Banks acted as ADC to Mr A. D. Younghusband CSI, Commissioner in Scinde, during the visit of the Prince of Wales to India in 1906. In the January of that year he was promoted to lieutenant and in October 1912 to captain.

Posted to France in January 1915, he was then attached to the 57th Wilde's Rifles. In April 1915 the Lahore Brigade, of which his regiment formed part, was hurried to Neuve Chapelle to support the assault there. In the course of an advance over two miles of open ground on 26 April 1915, and in the face of a murderous fire, Captain Banks managed to drag two brother officers who had been wounded into a shell hole. He also managed to do the same for his wounded servant and another NCO before trying to cover them while they took shelter. Unfortunately, while doing this Captain Banks was shot in the head and killed. Refusing to leave his officer, Banks' servant carried him back to the British lines on his back while still under fire. For this act of selfless bravery his servant was awarded the Distinguished Conducted Medal and later the Russian Order of Saint George. For his bravery in attempting to cover his brother officers, Banks was Mentioned in Sir John French's Despatches of 30 November 1915. In a letter to his parents his commanding officer described him as:

> an able man and a most promising officer, was possessed of exceptional tact and charm of manner that endeared him to his comrades and friends to a remarkable degree, while his native NCOs and men almost worshipped him.

He is commemorated on the Ypres (Menin Gate) Memorial, Panel 1.

Batting and fielding averages

	Mat	Inns	NO	Runs	HS	Ave	100	50	Ct	St
First-class	7	14	1	161	30	12.38	0	0	1	0

Bowling averages

	Mat	Balls	Runs	Wkts	BBI	BBM	Ave	Econ	SR	4w	5w	10
First-class	7	-	-	-	-	-	-	-	-	-	-	-

Captain George Amelius Crawshay Sandeman
Hampshire
3rd Bn (att'd 1st) The Hampshire Regiment
Died 26 April 1915
Aged 32
Left handed bat/Slow Left-Arm Orthodox.

'Holding out to the last he lost his life'

George Amelius Crawshay Sandeman was born on 18 April 1883 in Westminster, London, the only child of Lieutenant Colonel George Glas Sandeman and Amy Sandeman of Fonab, Pitlochry, Perthshire; his mother died a few days after his birth. He was educated at Cheam School, Sutton, Surrey, before going to Eton. About this time the artist Charles Martin Hardie (1858–1916) painted the thirteen-year-old Sandeman in his cricket whites in a bowling pose (see attached). On leaving Eton he went up to Christ Church Oxford in 1902, took his degree in 1907 and was called to the Bar at the Inner Temple in 1913. After his father's death in 1905, he inherited the Fonab Estate at Moulin, Perthshire, and became a partner in the wine merchants and shippers David Sandeman and sons of Pall Mall. The 1911 census shows him living in the family home at 34 Grosvenor Gardens, London, with five servants.

As a slow left-arm orthodox bowler he was in the Eton XI in 1901 and 1902. In his last year he took all ten wickets for 22 in the first innings against Winchester and 6 for 26 in the second. His thirty-five wickets for Eton in 1902 cost 11.62 runs each. At Oxford he was chosen for the Freshmen's match, but did not obtain his Blue.

Sandeman made six first-class appearances between June 1913 and June 1914. He made his debut for Hampshire against Nottinghamshire in the County Championship on 19 June 1913 at the County Ground, Southampton. He made no runs (although to be fair he was not out in his second innings) and took no wickets. He went on to represent Hampshire on two further occasions. Against Sussex on 23 June 1913, he made 0 and 4 but did catch Percy

Fenner off the bowling of George Brown for 80 and took the wicket of Herbert Chaplin for eleven. Sussex won by 155 runs. His final match for Hampshire was against Kent on 26 June 1913, again in the County Championship. He scored 5 and 0 and took the wickets of Harold Hardinge for 168 and Charles Hatfield (lbw) for 8, Kent winning by an innings and 75 runs. Sandeman made his debut for the Marylebone Cricket Club (MCC) on 28 May 1914, representing them in a single first-class match against Oxford University. He scored 0 in his single innings and took one wicket for 14 off 6 overs. The MCC won by 48 runs.

He also represented the Free Foresters against Oxford University on two occasions, on 1 June 1914 at University Parks, Oxford. Oxford won by 6 wickets and in his final first-class appearance on 8 June 1914 against Cambridge University at Fenners, Cambridge University won by one wicket. During his first-class career he made 18 runs his highest score being against Kent on 26 June 1913. He also took five wickets for 242 runs his best figures being 2 for 73. He took three catches.

Sandeman had been commissioned in the 3rd Battalion Hampshire Regiment on 19 December 1903 and was promoted to lieutenant on 5 September 1905, and to captain on 2 September 1914. During the war he served as a captain in the 1st Hampshire Regiment and travelled with them to France on 27 August 1914. Sandeman was killed in action at Zonnebeke, Belgium, on 26 April 1915 during the Second Battle of Ypres. The regiment's commanding officer, Lieutenant Colonel F. R. Hicks, described how Sandeman lost his life in his report:

> At 2.25 a.m. on the 26th we reached the top of a slight ridge: we knew we must be near the Royal Fusiliers and there was only an hour of darkness left. There was no time to lose and we started to dig. The men were tired out. They dug like bricks. Most of them knew that their lives depended on their being underground by dawn. Luckily for us we found some old trenches, some French, some perhaps support trenches of the Canadians facing all ways and more lucky still, the morning was misty, so we were able to go on digging for another couple of hours which made all the difference. But before this we had met the enemy in our centre opposite Captain Beckett and C. Coy. A large party advanced through the misty moonlight shouting 'Ve vos de Royal Fusiliers'. One of our own patrols was caught sheep like, but Captain Beckett was not so simple and quickly disposed of these Royal Fusiliers, who withdrew below the ridge. On the left, where A Coy. under Captain Sandeman, had occupied a few houses, we were not so fortunate. A surprise attack in the mist drove out the party holding the houses who pressed into the half-finished trench and caused some confusion. Captain Sandeman, Captain Chapman and others were killed, but Sergeant Ley and a few others gallantly formed a line across the trench and stopped the enemy's rush. When the mist lifted at 7, we were holding a curved line, C. Coy. on the right facing north-east, with a gap of some 400 yards between them and a small wood on the right front, held by the Royal Fusiliers with whom, by now Lt Stevens and a patrol had got in touch. In the centre D Coy. on the crest of the ridge, faced north and the left A Coy. faced nearly west with their left thrown back. B Coy. was in a second trench a little way back partly behind the crest and Headquarters in the right end of the same trench and their left still more thrown back.

His body was never recovered or recognized and he is commemorated on the Ypres (Menin Gate) Memorial, West-Vlaanderen, Belgium, Panel 35.

There is a memorial plaque to him inside Holy Trinity Episcopal Church, Pitlochry, and his name is on the War Memorial at Grange Cricket Club Edinburgh.

He wrote two books, *Metternich* and *Calais under English Rule*, and was a governor of St Mark's Hospital.

Batting and fielding averages

	Mat	Inns	NO	Runs	HS	Ave	100	50	Ct	St
First-class	6	11	7	18	5*	4.50	0	0	3	0

Bowling averages

	Mat	Runs	Wkts	BBI	Ave	5w	10
First-class	6	242	5	2/73	48.40	0	0

Major Bernard Maynard Lucas Brodhurst
Hampshire
1/4th Gurkha Rifles
Died 27 April 1915
Aged 41
Right-handed Bat/Right-arm Fast-Medium Bowler

'Would be a most destructive bowler if he could only bowl with the
same confidence and luck with which he bats'

Bernard Maynard Lucas Brodhurst was born on 6 August 1873 at Benares (now Varanasi) Uttar Pradesh, India, the youngest son of the late Maynard Brodhurst ICS Judge of the High Court, North West Province, India and Mary Brodhurst. Bernard was educated at Clifton College, where he was in the First XI playing as a fast bowler from 1889 to 1891, his best season being 1890 when he took thirty wickets at 14.66. A local paper commented:

> *"Would be a most destructive bowler if he could only bowl with the same confidence and luck with which he bats: he has improved in fielding."*

On entering the Royal Military College, Sandhurst in 1892 he was once again selected for the First XI. He made one first class appearance for Hampshire against Leicestershire in the County Championship on 26 August 1897 at the County Ground, Southampton. in the final match of the season. He scored nine in his one innings and caught Ralph Joyce off the bowling of Harry Baldwin for 10. He also played for the MCC, (a member since 1905), Old Cliftonians, and the Gurkha Brigade in India.

On passing for the Indian Army he was gazetted to the unattached list in September 1892 and served for a year in India with the 2nd Bn The Border Regiment. In January 1894 he was appointed to the 1/4th Gurkhas, becoming lieutenant in December of the same year. In 1900 he was made adjutant of his battalion, and was promoted captain in September 1901. He took part in the Waziristan Expedition, 1894–95 and saw service in China in 1900. From 1903 to 1906 he was Inspector of Signalling to the Imperial Service troops, having been the first officer to hold the appointment. He obtained his majority in September 1910.

Soon after the start of the war, the 1st Bn 4th Gurkha Rifles (1/4 GR) was deployed to France, as part of the Sirhind Brigade in 3rd (Lahore) Division of the Indian Corps as part of the Indian Expeditionary Force, to reinforce the British Expeditionary Force in France. The order of battle of the Sirhind Brigade included two British infantry battalions, and two Indian battalions, 1/1st and 1/4th Gurkha Rifles. The battalion arrived at Marseilles from Egypt on 30 November, before being deployed quickly to the Western Front in December 1914 with the Sirhind brigade. They saw action in the battles of Givenchy, Neuve Chapelle, and Ypres.

Major Brodhurst was killed in action while engaged in fighting near the Belgian city of Ypres on 27 April 1915 whilst in temporary command of his battalion.

He is buried in la Brique Military Cemetery No. 2, Ieper, West-Vlaanderen, Belgium, Plot I, Row G, Grave 21.

Batting and fielding averages

	Mat	Inns	NO	Runs	HS	Ave	100	50	Ct	St
First-class	1	1	0	9	9	9.00	0	0	1	0

Bowling averages

	Mat	Balls	Runs	Wkts	BBI	BBM	Ave	Econ	SR	4w	5w	10
First-class	1	35	23	0	-	-	-	3.94	-	0	0	0

Captain George King Molineux
Oxford University/Gentleman of England
2nd Bn The Northumberland Fusiliers
Died 5 May 1915
Aged 28
Right-hand bat/ unknown arm slow

'Stood his ground even when the position was impossible'

George King Molineux was born on 15 April 1887 at Meads, Eastbourne, Sussex, the first son of Major Harold Parminter Molineux JP and Rosa Molineux, née King. Educated at St Vincent's School, Eastbourne, and Winchester College, he was a Commoner Prefect at Winchester and captain of the Commoner VI in 1905, playing centre-half for the Association XI in 1906. He was also in the cricket XI in 1906.

In 1906 he went up to Magdalen College Oxford where he played in four first-class matches between May 1907 and July 1908. His debut first-class match was for Oxford University against Worcestershire in a university match played at The University Parks, Oxford, on 23 May 1907. He made 4 and 0 and took one wicket for 17 off 6 overs in the first innings and 3 wickets for 18 off 9.1 overs in his second. Oxford University won by 86 runs. Molineux next played against the South Africans in the British Isles on 30 June 1907 at the New College Ground, Oxford, scoring 11 in his one innings. The match was drawn. His next two first-class appearances came for the Gentlemen of England against Oxford. The first match was played on 28 May 1908 and the second on 2 July 1908 both were university matches. During his first-class career Molineux scored 127 runs, his highest score being 78 not out against Oxford University on 2 July 1908. He also took eleven wickets for 308 runs, his best figures being 4 for 62, again against Oxford University. He became a member of the MCC in 1912.

In 1909 he passed from the Special Reserve into the Regular Army, joining the 2nd Battalion Northumberland Fusiliers. He was gazetted ADC to the Viceroy of India in 1914 but resigned this appointment in November to join his regiment in France. His battalion was on the northern flank of the Ypres salient when a fresh phase of the Second Battle of Ypres began on 22 April 1915.

On 8 May there was fierce fighting on the Frezenberg Ridge and at one point the entire British line was in danger of collapse. By 1.00pm the line had begun to crumble with the Germans getting behind the 2nd Northumberland Fusiliers. By late that evening the commanding officer decided that their position was untenable and ordered them to 'hold on' until dusk. At 7.00pm the shelling abruptly stopped and the Battalion was almost overrun by the enemy. The CO and the adjutant were captured but the 2nd Northumberlands held their ground until darkness fell. Molineux was last seen, wounded and unconscious, in the trench which his unit was holding, but had to be left behind when the men were forced to fall back.

His body was never recovered and he is commemorated on Panels 8 and 12 of the Menin Gate Memorial, Ypres.

Batting and fielding averages

	Mat	Inns	NO	Runs	HS	Ave	100	50	Ct	St
First-class	4	7	1	127	78*	21.16	0	1	2	0

Bowling averages

	Mat	Balls	Runs	Wkts	BBI	Ave	Econ	SR	5w	10
First-class	4	520	308	11	4/62	28.00	3.55	47.2	0	0

Corporal Charles Reginald Handfield
Transvaal
Natal Light Horse
Died 6 May 1915
Aged 36
Unknown

'Always there when needed'

Charles Reginald Handfield was born in South Yarra, Melbourne on 26 August 1898, the son of Frederick Oliver Handfield and Mary Ellen Handfield (nee Tatham) and was educated at East Malvern Grammar School. In 1901 the family moved from Australia to seek fresh opportunities in South Africa.

Handfield played one first class match on 23 Match 1909 in the Currie Cup for Transvaal against Border at the Newlands Rugby Ground, Cape Town. He scored 5 in his one innings and caught both Charles Johnson off the bowling of Vogler for 1 and Norman Norton again off the bowling of Vogler for 15. Transvaal won by an innings and 12 runs.

In 1914, on the outbreak of the war, Handfield joined the Natal Light Horse and was seriously wounded with them at the battle of Gibeon, German South West Africa on 27 April 1915. He succumbed to his wounds just over a week later on 6 May.

He is buried in Gibeon Station Cemetery in what is now Namibia.

Batting and fielding averages

	Mat	Inns	NO	Runs	HS	Ave	100	50	Ct	St
First-class	1	1	0	5	5	5.00	0	0	2	0

Bowling averages

	Mat	Balls	Runs	Wkts	BBI	BBM	Ave	Econ	SR	4w	5w	10
First-class	1	-	-	-	-	-	-	-	-	-	-	-

Lieutenant Edward Stone Phillips
Cambridge University
1st Bn The Monmouthshire Regiment
Died 8 May 1915
Aged 32
Right-handed-Bat

'He always came through everything'

Edward Stone Phillips was born on 18 January 1883 in Newport, Monmouth, the eldest son of Edward and Elizabeth, née Stone, Phillips. Educated at Marlborough College, he was in the Marlborough XI for three years and, from Marlborough, went up to Pembroke College, Cambridge.

He made ten first-class appearances, all for Cambridge University, between May 1903 and July 1904. He made his debut against HDG Leveson-Gower's XI on 11 May 1903 at Fenners. He scored 22 and 0, HDG Leveson-Gower's XI winning by an innings and 42 runs. He went on to play against GJV Weigall's XI, London County, South Africans, Surrey, Sussex, MCC and Oxford University. He made his final first class appearance against Warwickshire on 7 July 1904 at Edgbaston. He made 14 in his one innings and caught Thomas Watson off the bowling of Percy May for 12. The match was drawn. During his first-class career Phillips scored an impressive 422 runs, his highest score being 107 against G. J. V. Weigall's XI on 19 May 1904. He also played successfully for Monmouth (Minor Counties) making 133 not out against Glamorganshire at Cardiff in 1905, putting on 284 for the second wicket with Arthur Silverlock (155 not out), Monmouth winning by an innings and 16 runs. Phillips became a member of the MCC in 1908. Phillips was also a fine golfer, being a former amateur ex-champion of England. After leaving university he became a director of the Newport brewery, Messrs Philips and Sons, Ltd.

At the outbreak of the war he obtained a commission as a second lieutenant into the Monmouthshire Territorials, being promoted to lieutenant in October 1914. Travelling with his battalion to France in February 1914 he was killed in action at Ypres on 8 May 1915. He was buried close to where he fell, but the ground was fought over for many years and in the subsequent fighting his body was lost. An account of his death can be found in the 1/12th London Regiment's official history under the title of *The Stand and Annihilation of the 84th Brigade: Counter attack of the 1/12 London Regiment (Rangers)*:

On the night of May 2nd-3rd, the Battalion was sent to dig a trench line, fire and support trenches, on the Frezenburg ridge, and to man this, which was to become the front line in the event of a retirement from the salient at Zonnebeke taking place. This retirement took place the following night (May 3rd-4th) on which night the new line was improved.

The German artillery soon found the new line on the Frezenburg ridge, and shelled it repeatedly, causing numerous casualties. Relief by the Monmouths, eagerly looked for by the troops now wearied with the strain of many days under continual shell fire, took place on the night May 7th-8th, and the Battalion retired to dug-outs behind the GHQ line, arriving about 4 a.m. Heavy shelling of these dug-outs from about 6 a.m. onwards caused numerous casualties and forbade rest. At 11.15 a.m. came the order to advance in support of the Monmouths, the right of the Brigade line having been broken by the German advance. The Battalion, now about 200 strong, advanced with A, B and C Companies in the front line, led by Major Challen and Major Foucar, and D Company, under Captain Jones, in support, the Machine Gun Section with one gun only left, moving independently on the left flank.

The Battalion had to pass through a gap in the barbed wire in front of the GHQ line on which German machine guns were trained, and suffered heavily in its passage. The whole of the ground over which the further advance took place was heavily shelled, and in places exposed to heavy rifle and machine-gun fire, so that the Battalion rapidly dwindled. A small remnant pushed forward to the rise where the trench line had been and there dug in, and stayed the German advance. (A captured British officer watching from the German lines records that 'they came through a barrage of high explosive shells which struck them down by the dozens, but they never halted for a minute and continued the advance until hardly a man remained.')

Of survivors there were ultimately collected by Sergeant W. J. Hornall (every officer having been killed, wounded, or taken prisoner), 53, mainly pioneers and signallers. All the remainder were either taken prisoner, killed, missing or wounded.

Lieutenant Phillips is commemorated on the Ypres Menin Gate Memorial, Panel 50.

His younger brother Captain Leslie Philips, 1st Welsh Regiment, died at Frezenberg, Ypres, on 25 May 1915.

Batting and fielding averages

	Mat	Inns	NO	Runs	HS	Ave	100	50	Ct	St
First-class	10	18	0	422	107	23.44	1	1	3	0

Bowling averages

	Mat	Balls	Runs	Wkts	BBI	BBM	Ave	Econ	SR	4w	5w	10
First-class	10	-	-	-	-	-	-	-	-	-	-	-

Captain Anthony (Tony) Frederick Wilding
Canterbury
Corps of Royal Marines
Died 9 May 1915
Aged 31
Right-handed Bat/Medium-pace Bowler

'he had displayed the greatest bravery '

Anthony (Tony) Frederick Wilding was born in Christchurch, Canterbury, on 30 October 1883, the second of five children born to Frederick Wilding and Julia Anthony. Both his parents were British and had emigrated to New Zealand from Hereford in England in 1879. His father Frederick practised law in Christchurch and was also a fine sportsman, playing cricket for New Zealand. Anthony Wilding was brought up in some comfort in a large house called 'Fownhope', which had a swimming pool, tennis courts, a croquet green and a cricket wicket.

Anthony, like his father, was a good all-round sportsman, excelling at cricket, tennis and swimming. He was sent to Mr Wilson's school in Cranmer Square, Christchurch, for three years where his sporting prowess soon became obvious and he made his first century (126) at the age of 12. A middle-order batsman and a decent medium-pace bowler with an off break, he played for his father's old team, Lancaster Park, and made two first-class appearances for Canterbury. His first match was played on 4 January 1901 at Lancaster Park, Christchurch, against Auckland and he scored 28 in his only innings and took three wickets for 22 off ten overs; Canterbury won by six wickets. His second match was played against Hawke's Bay on 4 January 1902, once again at Lancaster Park. Wilding scored 13 and 19 and failed to take a wicket. Hawks Bay won by six wickets. As well as cricket he excelled at tennis and, in October 1901 at the age of 17, won the Canterbury Tennis Championships. Wilding left New Zealand in 1902 to attend Cambridge University where he hoped to gain a Blue for cricket. However, once there he began to play more tennis than cricket. During the summer holidays of 1903, Wilding decided to play tennis on the tournament circuit with players who had enough of a private income to allow them to spend their time playing the game.

Despite his sporting activities, he still managed to pass his law examinations, graduating with a BA in 1905. In the same year he made his debut in the Davis Cup as a member of the Australian team. Returning to New Zealand, he joined his father's law firm but, after winning the New Zealand national tennis title in 1906, he returned to England and was admitted to the Bar at the Inner Temple. In this year he also won the Australian Open single and double titles. Between 1907 and 1909 he helped the Australasian team win the Davis Cup and won his second Australian Open in 1909, the same year he qualified as a barrister and solicitor at the Supreme Court of New Zealand. Returning to England, between 1910 and 1913 he won four successive Wimbledon titles, losing the 1914 final to Norman Brookes. He also won four doubles crowns, and in 1914 returned to Davis Cup competition, leading the Australasian side to another success.

Anthony also represented New Zealand in the Stockholm Olympics of 1912, winning a bronze medal. Unusually for the times, Wilding did not smoke or drink alcohol, and followed a strict training programme to keep up his level of fitness. He was not regarded as a naturally brilliant player but succeeded because he worked hard on improving his game, and was more consistent in his play than other players. In 1912 he wrote a book describing this life called *On the Court and off.*

At the outbreak of the First World War Winston Churchill advised Wilding to join the Royal Marines and in October 1914 he was gazetted as a second lieutenant in the Corps. He was attached to the Intelligence Corps before joining the Royal Naval Armoured Car Division in northern France, where he had thirty men, three guns, and armoured cars under his command. He was promoted to lieutenant and then in February 1915 served under the Duke of Westminster as an officer in a new squadron of Rolls Royce armoured cars. On 2 May Wilding received his captaincy and on 8 May wrote home to his parents, it was to be his final letter:

> For really the first time in seven and a half months I have a job on hand which is likely to end in gun, I, and the whole outfit being blown to hell. However, if we succeed we will help our infantry no end.

The following day, 9 May, he was killed in action at 4.45pm while taking part in the battle of Aubers Ridge at Neuve Chapelle when a shell exploded on the roof of the dug-out in which he was sheltering. A description of his death was later outlined in a report from his commander, Reginald Gregory, R.N.

> the gun's crew was sent to the trenches for shelter, Captain Wilding and three Army officers retiring to a dug-out close by.
>
> This was, however, shortly afterwards struck by a large shell, which killed the officers there, Captain Wilding dying in such a manner that his death must have been instantaneous.
>
> I beg to draw your attention to the fine work carried out by this officer. His loss will be greatly felt from a technical point of view, as he was carrying out experiments of great importance. On every occasion he had displayed the greatest bravery, exposing himself to every risk whilst working the armoured cars with the advanced forces of the Army. His loss is much regretted by the officers and men of the Armoured Car Division under my command.

Captain Tony Wilding was buried the following day at the front but was later re-interred at the Rue-des-Berceaux Military Cemetery in Richebourg-l'Avoue, Pas-de-Calais, France, Grave Reference II. D. 37.

Shortly before leaving for the front he had become engaged to the famous Broadway actress Maxine Elliott. After the First World War the Canterbury Lawn Tennis Association bought land in Woodham Road for tennis courts and named their new centre for Canterbury tennis Wilding Park. In 1978, Wilding was elected to the International Tennis Hall of Fame.

Batting and fielding averages

	Mat	Inns	NO	Runs	HS	Ave	100	50	Ct	St
First-class	2	3	0	60	28	20.00	0	0	0	0

Bowling averages

	Mat	Runs	Wkts	BBI	Ave	5w	10
First-class	2	52	3	3/22	17.33	0	0

Second Lieutenant Cecil Banes-Walker
Somerset
2nd Bn The Devonshire Regiment
Died 9 May 1915
Aged 26
Right-handed Bat

'Fell at the head of his men'

Cecil Banes-Walker was born 19 June 1888 at North Petherton, Somerset. Originally, he was called Frederick but somewhere along the way this name seems to have been dropped. He was the eldest son of Mr H. Banes-Walker CC of 'Verriers', North Petherton, Bridgwater, and was educated at Mr Coplestone's School at Exmouth and afterwards at Tonbridge.

Banes-Walker made his name at Long Ashton Cricket Club, North Somerset (established 1870) and Bridgewater Cricket Club. Walker made five first-class appearances for Somerset during the 1914 season in the County Championship. His first-class debut was for Somerset on 9 July 1914 at Gravesend against Kent. Batting at number nine Cecil made 5 and 28; Somerset lost by nine wickets. He next played against Yorkshire. This time he was moved up the batting order to number three and scored 5 and 15 not out, as Somerset were defeated by an innings and 155 runs. Against Worcestershire on 13 August 1914 he managed 8 and 21, Somerset eventually losing by ten wickets. His best score was 40 against Hampshire during his debut on his home ground on 17 August. He made a further 15 in his second innings but Somerset still went down by an innings and 47 runs. In his final match against Essex, on 31 August 1914, Somerset lost by ten wickets in a game played at Clarence Park, Weston-super-Mare, Cecil managing 21 and 14. Cecil was to finish his first-class career without ever being on the winning side. In his ten first-class innings he made a total of 172 runs with a high score of 40 against Hampshire. He also played rugby for Clifton Rugby Football Club and hockey for Gloucestershire.

At the outbreak of the First War, Cecil enlisted into the Gloucestershire Regiment as a private soldier as did many public schoolboys keen to get into the Army and take part in the 'big adventure' in France. However, once again, as was the experience of many young public schoolboys, on 7 October 1914 he was gazetted as a second lieutenant in the Devonshire Regiment. He completed a machine-gun course before being sent to the 2nd Battalion The Devonshire Regiment as a machine-gun officer in March 1915. At the Battle of Aubers Ridge the 2nd Devons were in support. However, at some point in the battle the Devons were ordered to advance and occupy the British front-line trenches in support of the main attack. The 2nd Devons' war diary records that as they did they came under heavy machine-gun and shellfire from the German lines and that between 6.45 and 7.30, together with another second lieutenant, Cecil Banes-Walker was killed. The battalion suffered total casualties of eight officers and 235 other ranks.

Cecil is commemorated at le Trou Aid Post Cemetery, Fleurbaix, France, grave reference F.1.

At the time of Cecil's death, his younger brother Gerald was serving as a lieutenant in the Somerset Light Infantry in India. He rose to the rank of captain and was transferred to Egypt where he was killed in action during the Palestine Campaign on 22 November 1917, aged 28.

Batting and fielding averages

	Mat	Inns	NO	Runs	HS	Ave	100	50	Ct	St
First-class	5	10	1	172	40	19.11	0	0	3	0

Bowling averages

	Mat	Balls	Runs	Wkts	BBI	BBM	Ave	Econ	SR	4w	5w	10
First-class	5	-	-	-	-	-	-	-	-	-	-	-

Lieutenant Wilfred Stanley Bird
Middlesex/Oxford University
5th (attd 2nd) Bn King's Royal Rifle Corps
Died 9 May 1915
Aged 31
Right-handed Bat/Wicket-keeper

'He is the best wicket keeper I ever saw'

Wilfred Stanley Bird was born on 28 September 1883 at Yiewsley Vicarage, Yiewsley Middlesex, the son of the Reverend Henry George Bird MA, Rector of Newdigate, Surrey and Henrietta Maria Bird (née Greenham). He was educated at the Grange (Preparatory) School, Eastbourne, where he was the captain of both the cricket and football XIs. From the Grange he went to Malvern, representing his college at cricket in 1900, 1901 and 1902, as well as at fives and football. His company also won the college cup for military drill.

In 1902 Bird went up to New College, Oxford. Between May 1904 and September 1913 Bird made fifty-five first class appearances playing mainly for Oxford University and Middlesex. He represented Oxford in cricket on three successive seasons. Bird should have stepped straight into the eleven as wicket-keeper, but in 1903 Oxford had a first class wicket-keeper in W. Findlay. However, Bird did keep wicket for Oxford in 1904, 1905 and 1906, being captain of the eleven in his last year. It was said of him that, as a wicket-keeper, he had not the genius of Martyn or Macgregor, but was decidedly above the average, although at least one England captain said of him, 'He is the best wicket-keeper I ever saw.'

He made his debut first class appearance for Oxford University against Yorkshire on 19 May 1904 at the Christ Church Ground, Oxford. He made 30 not out in his one innings, and caught Wilfred Rose off the bowling of George Branston for 8. The match was drawn.

He made his debut for Middlesex against Lancashire on 20 July 1905 in the County Championship at Lord's. Bird scored 4 and 11 (not out in both innings) and playing as wicket keeper stumped Reginald Spooner the Lancashire opener for 67 off the bowling of Bernard Bosanquet in the first innings and Albert Hornby off the bowling of Albert Trott for 8 in the second. He also caught John Sharp off the bowling of Trott again for 4. The match was drawn. Bird made his final first class appearance for Lord Londesborough's XI against Kent on 8 September 1913 at North Marine Road, Scarborough. Bird scored 0 (not out) and 10. He also stumped Frederick Huish off the bowling of Sydney Barnes for 7 and caught John Mason off the bowling of Barnes again for 2. Lord Londesborough's XI won by 337 runs. Bird also played for HDG Leveson-Gower's XI, MCC, Gentlemen (against Players) and CI Thornton's XI. As well as County and University matches Bird turned out against South Africa and Australia. He had been a member of the MCC since 1905. During his first class career Bird made 969 runs, his highest score being 57. He made ninety-three catches and seventeen stumpings as a wicket-keeper.

After leaving Oxford he became a master at Ludgrove where he spent the last eight years of his life. A member of the OTC, he was gazetted lieutenant in the 5th Bn The King's Royal Rifle Corps on 29 December 1914 and was afterwards attached to the 2nd Battalion at the front. Lieutenant Bird was killed on the opening day of the Battle of Aubers Ridge

– 9 May 1915 – while gallantly leading his platoon near Richebourg St Vaast. His company commander wrote of him:

> Bird was gallantly leading his men when he was shot, and died instantly. Bird was a splendid fellow, and a very promising officer and very popular with officers and men alike. I am more than sorry to lose him.

His body was never recovered or identified and he is commemorated on the le Touret memorial, Pas-de-Calais, France, Panels 32 and 33.

Batting and fielding averages

	Mat	Inns	NO	Runs	HS	Ave	100	50	Ct	St
First-class	55	92	16	969	57	12.75	0	2	93	17

Bowling averages

	Mat	Balls	Runs	Wkts	BBI	BBM	Ave	Econ	SR	4w	5w	10
First-class	55	-	-	-	-	-	-	-	-	-	-	-

Captain Wilfred John Hutton Curwen
Oxford University/Surrey/MCC
6th (att'd 3rd) Bn Royal Fusiliers (City of London Regiment)
Died 9 May 1915
Aged 32
Right-handed Bat/Right-arm Fast Medium

'He died bravely while doing his duty'

Wilfred John Hutton Curwen was born on 14 April 1883 at Beckenham, Kent, the son of John and Maria Curwen of The High House, Thames Ditton, Surrey, and of 53, Carlisle Mansions, South-West London. Educated at Charterhouse School, he was in the XI in both 1901 and 1902, averaging 22.66 in 1901 and 26.00 in 1902. In 1901 he also took seventeen wickets for 18.23 runs, the second highest that season. Curwen also played football, becoming a keen member of the Old Carthusians, and rackets for the school. After leaving Charterhouse he went up to Magdalen College Oxford where he obtained his Blue for Association Football in 1905 and 1906.

He made twenty-five first-class appearances between May 1906 and May 1910. As well as nine appearances for Oxford University he was selected to go on the MCC tour of New Zealand between November 1906 and March 1907 where he played in eight matches against Auckland (2), Canterbury (2), Otago (2), Hawke's Bay and New Zealand. On his return to England he played four further matches for the MCC against Hampshire, Leicestershire, Oxford University, Nottinghamshire. He also made four first class appearances for Surrey against Warwickshire, Oxford University, The Australians in the British Isles and Northamptonshire. During his first-class career he made 511 runs, his highest score being 76 against Canterbury in New Zealand on 29 December 1906. He also took twenty-six wickets for 851 runs, his best figures being five for 81. He took 12 catches. He was a member of the I Zingari, the Free Foresters, the Harlequins, and the MCC and was also a member of the Bath Club.

He went to Australia as ADC to Sir John Fuller, Lord Denman and Sir Munro-Ferguson and was unable to play for the MCC team at Geelong and Ballarat. When the war broke out he was still serving as ADC to the Right Honourable Sir R. C. Munro-Ferguson GCMG, Governor-General and Commander-in-Chief of the Commonwealth of Australia. Curwen was then a lieutenant in the 2nd Battalion The London Regiment (TF), having been commissioned in the Londons in April 1911 and promoted to lieutenant in July 1912. At the outbreak of the war he obtained permission to resign his appointment as ADC to Sir R. C. Munro-Ferguson and return to England. Promoted to captain, he joined the 6th Battalion Royal Fusiliers on Christmas Day 1915.

He was killed in action on 9 May 1915 in the Second Battle of Ypres, while acting adjutant of his battalion, at a critical moment in the fighting, when he was gallantly directing some of his men.

His Commanding Officer later wrote concerning his death, 'He died bravely while doing his duty.'

Captain Curwen was buried close to where he was killed. However, his body was not recovered after the war, and he is commemorated on Ypres (Menin Gate) Memorial, Ieper, West-Vlaanderen, Belgium, Panels 6 and 8.

Batting and fielding averages

	Mat	Inns	NO	Runs	HS	Ave	100	Ct	St
First-class	25	44	5	511	76	13.10	0	12	0

Bowling averages

	Mat	Runs	Wkts	BBI	Ave	5w	10
First-class	25	851	26	5/81	32.73	1	0

Captain John Edmund Valentine Isaac DSO
Orange Free State/ Worcestershire
2nd Bn The Prince Consort's Own (Rifle Brigade)
Died 9 May 1915
Aged 35
Right-hand Bat

'He has shown conspicuous gallantry on all occasions, and has always obtained reliable and valuable information when required'

John Edmund Valentine Isaac was born on 14 February 1880 at Powyke Court, near Worcester, the third son of John Swinton Isaac, Esq., DL, a banker of Boughton Park, Worcester, and his wife Alice. Educated at Wixenford Prep School, Wokingham, and Harrow School, he was gazetted in the 2nd Battalion Northumberland Fusiliers from the Militia in April 1900. The following June he sailed to South Africa to join his battalion. In December 1900 he was severely wounded at Nooitgedacht while taking part in the Second Boer War. Present at operations in the Transvaal, Orange River Colony and Cape Colony between May 1900, and March 1901, he was promoted lieutenant in November 1900 and captain in April 1905. On the disbandment of his battalion of the Northumberland Fusiliers in June 1908 he was gazetted in the Rifle Brigade, subsequently serving with them in Malta and Egypt.

Isaac made ten first-class appearances between January 1906 and June 1908. He made his first class debut, on 12 January 1906 for the South African Army against the MCC, at Thara Tswane Officers' Club Ground, Pretoria. He made 0 and 8, the South African Army going down by an innings and 218 runs. The match is probably best remembered for Schofield Haigh's taking four wickets in as many balls in the Army's second innings; Schofield Haigh went on to develop the talents of Douglas Jardine while the cricket coach at Winchester College. Isaac then went on to play four first-class matches for the Orange Free State in 1906–07 in the Currie Cup, the main domestic first-class competition in South Africa, first contested in 1889–90 (now known as the Castle Cup), his highest score being 34 not out. In 1907 and 1908 Isaac made five appearances for Worcestershire, three in the County Championship and two University matches, his best score being a lowly 13. He played his last first-class appearance for Worcestershire on 11 June 1908 against Oxford University at the University Parks, Oxford, scoring 9 and 3; Worcestershire won by 332 runs. During his first-class career he scored 140 runs, his highest score being 34 against Western Province on 26 December 1906. He also took 2 catches.

In 1911 Captain Isaac retired from the Army and went to Vancouver, British Columbia, to engage in real estate. He also hunted and shot in the Yukon and played polo in California. On hearing that Britain was going to war he returned to England in August 1914, and rejoined the Rifle Brigade Reserve of Officers on 1 September. Shortly afterwards he was appointed ADC to Major General Sir T. Capper, commanding 7th Division, and proceeded to the front in October. Later he returned to his regiment and was wounded in the left arm on 24 October at the first Battle of Ypres. For his behaviour on that occasion he was awarded the

DSO, receiving the decoration from the hands of the King on 15 April 1915. The following is the official record of the award:

> John Edmund Valentine Isaac, Capt., Reserve of Officers, The Rifle Brigade (The Prince Consort's Own). He has shown conspicuous gallantry on all occasions, and has always obtained reliable and valuable information when required. On 24 Oct. he guided a unit to a critical point with great skill, which resulted in checking the enemy. He was wounded in the engagement. (*London Gazette*, 1 December 1914)

He was also mentioned in Sir John French's Despatch of 14 January 1915. With his arm still damaged from his wounds he returned to duty on the staff on 19 December. In May 1915 he rejoined the 2nd Battalion Rifle Brigade and was killed in action four days later leading his men on the Fromelles Ridge during the battle of Aubers Ridge. He fell just after they took the German trench.

At the time of his death General Sir T. Capper, KCMG, commanding 7th Division, wrote to his family:

> Johnnie is more to me than an A.D.C, a very dear friend and companion ... he is a gallant soldier too. Sir H. Rawlinson writes to me that he was last seen leading his men to the second assault with great dash – a noble and gallant spirit.

Brigadier General Walter Long also wrote:

> His courage was phenomenal, as his return to his Regiment affords ample proof. Everyone who came in contact with him felt the better for his presence – he really had a most wonderful personality. ... His bravery was really remarkable, and it was a bye-word in his Division; he performed some wonderful deeds out here.

It was not possible to recover his body and he was initially posted as missing. However, six years later in April 1921, his body was discovered and identified by his medal ribbons. He was subsequently reburied at New Irish Farm Cemetery, Ieper, West Vlaanderen, Belgium, Grave reference XXXI, F. 13.

Isaac's brother Arthur also played first-class cricket and lost his life with the 5th Worcestershire Regiment on 7 July 1916. Previous to that, in March 1915, his brother-in-law, Lieutenant Colonel Ernest Charles Wodehouse DSO was also killed. Captain Isaac was a member of the Bath Club, the I Zingari, the Free Foresters and the MCC. He was also a good rider and won the Cairo Grand National in February 1911 while with his regiment in Egypt.

Batting and fielding averages

	Mat	Inns	NO	Runs	HS	Ave	100	50	Ct	St
First-class	10	17	1	140	34*	8.75	0	0	2	0

Bowling averages

	Mat	Runs	Wkts	BBI	BBM	Ave	SR	4w	5w	10
First-class	10	-	-	-	-	-	-	-	-	-

4/72A Sergeant Major Alan Wallace
Auckland
New Zealand Engineers
Died 10 May 1915
Aged 24
Right-handed Bat

'shown the greatest gallantry ever since his arrival at the front'

Alan Wallace was born on 1 April 1891, the fifth of seven sons born to George Wallace, manager of the Devonport Gasworks, and Florence Wallace, née Creighton, of Devonport, Auckland. Educated at Ponsonby Public School and Auckland Grammar School, which he entered as a Foundation Scholar in 1903, he went up to Auckland University. A brilliant student, winning numerous prices in mathematics, science and languages, he won the senior district scholarship and the senior national scholarship. In 1907 he won a junior university scholarship, being second in the Dominion. While at university he won the Sir George Grey Scholarship in chemistry, mathematics and astronomy and also won three senior university scholarships in pure mathematics, mechanics and chemistry. He took his BA in 1910, sitting for honours in 1911 in both mathematics and chemistry. On 13 December 1912 he had the distinction of being selected as a Rhodes Scholar, at the tender age of 20 the youngest ever to be selected from New Zealand. Leaving New Zealand, he set up shop at Balliol College Oxford.

Wallace made three first-class appearances between March 1911 and February 1912. He made his debut first class appearance on 3 March 1911 for Auckland against Hawke's Bay, at Victoria Park, Auckland. He made 72 in his single innings and managed to hang on to a catch from John Board off the bowling of Andrew Snedden for 26. Auckland won by an innings and 275 runs. His second match, played on 9 February 1912 in the Plunket Shield, was against Canterbury at Lancaster Park, Christchurch. Wallace made 0 and 13; Auckland won by two wickets. Wallace played his final first-class match on 23 February 1912, against Wellington at the Basin Reserve, Wellington. He scored 1 and 16 not out. Auckland won by one wicket; it was in this match that Andrew Snedden took eight Wellington wickets for 94. Wallace also played association football for the North Shores Association Football Club, being a very fine striker. While at Balliol Wallace played both rugby and football for his college and took part in the Freshman's cricket match of 1913.

When war broke out he was still at Oxford and initially enlisted into the Royal Engineers before transferring to the New Zealand Engineers. Although not commissioned, he rose quickly through the ranks becoming a sergeant major. He took part in the landings with the New Zealand Anzacs on 25 April 1915 but had only been there a fortnight when he was wounded in the head and shoulder by shrapnel. He died three days later on 10 May 1915 without gaining consciousness. He was buried at sea from the HMT *Lutzow*. His commanding officer wrote of him:

> I should like to write a line to express the deep regret of myself and all the officers and
> men of the NZ Engineers at the death of Sergt Wallace. It may be some consolation,

and at any rate a matter of pride, to know that he had done the most excellent work, and shown the greatest gallantry ever since his arrival at the front. His name is being forwarded to the General Commanding the Division, as one of the NCOs who did especially good work during the arduous fortnight we have been on shore. He died a soldier's death on duty.

Wallace was later Mentioned in Despatches for his brave work.

His body was never recovered or identified and he is commemorated on the Lone Pine memorial, Lone Pine Cemetery, Anzac, Turkey, Panel 72.

We can only wonder what heights this New Zealand academic and cricketer would have reached had his life not been cut so painfully short.

His brother Bertram 'Bert' Wallace, served as Gunner 2/1110 and was killed in action at the Somme fourteen months after Alan's death.

Batting and fielding averages

	Mat	Inns	NO	Runs	HS	Ave	100	50	Ct	St
First-class	3	5	1	102	72	25.50	0	1	2	0

Bowling averages

	Mat	Runs	Wkts	BBI	BBM	Ave	SR	4w	5w	10
First-class	3	19	0	-	-	-	-	0	0	0

Second Lieutenant Geoffrey William Van Der Byl Hopley
Cambridge University
2nd Bn Grenadier Guards
Died 12 May 1915
23 years
Right-handed Bat

'I am afraid. Sir I shall not be much use to you, I am sorry,
especially as we are so short-handed'

Geoffrey William Van Der Byl Hopley was born on 9 September 1891 at Kimberley, Cape Province, South Africa, the second son of the Honourable W. M. Hopley, until recently a Puisne Judge of the Supreme Court of South Africa, but by now a Senior Judge in Southern Rhodesia. Educated at Harrow School, Geoffrey was in the XI in both 1909 and 1910, being second in the batting averages in 1910 with 27.18. In his two matches against Eton, he scored 1 and 23, 35 and 8. Proceeding to Trinity College Cambridge to read History, he obtained his Blue for cricket in 1912.

Between May 1911 and June 1914 Hopley made fifteen first-class appearances, mostly for Cambridge University although he also represented the Free Foresters and LG Robinson's XI. Hopley made his debut first class appearance on 8 May 1911 against Surrey, Fenner's, Cambridge. He scored 16 and 8, Surrey taking the game by 83 runs. He also played against Sussex, Hampshire, HDG Leveson-Gower's XI, MCC, Oxford University, Free Foresters, and Middlesex. His final first-class match was played on 11 June 1914 against the Army, once again at Fenner's. Playing together with his great friend Reginald Lagden (killed in action 3 March 1915), he made 4 in his only innings and caught Harold Fawcus off the bowling of Edward Baker for 56. Cambridge University won by an innings and 80 runs. During his first-class career he made 309 runs, his highest score being 42 against Sussex on 20 June 1912. He also took one wicket for 21 and made 23 catches. He became a member of the MCC in 1911. The following year he became Cambridge University's heavyweight boxing champion.

At the beginning of the war Hopley, on the advice of his friend Arthur Lang, (first-class cricketer for Cambridge University and Sussex), took a commission into the Grenadier Guards. When they reached France however the two friends were separated, Lang going to the Scots Guards, where, on 25 January 1915, he and Gerald Crutchley, another first-class cricketer (Middlesex and Oxford University), had a German trench mine explode under them. Crutchley was wounded and taken prisoner while nothing more was heard of Lang and his death was assumed to have taken place on that day.

A few weeks later, on 3 February 1915, Hopley, while outside his trench, was shot in the arm and thigh. He rolled down into a shell-crater behind the trench and lay there for some time. At length, and with the greatest difficulty, he crawled out of the crater and made his way back into his own trench. As badly wounded as he was, his first thought was not of himself. He made his report, 'I am afraid, Sir, I shall not be much use to you; I am sorry, especially as we are so short-handed.'

He was evacuated and spent fourteen weeks in hospital. At first there was hope that he would recover, but his condition gradually began to deteriorate. His last wish was that he should be buried at Harrow. He wrote to his brother John the day before he died:

> I am afraid I am just about done for, but this is not a real parting. Please don't worry about me old thing. It is I who am to be envied. I am sure that this life here is just a flash in the fire and that our real existence comes later. The very best of love and luck to you, my darling old John. Thank God we have always been such good pals.

He died with his mother beside him in the Military Hospital, Boulogne, on 12 May 1915 and, in accordance with his wishes, his body was brought back to England and buried by the Hill he loved so well.

He is buried in Harrow Cemetery, grave reference 19. I. 3306.

His grave isn't in great condition. Always worth a visit, a clean-up and a few flowers.

Batting and fielding averages

	Mat	Inns	NO	Runs	HS	Ave	100	50	Ct	St
First-class	15	29	4	309	42	12.36	0	0	23	0

Bowling averages

	Mat	Balls	Runs	Wkts	BBI	Ave	Econ	SR	5w	10
First-class	15	25	21	1	1/21	21.00	5.04	25.0	0	0

His brother John Hopley was also a first-class cricketer, making twenty-seven first-class appearances for Cambridge University, the MCC, Western Province, and H. D. G. Leveson-Gower's XI. He died in 1951.

Lieutenant Kenneth Herbert Clayton Woodroffe
Cambridge University/Hampshire/Sussex
6th Bn The Prince Consort's Own (Rifle Brigade), attd 2nd
Welsh Regiment
Died 13 May 1915
Aged 22
Right-handed Bat/Right-arm Fast

'He was killed in the way that every soldier would wish to be killed'

Kenneth Herbert Clayton Woodroffe was born on 9 December 1892, at Wallands Park, Lewes, East Sussex, the son of Henry Long Woodroffe and Clara Woodroffe, née Clayton, of Thorpewood, Branksome Avenue, Bournemouth. He was educated at Rose Hill School, Banstead, Marlborough College and Pembroke College Cambridge, where he was a Classics Exhibitioner.

While at Marlborough College, Woodroffe was a senior prefect, captain of the OTC and captain of the XI (1909–12). It was his bat that turned the match against Rugby at Lord's in 1912. He was also in the hockey XI and rugby XV. Going up to Pembroke College Cambridge, Woodroffe concentrated on his bowling and was of a good enough standard to be given his Blue as a freshman in 1913. He made eighteen first-class appearances between September 1912 and August 1914. Fifteen of those were University matches, playing for Cambridge University, while one was for Hampshire against the South Africans in the British Isles and he turned out twice for Sussex. His debut first-class match was for Hampshire against the touring South Africans at Dean Park, Bournemouth where he scored 9 in his only innings and took 5 wickets for 33 runs; the match was drawn. In his debut match against Oxford University, at Lord's on 7 July 1913, he took six wickets for 55 and scored 2 in his only innings; Cambridge won by four wickets. His final first-class match came on 3 August 1914 in the County Championship for Sussex against Kent during which he scored 1 in his only innings and took no wickets. Sussex won by 34 runs. He also played against Northamptonshire, Hampshire, Free Foresters, Sussex, HDG Leveson Gower's XI, MCC, Middlesex and the Army. He made a total of 172 runs, his highest score being 22 against the Army on 11 March 1914. He also took fifty-five wickets for 1,500 runs, his best figures being six for 43. He made 5 catches.

On 15 August 1914, at the outbreak of the war, he was gazetted to the 6th Rifle Brigade as a second lieutenant. He went to France in November 1914 and was promoted to lieutenant on 15 April 1915. While in France he was attached to the 2nd Battalion Welsh Regiment, and was killed in action with them during an attack on the German trenches at Neuve Chapelle on 9 May 1915. One of his commanders, Captain Gilbey, wrote to his family concerning his death:

> Your son was killed yesterday in an attack near Neuve Chapelle. He was with the leading platoon and was the man to get nearer the German front line trenches than any other. He was killed in the way that every soldier would wish to be killed, leading his platoon gallantly in the attack. His death was quite instantaneous, he was shot

through the head. By his death I personally have lost a very good and true friend, and the regiment a fine and most gallant officer. At Festubert before Christmas he commanded one of our companies in an attack with great success, for which his name was included in our list of recommendations sent to Brigade. Later at Givenchy, against the German attack on 25 January, he brought up his platoon under heavy fire, leading his men most gallantly.

He was mentioned in Lord French's Despatches of 5 April-31 May (*London Gazette*, 22 June 1915).

His body was never recovered or identified and he is commemorated on the le Touret Memorial, Panel 44.

His parents were to lose three sons during the war: Second Lieutenant Sidney Clayton Woodroffe VC, 14th attd 8th Battalion The Rifle Brigade was killed in action on 30 July 1915, aged 19 years, and Captain Leslie Woodroffe MC, 8th Battalion The Rifle Brigade, died of wounds on 4 June 1916. Between them the brothers earned won a Victoria Cross, a Military Cross and a Mention in Despatches. We can only speculate on the effect of losing their sons in such tragic ways on their parents.

Batting and fielding averages

	Mat	Inns	NO	Runs	HS	Ave	100	50	Ct	St
First-class	18	29	8	172	22*	8.19	0	0	5	0

Bowling averages

	Mat	Runs	Wkts	BBI	Ave	5w	10
First-class	18	1500	55	6/43	27.27	2	0

Major Eustace Frederick Rutter
Europeans (India)
1st Bn East Lancashire Regiment
Died 13 May 1915
Aged 44
Not Known

'All who have returned to us from the Front tell tales of his goodness'

Eustace Frederick Rutter was born on 20 June 1870, at Hillingdon, Middlesex, England, the eldest son of Frederick John Rutter, a manufacturer, of Parkfield, Hillingdon, Uxbridge, and of Elizabeth his wife. He was educated at Rugby School, entering school in 1884 and was a member of the cricket XI between 1887 and 1889. From Rugby he went up to Trinity Hall Cambridge and while at Cambridge decided on a career in the Army. He entered the Royal Military College Sandhurst and in 1892 was commissioned in the 1st Battalion East Lancashire Regiment and saw active service on the North-West Frontier of India in 1897 and 1898. He also served in the Second Boer War from 1899 to 1902, where he took part in operations in the Orange Free State, Natal and the defence of Ladysmith.

While in India between 11 September 1905 and 21 September 1908 Rutter made eight first-class appearances, all for the Europeans playing for the Bombay Presidency XI. Six against the Parsees and two against the Hindus. He made his debut on 11 September 1905 against the Parsees at the Deccan Gymkhana Ground, Poona. Rutter scored 3 in his only innings. The Parsees won by an innings and 226 runs. Rutter's final first class appearance came on 21 September 1908 in the final of the Triangular Tournament against the Hindus at the Gymkhana Ground, Bombay. Rutter scored two ducks, the Europeans going on to win by 119 runs.

During his first class career Rutter made 142 runs, his highest score being 23 against Parsees on 27 August 1907. He took three catches. He also turned out for the MCC and the Free Foresters in 1892–93 (not first class matches).

At the beginning of the First World War he went out to France with the East Lancashire Regiment and was promoted major in December 1914. On 31 May 1915 he was Mentioned in Despatches for bravery in the field. Rutter was killed in action at Ypres on 13 May 1915 while repelling an attack on his trench. It was reported that he was firing over the parapet at the oncoming German infantry when he was shot through the head, dying instantly. His colonel later wrote:

> Since he has been out here he has been my Second in Command and rendered me invaluable aid. I feel his loss greatly, and so does everyone in the Regiment, for he was a great favourite with all ranks.

The wife of one of his brother officers also later wrote, 'All who have returned to us from the Front tell tales of his goodness.'

Rutter's body was never recovered and he is commemorated on Ypres (Menin Gate) Memorial, Ieper, West-Vlaanderen, Belgium, Panel 34.

Batting and fielding averages

	Mat	Inns	NO	Runs	HS	Ave	100	50	Ct	St
First-class	8	15	2	142	23	10.92	0	0	3	0

Bowling averages

	Mat	Balls	Runs	Wkts	BBI	BBM	Ave	Econ	SR	4w	5w	10
First-class	8	-	-	-	-	-	-	-	-	-	-	-

Captain Gordon Belcher MC
Hampshire
3rd (attd 1st) Bn Princess Charlotte of Wales's (Royal
Berkshire Regiment)
Died 16 May 1915
Aged 29
Right-handed Bat/Right-arm Medium

'No family should suffer so much. No country should loose so much talent'

Gordon Belcher was born on 26 September 1885 at Keep Town, Brighton, Sussex, the youngest son of the Reverend Thomas Hayes Belcher, headmaster of Brighton College, who won his cricket Blue at Oxford in 1870 and was also the second victim of Cobden's famous hat-trick when Oxford, requiring just four to win off the last over with three wickets left, were bowled out. Gordon was educated at Brighton College, where he was in the XI in 1901, 1902, 1903 and 1904, captaining the side in 1903–4.

On leaving school in 1904 he want up to St Catherine's College Cambridge but, although played in the Freshmen's match, did not win his Blue. He played frequently for Berkshire, his best seasons coming in 1910 and 1911, when his averages were 27.00 and 26.60 respectively. First in the county's bowling in 1912 and second in 1911, his highest innings for Berkshire was 112 not out against Wiltshire at Reading in 1910, and 104 not out against Carmarthen on the same ground the following year. Belcher played in one first-class match on 24 August 1905 for Hampshire against Warwickshire at the County Ground, Southampton. He was dismissed twice for a duck. Warwickshire won by ten wickets.

He became a master at Reading School where he was commissioned into the School Officer Training Corps (OTC) as a second lieutenant on 5 December 1908. Later he moved to Brighton College, his old school, where he continued his work with the OTC.

He was gazetted to a lieutenancy in the 3rd (Reserve) Battalion Princess Charlotte of Wales's (Royal Berkshire Regiment) becoming a captain and later going out to France with the 1st Battalion. During the fighting he was decorated with the Military Cross but was killed in action on 16 May 1915 near Richebourg l'Avoue, Belgium.

He is buried in the Rue-des-Berceaux Military Cemetery, Richebourg l'Avoue, grave reference I.A.15.

Gordon Belcher was one of three brothers to die during the war, the others being Lieutenant Colonel Harold Thomas DSO RFA, who was killed in action on 8 July 1917, aged 42, and Major Raymond Belcher DSO MC RFA, who died of wounds on 7 December 1917, aged 34.

1915

Batting and fielding averages

	Mat	Inns	NO	Runs	HS	Ave	100	50	4s	6s	Ct	St
First-class	1	2	0	0	0	0.00	0	0	0	0	0	0

Bowling averages

	Mat	Balls	Runs	Wkts	BBI	BBM	Ave	Econ	SR	4w	5w	10
First-class	1	6	3	0	-	-	-	3.00	-	0	0	0

Lieutenant Frank Miller Bingham MRCS, LRCP
Derbyshire
Royal Army Medical Corps
5th Bn King's Own Royal Regiment (Lancaster)
Died 22 May 1915
Aged 40
Right-handed Bat

'Died as he had lived caring for others'

Frank Miller Bingham was born on 17 September 1874 at Alfreton, the second son of Dr Joseph and Mrs Bingham, of Alfreton, Derbyshire. He was educated at St Peter's School, York, where he played in the school XI and St Thomas's Hospital Medical School, London. Having qualified as a doctor, he took a practice in Blackwell, Alfreton, and Derbyshire, having a strong association with the Blackwell Collieries. He left this practice four years later to set up a surgery in Lancaster. While there he also found time to meet and marry Ruth Morley and set up home at Highfield House, Lancaster.

A good all-round sportsman, Bingham played cricket for Derbyshire. He made one first-class appearance on 28 May 1896 against the Marylebone Cricket Club (MCC) at Lord's, making 6 and 11, Derbyshire winning by one wicket. He was also a good rugby union player, turning out for Blackheath FC and Middlesex.

Keen on the Territorials, he was first commissioned as a medical officer with the rank of lieutenant in the Royal Army Medical Corps on 24 March 1910. However, perhaps because he wanted his military duties to be different to his civilian occupation, he transferred to the 5th Battalion, King's Own Royal Regiment (Lancaster) on 26 November 1910. Promoted to captain in May 1914, he took command of a company. He took part in the Second Battle of Ypres in May 1915, becoming acting second in command of his battalion. He was given three days' home leave and, on the day after his return to the front, was killed in action on 22 May. He had been reconnoitring some new trenches close to Sanctuary Wood that his battalion were to occupy the following day. As he and other

officers were leaving, before daybreak, they came across a man half buried by the side of a trench which had been blown in. Bingham insisted on stopping to dig the man out himself, which took some time. It was therefore daylight before he began to leave the trenches. Unfortunately the party were spotted by the Germans who opened fire, Bingham receiving a bullet through the heart which killed him instantaneously.

He was buried initially on the edge of a wood close to the front. However, after years of heavy fighting, his grave was subsequently lost. He is commemorated on the Ypres (Menin Gate) Memorial, Panel 12.

Later that same year a bronze tablet was erected in his memory by the medical profession of Lancaster and district on the outer wall of the Royal Lancaster Infirmary and unveiled on 2 December 1915 by Dr G. R. Parker, the senior member of the medical profession in Lancaster.

Batting and fielding averages

	Mat	Inns	NO	Runs	HS	Ave	100	50	Ct	St
First-class	1	2	0	17	11	8.50	0	0	0	0

Bowling averages

	Mat	Balls	Runs	Wkts	BBI	BBM	Ave	Econ	SR	4w	5w	10
First-class	1	-	-	-	-	-	-	-	-	-	-	-

Major Francis Stuart Wilson
Jamaica
HQ Staff 1 Brigade Royal Marine Light Infantry
Died 24 May 1915
Aged 32
Right-handed Bat

'An officer of strong personality and marked organizing capability'

Francis Stuart Wilson was born on 18 January 1883 at Campden Hill, London, the son of Henry Wilson, Gentleman, and Mrs A. A. Wilson of 85 Inverness Terrace, Hyde Park, London. His brother was Lieutenant Colonel Leslie Wilson RMLI MP officer commanding Hawk battalion.

Joining the Army he spent some time in Jamaica and while there played five first class matches for Jamaica during the 1905 season. He made his debut against Lord Brackley's XI on 12 January 1905 at Sabina Park, Kingston. Wilson scored 55 and 1 and caught Charles Ebden off the bowling of M Moyston for 16. The match was drawn. He made his final first class appearance on 16 August 1905 against Trinidad again at the Sabina Park, Kingston. He made 14 and 10. He also caught JA Pinder off the bowling of Robert Hutton for 71. Trinidad won by 289 runs. During his first class career Wilson made 197 runs his highest score being 63 against Lord Brackley's XI on 19 January 1905. He also made 2 catches. He was also a first-class shot and fine hockey player.

On 29 May 1913 he obtained his pilot's certificate at the Bristol School, Brooklands (certificate number 497). He became adjutant at the depot in Walmer, a post he held for three years. During this time he organized military pageants, which were both popular and quite spectacular for their time. The pageant fixed for 6 August 1914 was one of the many events in the first week of the war that had to be postponed, a fact which Captain Wilson particularly regretted after all the work he had put in preparing for it. As commandant of the Depot Cadet Corps, he was much interested in the lads who were members of it, and did much to promote their proficiency.

When 1 Brigade of the Royal Naval Division was in camp at Walmer, Captain Wilson was attached to the headquarters staff and, in this capacity, went with the Royal Naval Division to Antwerp at the beginning of October. He was appointed brigade major on 16 October. He also accompanied the brigade on their second and greater expedition, to the Dardanelles. While there he was Mentioned in Despatches (*London Gazette* 5 August 1915) by Brigadier General Mercer: 'He performed his duties with great zeal, ability & tact. He is always cheerful & worked very hard. I have the highest opinion of this officer.'

Major Wilson was killed in action on 24 May 1915 (initially reported killed in action on the 19th) while on a visit to the trenches. Originally buried at Backhouse Post, he is now buried at Skew Bridge Cemetery, Helles, grave reference II. B. 7.

His commanding officer later wrote:

An officer of strong personality & marked organizing capability was lost to the Service when in the operations in the Dardanelles on the 26th of May 1915, Major F. S. Wilson, RMLI was killed.

Batting and fielding averages

	Mat	Inns	NO	Runs	HS	Ave	100	50	Ct	St
First-class	5	10	0	197	63	19.70	0	2	2	0

Bowling averages

	Mat	Runs	Wkts	BBI	BBM	Ave	SR	4w	5w	10
First-class	5	23	0	-	-	-	-	0	0	0

Captain Edmund Marsden
Gloucestershire
64th Pioneers, Indian Army
Died 26 May 1915
Aged 34
Right-handed Bat

'Forgotten for eighty years his memory lives on'

Edmund Marsden was born on 18 April 1881, Madras (now Chennai), India and attended Cheltenham College between 1896 and 1898 before deciding to take up a career with the military. He was accepted at the Royal Military College Sandhurst and was granted a commission on the Unattached List in 1900 before joining the Indian Staff Corps in 1901. Eventually he was attached to the 64th Pioneers, Indian Army and while serving with them died of malarial fever at Myitkyina, Burma on 26 May 1915.

Marsden played two first-class matches for Gloucester in 1909 both in the County Championship. He made his debut first class appearance against Nottinghamshire on 7 June 1909 at the Spa Ground, Gloucester. He scored 7 and 11, Gloucestershire going down by two wickets. His next match was against Northamptonshire on 10 June 1909 once again at the Spa Ground. Marsden's form improved and he opened the batting scoring 38 and 23, Gloucestershire going on to win by 25 runs.

His grave was eventually lost among hundreds of others and for years he wasn't recorded as a war casualty. For some reason his name was not forwarded to the CWGC when the Debt of Honour Register was compiled in the 1920s. However, in 2006 this error was rectified, his name was added to the register and he was finally classified as a war casualty over eighty years after he lost his life.

He is now commemorated by a plaque in Plot 27.J.2 in the Taukkyan War Cemetery, Myanmar. He is also commemorated on the Cheltenham War Memorial, the Cheltenham College Roll of Honour and in the Chapel at the Royal Military Academy, Sandhurst.

Batting and fielding averages

	Mat	Inns	NO	Runs	HS	Ave	100	50	Ct	St
First-class	2	4	0	79	38	19.75	0	0	0	0

Bowling averages

	Mat	Balls	Runs	Wkts	BBI	BBM	Ave	Econ	SR	4w	5w	10
First-class	2	-	-	-	-	-	-	-	-	-	-	-

Lieutenant Hubert Frederick Garrett
Somerset
9th Bn East Yorkshire Regiment, attd 1st Bn Royal Dublin
Fusiliers
Died 4 June 1915
Aged 21
Right-handed Bat/Leg break

'Died like the gallant officer and gentleman he was'

Hubert Frederick Garrett was born on 13 November 1894 at Chesterfield Avenue, Malvern (a suburb of Melbourne), Australia and was educated at Melbourne Grammar School. He entered the school in 1905 and had a distinguished school career, becoming a Witherby Scholar in 1907. He was in the athletic team which won *The Argus* and *The Australasian* Cup in 1909, Garrett winning the quarter mile (under 16). In the First XI in 1910 and 1911, he had the reputation of being a first-class bat and an effective leg spinner, as well as being the captain of the lacrosse team. Academically brilliant, he was accepted at Queen's College Cambridge in 1911.

Although a gifted cricketer, he failed to get his Blue, although this might have been due to an injury to his arm.

He played in eleven first-class matches between June 1913 and June 1914. His first-class début came for H. D. G. Leveson Gower's XI in two festival matches against Cambridge and Oxford Universities at Eastbourne in June 1913. His leg-break and googly bowling proved very effective. Against Cambridge, which was a 12-a-side first-class match, he took eight wickets for 70 runs, including a second innings total of five for 39. He improved on these figures in the 11-a-side match against Oxford, taking six for 60 and four for 32, his total match figures being 10 for 92. In all first-class matches that season he made 209 runs and took thirty-two wickets for 20.93 runs apiece. The county side Somerset, seeing his potential, signed him up and he played in eight first-class matches for them late in the 1913 season. However, he was unable to repeat his Eastbourne success, and was only able to take fourteen wickets in the eight matches. He also made a single first-class appearance for the MCC on 4 June 1914 in the match against Cambridge University, scoring 0 and 11 and taking two wickets for 85 runs. Cambridge University won by 177 runs. It was to be his last first-class match.

In October 1914, shortly after the outbreak of the Great War, he joined the Cambridge Officer Training Corps (OTC). The following month, he was gazetted as a second lieutenant in the 9th Battalion East Yorkshire Regiment. His potential was quickly recognized and only a few weeks later, in December, he was promoted to lieutenant and adjutant of his battalion. He, together with two other officers, was transferred and attached to the 1st Battalion Royal Dublin Fusiliers, travelling to Gallipoli to help make up the losses they had suffered during the campaign. A few days later he took part in the third Battle of Krithia and was reported missing during an advance near Achi Baba. It was later confirmed that he had been killed in action during the advance on 4 June 1915. A brother officer later wrote:

We have had very sad news about Hubert. It appears that a staff officer came into the trench his company was occupying and said that the trench immediately in front of them was not being held by the enemy and must be occupied by our own men. However, a machine gun on our left was holding up progress. He thereupon ordered two platoons to be sent forward to occupy the trench and enfilade the gun and put it out of action. Hubert led his platoon forward, but no sooner had they crossed the parapet than three machine guns opened fire from the supposedly unoccupied trench with murderous effect. The men were seen to stagger and fall, and among them were the two boys. They died like gallant officers and gentlemen. Out of the two platoons 70 were missing.

His body was never recovered or identified and he is commemorated on the Helles Memorial, addenda panel.

Batting and fielding averages

	Mat	Inns	NO	Runs	HS	Ave	100	50	Ct	St
First-class	11	21	3	220	37*	12.22	0	0	4	0

Bowling averages

	Mat	Balls	Runs	Wkts	BBI	Ave	Econ	SR	5w	10
First-class	11	1277	755	34	6/60	22.20	3.54	37.5	2	1

He was not, as many have supposed over the years, the son of the famous Australian Test cricketer Tom Garrett.

Captain Francis Hunt Gould
Europeans (India)
Middlesex Regiment (Duke of Cambridge's Own)
Died 6 June 1915
Aged 32
Right-handed Bat

'Always at hand, the very best of men'

Francis Hunt Gould was born on 16 October 1881 at Ross, Herefordshire, the son of Captain and Mrs Louis P. Gould of Wolverdene, Andover, Hants. He was educated at Repton School, Derbyshire, where he was in the XI and was head of the batting averages in 1899, scoring 285 runs with an average of 28.50; he made 19 and 63 versus Malvern and 34 and 19 versus Uppingham.

On 13 March 1900 he was commissioned in the 3rd Battalion Middlesex Regiment. While serving in India he played for the Ballygunge Cricket Club and made one first-class appearance on 28 August 1913 during the Bombay Presidency match at the Deccan Gymkhana Ground, Poona, playing for the Europeans against Hindus. He scored 4 and 27, despite Gould's best efforts, Hindus won by six wickets.

Gould was promoted captain in the 1st Battalion in August 1914, going to France with his regiment at the outbreak of the war. He was accidentally killed at Armentières on 6 June 1915 at the age of 33.

He is buried at Cite Bonjean Military Cemetery, Armentières, grave reference IX. C. 13.

Batting and fielding averages

	Mat	Inns	NO	Runs	HS	Ave	100	50	Ct	St
First-class	1	2	1	31	27*	31.00	0	0	1	0

Bowling averages

	Mat	Balls	Runs	Wkts	BBI	BBM	Ave	Econ	SR	4w	5w	10
First-class	1	-	-	-	-	-	-	-	-	-	-	-

Second Lieutenant Claude Lysaght Mackay
Gloucestershire
2nd Bn The Worcestershire Regiment, attd 2nd Bn The
Manchester Regiment
Died 7 June 1915
Aged 20
Right-handed Bat/Right-arm medium-fast bowler

'I do not think he will ever be forgotten'

Claude Lysaght Mackay was born on 29 October 1894 in Rajkot, Kithiawar, India to Edward Vansittart Mackay, late of the Indian Police, and Jane (Nina) Mackay of 10 College Road, Clifton, Gloucestershire. He was educated at Clifton College, Bristol, where he was an important member of the cricket XI in 1912 and 1913. In the latter year he made 400 runs with an average of 36.33 and a high score of 71 against Cheltenham. Mackay also took twenty wickets for 15.45 runs each. A good all-round cricketer he had a good reach and would undoubtedly have made a name for himself had he been able to devote himself to first-class cricket. Good at most sports he took up, he won the Challenge Cup at Athletics and the Public Schools' heavyweight boxing competition at Aldershot in 1913. The *Sportsman* magazine said of him after his victory that it 'had never seen such an electrifying performance'.

While in the Clifton XI Mackay proved himself a fine free-hitting bat and a useful fast bowler. He also got his football cap. On leaving school, he made a single first-class appearance for Gloucestershire against Kent on 20 July 1914 at Mote Park, Maidstone. He made 13 and 15 and caught James Seymour off the bowling of Francis Ellis for 0. Kent won by 323 runs.

From Clifton College, having won the Leaving Exhibition, he went to Cambridge, winning a Classic Exhibition into Corpus Christi College where he distinguished himself in athletics. On the day war was declared Claude was on tour with Old Cliftonians but joined up immediately and was gazetted into the 5th (Reserve) Battalion, Worcestershire Regiment on 15 August. He joined the Expeditionary Force on 1 January 1915 when he was posted to the 2nd Battalion. He then became attached to the 2nd Battalion Manchester Regiment. On 28 May 1915, while in command of a company, he was seriously wounded and died in hospital at Boulogne just over a week later on 7 June.

Among the many letters his family received was one from a sergeant in his platoon:

I do not think he will ever be forgotten. There was no braver officer, he always did his duty, and more than his duty, staying out when on patrol duty very close to the enemy trenches, and when our trenches were being shelled he was always near at hand, bandaging up the wounded and cheering his men on and sometimes, when we would be all wet through and in a thoroughly dismal condition, up he would come with cigarettes, and then he would receive the smiling thanks of the men – nothing like a cigarette to put a smile on our faces! He was very popular with us all, always doing what was in his power to make things as pleasant as possible for us under very trying conditions.

He is buried in Boulogne Eastern Cemetery, Grave reference II. A. 31.

Batting and fielding averages

	Mat	Inns	NO	Runs	HS	Ave	100	50	Ct	St
First-class	1	2	0	28	15	14.00	0	0	1	0

Bowling averages

	Mat	Balls	Runs	Wkts	BBI	BBM	Ave	Econ	SR	4w	5w	10
First-class	1	30	24	0	-	-	-	4.80	-	0	0	0

Private Hugh Latimer Tuke
Hawke's Bay
Auckland Regiment, New Zealand Expeditionary Force
6 (Hauaki) Company, Auckland Regiment
Died 7 June 1915
Aged 31

'Loved his country more than any man I knew'

Hugh Latimer Tuke was born on 6 April 1885 at Taradale, Hawke's Bay, New Zealand, the second son of the Reverend Charles Laurence and Mary Eleanor Tuke, of 22 Omahu Road, Remuera, Auckland. Educated at the Heretaunga School, he later worked for Messrs William and Kettle before taking a job with the local council, working on the roads. Tuke also served with the Old Napier Guard, rising to the rank of corporal and becoming a crack shot. After being invited to study farming and live in America by a relative, he remained there for five years, later returning to New Zealand to take up land in the Thames Valley.

He represented Hawke's Bay in one first-class match on 24 March 1905 against Auckland at the Auckland Domain, Auckland. Tuke scored 3 and 4 (not out), Auckland winning by an innings and seventeen runs. He also played football for Hawke's Bay.

At the outbreak of the First World War Hugh Tuke joined the Auckland Regiment and was assigned to 6 (Hauaki) Company. He embarked on the *Star of India* (or *Waimana*) for Suez in Egypt on 16 October 1914. Later offered a commission he declined this, preferring to stay with his friends in the Hauaki Company. He was badly wounded during the fighting at Quinn's Post and evacuated to HMS *Sicilia* where he died of his wounds on 7 June 1915 and was buried at sea.

He is commemorated on the Lone Pine Memorial, Turkey.

Batting and fielding averages

	Mat	Inns	NO	Runs	HS	Ave	100	50	Ct	St
First-class	1	2	1	7	4*	7.00	0	0	0	0

Bowling averages

	Mat	Balls	Runs	Wkts	BBI	BBM	Ave	Econ	SR	4w	5w	10
First-class	1	-	-	-	-	-	-	-	-	-	-	-

Lieutenant Douglas (Druce) Robert Brandt
Oxford University
6th Bn, attd 1st Bn The Prince Consort's Own (Rifle Brigade)
Died 6 July 1915
Aged 27
Right-handed Bat/Wicketkeeper

'All the gifts of the gods were his'

Douglas (Druce) Robert Brandt was born on 20 October 1887 in Streatham, London, the youngest son of Robert E. Brandt and Mrs Florence Brandt of 15 Lennox Gardens, London. Educated at Mrs Bailey's preparatory school at Hazelwood, Limpsfield, before going up to Harrow School in 1901 (Mr Davidson's house), he became a Leaf Scholar in 1906. Brandt won most of the school prizes including the *prize ob studia uno temore feliciter peracta*, only ever awarded eight times before in the school's history. His House Master wrote of him, 'came nearer to being my ideal of a boy than any boy I have ever known'.

He was in the cricket XI from 1904 to 1906, the football XI from 1903 to 1905 (Captain 1904–05) and won the lightweight Public Schools' boxing championship in 1903 and became famous throughout the school for throwing a cricket ball over 120 yards during school sports day. Perhaps the most dramatic of his individual feats was his carrying of a relatively weak House XI to victory in the Cock House Match of 1906, when he not only scored 61 out of the 136 runs made in the first innings, followed by 120 out of 266 in the second but also took eleven wickets in the two innings, with the result that his House won by five wickets. Hurrying, late, into the speech room for prize-giving after the match he was spontaneously applauded and cheered. A tiny incident, perhaps, but one probably unique in its way, and eloquent by its very spontaneity.

In 1904 he was elected to a Domus Classical Exhibition at Balliol College Oxford and achieved the top first in honour moderations of his year. He went on to be a fellow and lecturer at Brasenose College Oxford in 1910.

Brandt played in eight first-class matches between May 1907 and June 1908. He made his debut for Oxford University against Lancashire on 16 May 1907 at the Christ Church Ground, Oxford. Brandt scored 5 and 7 Lancashire won by 9 wickets. He made his final first class appearance on 25 June 1908 against Surrey at the Kennington Oval. Brandt scored 10 and 0 and caught Walter Lees off the bowling of John Lowe for 13. Surrey won by 6 wickets. He also played against the MCC, Sussex, Cambridge University, and Worcestershire. He made 105 first class runs, his highest score being 23 against Sussex on 1 July 1907. A decent wicket keeper he also took six catches and made three stumpings.

In 1911 Brandt took a commission in the university OTC and when, in the summer of 1913, he resigned his fellowship, he went at once to a course of training with the Special Reserve. At the outbreak of the war he was posted to the 6th Battalion Rifle Brigade and began his training at Sheerness. He went to the front in May 1915, attached to the 1st Battalion. On 6 July 191 5 he was put in command of a company detailed to capture a

German trench in Flanders, and fell on the German parapet cheering on his men. The day before he died Brandt wrote, 'It's very difficult to think of anything beyond to-morrow.'

He has no known grave and is commemorated on Ypres (Menin Gate) Memorial, Ieper, West-Vlaanderen, Belgium, Panels 46 – 48 and 50

Batting and fielding averages

	Mat	Inns	NO	Runs	HS	Ave	100	50	Ct	St
First-class	8	15	3	105	23	8.75	0	0	6	3

Bowling averages

	Mat	Balls	Runs	Wkts	BBI	BBM	Ave	Econ	SR	4w	5w	10
First-class	8	-	-	-	-	-	-	-	-	-	-	-

Lieutenant James Frederick Sutcliffe
Hampshire
Royal Marine Light Infantry (Portsmouth Bn)
Died 14 July 1915
Aged 38
Right-handed Bat

'A beautiful voice silenced too soon'

James Frederick Sutcliffe was born on 12 December 1876 at Chatham in Kent, the son of James and Alice Sutcliffe. A man with a good voice, he was a member of St Thomas' church choir in Portsmouth. James followed his father into the Royal Marines, serving with the Portsmouth Battalion of the Royal Marine Light Infantry.

He was a middle-order batsman and had the distinction of being one of two colour sergeants who played for Hampshire in 1911, the other being Harold Forster. Sutcliffe played one first-class match on 17 August 1911 for Hampshire against Worcestershire in the County Championship at New Road, Worcester. Batting at number seven, he scored 16 and 8. Worcestershire won comfortably by eight wickets. He did well in the RMLI and was commissioned as a lieutenant. In 1912 he met and married Gladys Mills at Portsmouth and in 1914, whilst living in Alverstoke, Gosport, they had a son, James.

Sutcliffe travelled with his battalion to take part in the Gallipoli campaign and was killed on 14 July 1915. His body was never discovered or identified and he is commemorated on the Helles Memorial, Panels 2–7. His name is also listed on the memorial outside Portsmouth Cathedral. The local paper also remembered him, "His death (Sutcliffe) will be a great loss to St. Thomas' choir. We were proud of him when he obtained his commission from warrant rank since the outbreak of the war. Our deepest sympathy goes out to his relations in Gosport."

Batting and fielding averages

	Mat	Inns	NO	Runs	HS	Ave	100	50	Ct	St
First-class	1	2	0	24	16	12.00	0	0	0	0

Bowling averages

	Mat	Balls	Runs	Wkts	BBI	BBM	Ave	Econ	SR	4w	5w	10
First-class	1	-	-	-	-	-	-	-	-	-	-	-

163 Private Alan Marshal
Queensland/Surrey
15th Battalion Australian Infantry
Died 23 July 1915
Aged 32
Right-hand bat/ Right-arm fast-medium

The finest Australian bat ever to play in England

Alan Marshal was born 12 June 1883 in Warwick, Queensland, Australia, the son of Samuel (an immigrant from Lincolnshire) and Agnes Marshal of the Bungalow, Esk, Queensland. He was educated at the South Brisbane State School and the Brisbane Grammar School. He played in both school XIs and showed great promise from an early age. A big hitting middle order batsman he was also a first class fast medium bowler.

Alan Marshal made 119 first class appearances between April 1904 and December 1913, the majority for Queensland Australia and Surrey. He made his debut first class match for Queensland against New South Wales on 2 April 1904 at the Brisbane Cricket Ground, Woolloongabba, Brisbane. He made 22 and 0 and caught Ernest Jansan off the bowling of David Miller for 40 and Montague Noble again off the bowling of Miller for 12. He played for Queensland on two more occasions against Victoria and New South Wales before leaving for England in 1905. On arriving in England he played for Gentlemen of England, Gentlemen of the South, and WG Grace's XI. He made his debut for Surrey against WG Grace's XI on 2 May 1907 at the Kennington Oval. Marshal made 3 in his only innings, Surrey taking the match by 9 wickets. He went on to play for Surrey mostly in the County Championship making his final appearance for them on 23 May 1910 against Worcestershire at the War Memorial Ground, Amblecote. He made 0 and 13 and took 3 wickets for 19 off 4 overs. Worcestershire won by 316 runs. At the Oval in 1908 he took five wickets for 19 against Nottinghamshire during the August Bank Holiday match, and in the match against Derbyshire dismissed five men with thirteen balls without a run being scored. As a result in 1909 he was made Wisden Cricketer of the year. However it wasn't all good news. He was suspended by Surrey for a short while following an 'incident' at Chesterfield when Surrey was playing Derbyshire. Marshal together with some friends were kicking a ball about on their way back to their hotel when a police officer stopped them and demanded their names. Marshal told the officer where he could stick their names and was taken to the police station. The case was put before the Chief Constable who dismissed it. However after only a handful of games at the beginning of the 1910 season, Marshal's contract was surprisingly terminated.

On returning to Australia he began to play for Queensland once again. He not only made 8 first class appearances for them but also turned out for Australia against South Africa on 2 December 1910. The match was drawn. Marshal made a total of 5,177 first class runs including 8 centuries and 31 half centuries, his highest score being 176. He also took 119 wickets for 2,718 runs, his best figures being 7 for 41. He took 114 catches.

At the outbreak of the war Marshal enlisted into the 15th battalion Australian Infantry and like so many other Australians was sent to Gallipoli. There he managed to catch enteric fever. Despite being evacuated to Malta it was too late, the fever had too firm a grip. He died at the Imtarfa military hospital on 23 July 1915. Marshall is buried in the Pieta Military Hospital Cemetery Grave reference B III.1.

Alan Marshal, the well known Australian actor (1909–1961) was his great-uncle.

Batting and fielding averages

	Mat	Inns	NO	Runs	HS	Ave	100	50	Ct	St
First-class	119	198	13	5177	176	27.98	8	31	114	0

Bowling averages

	Mat	Balls	Runs	Wkts	BBI	Ave	Econ	SR	5w	10
First-class	119	5355	2718	119	7/41	22.84	3.04	45.0	7	1

Lieut-Colonel Cecil Howard Palmer
Hampshire-Worcestershire
9ᵗʰ Batt'n Royal Warwickshire Regiment
Died 26ᵗʰ July 1915
Aged 42
Right-Handed Bat

Died as he had lived, with his men

Cecil Howard Palmer was born on 14ᵗʰ July 1873 at Eastborne, Sussex. He was the son of the Reverend James Howard Palmer and Marian Palmer (nee Edwards) of East Worldham Rectory, Alton, Hants. He was educated at "Ashampstead" Upperton Road, an establishment for Young Gentlemen and later at St. Peters College, Radley, Abingdon, Berkshire. He represented the XI and was fourth in the Radley College averages in 1890 and third in 1891.

He played in nine first class matches between July 1899 and July 1907 all but one in the County Championship. Eight of them for Hampshire and one for Worcestershire. He played against Sussex, Yorkshire, Derbyshire, Kent, Somerset, Worcestershire and Warwickshire (twice). He made his debut for Hampshire against Sussex on 10 July 1899 at the County Ground, Hove. Palmer scored 16 and 1, Sussex winning by 57 runs. He went on to play against Yorkshire, Derbyshire, Kent, Oxford University and Somerset. He made one first class appearance for Worcestershire against Oxford University, in a university match, on 7 July 1904 at the County Ground, New Road, Worcester. Palmer scored 41 and 75 not out, Oxford University going on to win by 3 wickets. Palmer made his final first class appearance against Warwickshire on 5 July 1907 at Edgbaston, Birmingham. He scored 27 and 1, Hampshire winning by 95 runs. Palmer made 380 first class runs during his career his highest score being 75 for Worcestershire against Oxford University on 7 July 1904 (his highest score for Hampshire being 64 against Yorkshire at Bradford) He also made two catches.

He was commissioned as a second lieutenant into the Worcestershire Regiment in 1894. He was promoted to the rank of lieutenant on 1 February 1897 and Captain on 20 June 1900. During the Boer War he served with the Mounted Infantry and was mentioned-in-dispatches in 1901 (*London Gazette*, 10 September 1901).

On 1 November 1901 he was appointed Aide-de-Camp to Colonel (temporary Major-General) R. H. Murray, C.B., C.M.G. at Aldershot Infantry Brigade. In 1903 Cecil Howard Palmer married Hilda Beatrice Hall at Alton, Hampshire. On 18 November 1906 he was seconded for service as Adjutant of the 1st Volunteers Battalion Worcestershire Regiment. In 1908 under Lord Haldane's new administration for the Army the 1st Volunteer Battalion became the 7th Battalion, Territorial Force, and so on the 1st April 1908 Captain Cecil Howard Palmer was appointed Adjutant of the 7th Battalion Worcestershire Regiment for the remaining period of that appointment.

At the outbreak of the Great War in August 1914, he was appointed to command the 9th Battalion Royal Warwickshire Regiment and granted the temporary rank of Lieut. Colonel (19 August 1914, *London Gazette*, 2 September 1914). He sailed from Avonmouth on 24 June 1915. He landed with his battalion at "V Beach" Cape Helles on 13 July 1915 and moved inland to their front line positions at Fusiliers Post, taking up their positions on 15th July. Colonel Palmer was killed by a sniper near Hill Q, on 26 July 1915.

His body was never recovered or identified and he is commemorated on the Helles Memorial, panel 35–37.

Batting and fielding averages

	Mat	Inns	NO	Runs	HS	Ave	100	Ct	St
First-class	9	18	2	380	75*	23.75	0	2	0

Bowling averages

	Mat	Balls	Runs	Wkts	BBI	BBM	Ave	Econ	SR	4w	5w	10
First-class	9	-	-	-	-	-	-	-	-	-	-	-

Captain William Mackworth Parker
Army, Marylebone Cricket Club
8th Bn The Prince Consort's Own (Rifle Brigade)
Died 30 July 1915
Aged 28
Right-handed Bat

'Fell surrounded by his friends'

William Mackworth Parker was born on 1 September 1886 at Belgaum, India, the eldest son of Lieutenant Colonel William Frederick Parker, late Rifle Brigade, of Delamore, Ivybridge, Devon and Helinor Parker, née Stephen. Educated at Aysgarth School and Winchester College (1900–1905), William was in the Winchester XI in 1903 and the following two seasons. Against Eton he was not seen at his best, making only 48 runs in five innings. In his last year at school he was a commoner prefect, captain of the commoner VI and second captain at Lord's. He also represented the school at football.

After leaving Winchester he served for two years in the Royal North Devon Yeomanry before going to the Royal Military College Sandhurst where he won the Sword of Honour and was in the Sandhurst XI. He also played cricket for the Army, Rifle Brigade and the Free Foresters and joined the MCC in 1912. At Frensham Hill in August 1909, he scored 106 and 103 for Bordon Camp against C. E. N. Charrington's XI.

Parker made two first class appearances. He made his first class debut for the MCC against Oxford University on 3 July 1913 at Lord's. Parker scored 11 and 8 and caught Ion Campbell off the bowling of Peter Clarke for 24 and Charles Peat off the bowling of William Reeves for 8. The MCC won by 104 runs. His second match took place for the Army against the Navy on 25 June 1914 once again at Lords. He made 5 and 10, taking 3 wickets for 64 off 21 overs in the first innings and 1 wicket for 17 off 9 overs in the second. The Royal Navy won by 170 runs.

He married in 1912 Lilian Ursula Vivian, daughter of Sir Arthur Vivian KCB. They had a son, Frederick Anthony Vivian Parker, who came to Winchester (1926–1931), played for Lords and also joined the Rifle Brigade.

Gazetted in the Rifle Brigade, a few weeks after the outbreak of war Parker was appointed Adjutant of the 8th (Service) Battalion. He was posted to France, leaving on 18 May 1915. At Dickebusch, near Ypres, the battalion took over a sector of the front line for the first time in their own right. Until then, they had been attached to the North Midlands Brigade for instruction in trench warfare but by 5 June the battalion was ready for independent operations. On 23 July 8th Rifle Brigade moved to the Sanctuary Wood area, near Hooge, where it had its first real taste of battle.

Parker died at Hooge on 30 July 1915 (although the CWGC gives the date as 20 July). The 8th Battalion was involved in a costly action with several other old Wykehamists being killed or wounded. At about midnight on the night of 29 July the battalion came out of the line on being relieved by 8th Battalion King's Royal Rifle Corps and set out for Ypres, with Parker going into dug-outs near a site known as the White House. At 3.15am the site of the old château stables exploded with liquid flame pouring from the German trenches, each cloud of flame covering an area of over 100 feet. The 8th Rifle Brigade retreated to nearby Zouave Wood, and were joined shortly after by 8th KRRC with orders to prepare a counter-attack to recover the lost trenches. The Germans did not follow up their initial success but spent the morning and early afternoon fortifying their positions. A British counter-attack was launched but retaliatory German machine-gun fire caused it to fail with 8th Rifle Brigade finding it impossible to leave Zouave Wood. Eventually orders were received to abandon the attack. The battalion lost ten officers, including Parker, and 190 men.

The war diary records:

> The losses had been very heavy ... The medical arrangements were entirely inadequate. Dr Hawkes having been killed, only one doctor was available to cope with over five hundred cases. Great difficulties were experienced in finding and collecting the wounded in the thick woods, and when found in bringing them to dressing station. It being impossible to bring ambulances within nine hundred yards of the first aid station, many men had to remain out, exposed for over twenty-four hours. This, coupled with the fact that the battalion had had no rations for thirty-six hours, and suffered from want of water, caused the loss of many fine riflemen who might have been saved.

They were unable to recover or identify Parker's body and he is commemorated on the Menin Gate Memorial, Panels 46 to 48 and 50.

Batting and fielding averages

	Mat	Inns	NO	Runs	HS	Ave	100	50	Ct	St
First-class	2	4	0	34	11	8.50	0	0	2	0

Bowling averages

	Mat	Balls	Runs	Wkts	BBI	Ave	Econ	SR	5w	10
First-class	2	180	81	4	3/64	20.25	2.70	45.0	0	0

Captain Geoffrey Charles Walter Dowling
Sussex
7th Bn King's Royal Rifle Corps
Died 30 July 1915
Aged 23
Right-handed Bat

'Died for England but was Australian through and through'

Geoffrey Charles Walter Dowling was born in Melbourne, Australia on 12 August 1891, the son of Joseph and Rose Dowling. His father was born in Tasmania and his mother, as Rose Tuenich, in Blandford Forum, Dorset. They married in Australia. His father died when Geoffrey was still young and his mother remarried Colonel Foster Cunliffe and went to live at the Nunnery, a country estate south-west of Rusper.

Dowling was in the Charterhouse XI in 1908, 1909 and 1910, averaging 25.90 in 1908 and 28.60 in 1910. While playing for his school his highest scores were 78 not out, playing in the lower order versus Westminster in 1908, 57 versus Haverford in 1910, and 31 versus Wellington in 1908. He went up to Trinity College Cambridge where he made 60 in the Freshmen's match in 1911. Dowling made 4 first class appearances between May 1911 and May 1913. He made his debut first class match for Sussex against Cambridge University on 22 May 1911 at FP Fenner's Ground. Dowling scored 48 and 11 and caught Mervyn Baggallay off the bowling of George Cox for 2 and Harold Prest off the bowling of George Leach for 37. Cambridge University won by 41 runs. Dowling went on to play against Nottingham and Kent. He made his final first class appearance, like his debut, against Cambridge University on 15 May 1913 once again at Fenner's. He scored 14 and 3 Sussex finally winning by 5 wickets. He made 123 first class runs his highest score being 48 against Cambridge University 22 May 1911. He also took 1 wicket for 19 runs and made 4 catches. He became a member of the MCC in 1913. In the same year when playing for the club at Rye he scored 138, he and Roy Dundonald Cochrane (184) adding 294 together for the second wicket.

Captain Dowling was killed at Hooge, Belgium on 30 July 1915 during a British counter-attack following the German army's first use of flame-throwers on the Western Front.

His body was never discovered and he is commemorated on the Ypres (Menin Gate) Memorial, Panels 51 and 53.

Batting and fielding averages

	Mat	Inns	NO	Runs	HS	Ave	100	50	Ct	St
First-class	4	8	0	123	48	15.37	0	0	4	0

Bowling averages

	Mat	Balls	Runs	Wkts	BBI	Ave	Econ	SR	5w	10
First-class	4	36	19	1	1/19	19.00	3.16	36.0	0	0

Colonel Leslie William Davidson CB
Marylebone Cricket Club (MCC)
Royal Horse Artillery
Died 3 August 1915
Aged 65
Right-handed Bat

'The oldest first-class cricketer to die in the war'

Leslie William Davidson was born on 31 January 1850 in Ichmarlo, Kincardineshire, Scotland, the second son Patrick Davidson LLD JP DL of Inchmarlo, Kincardineshire,by his wife, Mary Anne, eldest daughter of William Leslie, 10th Laird of Warthill, Aberdeenshire. Deciding to make a career in the Army he entered the Royal Military Academy Woolwich passing out top of his year and was commissioned into the Royal Artillery as a lieutenant on 7 July 1869. He was promoted to captain on 24 January 1880 and achieved his majority on 7 June,1885. On 25 June 1896, he was promoted to lieutenant colonel and then to colonel on 23 January 1900. For some time Davidson was ADC to the Commander-in-Chief in India and subsequently to the Governor of Gibraltar. He served throughout the Zulu Campaign where he was Mentioned in Despatches, and wounded at Ulundi. He had charge of the Zulu King Cetewayo for some time in Cape Town.

Davidson served in the Afghan War in 1880 and in the Second Boer War in 1899 and 1900. He commanded the Royal Horse Artillery on the forced march to the Relief of Kimberley and was present at Paardeburg, Poplar Grove, Driefontein and Karoo Siding, before commanding the Bloemfontein defences. During the campaign, he received two further Mentions in Despatches.

Davidson made one first-class appearance for the MCC against Cambridge University on 17 May 1877 at F. P. Fenner's Ground, Cambridge, in a university match. Playing with the famous W. G. Grace, he scored zero in his only innings in a match that was eventually drawn.

Wisden said of Davidson that he was:

a fine, free hitter, and represented the Royal Artillery at cricket, football, rackets, and billiards. He had been a member of the MCC since 1873. He was dismissed for a duck when he played alongside W. G. Grace in 1877 in his one match for the MCC, against Cambridge University. In 1909 he was in the Woolwich XI, scoring 8 and 50 against Sandhurst.

He retired in 1907 and in 1913 was appointed Gentleman Usher to the King. On the outbreak of war in August 1914, although 63-years-old, he immediately volunteered for active service and was sent to command No. 4 General Base Depot at Rouen. There he fell a victim to over-exertion, dying from a heart attack on 3 August 1915, aged 65. A brother officer later wrote:

He died when in the fulfilment of a duty to his country, towards which he devoted a lifetime full of energy and heartiness. I felt sure that with his keen and vigorous sense of duty he would spare no pains to try and take his share of work in the Nation's task.

Another said, 'A soldier to the backbone, he leaves a very fine record.'

He was the oldest first-class cricketer to die in the war. Davidson was buried with full military honours in St Sever Cemetery, Rouen, Seine-Maritime, France. (Officers' section, Plot A. Row 1. Grave 3.)

His eldest son, Captain Donald Alastair Leslie Davidson MC, was killed in France on 30 April 1917, aged 25. His second son, Lieutenant Colonel Keppel Davidson CIE OBE, who had also served during the First World War and was a Clerk of the House of Lords, was killed in Tunisia on 2 March 1943, aged 47.

Batting and fielding averages

	Mat	Inns	NO	Runs	HS	Ave	100	50	4s	6s	Ct	St
First-class	1	1	0	0	0	0.00	0	0	0	0	0	0

Bowling averages

	Mat	Balls	Runs	Wkts	BBI	BBM	Ave	Econ	SR	4w	5w	10
First-class	1	-	-	-	-	-	-	-	-	-	-	-

Second Lieutenant Rowland Raw
Gentlemen of England
9th Bn Lancashire Fusiliers
Died 7 August 1915
Aged 31
Right-handed Bat

'Such great potential gone too soon'

Rowland Raw was born on 16 July 1884 at Pietermaritzburg, Natal, South Africa. The son of George H. and Edith S. Raw, he was educated at Clifton College where he was in the School XI in 1901 and 1902, averaging 22.00 in the former year and 20.71 in the latter. After Clifton in 1903 he went up to Trinity College Cambridge where, for some unknown reason, he failed to get his Blue.

After leaving Cambridge he married May Raw of Churchfield, Witley, Surrey, and they set up home at Umberleigh House. He made two first-class appearances during the 1905 season, both for The Gentlemen of England. He made his debut against Cambridge University at Crystal Palace on 19 June 1905. He scored 47 and 1, the Gentlemen of England losing by nine wickets. His second match took place on 29 June 1905 against Oxford University at the same venue; the match was drawn and Raw failed to bat.

During the war he was commissioned into the Lancashire Fusiliers becoming part of X Company in the 9th Battalion. On 7 July 1915 he sailed from Liverpool, landing at Alexandria, before moving onto Mudros and preparing for the landings on the Gallipoli mainland at Suvla Bay.

He was killed in action on 7 August 1915 during the landings at Suvla. It was during this action that Raw's Company Sergeant Major Thomas Bleackley, who had been Mentioned in Despatches earlier in the war, won the Distinguished Conduct Medal for leading his men ashore under heavy fire after his two officers (one being Raw) had been killed. Bleackley organised the platoon, leading them into the attack.

Rowland Raw is buried in Hill 10 Cemetery, Grave I. C. 19.

Batting and fielding averages

	Mat	Inns	NO	Runs	HS	Ave	100	50	Ct	St
First-class	2	2	0	48	47	24.00	0	0	0	0

Bowling averages

	Mat	Balls	Runs	Wkts	BBI	BBM	Ave	Econ	SR	4w	5w	10
First-class	2	-	-	-	-	-	-	-	-	-	-	-

Second Lieutenant Tomas (Hami) Marshall Percy Grace
Wellington
9th (Hawke's Bay) Company, Wellington Battalion
New Zealand Expeditionary Force
Died 8 August 1915
Aged 25
Unknown

'The first Maori to be commissioned'

Tomas Marshall Percy Grace was born on 11 July 1890 in Pukawa, Lake Taupo, New Zealand, the second son of Lawrence Marshall Grace of Government Buildings, Russell Terrace, Wellington, New Zealand, a well-known Maori interpreter, and an authority on most subjects appertaining to the Maori people. His maternal grandfather was the Ngati Tuwharetoa Paramount Chief Te Heuheu and his paternal grandfather was the Reverend Thomas Grace of the Church Missionary Society. Tomas was educated at Blenheim Borough School, Marlborough High School and Wellington College (1904–05). At school he played in both the first XV and first XI, which he captained. His figures of five for 66 and five for 29 against Wanganui Collegiate remain among the best ever bowling figures in this traditional fixture. He was also a first-class shot.

On leaving school he took up employment as a member of staff of the accountants' branch of the Post Office in Wellington, where he was held in the greatest esteem. He subsequently became a skilful and prominent member of the Old Boys' Cricket and Football Clubs, until he joined the Wellington Club, in which he distinguished himself as a sound three-quarter back. A B-representative footballer in 1910, the following year he was a member of the A team. In 1912 he visited Australia as a member of Parata's Native rugby team.

Grace made two first-class appearances for Wellington between 1911 and 1914. He made his debut on 23 December 1911 against Hawke's Bay at the Basin Reserve, Wellington. He scored 4 in his one innings and took one wicket for 34 off 7 overs. The match was drawn. His second first-class appearance took place on 9 January 1914 against Otago at Carisbrook, Dunedin. This time he was more successful, making 16 not out and 28, as well as taking four wickets for 6 runs off 7.1 overs. Wellington won by 85 runs.

Upon the outbreak of war in 1914, Grace joined the Wellington Regiment as a private, later being promoted to sergeant at Trentham camp before being commissioned as a second lieutenant on 29 May 1915. There was some disquiet about the use of Maori troops against European forces and most Maori soldiers were forced to provide support duties only. However, at least one New Zealand minister, James Allen, was unhappy about this and wrote to Major General Sir Alexander Godley, commander of the New Zealand Expeditionary Force, 'Although they are a coloured race I think it would be apparent on their arrival that they are different to the ordinary coloured race.'

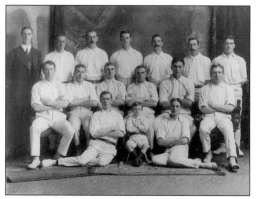

As a Maori who had been commissioned as a second lieutenant into a regular army regiment, Grace became a cause célèbre for his entire race. He trained in Egypt in preparation for the Gallipoli landings, which took place on 25 April 1915.

At Quinn's Post, Grace, a first-class shot, established a sniper team to rout out Turkish snipers who were causing large numbers of casualties among the New Zealand and Australian forces occupying and travelling along Monash Gully. Thirty to forty Australians a day were being sniped. Placing his men in pairs in concealed positions along the valley, Grace began systematically to mark down the positions and shoot the Turkish snipers. Within a few weeks the enemy's sniping had been stopped. An extract from a letter written by Captain J. A. Wallingford to Major M. Atkinson of Auckland, dated London 17 October 1915, describes the situation.

> When the New Zealanders occupied this was soon put a stop to. Snipers were organized, with Lieutenant Grace, a Trenthan, in command. They had their regular 'pot-holes', two in each, with a telescope. That did the trick …

Grace's ability as a bowler also came in useful when it came to bombing the enemy. He would take sacks full of grenades and, sneaking over to the Turkish trenches, throw them into their trenches with a good action. For one of these actions performed on 8 July 1915 Grace was Mentioned in Despatches. It is interesting to note that a white New Zealand officer who committed a similar act of bravery was awarded the Victoria Cross. The question has to be asked as to whether the fact that Grace was a Maori had any bearing on the award he was given.

Grace finally lost his life during his regiment's attack on Chunuk Bair in August 1915. He survived the initial attack only to fall to either a sniper or stray bullet later.

His body was never recovered and he is commemorated on the Chunk Bair (New Zealand) Memorial, Panel 17.

Batting and fielding averages

	Mat	Inns	NO	Runs	HS	Ave	100	50	Ct	St
First-class	2	3	1	48	28	24.00	0	0	0	0

Bowling averages

	Mat	Runs	Wkts	BBI	Ave	5w	10
First-class	2	58	5	4/6	11.60	0	0

Captain Norman Kingsley Street
Warwickshire
9th Bn The Worcestershire Regiment
attd 39 Infantry Brigade, General Headquarters Staff.
Died 10 August 1915
Aged 33
Right-handed Bat

'No braver soul wore the King's colours'

Norman Kingsley Street was born in Edgbaston, Birmingham, Warwickshire, on 13 August 1881, the only son of Thomas Richard and Marian Street, née Kloss, of Leacroft, Kidderminster, formerly of Edgbaston. Educated at Bromsgrove School, he was a member of the School XV in 1899 to 1900 and the School XI in 1898, 1899 and 1900. Deciding on a career in the Army he entered the Royal Military College Sandhurst, being commissioned in the Worcestershire Regiment on 8 May 1901. He was promoted to lieutenant on 20 March 1903 and captain on 18 June 1911.

During his career he travelled extensively, serving in Bermuda, Barbados, Jamaica, Malta, Egypt and Bareilly in India, as well as serving with the West African Frontier Force from 18 May 1910 until his recall to England in August 1914.

Street made five first-class appearances for Warwickshire during the 1908 County Championship. He made his debut against Leicestershire on 9 May 1908 at Aylestone Road, Leicester. He scored 4 and 5 and caught William Ward Odell off the bowling of Sam Hargreave for 3. Leicestershire winning by 173 runs; the damage was done by the Leicestershire bowlers William Astill, who took eight for 51 off twenty-seven overs, and William Ward Odell (killed in action 4 October 1917), who took four wickets for 52 off twenty-eight overs. He then played against Sussex (drawn), Surrey (drawn), Somerset (lost). He made his final first class appearance against Northamptonshire on 11 June 1908 at the County Ground, Northampton. He scored 0 in both innings, but he did catch William Wells off the bowling of Sam Hargreave for 19. Street was another of the unfortunate first-class cricketers who was never to be on the winning side having lost three and drawn two. He scored 43 first-class runs, his highest score being 14 against Surrey on 21 May 1908. He made three ctaches.

At the outbreak of the war he found himself attached to 9th battalion Worcestershire Regiment. In January 1915 he was appointed to headquarters staff of 39 Infantry Brigade and served with the Mediterranean Expeditionary Force in the Dardanelles from June 1915. Captain Street was killed in action on 10 August 1915. The action in which he was killed is best described in 'The Worcestershire Regiment in the Great War' by H. Fitz M. Stacke:

> At dawn on August 10th the enemy on the crest line above the position of the 9th Worcestershire opened fire and commenced a bombing attack. Great bombs were rolled down the mountainside to burst in our lines. Then the enemy came over the crest of the ridge in wave after wave of densely packed troops, their bayonets glittering

in the sun as they topped the ridge. Firing as rapidly as possible the 9th Worcestershire held their ground, meeting and repulsing rush after rush. For some three hours a desperate struggle raged. At last, when nearly all of the officers and most of the men were down, the remnant of 39 Brigade fell back from the exposed front line on the slope to the more sheltered position in the dead ground at the head of the ravine. There the 9th Worcestershire were re-organized by Captain Munnick.

On the left flank the garrison of Gurkha Redoubt, commanded by Captain W. D. Gibbon, beat off all attacks, and maintained their position until darkness fell.

Meanwhile every available man had been ordered up from reserve. C Company of the 9th Worcestershire were the only reserve unit of 39 Brigade, and its platoons had been dispersed as picquets over wells and dumps in the gully. When orders came down, these platoons made their way up the ravine, as also did every available man of Battalion Headquarters, led by the Quartermaster, Lieut C. H. Inwood. Lieut. Inwood led his collection of cooks and orderlies most bravely through a fierce and accurate fire along the gully and up the ravine to the firing line, bringing bandoliers of ammunition and tins full of water which enabled the defence to be continued.

In the re-organization of the defence, Captain N. K. Street of the Regiment, Staff Captain of 39 Brigade, was conspicuous by his bravery. He rallied stragglers of all regiments and led them up the hill to a level stretch known as 'The Farm', where the fighting was desperate. There he continued to direct and inspire their resistance until he was killed.

For his gallant actions on this day Captain Street was Mentioned in Despatches (*London Gazette*, 28 January 1916) by General Sir Ian Hamilton.

His body was never recovered or identified and he is commemorated on the Helles Memorial, Gallipoli, Turkey, Panels 104–113.

Batting and fielding averages

	Mat	Inns	NO	Runs	HS	Ave	100	50	Ct	St
First-class	5	9	0	43	14	4.77	0	0	3	0

Bowling averages

	Mat	Balls	Runs	Wkts	BBI	BBM	Ave	Econ	SR	4w	5w	10
First-class	5	-	-	-	-	-	-	-	-	-	-	-

Second Lieutenant Ronald Turner
Gloucestershire
1/5th Bn The Essex Regiment
15 August 1915
Aged 30
Unknown

'The finest footballer ever to play first-class cricket'

Ronald Turner was born on 19 June 1885 at Gillingham, Kent, the son of the Reverend Robert Stobbs Turner and Catherine Mary Turner of Tewkesbury, Gloucestershire. He was educated at Hurtspierpoint College, West Sussex where he played for and was captain of the XI. From there he went up to Queen's College Cambridge where he won a football Blue as well as playing for the English amateur national team. Although he didn't win his Blue for cricket while at Cambridge, he did play 3 first-class matches for Gloucestershire during the 1906 season. He made debut for Gloucestershire was on 11 June 1906 against Cambridge University at F.P. Fenner's Ground, Cambridge.

He scored 19 and 5, Cambridge taking the match by 54 runs. His second appearance was against Somerset at the Recreation Ground, Bath. He scored 3 and 1, the match was drawn. His final first-class appearance came against Surrey on 18 June 1906 at the Ashley Down Ground, Bristol; he scored 2 and 0, Gloucestershire going down by an innings and 22 runs.

At the outbreak of the First World War, Turner enlisted into the ranks of the 28th London Regiment (Artists Rifles) before being commissioned into the 1/5th Battalion The Essex Regiment (Territorial Force) as a second lieutenant. The 1/5th left Plymouth aboard the *Grampian* with a battalion strength of twenty-nine officers and 649 other ranks, commanded by Lieutenant Colonel J. M. Welch. The ship called at Malta on 30 July before sailing on to Alexandria, arriving on 2 August, and then Lemnos on the 6th, before moving onto Mudros Harbour. The battalion transferred to the *Hazel* on the 9th and sailed for Imbros, arriving at 5.00am the following day. In his history of the battalion, Major T. Gibbons recalls arriving at Imbros and hearing heavy firing from the peninsula; 'puffs of smoke could also be seen from shells bursting inland.' After sailing at 12.30pm, they landed at A Beach, Suvla, without casualties and concentrated a short distance inland. The battalion war diary then reads:

Moved forward to reserve positions 10 pm, ordered forward to second line trenches during night (12th), advanced in single file, halting at daybreak and forming two lines. Advanced to relieve 163 Brigade firing line 4 pm (14th), Major Gibbons records distance covered as being just over a mile, he also notes heavy shrapnel fire and snipers operating to the left

15 August 1915.
Relieved 1/5th Norfolks (Vanished Battalion) and 1/8th Hampshire in C Sector, line held being a fenced ditch facing Kuchuk Anafarta Ova. Casualties during the advance – 14 other ranks killed and 60 wounded, 2Lt Turner killed while out with patrol after dark.

Ronald Turner's body was never recovered or identified and he is commemorated on The Helles Memorial, Panels 144 to 150 or 229 to 233.

Batting and fielding averages

	Mat	Inns	NO	Runs	HS	Ave	100	50	Ct	St
First-class	3	6	0	30	19	5.00	0	0	0	0

Bowling averages

	Mat	Balls	Runs	Wkts	BBI	BBM	Ave	Econ	SR	4w	5w	10
First-class	3	-	-	-	-	-	-	-	-	-	-	-

2446 Lance Corporal Theodore Humphrey Fowler
Gloucestershire
Honourable Artillery Company (HAC)
Died 17 August 1915
Aged 35
Right-handed Bat/Wicketkeeper

'Always in the thick of the fighting'

Theodore Humphrey Fowler was born on 25 September 1879 at Cirencester, Gloucestershire, the youngest son of Dr Oliver Humphrey Fowler MRCS and Caroline Fowler of Ashcroft House, Cirencester. He was educated at Grange House School at Worth in Sussex before going up to Lancing College, West Sussex, where he was in School House from January 1894 to July 1897. A member of the Officer Training Corps (OTC), he played in the Football XI from 1895 to 1897 and was a member of the Cricket XI from 1894 to 1897. Appointed as a House Captain in 1896, for two years he won all the long-distance races at the college. On leaving school, he studied at St Bartholomew's Hospital from 1900 to 1902 and later worked as a brewer in Weymouth.

A fine cricketer he played 46 first-class matches for Gloucestershire between May 1901 and June 1914, mostly in the County Championship, but he also played in one University match against Cambridge, two matches against London County, one against South Africa in the British Isles and a single match against the Gentlemen of Philadelphia. He made his debut for Gloucestershire against Sussex on 27 May 1901 at the County Ground, Hove in the County Championship. He scored 14 and 48 Gloucestershire winning by 228 runs. He made his final first class match against Northamptonshire on 8 June 1914 against in the County Championship at the Ashley Down Ground, Bristol. He made 3 and 0 and caught Claud Woolley off the bowling of Edward Dennett for 44 and Walter Buswell off the bowling of Charles Parker for 9. Northamptonshire won by 143 runs. During his first class career Fowler made a total of 1,057 runs, including one century and five 50s. His highest score being 114 against the County of London on 4 June 1903 when he and Harry Wrathall who made 160, put on 277 for the first wicket at the Crystal Palace. A decent wicketkeeper he took 35 catches and made 1 stumping. He also played several minor county matches for Dorset.

At the outbreak of the First World War, Fowler enlisted into the University and Public Schools Corps at Epsom. From there he enlisted into the ranks of the Honourable Artillery Company (HAC). After training Fowler was posted to the 1st Battalion, joining C Company in France on 13 January 1915. Soon in the thick of the fighting, he was wounded on 12 March but not badly enough to be evacuated back to England. He was promoted to lance corporal on 16 March 1915. He was shot and wounded in the face at Dickebusch on 17 April and evacuated to 14 General Hospital at Boulogne before being transferred to 9 General Hospital, Rouen. On recovering from his wounds he returned to his unit on 26 April. Two months later he was evacuated again, this time suffering from shellshock after the HAC's attack on Hooge. He was also suffering from a hernia. Unable to receive the treatment he needed in France he was evacuated to England and was taken to the County of London

War Hospital at Epsom. He died of pyrexia at 7.45pm on 17 August following an operation for his hernia.

He was buried with full military honors at Cirencester Cemetery, grave reference Row R, Grave 75. Once again, if you're passing or live locally, pop over and pay your respects.

Batting and fielding averages

	Mat	Inns	NO	Runs	HS	Ave	100	50	Ct	St
First-class	46	78	4	1057	114	14.28	1	5	35	1

Bowling averages

	Mat	Balls	Runs	Wkts	BBI	BBM	Ave	Econ	SR	4w	5w	10
First-class	46	54	36	0	-	-	-	4.00	-	0	0	0

Lieutenant Colonel Maximillian David Francis Wood DSO
Europeans (India) Hampshire
9th Bn The Prince of Wales's Own (West Yorkshire
Regiment)
Died 21 August 1915
Aged 42
Right-handed Bat Right-arm Fast-Medium

'A pleasure to watch him bowl'

Maximillian David Francis Wood was born on 22 February 1873 at Kamptee (now Kamthi), Maharashtra, India, the son of Captain Charles Watkins Arthur Harcourt Wood of Pontefract Yorkshire, West Riding, and Maria Louisa Wood, née Grace. He was educated at Wellington College where he was in the XI and considered one of the best bats Wellington had ever produced. Deciding on a career in the Army he entered Sandhurst where he was in the XI and XV in 1892.

He was commissioned into the West Yorkshire Regiment in 1893, becoming a lieutenant in 1895, and a captain in 1900 when he was also appointed ADC to the Governor of Bombay. He served in the Second Boer War, being awarded the Queen's Medal with six clasps and the King's Medal with two clasps.

Wood made his ten first-class appearances between September 1897 and June 1909. Seven were for the Europeans (India) against Parsees, all Bombay Presidency matches, one for Hampshire against Yorkshire and two for H. D. G. Leveson-Gower's XI against Oxford (May 1909) and Cambridge (June 1909). Wood made his debut for the Europeans (India) against the Parsees on 16 September 1897 at the Deccan Gymkhana Ground, Poona. He made 23 and 0. The Parsees won by 308 runs. Returning to England he made his debut in the County Championship for Hampshire against Yorkshire on the 27 May 1907 at the Park Avenue Cricket Ground, Bradford. He scored 5 and 4 and caught Harold Kaye off the bowling of William Langford for 11. The match was drawn. He made his final first class appearance for HDG Leveson Gower's XI against Cambridge University on 10 June 1909 at Fenner's. Wood scored 2 and 10. The match was drawn. Wood made 196 runs, his highest score being 30 against Parsees on 13 September 1900 at the Deccan Gymkhana Ground. He also took 34 wickets for 483 runs, his best figures being 6 for 51 against the Parsees on 17 August 1900 at the Gymkhana ground, Bombay. He made 8 catches. Two years later, on 30 December 1911, Wood married Eugenie Sybil Ward, daughter of William Humble Dudley Ward and the Honourable Eugenie Violet Adele Brett.

On 3 July 1915 he sailed with his battalion from Liverpool to Mudros. The battalion first saw action during the landings at Suvla Bay, Gallipoli, on 6 August 1915. On 21 August he was reported missing at Ismail Oglu Tepe and it was later assumed that he had been killed on that date. He was awarded the Distinguished Service Order (DSO) for his services in Gallipoli (*London Gazette*, 2 February 1916).

His body was never recovered and he is commemorated on the Helles Memorial Gallipoli, Turkey, Panels 47–51.

Batting and fielding averages

	Mat	Inns	NO	Runs	HS	Ave	100	50	Ct	St
First-class	10	19	0	196	30	10.31	0	0	8	0

Bowling averages

	Mat	Runs	Wkts	BBI	Ave	5w	10
First-class	10	483	34	6/51	14.20	1	0

Captain Harold Wright
Leicestershire/Marylebone Cricket Club
6th Bn Loyal North Lancashire Regiment
Died 14 September 1915
Aged 31
Left-handed Bat/Slow left-arm orthodox

'Everybody loved him'

Harold Wright was born on 19 February 1884 at Woodthorpe, Barrow-on-Soar, Leicestershire, the son of William and Agnes Wright. He attended Mill Hill School, London from 1898, where he was a member of School House and played in the Mill Hill School XI in 1899, 1900 and 1901, being captain in 1901. With a batting average of 23.30, among his scores that season were 61 against Wellingborough Grammar School, 51 against Royal Naval School, and 47 against Bedford Modern. Wright was also a school monitor and a member of the Officers Training Corps at Royston.

He made eleven first-class appearances between May 1912 and June 1914, ten for Leicestershire in the County Championship and one for the MCC against Cambridge University. His made his first class debut against Nottinghamshire on 16 May 1912 at Trent Bridge, Nottingham. Wright scored 9 and 44, Nottinghamshire going on to win by an innings and 12 runs. He went on to play against Lancashire, Northamptonshire, Essex, Hampshire, Warwickshire and Worcestershire. Wright made his final first-class appearance for the MCC against Cambridge University on 4 June 1914 at F. P. Fenner's Ground. Wright made 14 and 11 and caught George Wood off the bowling of Peter Clarke for 75. Cambridge University won by 177 runs. Wright scored a total of 243 first-class runs, his highest being 44 against Nottinghamshire on 16 May 1912 at Trent Bridge. He made 10 catches. Wright became a member of the MCC in 1913.

Before the war he was involved in the running of Wright's Elastic Webbing factory, which is still based in Quorn today.

On 14 September 1914, shortly after the outbreak of the First World War, Wright was commissioned into the 6th Battalion Loyal North Lancashire Regiment. He served in Gallipoli with his battalion, being seriously wounded on 28 July 1915. Evacuated to England, he died of wounds on 14 September 1915 at Marylebone, London.

Captain Wright was buried with full military honours on 17 September 1915 in St Bartholomew, Church Yard, Quorn, Leicestershire. Once again well worth a visit and a few flowers.

Batting and fielding averages

	Mat	Inns	NO	Runs	HS	Ave	100	50	Ct	St
First-class	11	21	4	243	44	14.29	0	0	10	0

Bowling averages

	Mat	Balls	Runs	Wkts	BBI	BBM	Ave	Econ	SR	4w	5w	10
First-class	11	18	20	0	-	-	-	6.66	-	0	0	0

Captain Hugh Montagu Butterworth
Oxford University and MCC
9th Bn The Prince Consort's Own (Rifle Brigade)
Died 25 September 1915
Aged 29
Right-handed Bat

'I am posting this myself just before leaving. Perhaps I shan't be killed!!'

Hugh Montagu Butterworth was born on 1 November 1885, the only son of Mr and Mrs G. M. Butterworth of Christchurch, New Zealand, formerly of Swindon, England. He was educated at Hazelwood and Marlborough College. A natural sportsman while at school he was in the cricket XI, rugby XV, and hockey XI as well as being captain of the rifle club, and racquets. On leaving school in 1904 he went up to University College Oxford where he won the athletic championship cup. He was a very good, but unlucky, all-round athlete. At different times he represented his university at cricket, football and hockey, and won the Freshman's 100 yards, but an injured knee only permitted him to obtain his Blue at racquets.

He made three first class appearances in 1906, two for Oxford University and one for the MCC. He made his debut appearance for Oxford University against HDG Leveson-Gower's XI on 14 May 1906 at the University Parks, Oxford. He scored 2 and 30 and caught Kingsmill Key off the bowling of Alan Fyffe for 29. Oxford University won by four wickets. He next appeared for Oxford University against Lancashire on 17 May 1906 at the Christ Church Ground, Oxford. He scored 0 and 6 and managed to hang onto a catch from William Findlay of the bowling of Alan Fyffe for 7, Lancashire winning by 141 runs. His final first class match took place for the MCC against Oxford University on 21 May 1903 at the University Parks, Oxford. Butterworth scored 31 and 9, the MCC going on to win by 134 runs. He also played for Wiltshire in the Minor Counties Championship.

In 1907 he went to New Zealand and became assistant master at the Collegiate School, Wanganui. During the war he returned to England and was commissioned into the 9th Battalion of The Rifle Brigade, travelling out to France with his battalion. He was killed in action during the Battle of Loos on 25 September 1915. His letters from the front were later published by Wanganui School as *Letters from Flanders* by H. M. B. (now available as *Blood and Iron Letters from the Western Front* by Hugh Montagu Butterworth, edited by Jon Cooksey). In one of his earlier letters home he wrote:

I am leaving this in the hands of the transport officer, and if I get knocked out, he will send it on to you. We are going into a big thing. It will be my pleasant duty to leap lightly over the parapet and lead D Company over the delectable confusion of old trenches, crump holes, barbed wire, that lies between us and the Bosche, and take a portion of his front line. Quo facto, I shall then proceed to bomb down various communication trenches and take his second line. In the very unlikely event of my being alive by then I shall dig in like the blazes and, if God is good, stop the

Bosche counter-attack, which will come in an hour or two. If we stop that I shall then in broad daylight have to get out wire in front under machine-gun fire and probably stop at least one more counter-attack and a bomb attack from the flank. If all that happens successfully and I'm still alive, I shall hang on until relief. Well, when one is faced with a programme like that, one touches up one's will, thanks heaven one has led a fairly amusing life, thanks God one is not married, and trusts in Providence. Unless we get more officers before the show, I am practically bound to be outed as I shall have to lead all these things myself. Anyway if I do go out I shall do so amidst such a scene of blood and iron as even this war has rarely witnessed. We are going to bombard for a week, explode a mine and then charge. One does see life, doesn't one? Of course there is always a chance of only being wounded and the off-chance of pulling through. Of course one has been facing death pretty intimately for months now, but with this ahead, one must realise that, in the vernacular of New Zealand, one's numbers are probably up. We are not a sentimental crowd at the Collegiate School, Wanganui, but I think in a letter of this sort, one can say how frightfully attached one is to the old brigade. Also I am very, very much attached to the School, and to Selwyn in particular.

There are two thousand things I should like to say about what I feel, but they can't be put down, I find. Live long and prosper, all of you. Curiously enough, I don't doubt my power to stick it out, and I think my men will follow me.

His obituary describes his life in a rather more moving manner than ever I could.

Schoolmaster at Wanganui Collegiate

For rather more than seven years a master here, joined the staff in September, 1907, and immediately endeared himself to everybody with whom he became associated. In the face of what is now so well known of his life and work among us, it would be superfluous to add further expressions of the honour in which he was held. Leaving for England in January 1915, he was given a commission in the 9th Battalion Rifle Brigade, and left for 'Bulletville', as he humorously described it, towards the end of May. During the few weeks of training he received at Aldershot, and indeed up to the actual date of his death, he wrote almost without interruption, and described in detail his experiences of military life in an altogether delightful style. Cheerful under all conditions, and full of enthusiasm for everything he undertook, he faced the war in a true spirit of self-sacrifice, his personality winning for him an affection that can never be adequately described. He saw but four months of active service, and this in the neighbourhood of Ypres, being killed in action on September 25th, 1915. The news of his death caused universal sorrow, but his life of unselfish devotion to duty will serve as a pattern for many years to those who had the good fortune to know him. His father, in a letter, alluded to him in these few words, which seem peculiarly appropriate: 'If he died as we believe he did, charging at the trenches, do you pity him? I cannot. Fancy trying to keep up with him! At that supreme moment as he glanced at his men whom we know loved him and would follow him anywhere, he tasted life's elixir, and what mattered it whether it lasted only for seconds. It was the rapture of a lifetime!'

(In Memoriam, 1914–1918 [Wanganui Collegiate School])

In his last letter home he wrote, 'I am posting this myself just before leaving. Perhaps I shan't be killed!!'

His body was never discovered or identified and he is commemorated with thousands of others on the Ypres (Menin Gate) Memorial, Panels 46–48 and 50.

Batting and fielding averages

	Mat	Inns	NO	Runs	HS	Ave	100	50	Ct	St
First-class	3	6	0	78	31	13.00	0	0	2	0

Bowling averages

	Mat	Balls	Runs	Wkts	BBI	BBM	Ave	Econ	SR	4w	5w	10
First-class	3	-	-	-	-	-	-	-	-	-	-	-

Captain James Henry Aloysius Ryan MC
1st Bn The King's (Liverpool Regiment)
Northamptonshire/Ireland
Died 25 September 1915
Aged 23
Right-handed Bat/Right-arm Medium Pace

'I don't believe anyone else could have led his men across that terrible piece of ground,
but they would follow him anywhere'

James Henry Aloysius Ryan was born on 15 September 1892 at Roade, Northamptonshire, England. The son of Walter H. Ryan, of Roade, Northampton, he was educated at Downside School. A good athlete he was captain of the cricket XI, football and hockey and was also considered to be a fine classical actor. Ryan won entrance to Sandhurst, where he again excelled at football, hockey and cricket. He continued to play soccer and hockey for the Army and found time to win the Officers' Half Mile at The Army Athletic Meeting in 1913.

He made 8 first class appearances for Northamptonshire and 1 for Ireland between August 1911 and June 1914. He made his first class debut on 10th August 1911 in the County Championship against Sussex at the County Ground, Northampton. He made 4 and 17 and caught Robert Relf off the bowling of George Thomson for 75. Northampton won by 138 runs. He went on to play against Gloucestershire, Warwickshire, Kent and Derbyshire.

Ryan was selected to play for Ireland against the visiting South Africans on 25 July 1912, at the Woodbrook Cricket Club Ground, Bray. Ryan made 5 and 0, South Africa winning by an innings and 169 runs. He made his final first class appearance against Somerset on 24 June 1914 once again at the County Ground, Northampton. Ryan scored 41 in his only innings and took 1 wicket 27 off 8 overs. Northamptonshire won by an innings and 127 runs. Ryan made a total of 119 first class runs his highest score being 41 against Somerset 24 June 1914. He also took 4 wickets for 152 runs his best figures being 2 for 51. He made 2 catches.

At the outbreak of the war he travelled to France with the 1st Bn The King's (Liverpool Regiment). Showing great leadership and courage he was awarded the Military Cross (MC) for gallantry in January 1915 (*London Gazette*, 17 February 1915) the official citation reading 'For gallantry and great ability'.

He was also promoted captain and later Mentioned in Despatches (*London Gazette*, 17 February 1915). On 25 September 1915 Ryan was killed in action while attacking Hill 70 at Loos in France. A fellow officer later wrote to his parents, 'I don't believe anyone else could have led his men across that terrible piece of ground, but they would follow him anywhere.'

James Ryan was buried at Cambrin Military Cemetery, grave reference D. 16.

Batting and fielding averages

	Mat	Inns	NO	Runs	HS	Ave	100	50	Ct	St
First-class	9	15	1	119	41	8.50	0	0	2	0

Bowling averages

	Mat	Balls	Runs	Wkts	BBI	Ave	Econ	SR	5w	10
First-class	9	229	152	4	2/51	38.00	3.98	57.2	0	0

Second Lieutenant James Elliot Balfour-Melville
Scotland
3rd (attd 2nd) Bn Black Watch (Royal Highland Regiment)
Died 25 September 1915
Aged 33
Right-handed Bat/Wicket-keeper

'He was a fine and fearless leader'

James Elliot Balfour-Melville was born on 8 July 1882 in Edinburgh, Scotland, the son of Leslie Melville Balfour, one of the most famous golfers and perhaps the best all-round athlete that Scotland ever produced, of 3 Learmouth Terrace, Edinburgh, and Jeannie Amelia, daughter of Dr William Wilson, of Florence. Leslie Melville Balfour, whose family changed its name to Balfour-Melville in 1893, was a Writer to His Majesty's Signet (a society of Scottish solicitors). James was educated at Cargilfield Preparatory School, the Edinburgh Academy, Malvern College, Oriel College, Oxford missing out on his Blue and Edinburgh University. He was a useful bat and a first-class wicket-keeper and was in the Malvern College XI in 1901, averaging 23.91. In that same year he scored 51 against Uppingham School.

Melville made 2 first class appearances both for Scotland in 1913. He made his debut for Scotland against Oxford University on 13 June 1913 at the University Parks, Oxford. He made 0 and 13 and caught William Boswell off the bowling of Robert Sievwright for 10. Oxford University won by 34 runs. He made his second and final first class match against Surrey on 12 June 1913 at the Kennington Oval. Melville scored 32 and 1 Surrey winning by 7 wickets. He was a member of the MCC, I. Zingari, Oxford Authentics, and the Grange Cricket Clubs. While at Oxford he got his Blue for association football, playing on the right wing from 1901 to 1905 and captaining the side in 1905. A keen golfer, he was a member of the Royal and Ancient Club, St Andrews, and the Honourable Company of Edinburgh Golfers, Muirfield. On completing his studies he became a chartered accountant working in Edinburgh, employed by Messrs Lindsay, Jameson and Haldane before moving to Messrs Guild and Shepherd.

On the outbreak of the war Balfour-Melville applied for a commission, and was gazetted second lieutenant in the 3rd Battalion of the Black Watch on 3 November 1914. He completed his training at Nigg before being attached to the 2nd Battalion in France on 15 May 1915. Balfour-Melville was killed in action in the charge of the Scottish Division at Loos on 25 September 1915, after reaching the fifth line of German trenches. The commanding officer of his battalion later wrote of him:

He was not only popular though, he was a thoroughly capable officer. I feel his loss personally as a friend and also as commanding the battalion, for he was a fine and fearless leader. It is a consolation that he died painlessly in the hour of victory. I saw him lying in the enemy's fourth-line trench, which his company had been among the first to capture, your son leading. It was greatly due to the bold leading of your son and others like him that the Regiment earned the praise of all three Generals …

A fellow officer also wrote:

> He was sniped through the head and killed instantaneously at the furthest point
> reached by the Regiment in their charge. To have kept his men together and reached
> such a point is a feat of gallantry and dash beyond all praise. It was in front of the fifth
> line of German trenches that Elliot fell, explaining to his men the work to be done
> to put the captured trench into a defensive one, evidently exposing himself fearlessly.

He has no known grave and is commemorated on the Loos Memorial, Pas-de-Calais,
France, Panels 78 to 83.

Batting and fielding averages

	Mat	Inns	NO	Runs	HS	Ave	100	50	Ct	St
First-class	2	4	0	46	32	11.50	0	0	1	0

Bowling averages

	Mat	Balls	Runs	Wkts	BBI	BBM	Ave	Econ	SR	4w	5w	10
First-class	2	-	-	-	-	-	-	-	-	-	-	-

Captain Arthur Corbett Edwards
Europeans (India), Orange Free State
8th Bn Queen's Own (Royal West Kent Regiment)
Died 25/26 September 1915
Aged 44

'An inspiration to all that met him'

Arthur Corbett Edwards was born on 10 September 1871 in Portsmouth, Hampshire and was educated at Eton College and St Edmund's Hall, Oxford. At Eton he was in the First XI playing against Winchester in 1890 but failed to score. In 1895 he represented the Kent Second XI against the Middlesex Second XI, this time scoring 75 and 34 at Hythe. Playing for Folkestone Cricket Club in June 1911 against Hythe at Folkestone, he scored a big hitting 169.

In 1904, playing for Folkestone against Shorncliffe Garrison at Shorncliffe, he bowled unchanged through the home side's innings of 118, taking seven wickets for 45, before going on to score a very respectable 49. He became a member of the MCC in 1909. He made 2 first class appearances between September 1902 and January 1904. He made his debut first class appearance for the Europeans against the Parsees on 11 September 1902 at the Deccan Gymkhana Ground, Poona in a Bombay Presidency match. He scored 1 and 13 and caught JF Umrigar off the bowling of John Greig for 3. The Europeans won by 4 wickets. He made his second and final first class appearance for the Orange Free State against the Transvaal on 1st January 1904 at the Ramblers Cricket Club Ground, Bloemfontein in the Currie cup. Edwards scored 10 and 0 and took 2 wickets for 59 off 12 overs. Transvaal won by an innings and 327 runs.

Edwards served with the 8th Bn Royal West Kent Regiment during the First World War and travelled with them to France, landing on 1 September 1915. After spending two days in Boulogne they were marched to the training camp at Étaples. On 25 September they marched to Béthune to take part in the Battle of Loos. They were then ordered to move to Vermelles for a night attack which was in the end cancelled. Instead the battalion was ordered to attack the following morning. The attack began at 10:30am and the battalion was ordered to take an objective at Hulluch. To do this the attacking infantry had to cross a stretch of no man's land more than a mile wide. Despite being badly machine gunned, the West Kents reached their objective, only to discover that the wire in front of it was still intact. Despite this, the battalion continued to engage the Germans from in front of the German wire. The division to their right then withdrew, having suffered heavy casualties, leaving the right flank open with machine-gun fire coming through it. The Germans then started shelling. The battalion withstood this for four hours before being forced to withdraw, taking further casualties as they did. Their casualties were high and only one officer was left alive to bring them out; the casualty figures were twenty-four officers and 610 other ranks, the highest they had ever suffered. Edwards's body was never recovered and his name is commemorated on the Loos Memorial, Panels 95 to 97.

Batting and fielding averages

	Mat	Inns	NO	Runs	HS	Ave	100	50	Ct	St
First-class	2	4	0	24	13	6.00	0	0	1	0

Bowling averages

	Mat	Balls	Runs	Wkts	BBI	Ave	Econ	SR	5w	10
First-class	2	78	62	2	2/59	31.00	4.76	39.0	0	0

Lieutenant Charles Howard Eyre
Cambridge University/MCC
6th (wattd 2nd) Bn King's Royal Rifle Corps
Died 25 September 1915
Aged 32
Right-hand Bat

'A Rising Star of England'

Charles Howard Eyre was born on 26 March 1883 at Toxteth, Liverpool, Lancashire, the youngest son of the Archdeacon of Sheffield and of Mrs Eyre. Educated at Harrow School, where he was an Entrance Scholar, he was Head of School in 1901 and in the cricket XI between 1900 and 1902, being captain in 1902. His most successful season was 1901, when he scored 302 runs with an average of 30.20, his highest scores being 105 against I. Zingari and 100 against the Old Harrovians. Eyre was also in the football XI in 1901, was the winner of the Ebrington Racket Cup 1901, and a Fives player in 1902. On leaving Harrow he went up to Pembroke College, Cambridge, becoming a Bell University Scholar in 1903. He took his BA in 1905 and his MA in 1910. While at Pembroke he got his Blue for cricket. Between June 1903 and July 1906 Eyre made 30 first class appearances mostly for Cambridge University. He made his debut for Cambridge against Worcestershire on 4 June 1903 at Fenner's. He scored 7 in his one innings the match was drawn. He travelled with the MCC during their tour of North America in 1905 but only played in one game against the Gentlemen of Philadelphia on 22 July 1905 at Germantown Cricket Club Ground, Manheim, Philadelphia. Eyre scored 0 in his only innings. The MCC won by 7 wickets. His great feat was to make 153 in three-and-a-half hours for the University against Yorkshire at Cambridge on 14 May 1906. Eyre made his final first class appearance on 5 July 1906 against Oxford University at Lords. Eyre made 20 and 17 and caught Cecil Payne off the bowling of Guy Napier (killed in action 25 September 1915). For 3 and George Branston off the bowling of Percy May for 34. Cambridge University won by 94 runs. He became Captain of Cambridge University in 1906. During his first class career Eyre made 1092 runs his best score being 153 against Yorkshire on 14 May 1906. He also took 2 wickets for 50 runs and made 40 catches. He became a member of the MCC in 1904.

On leaving Cambridge he returned to Harrow as an assistant master and also became the honorary secretary of the Harrow Association.

Eyre was commissioned as a second lieutenant in the King's Royal Rifle Corps shortly after the outbreak of the war, joining up with his Harrow friend and fellow master Ronald Lagden. For some time they were at Sheerness together, where they were joined by another old school friend and assistant master, Charles Werner (all three were to lose their lives in the war). He was promoted to lieutenant and went out to France with his battalion in December 1914. He soon found himself in the thick of it and closer to the enemy than he would have expected, 'one point of the trenches held by us at this time being only ten yards from the Germans'.

Despite his proximity to the Germans, his sector was quiet and he saw little action. He wrote home again in March 1915:

I see you still have strikes. That on top of Russian reverses is rather depressing to read. But as long as no one in England talks about peace till we have won 'really won' all is well. The next generations must be spared the horrors of modern war. ... Make the boys realize what a big thing we are in for.

In the last letter to Harrow sent on 19 September 1915, he wrote:

I shall be thinking of you all rallying on the Old Hill this week. I have tried to do my best for it according to my lights ... I shall be proud and happy to be among the Old Harrovians who fell in the Great War.

Six days later, on 25 September 1915, while leading his company of the 2nd King's Royal Rifle Corps, he was the first to reach the enemy's barbed wire and was there shot through the head.

Lieutenant Colonel Priaulx wrote:

It was with great pleasure that I gave him the command of D Company a few days before the attack. We had a very difficult job, as the wire in our sections was not cut by our shells. The last time I saw Charles he was leading his Company to the attack. He died, like a true Rifleman, at the head of his men. We were both of us Harrovians.

Charles is buried in Dud Corner Cemetery, Loos, Pas-de-Calais, France, Plot V, Row E, Grave 8.

In the Harrow Chapel the eight Masters' stalls in oak which stand against the west wall at the back of the Nave commemorate Charles Howard Eyre (OH), Charles Augustus Werner, and Ronald Owen Lagden, the three friends and Masters who died in the Great War.

Batting and fielding averages

	Mat	Inns	NO	Runs	HS	Ave	100	Ct	St
First-class	30	53	2	1092	153	21.41	1	40	0

Bowling averages

	Mat	Balls	Runs	Wkts	BBI	Ave	Econ	SR	5w	10
First-class	30	66	50	2	1/9	25.00	4.54	33.0	0	0

Captain Joseph Edward Lynch
Gentlemen of Ireland
10th Bn The Princess of Wales's Own (Yorkshire) Regiment
25 September 1915
Aged 35
Right-handed Bat/Right-arm Medium Fast Bowler

'Ahead of his battalion as ever, he fell'

Joseph Edward Lynch was born on 26 April 1880 in Monkstown, County Dublin, the second son of Michael Palles Lynch (barrister at law), and Annie Josephine, his wife, of 4 Clifton Terrace, Monkstown.

He was educated in Clongowes Wood College from 1892 to 1897 and, later, Trinity College Dublin. Joseph Lynch did not find a regular place in the University XI until his last summer term in 1905, at the beginning of which he also became a commissioned officer in the Army; however, he still managed to play a full season. He also played for the University Past and Present XI against the visiting Australians

On 19 June 1905 at College Park, Dublin, Lynch only scored 0 and 8 but his bowling figures were better, taking four wickets for 113 runs. In 1905 Lynch had been gazetted as a second lieutenant in the 2nd Bn Royal Irish Fusiliers who were at that time stationed in India. Unfortunately, however, while serving with his regiment he suffered from enteric fever and malaria. This became so severe that he was eventually invalided home and shortly afterwards resigned his commission.

He was not involved again in Irish cricket until 1909 when he was selected for Frank Browning's side that toured the USA and Canada. Lynch's American tour was not a success. In his first match against 'All New York' on Staten Island Lynch failed to score while Ireland went on to win by an innings. It was during this tour, however, that Lynch was to play his only first-class match, on 17 September 1909, when he turned out for the Gentlemen of Ireland against the Gentlemen of Philadelphia at Merion Cricket Club Ground, Haverford. Lynch scored 1 and 11. The Gentlemen of Philadelphia won by an innings and 168 runs.

On the outbreak of the First World War Lynch joined up once again, this time being gazetted as a second lieutenant in the 10th Bn The Princess of Wales's (Yorkshire) Regiment, better known as the Green Howards, in September 1914. He was later promoted to lieutenant and then to captain on 3 April 1915. On 9 September the battalion left Witley Camp, where they had been training, for France, arriving in Boulogne on the 10th. Captain Lynch was in command of D Company. A little over two weeks later Lynch was dead. Details of Lynch's demise during the battalion's first action of the war are outlined in the Regimental History:

> Very little time was spent in the rest camp at Boulogne, for in the early hours of the 11th the Battalion marched to the railway station and took the train for Watten, where it arrived at about 7.40 A.M., and then marched to Noeux-les-Mines, halting and bivouacking en route at Houlle, Wittes, Ames and Burbure. Noeux-les-Mines was reached at 1 A.M. on the 25th, and all lay down in a very wet bivouac for such of the night remained, marching on the same day to Vermelles and crossing the Béthune-Lens Road where, for the first time the 10th Yorkshire Regiment came under shell fire and adopted an open formation.

On the afternoon of Saturday the 25th, the division passed through the village of Loos, with 62 Brigade leading, and the battalion arrived at the front trenches, then held by the 18th London Regiment, about dusk.

We inquired of the Londoners what they were doing, and they said they had decided to dig in for the night, so we did likewise except two platoons of D Company who pushed on a little further and it was then that Captain Lynch, previously shot through the wrist but carrying on, was killed. These then fell back into the line with the rest.

After his son's death Lynch's father received a letter from a fellow officer regarding his death.

October 1915,
Dear Mr Lynch,
Many thanks for yours of the 3rd inst. I can give you a few more details but only a few. I can assure you that it is no trouble to me at all, I am only glad to be able to tell you something, knowing what sorrow you will be in. Your son was first wounded in the wrist, just before entering the village of Loos and went on with us to the assault of Hill 70. It was growing dusk at this time. We charged past the troops who had attacked on the morning of Saturday, and it was during this charge that your son was fatally wounded on the German side of our trenches. We however got him in during the night, and laid him near the side of the Slag Heap at Loos Pylons. We ourselves were unable to bury any of our comrades much to our sorrow, not even our C.O. and our 2nd in command who both fell. He was in the best of spirits all the day before the action as in fact he always was. We had a good long march before going into action, but all the battalion did well, though hungry and wet through the rain. I am afraid I can give you no hope of being able to identify the grave. I should not like to tell you that our comrades are not buried yet but owing to the continuous bombardment of Hill 70 where we laid our comrade the burial parties have been unable to work, but I personally could almost exactly show you were he fell and where he was placed but that does not help you much. I only had the chance to say good bye to him about four miles before we went into action. I had very little chance of having a word with him after that. You will be receiving his kit etc. back through the [War Office]. It has already been sent on to the base and will be sent on from there to you. If as I say, fate or fortune sends me ever your way, I shall not forget to see you, or if you come to England and have time to come to Scarborough. I shall be glad to see you. I miss your son.
Yours very faithfully,
V. Fowler
Captain York Regiment

(Captain Valentine Fowler was later killed in action in 1917.)

Joseph Lynch's body was never recovered and he is commemorated on the Loos Memorial, Panels 44 and 45.

Batting and fielding averages

	Mat	Inns	NO	Runs	HS	Ave	100	50	Ct	St
First-class	1	2	0	12	11	6.00	0	0	0	0

Bowling averages

	Mat	Runs	Wkts	BBI	BBM	Ave	SR	4w	5w	10
First-class	1	29	0	-	-	-	-	0	0	0

Lieutenant Guy Greville Napier
Cambridge University, Europeans (India), Marylebone
Cricket Club, Middlesex
35th Sikhs (attd 47th Sikhs)
Died 25 September 1915
Aged 31
Right-handed Bat/Right-arm Medium

'One of the best medium pace bowlers seen in the University
match in his own generation'

Guy Greville Napier was born on 26 January 1884, the son of Thomas Bateman Napier and Florence Emily Napier of 7 New Square, Lincoln's Inn, London. He was educated at Marlborough College and Pembroke College, Cambridge. While at Marlborough was in the XI for three years between 1899 and 1901, taking nine wickets in his last match for the college against Rugby. Considered to be one of the finest medium-pace bowlers ever to represent Cambridge University, he obtained his Blue for cricket.

Between May 1904 and September 1913 Napier made 81 first class appearances mostly for Cambridge University, Europeans (India), the MCC, and Middlesex. He made his debut for Cambridge against Yorkshire on 12 May 1904 at Fenner's. Napier scored 0 and 3 and took 4 wickets for 97 off 33.4 overs. He also caught John Brown off the bowling of Percy May for 52. Yorkshire won by 118 runs. He made his debut for Middlesex in the County Championship against Lancashire on 18 July 1904 at Old Trafford, Manchester. Napier scored 17 and 11 and took 2 wickets for 78 off 23 overs in the first innings and I wicket for 51 off 7 overs in the second. Lancashire won by 8 wickets. He went on the MCC tour of North America in 1905 representing the MCC twice against the Gentlemen of Philadelphia on 22 July 1905 at Germantown Cricket Club Ground, Manheim Philadelphia. Napier scored 4 in his only innings, took 3 wickets for 31 off 18.1 overs and caught Charles Morris off the bowling of Kenneth Hunter for 21. MCC won by 7 wickets. His second match against the Gentlemen of Philadelphia came on 28 July 1905 at the Merion Cricket Club Ground, Haverford. Napier made two ducks and took 2 wickets for 77 off 25 overs in the first innings and 2 for 77 of 17 overs in the second. Gentlemen of Philadelphia won by 61 runs. At Lord's in 1907, playing for the Gentlemen, he took six wickets for 39 runs in the Players' second innings, this being the best performance of his life.

He made his final first class appearance on 4 September 1913 for the Gentlemen against the Players at North Marine Road, Scarborough. Napier made 0 and 1, took 2 wickets for 46 off 17 overs in the first innings and 3 wickets for 64 off 22 overs in the second. He also caught Colin Blythe (killed in action 8 November 1917) off the bowling of Gilbert Jessop for 4. Gentlemen won by 6 runs.

After Cambridge he took a commission in the Indian Army, joining the 36th Sikhs in Quetta, and serving on the North-West Frontier. While in India in 1909 he made two first class appearances for the Europeans (India) against the Parsees. One a Bombay Presidency match the Europeans won by an innings and 71 runs. The other in the Bombay Triangular

Tournament was drawn. He made a total of 854 first class runs, his highest score being 59. He also took 365 wickets for 7787 runs his best figures being 9 for 17. He took 84 catches.

At the outbreak of the First World War Napier transferred to the 47th Sikhs, landing in France in September 1914. He survived Ypres and was then granted leave to return home and marry his fiancée, Constance Mary Brock. The honeymoon was short and Napier was soon back at the front. He was killed in action during the battle of Loos on 25 September 1915.

He is buried at Cabaret-Rouge British Cemetery, Souchez, grave XVII, A. 40.

Batting and fielding averages

	Mat	Inns	NO	Runs	HS	Ave	100	50	Ct	St
First-class	81	127	29	854	59	8.71	0	1	84	0

Bowling averages

	Mat	Runs	Wkts	BBI	Ave	5w	10
First-class	81	7787	365	9/17	21.33	23	5

Lieutenant Burnet James
Gloucestershire
Royal Field Artillery, attd No. 7 Squadron Royal Flying Corps
Died 26 September 1915
Aged 28
Left-handed Bat/Left-arm Slow Bowler

'All that he had he gave'

Burnet James was born on 26 October 1886, the son of Sir Edward Burnet James, a tobacco manufacturer, and Lady James, of Springfort, Stoke Bishop, Bristol. He was educated at Charterhouse between 1905 and 1910 where he was in the first XI. A good all-round sportsman, he also played rugby for Clifton Rugby Football Club from 1908. For five years he played cricket for Bristol Imperial Cricket Club for which his batting average in 1914 was over 100. In addition, he played both hockey and first-class cricket for Gloucestershire. He made 3 first class appearances in the County Championship for Gloucestershire during the 1914 season. He made his debut on 21 May 1914 against Warwickshire at the Ashley Down Ground, Bristol. He made 6 and 10, Warwickshire won by 10 wickets. His second match came on 8 June 1914 against Northamptonshire once again at the Ashley Down Ground, Bristol. James scored 4 and 1, Northamptonshire won by 143 runs. He made his final first class against Warwickshire on 18 June 1914 at the Bulls Head Ground, Coventry. Napier scored 3 and 3 not out and caught William Quaife off the bowling of Alfred Dipper for 134. Warwickshire won by an innings and 197 runs.

James was also keen on the military and, in 1907, enlisted in the 1st Gloucestershire Royal Garrison Artillery Volunteers. However, after serving for five years, he resigned in 1912. At the outbreak of the First World War he once again volunteered his services with his old unit, who by then had changed their names to the 1st South Midland Brigade RFA (TF) of the 48th (South Midland) Division. James arrived in France in March 1914 and quickly became interested in the idea of flying, joining No. 7 Squadron Royal Flying Corps. In July 1915, as an observer, he had his first taste of action when he forced down a German Scout five miles south-east of Ypres while flying in a Voisin LAS, numbered 5028, at 7,000 feet; the aircraft was flown by Second Lieutenant Louis William Yule. On 31 August his aircraft, a BE2c, was flying over Douai when it was engaged in a combat with a German Scout which shot his engine up and wounded James. However, the pilot, Second Lieutenant Fairburn, managed to get the plane back to their base and land it safely. On 26 September, during the Battle of Loos, James's aircraft, a BE2c, number 1719, developed engine trouble and crashed, killing both James and his pilot, Yule.

James and Yule were buried together in a German cemetery behind the lines. They now lie in neighbouring graves in Cement House Cemetery, Langemarck, Belgium, grave reference XIII. D. 37.

Batting and fielding averages

	Mat	Inns	NO	Runs	HS	Ave	100	50	Ct	St
First-class	3	6	1	27	10	5.40	0	0	1	0

Bowling averages

	Mat	Balls	Runs	Wkts	BBI	BBM	Ave	Econ	SR	4w	5w	10
First-class	3	-	-	-	-	-	-	-	-	-	-	-

Major Kenelm Rees McCloughin
Europeans (India), Free Foresters, R. D. Robinson's XI, Army
14th King George's Own Ferozepore Sikhs, attd 11th Bn
Royal Scots
Died 26 September 1915
Aged 31
Unknown

'A most popular boy'

Kenelm Rees McCloughin was born on 18 August 1884 in Bombay (now Mumbai), Maharashtra, India, the son of Thomas John and Mary Kathleen McCloughin. He was educated at Dulwich College, where he was in the First XI, and the Royal Military Academy Woolwich. He made five first-class appearances between September 1909 and July 1914. He made his debut in a Bombay Presidency match on 6 September 1909 playing for the Europeans against the Parsees at the Deccan Gymkhana ground, Poona. He scored eight in his only innings, took 1 wicket for 4 off 3 overs and caught MD Parekh off the bowling of Guy Napier (Killed in action 25 September 1915) for 0. The Europeans won by an innings and 71 runs. On returning to England he turned out for the Free Foresters 1 June 1914 against Oxford University at The University Parks, Oxford. He scored 45 and 9 and caught Orme Bristowe off the bowling of John Burrough for 34. Oxford University won by 6 wickets. He went on to play for the Free Foresters against Cambridge University (Cambridge won by 1 wicket) and the Army against Cambridge University (Cambridge University won by an innings and 80 runs). McCloughin made his final first class appearance for LG Robinson's XI against Oxford University on 2 July 1914 at Old Buckenham Hall, Attleborough. He scored 0 and 21. The match was drawn. McCloughin made a total of 158 first class runs, his highest score being 57 against Cambridge University on 8 June 1914. He took 1 wicket for 52 runs his best figures being 1 for 4. He made 2 catches. He was a member of the MCC from 1914.

On leaving school McCloughin attended the Royal Military Academy Woolwich before being commissioned into the Royal Garrison Artillery in 1903. While in India he transferred to the 14th King George's Own Sikhs and then, shortly after the outbreak of war, once again transferred, to the 11th Bn Royal Scots. It was while serving with the Royal Scots that he was killed in action on 26 September 1915. A valiant soldier, he was also Mentioned in Despatches for his bravery in the field.

His body was never recovered and he is commemorated on the Neuve-Chapelle Memorial, Panel 18.

Final Wicket

Batting and fielding averages

	Mat	Inns	NO	Runs	HS	Ave	100	50	Ct	St
First-class	5	9	0	158	57	17.55	0	1	2	0

Bowling averages

	Mat	Runs	Wkts	BBI	Ave	5w	10
First-class	5	52	1	1/4	52.00	0	0

Captain Geoffrey Boisseller Davies
Cambridge University, Essex
11th Bn The Essex Regiment
Died 26 September 1915
Aged 22
Right-handed Bat, Right-arm Slow-Medium, Legbreak
Essex Cricket Club

'Are very proud of Geoffrey Davies'

Geoffrey Boisseller Davies was born on 26 October 1892, in Poplar, London. He was educated at Rossall School, Fleetwood, Lancashire where, between 1909 and 1912, he was in the Rossall XI, being captain in his final year. In 1910 he was second in the batting averages with 31.07 and first in 1911 with 27.57. His most successful year was 1912 when he scored 468 runs with an average of 33.42. In 1913 he went up to Selwyn College Cambridge and played in the Freshman's match, scoring 81 and 18 and taking five wickets in the second innings. He received his Blue.

Davis made 54 first class appearances between August 1912 and August 1914 playing mostly for Cambridge University and Essex in the County Championship. He made his debut for Essex on 8 August 1912 against Yorkshire at the County Ground, Leyton. He scored 7 and 45 not out and caught the English Test cricketer Major William Booth (killed in action 1 July 1916 first day of the Somme) off the bowling of Claude Buckenham for 9. Yorkshire won by 10 wickets. He made his debut for Cambridge against Middlesex on 7 May 1913 at Fenner's. He scored 16 in his one innings, Cambridge University winning by 9 wickets. He made his final first class appearance on 31 August 1914 for Essex against Somerset at Clarence Park, Weston-super-Mare. He seems to have left his best to last. He scored 118 in his only innings this also being his highest ever first class score. Took 4 wickets for 18 off 3 overs in his first innings and caught and bowled James Bridges for 31 in his second. Essex won by 10 wickets. During his first class career Davies made 1487 runs including 2 centuries his highest score being 118 against Somerset on 31 August 1914. He also took 141 wickets for 2935 runs his best figures being 8 for 67 and made 43 catches.

At the outbreak of war Davies was commissioned into the Essex Regiment, rising to the rank of captain. He landed in Boulogne with his battalion on 30 August 1915 but wasn't to survive a month. He was killed in action during the Battle of Loos on 26 September 1915, attacking the German second line near the Chalk Pit. The battalion suffered 371 casualties including eighteen officers during the battle, one of whom was the brave Geoffrey Davies.

His body was never recovered and he is commemorated on the Loos Memorial, Panels 85 to 87.

Batting and fielding averages

	Mat	Inns	NO	Runs	HS	Ave	100	Ct	St
First-class	54	90	9	1487	118	18.35	2	43	0

Bowling averages

	Mat	Runs	Wkts	BBI	Ave	5w	10
First-class	54	2935	141	8/67	20.81	4	1

Captain Bernard Henry Holloway
Sussex, MCC
9th Bn The Royal Sussex Regiment
Died 27 September 1915
Aged 27
Right-handed Bat/Right-arm Fast Medium

'A sportsman to the end'

Bernard Henry Holloway was born on 13 January 1888 at Burntwood Grange, Wandsworth Common, London. The son of Sir Henry and Lady Holloway, of Draxmont, Wimbledon Hill, London, he was educated at the Leys School from 1899 where he was in North A House. A senior prefect, Bernard won Tri-colours and was captain of the First XI. He was third in the batting averages in 1904, second in 1905 and 1906 – in '06 with 35.81 – and top in 1907, when his figure was 35.75. From there Holloway went up to Jesus College Cambridge where he became captain of the college XI but for some reason didn't get his Blue. He did little in the trial games save in 1911 when, in the Seniors' match, he scored 52 and made 133 for the first wicket stand with C. G. Forbes-Adam. Holloway also played rugby for Cambridge against Oxford in 1907 and 1909, as well as representing his university in the lacrosse XII in 1908, 1909 and 1910, being captain in 1910, the year in which he represented England at the game.

On leaving Cambridge Bernard Holloway went on to train as a solicitor. He made his first class debut for the MCC against Barbados on the 6 February 1911 at the Kensington Oval, Bridgetown during the MCC tour of the West Indies in 1910–11. He scored 19 in his one innings having to leave the field hurt and unable to continue. Barbados won by an innings and 103 runs. He went on to play against West Indies (x3), British Guiana, Trinidad (x2), Jamaica (x3). On returning to England he began to play for Sussex County Cricket Club. He made his debut for them on 22 June 1911 against Essex in the County Championship at the County Ground, Leyton. He made 0 and 4, Sussex won by 4 wickets. He also turned out against Cambridge University, Yorkshire, Somerset and Derbyshire. He made his final first class appearance for the MCC against Oxford University on 28 May 1914 at the University Parks, Oxford. Holloway made 39 and 14, the MCC winning by 48 runs. He made a total of 701 first class runs, his highest score being 100 against British Guiana on 23 February 1911. He made 13 catches.

At the outbreak of war Holloway gained a commission in the Royal Sussex Regiment and was quickly promoted to captain. He was killed in action during the Battle of Loos on 27 September 1915.

His body was never recovered and he is commemorated on the Loos Memorial, Pas de Calais, France, Panels 69 to 73.

He was the brother of N. J. Holloway, a Cambridge Blue and first-class cricketer.

Batting and fielding averages

	Mat	Inns	NO	Runs	HS	Ave	100	Ct	St
First-class	19	33	2	701	100	22.61	1	13	0

Bowling averages

	Mat	Balls	Runs	Wkts	BBI	BBM	Ave	Econ	SR	4w	5w	10
First-class	19	-	-	-	-	-	-	-	-	-	-	-

Captain Arthur Jaques
Hampshire/MCC
12th Bn Prince of Wales's Own (West Yorkshire Regiment)
Died 27 September 1915
Aged 27
Right-handed bat/Leg break, Medium pace

'Two of the finest brothers the Regiment have ever seen, both
died on the same day'

Arthur Jaques was born 7 March 1888 in Shanghai, China. He was the son of Mrs Allan Greene (formerly Jaques), of Red Lodge, Bassett, Southampton, and Joseph Jaques. Educated at Aldenham School, Hertfordshire where, between 1905 and 1907, he was in the Aldenham XI, heading the bowling averages in his final year with forty-three wickets at an average of 10.74. From Aldenham, Jaques went up to Trinity College Cambridge. Although he didn't get his Blue at Cambridge, or play in any first-class matches, he did, however, take part in the MCC's tour of the West Indies in 1912/13. He made 60 first class appearances between January 1913 and August 1914 the majority for the MCC and Hampshire. He made his first class debut against Barbados 30 January 1913 at the Kensington Oval, Bridgtown. He scored 1 in his only innings, took 1 wicket for 45 off 10 overs and caught Frederick Archer off the bowling of William Smith for 20. Barbados won by an innings and 29 runs. He went on to ply against the West Indies (x3), Trinidad (x2) and British Guiana (x2). During the tour Jaques scored 106 runs averaging 11.77, his highest score being 48 against the West Indies on 6 March 1913. He also took five wickets with an average of 29.00, his best figures being 2 for 31.

He made his debut for Hampshire against Derbyshire on 15 May 1913 in the County Championship at the County Ground, Southampton. Jaques scored 9 and 22, took 2 wickets for 26 off 7.1 overs and caught Richard Baggallay off the bowling of Arthur Hill for 33. Derbyshire won by 8 wickets. He also played for LG Robinson's XI and the Gentlemen against the Players on two occasions. He made his final first class appearance on 31 August 1914 for Hampshire against Kent at the Dean Park, Bournemouth. Like so many others he saved his best for last. Although he only made 4 runs he took 6 wickets for 55 off 23 overs in the first innings and 3 wickets for 31 off 12 overs in the second. Hampshire winning by an innings and 83 runs. During his first class career he made 982 runs his highest score being 68. He also took 175 wickets for 3835 runs his best figures being 8 for 21 and made 40 catches.

Wisden said of him,

Doubtless his unusual methods contributed much to his success, for, placing nearly all his field on the on-side, he pitched on the wicket or outside the leg-stump, and, swinging-in and getting on an off-break, cramped the batsmen so much that many of them lost patience and succumbed.

At the beginning of the First World War he was commissioned in the 12th Bn Royal West Kent Regiment. He was promoted to captain and was killed in action with his battalion at Bois Hugo during the Battle of Loos on 27 September 1915.

His body was never recovered and he is commemorated on the Loos Memorial, Pas de Calais, France, Panels 39 and 40.

Tragically, his brother Joseph Jacques, a major in the same regiment, was killed on the same day. We can only imagine the pain of his family.

Batting and fielding averages

	Mat	Inns	NO	Runs	HS	Ave	100	Ct	St
First-class	60	99	22	982	68	12.75	0	40	0

Bowling averages

	Mat	Runs	Wkts	BBI	Ave	5w	10
First-class	60	3835	175	8/21	21.91	10	3

**Lieutenant Colonel George Henry Neale
3rd Bn The Middlesex Regiment (Duke of Cambridge's
Own)
Marylebone Cricket Club
Died 28 September 1915
Aged 46
Right-handed Bat**

'Leading from the front as ever, he died'

George Henry Neale was born on 31 January 1869, in Reigate, Surrey, the son of Sisson Watts Neale, a brewer, and Mary A. Neale of De Vere Gardens, Reigate. He was educated at Lancing College where he was in Seconds House from September 1883 to July 1888. A member of the First XI between 1887 and 1888, he was a first-class batsman, averaging 14.50 and 25.50 in the years he played for the school XI.

On leaving school he decided to pursue a career in the Army and was commissioned in the King's Own Yorkshire Light Infantry as a second lieutenant on 26 January 1889. Promoted to lieutenant on 23 November 1892, by 1897 he had transferred to The Queen's (Royal West Surrey Regiment). He was promoted to lieutenant on 21 April 1897 and then to captain on 17 December 1898, achieving his majority on 17 June 1911. By 1914 he had transferred into the 3rd Bn The Middlesex Regiment (Duke of Cambridge's Own), based in Cawnpore, India. The Middlesex Regiment was one of a small number of regiments that had four battalions at this time.

Neale continued to play cricket when he was in the Army. In 1903, when he was based in Peshawar, India, he made 55 and 124 not out against Oxford University Authentics. The following month, in a match between the Queen's Regiment and the Gordon Highlanders, Neal scored 267 runs from a total team score of 607. He joined the MCC in 1902. He played one first-class match for the MCC at Lords against London County on 12 May 1902. but failed to score in both innings. London County won by 10 wickets.

He saw action in the Niger Soudan Expedition in 1896–97 where he was present at the expeditions to Egbon, Bida and Ilorin and was in command of No. 6 Company, Royal Niger Constabulary, to which he had been seconded in November 1896. Neale also served in the Tirah Expedition of 1897–98, on the North-West Frontier of India in the same years, in Waziristan in 1902 and Tibet between 1903 and 1904. Serving as Transport Officer in Tibet, he was Mentioned in Despatches. During all this action he still managed to find time to marry Agatha Augusta Downie (neé Smail) Neale; they lived at 57 The Pryors, Hampstead in London NW3.

At the outbreak of the Great War the battalion was in India but sailed for Britain, arriving on Christmas Eve 1914. After being re-equipped, Neale sailed with his battalion to France, arriving at le Havre on 28 January 1915, after which the battalion moved north to Ypres and saw action during the Second Battle of Ypres where George Neale was put in command of B and D Companies. During the heavy fighting on 23 April 1915, Neale's commanding officer, Lieutenant Colonel Ernest William Rokeby Stephenson, was killed and Neale assumed command of the battalion. The 3rd Middlesex also saw heavy fighting at the Battle of the Frezenberg Ridge, where the battalion suffered heavy casualties. Neale was promoted lieutenant colonel in May 1915.

At 2.00am on 28 September 1915, during the Battle of Loos, 3rd Middlesex were ordered to support a battalion of the East Kent Regiment who were detailed to attack the German positions known as the Dump and Fosse 8. Due to overcrowding in the front trenches, the attack was delayed until 9.30am when the East Kents went over, following an artillery bombardment on the German front line. While the East Kents (The Buffs) moved across no man's land in the open, the Middlesex moved along South Face Trench and into Dump Trench, launching a bombing attack against the left of the German line. Although they made good progress initially, their supply of bombs gave out and urgent messages were sent back for more. While this was being done the Germans counter-attacked and soon the Middlesex began taking heavy casualties. Realising his men were in great danger in the narrow, congested trench, Neale ordered them to withdraw slowly. By now, they were under heavy machine-gun fire in enfilade and any man who showed himself above the parapet was soon cut down. It was about this time that George Neale was killed. He was Mentioned in Despatches for this action (*London Gazette*, 1 January 1916). At this time, the only gallantry awards that could be given posthumously were the Victoria Cross and the Mention in Despatches.

Lieutenant Colonel Neale's body was never recovered or identified and he is commemorated on the Loos Memorial, Panels 99 to 101.

Batting and fielding averages

	Mat	Inns	NO	Runs	HS	Ave	100	50	4s	6s	Ct	St
First-class	1	2	0	0	0	0.00	0	0	0	0	0	0

Bowling averages

	Mat	Balls	Runs	Wkts	BBI	BBM	Ave	Econ	SR	4w	5w	10
First-class	1	-	-	-	-	-	-	-	-	-	-	-

Lance Corporal Wilfred Francis Reay
Gentlemen of England
10th Bn The Royal Fusiliers (City of London Regiment)
Died 8 October 1915
Aged 24
Fast/Medium Bowler

'Although never found he will always be with us'

Wilfred Francis Reay was born at Wallington Surrey on 12 June 1891 at Wallington, in Surrey, the son of Mr J. H. A. Reay a former civil servant. He was a first-class bowler and, while playing for both Beddington and Purley Cricket Clubs, took hundreds of wickets. In September 1912 he took all ten wickets in an innings for 30 runs for Beddington against Honor Oak on the latter's ground. He made one first class appearance on 30 June 1910 for the Gentlemen of England against Oxford University at The Saffrons, Eastbourne. Reay scored 5 not out and 0 not out and took one wicket for 51 off 11 overs. The Gentlemen of England won by 113 runs.

Reay was employed as an authorized clerk in the Stock Exchange and later married Dorothy Katherine Livermore, of 67 Elm Park Mansions, West Brompton, London.

At the outbreak of war he enlisted in the ranks of the 10th Bn Royal Fusiliers (City of London Regiment) which was raised in the City of London in August 1914 as an independent unit named The Stockbrokers' Battalion. He proceeded to France with his battalion, landing at Boulogne on 30 July 1915 and concentrating near Tilques. Lance Corporal Reay was killed in action on 8 October 1915. He has no known grave and is commemorated on the Thiepval Memorial, Somme, France, Piers and Faces 8C 9A and 16A.

Batting and fielding averages

	Mat	Inns	NO	Runs	HS	Ave	100	50	Ct	St
First-class	1	2	2	5	5*	-	0	0	0	0

Bowling averages

	Mat	Balls	Runs	Wkts	BBI	Ave	Econ	SR	5w	10
First-class	1	66	51	1	1/51	51.00	4.63	66.0	0	0

Lieutenant Geoffrey Dayrell Wood
Oxford University
7th Bn The Suffolk Regiment
Died 13 October 1915
Aged 24
Slow Left-arm Orthodox

'The first of three brothers to fall for their country'

Geoffrey Dayrell Wood was born on 17 August 1891 at Hampstead, London, the second of six boys born to Ernest Richard and Katherine Grace Wood, of Melton Hall, Melton, Suffolk. He was educated at Eaton House, Aldeburgh, and Cheltenham College. While at Cheltenham he was head of his house, played for the Cheltenham XI in 1908, 1909 and 1910 and was captain in 1909–10. A useful batsman, he also bowled well and in his last season headed the bowling with a record of forty-five wickets for 15.17 runs each. He was also captain of the school rugby XV and played for the school hockey team.

After leaving Cheltenham, Wood went up to Exeter College Oxford. He played in the Freshmen's trial match in 1911, and the Seniors' trial match in the following year, taking six wickets for 23 runs in the first innings. A member of the Oxford Authentics and the MCC from 1911. He played a single first-class match for Oxford University against the MCC on 3 June 1912 at The Parks, Oxford. Wood took 2 wickets for 36 runs and made no runs; the match was drawn. He also played for Suffolk three times in Minor County matches between 1910 and 1911.

While at Oxford in 1911 he joined the Officer Training Corps and at the outbreak of hostilities volunteered for foreign service. He was commissioned as a second lieutenant in the 7th Bn Suffolk Regiment on 26 August 1914 and was promoted to lieutenant on 8 March 1915 before going to France at the end of May 1915. Lieutenant Wood was killed in action at the Hohenzollern Redoubt five months later on 13 October 1915 and was buried where he fell.

His body was never discovered after the war and he is commemorated on the Loos Memorial, Pas de Calais, France, Panels 37 and 38.

Two of his five brothers were also killed during the war: Lieutenant Colonel Richard Poingdestre Wood MC, commanding 2nd Bn The York and Lancaster Regiment, died on 9 October 1916, aged 26; and Second Lieutenant Robert Basil, serving with the Border Regiment, died three days later on 12 October 1916, aged 23.

Batting and fielding averages

	Mat	Inns	NO	Runs	HS	Ave	100	50	4s	6s	Ct	St
First-class	1	1	0	0	0	0.00	0	0	0	0	0	0

Bowling averages

	Mat	Balls	Runs	Wkts	BBI	Ave	Econ	SR	5w	10
First-class	1	72	36	2	1/16	18.00	3.00	36.0	0	0

Second Lieutenant Ralph Eustace Hemingway
Nottinghamshire
8th Bn The Sherwood Foresters (Nottinghamshire and
Derbyshire Regiment)
Died 15 October 1915
Aged 37
Right-handed Bat

'I led them to the end'

Ralph Eustace Hemingway was born on 15 December 1877 at Foden Bank, Sutton, Macclesfield, Cheshire. He was the tenth and youngest son of James Hemingway of Roath, Cardiff, and was educated at Rugby School (School House), entering the school in 1892. He failed to be selected for the XI while there.

On leaving the school in 1895, he became an Associate of the Royal Institute of British Architects, and practised in Nottingham. While there he played for Nottinghamshire County Cricket Club. Hemingway made 32 first class appearances mostly for Nottinghamshire in the County Championship between July 1903 and September 1905. He also put in appearances for The North in a North versus South match (28 August 1905) and for the Gentlemen of the South versus the Players of the South (4 September 1905). He made his debut for Nottinghamshire against Kent on 30 July 1903 at Trent Bridge. He scored 17 and 39 and caught Arthur Fielder off the bowling of John Gunn for 12. Nottinghamshire won by an innings and 36 runs. In the 1904 season he scored 300 runs in first-class cricket with an average of 23.07. He opened the batting together with George Gunn against the visiting South Africans at Trent Bridge on 8 August 1904 and scored 85, with George Gunn knocking up 143, and 30. Despite this remarkable stand, South Africa still came out on top by an innings and 49 runs. Hemingway played his final first-class match on 4 September 1905 for the Gentlemen of the South against the Players of the South at Dean Park, Bournemouth. He made 10 not out and zero and took one wicket for 37 off fourteen overs as well as having the distinction of catching the great W. G. Grace off the bowling of Albert Relf for 43. Ill health finally forced Hemmingway to give up his cricketing career. A sad and early loss to the game.

Hemingway obtained a commission in the 8th Battalion Nottinghamshire and Derbyshire Regiment at the outbreak of the war and went with them to France in June 1915. He was present at the Battle of Hooge in July, at 'The Bluff' during the attack on 25 September and was wounded on 27 September. Taking part in the attack on the Hohenzollern Redoubt, he was killed there on 15 September.

From letters received by his family after his death it appears that he and seventy-five other members of the battalion had been attached to the Lincolnshire Regiment, and that he was pleased at the idea of being the first into action. His party had to follow up the attack immediately, and he and his bombers at once got into the Hohenzollern Redoubt and began to bomb up the trenches according to orders. They drove the Germans a long way back, but the difficulty of getting bombs up prevented them from getting on farther and they had to gradually give way. Lieutenant Hemingway was then wounded by a German bomb and was carried some way back along the trench, where he died. Survivors said that his last words were, 'I led them to the end, they wavered I tried to keep them together.'

His body was never recovered and Hemingway is commemorated on the Loos Memorial, Panels 87 to 89.

Batting and fielding averages

	Mat	Inns	NO	Runs	HS	Ave	100	50	Ct	St
First-class	32	50	2	976	85	20.33	0	6	17	0

Bowling averages

	Mat	Balls	Runs	Wkts	BBI	BBM	Ave	Econ	SR	4w	5w	10
First-class	32	6	6	0	-	-	-	6.00	-	0	0	0

Lieutenant Eric Frank Penn
Cambridge University/MCC
Grenadier Guards
Died 18 October 1915
Aged 37
Right-hand Bat/Right-arm Slow

'No one could fail to love and honor him for his noble qualities'

Eric Frank Penn was born on 17 April 1878 in Hanover Square, Westminster, London, the eldest son of William and Constance Penn of Taverham Hall, Norwich. He was educated at Eton between September 1891 and July 1897 where he was in the School XI, Field XI, Mixed Wall 1896 and Oppidian Wall 1895–96, as well as winning the throwing the cricket ball competition. Eric also played football for the college and won the School Quarter Mile.

Penn went up to Trinity College Cambridge on 25 June 1897 playing in the Freshman's match and and winning his Blue. He made 22 first class appearances all for Cambridge University between May 1898 and June 1903. Most were University Matches but he also played against Australia in England in 1899, Australia in the British Isles in 1902 and Ireland in England in the same year. He made his debut for Nottinghamshire on 19 May 1898 against Middlesex at Fenner's. Penn scored 7 in his one innings and caught John Head off the bowling of Herbert Hawkins for 43. The match was drawn. Penn went on to play against, Yorkshire, AJ Webbe's XI, the MCC, Sussex, Surrey, Oxford University and London County. Penn made his final first class appearance against for the MCC against Cambridge University on 25 June 1903 at Lord's. Penn scored 10 in his only innings. The MCC won by an innings and 161 runs. Penn made 449 first class runs during his career his highest score being 51. He also took 34 wickets for 1076 runs his best figures being 5 for 47. He made 13 catches. He also turned out 10 times for Norfolk in the minor counties.

He served as a second lieutenant in the 3rd (Militia) Bn Royal Scots, which he joined while still at Eton and went out to South Africa with them during the Boer War. He was invalided home in 1901 with the rank of captain. On leaving university he went into the City and became a partner in the firm of Sir R. W. Carden and Co., becoming a member of the Stock Exchange in 1905. In 1906 he married Gladys Penn of Baldslow Place, Baldslow, Sussex. They had one son who was, like thousands of others, born after his father's death.

At the outbreak of the war Captain Penn served with the Norfolk Yeomanry before transferring to the 4th Grenadier Guards as a second lieutenant. After the Battle of Loos, during which he was Mentioned in Despatches for bravery in the field, he was promoted back to captain. He was killed in action on 18 October 1915 at the Battle of the Hohenzollern Redoubt, at Auchy-les-Mines, France.

A writer in the *Eton Chronicle* said of him:

Prominent in games and with a stainless record, always cheerful and full of grit, he attracted to himself all that was best at Eton. No one could fail to love and honour him for his noble qualities.

One of his brother officers wrote:

> I can never forget what his example has been to me, and I know that it has helped many along the road.

Another wrote

> He was an exceptionally fine company commander and his men would have done anything for him.

He is buried in Vermelles British Cemetery, Pas de Calais, France, Plot I, Row K, Grave 11.

Batting and fielding averages

	Mat	Inns	NO	Runs	HS	Ave	100	50	Ct	St
First-class	22	36	6	449	51*	14.96	0	1	13	0

Bowling averages

	Mat	Balls	Runs	Wkts	BBI	Ave	Econ	SR	5w	10
First-class	22	2086	1076	34	5/47	31.64	3.09	61.3	1	0

Captain John Wyndham Hamilton McCulloch
Middlesex
8th Bn The Border Regiment
Died 21 October 1915
Aged 20
Right-handed Bat

'In duty he fell'

John Wyndham Hamilton McCulloch was born on 4 December 1894 in Calcutta (now Kolkata), Bengal, India, the son of J. E. McCulloch of Richmond House, St Mary's Terrace, Paddington. Educated at Westminster School where he got a double 'pink' in football and cricket, he played for the school XI in both 1912 and 1913.

He made two first-class appearances for Middlesex, both university matches during the 1914 season. He made his debut on 11 May 1914 against Oxford University at the University Parks, Oxford. He scored 0 and 4; Middlesex won by 234 runs. His second and final first-class match took place on 14 May 1914 against Cambridge University at F. P. Fenner's Ground Cambridge when McCulloch scored 14 in his only innings, Middlesex winning by eight wickets.

He served with the 8th Battalion Border Regiment during the war and died of wounds received in action on 21 October 1915 at Bailleul, Lille, France. The regimental diary explains in a little more detail.

20th October – 8pm. A noisy night, much more firing on German side, apparently due to new reliefs. Captain McCulloch severely wounded in the leg about 5am. Another casualty in B W the same night. A quiet day, and work proceeded as usual. Hope we have located a German battery which has been shelling our trenches and informed the artillery.

21st – 8pm. A quiet night. Heard of Captain McCulloch's death at No. 2 Clearing Station from collapse. Relief was completed by 5pm and trenches handed over to 10th Cheshires.

On the 22nd October a service was held in memory of Captain McCulloch.

He is commemorated in the Bailleul Communal Cemetery Extension, Nord, Grave reference, I. C. 125

Batting and fielding averages

	Mat	Inns	NO	Runs	HS	Ave	100	50	Ct	St
First-class	2	3	0	18	14	6.00	0	0	0	0

Bowling averages

	Mat	Balls	Runs	Wkts	BBI	BBM	Ave	Econ	SR	4w	5w	10
First-class	2	-	-	-	-	-	-	-	-	-	-	-

Assistant Paymaster Francis Hugh Bacon
Royal Naval Reserve
Royal Yacht Squadron's Steam Yacht *Aries*
Hampshire
Died 31 October 1915
Aged 46
Right-handed Bat/Right-arm Slow Bowler.

'Small in stature he had the courage of a lion'

Francis Hugh Bacon was born on 24 June 1869 in Colombo, Ceylon (now Sri Lanka), the son of the Reverend James Bacon, of Colombo, Ceylon. He was educated at St Augustine's College, Canterbury where he was in the XI. On leaving school he settled in Basingstoke. During the first few months of 1894, on the strength of three not-out innings of 101 for Basingstoke, he was tried for Hampshire. It was a very good decision by Hampshire; in his first match for the county against Warwickshire at Edgbaston, Bacon scored 114 in 130 minutes. However it wasn't until the following season that Bacon was to start making regular first class appearances for the county. He made 75 first class appearances for Hampshire between May 1895 and July 1911 all but 1 in the County Championship. He made his first class debut for Hampshire on 30 May 1894 against Somerset at the County Ground, Taunton. He made a good start catching the Somerset opener Lion Palairet off the bowling of Harry Baldwin for 96. He then caught Charles Winter once again of the bowling of Baldwin for 9. He did well with the bat to scoring 15 and a very impressive 92. With out doubt it was Bacon's second innings score of 92 that led Hampshire to wining the match by 11 runs. A fine start to any cricketing career. His most successful season was 1903 when he scored 357 runs at a batting average of 18.78, with a high score of 39. In terms of batting average, the 1906 season was Bacon's best with 308 runs at a batting average of 23.69, with three fifties and a high score of 60. He made his final first class appearance against Lancashire on 3 July 1911 at Old Trafford, Manchester. He made 7 in his only innings and took 2 wickets for 23 runs off 3 overs. Lancashire won by an innings and 455 runs. During his first class career Bacon made 1909 runs his highest score being 110 against Leicestershire in 1907. He also took 6 wickets for 190 runs his best figures being 2 for 23. He took 34 catches.

Bacon wasn't a big man, standing only 5 foot 5 inches in his stocking feet, but he was a big hitter. To add to his numerous talents he was considered the best cover-point-in England and had the rare distinction of being one of the few cricketers who started as a professional and finished as an amateur. From 1903 until his death he was secretary of the Hampshire County Cricket Club and was much liked and highly thought of by all who knew him. He also found time to marry Fanny Bacon of Ashdene, Regents Park, Southampton.

An officer in the Royal Naval Reserve, Bacon was unfortunately killed on 31 October 1915 when the Royal Yacht Squadron's Steam Yacht *Aries* hit a sea mine near the South Goodwin Lightship. The Yacht was commanded at the time by Commander H Caulder. Observing what he believed to be an enemy mine inshore of him, he steamed towards it to destroy it. In so doing, he must have bumped another mine which caused the vessel to break in two, and to sink in about a minute. The commanding officer, four officers and seventeen men were drowned. One officer and four men were saved, two of the latter having broken ribs. The mines had been laid by the German Submarine *UC-6*, under command of Matthias Graf von Schmettow.

Bacon's body eventually washed up and he was buried in Borsmose Churchyard (Borsmose is a small village in west Jutland, west of the town of Varde).

Batting and fielding averages

	Mat	Inns	NO	Runs	HS	Ave	100	Ct	St
First-class	75	132	11	1909	110	15.77	1	34	0

Bowling averages

	Mat	Balls	Runs	Wkts	BBI	Ave	Econ	SR	5w	10
First-class	75	217	190	6	2/23	31.66	5.25	36.1	0	0

Second Lieutenant Frank Noel Tuff
Oxford University/Free Foresters
Royal East Kent Mounted Rifles
Died 5 November 1915
Aged 25
Right-handed Bat/Right-arm Medium-Fast

'His father never recovered from his loss'

Frank Noel Tuff was born on 26 November 1889 at Rochester, Kent. He was the son of Charles Tuff JP and Mary Ann Tuff (née Gill) of Westfield, Singlewell, Gravesend, Kent. He was educated at the Abbey School, Southend Road, Beckenham, Kent and Malvern College where he was in the XI for three years. Tuff was Malvern's senior bowler – medium-paced – in 1906 and headed the averages in each of the following seasons. He was also in the soccer XI. After leaving Malvern Tuff went up to Brasenose College Oxford where he studied law. During the Freshmen's match in 1909 he scored 29 not out and 36; he also took three wickets. The following year Tuff obtained his Blue against Cambridge. Tuff made 11 first class appearances between June 1910 and June 1914, all but one University matches. He made his debut for Oxford against the Gentlemen of England on 6 June 1910 at the University Parks, Oxford. Tuff made 1 not out and 6 not out. He also took 5 wickets for 28 off 17 overs in the first innings and 2 wickets for 18 off 8 wickets in the second. Oxford University won by 167 runs. Tuff went on to play against the MCC, Sussex, Cambridge University, Surrey, Kent and Oxford and Cambridge against the Army and Navy. He made his final first class appearance on 1 June 1914 for the Free Foresters against Oxford University at The University Parks, Oxford. He scored 0 and 35. Oxford University won my 6 wickets. During his first class career Tuff scored 190 runs his highest score being 35 against Oxford University on 1 June 1914. He also took 25 wickets for 670 runs his best figures being 7 for 47. He made 6 catches. He also played for the Kent 2nd XI, Band of Brothers and the Corinthians and represented Oxford at association football in 1909, 1910 and 1911. In 1912 he married Muriel Mary Smith at St Michael's, Chester Square, London.

Tuff received a commission into the Royal East Kent Yeomanry on 1 June 1915. The following September he went to Gallipoli with his regiment and was seriously wounded in a bomb accident at Helles on 23 October. Unfortunately he died of his wounds at Imtarfa, Malta on 5 November 1915. He is buried in Pieta Military Cemetery, grave reference D. II. 1.

Frank Tuff's brother, Captain Cecil Thomas Tuff, Royal West Kent Regiment, was killed on 20 April 1915. Their father never recovered from the loss of two of his four sons.

Batting and fielding averages

	Mat	Inns	NO	Runs	HS	Ave	100	50	Ct	St
First-class	11	20	7	190	35	14.61	0	0	6	0

Bowling averages

	Mat	Balls	Runs	Wkts	BBI	Ave	Econ	SR	5w	10
First-class	11	1359	670	25	7/47	26.80	2.95	54.3	2	0

Captain George Lumley Whatford
Sussex
Died 22 November 1915
Aged 37
66th Punjabis
Not Known

'The regiment will not be the same without him.
We shall miss him sadly'

George Lumley Whatford was born on 20 July 1878 in Eastbourne, Sussex, the son of Jack Henry Whatford and Rose Whatford (née Linkwood). Educated at Harrow and Trinity College Cambridge, in 1902, on leaving Cambridge, he took up a career in the Army, and was commissioned in the South Staffordshire Regiment as a second lieutenant. Whatford played cricket for Eastbourne and in 1904 got his trial for Sussex after scoring 101 for the Sussex Second XI against Kent's Second XI at Brighton. He made his first-class debut for Sussex against Somerset at the Recreation Ground, Bath, in 1904 but the match was rained off before Whatford could bat. He made two first class appearances during the 1904 season both in the County Championship. He made his debut against Somerset at the Recreation Ground, Bath on 28 July 1904. He failed to bat and the match was drawn due to the weather. He made his second and final first class appearance on 1 August 1904 against Gloucestershire at the Ashley Down Ground, Bristol. Whatford scored 8 and 13, Gloucestershire won by 168 runs.

He travelled to India with his regiment and transferred to the 66th Punjabis. In India he continued to play cricket and made several good scores at Peshawar. He was promoted to lieutenant in 1904 and, in 1909, was made adjutant and captain. Between 1910 and 1912 he became adjutant of the Eastern Bengal Railway Volunteers and at the outbreak of the war was appointed censor at Mergui, Burma. He went to Mesopotamia in the winter of 1914 and was killed in action on 22 November 1915 at the Battle of Ctesiphon, while attempting to capture Baghdad.

His colonel wrote, 'Your son was a fine sportsman a good soldier and a great gentleman.' A brother officer also wrote:

Your son died a soldier's death in its truest sense, leading his company under a heavy fire. The regiment will not be the same without him. We shall miss him sadly.

Prior to his death he was due to be promoted to major. His body was never recovered and his name is commemorated on the Basra Memorial, Panels 47 and 68.

Batting and fielding averages

	Mat	Inns	NO	Runs	HS	Ave	100	50	Ct	St
First-class	2	2	0	21	13	10.50	0	0	0	0

Bowling averages

	Mat	Balls	Runs	Wkts	BBI	BBM	Ave	Econ	SR	4w	5w	10
First-class	2	-	-	-	-	-	-	-	-	-	-	-

Captain Frederick James Cook
South Africa/Eastern Province
10th Bn The Border Regiment
Attd 1/4th (Queen's Edinburgh Rifles) Royal Scots
Died 30 November 1915
Aged 45
Right-handed Bat

'A fine South African who died for his mother country'

Frederick James Cook was born in 1870, in Java, Dutch East Indies, the son of John Groom Cook and Emily Cook. He made 5 first class appearances for Eastern Province between March 1894 and December 1904 all in the Currie cup, although his appearances were infrequently over the twelve-season period between 1893–94 and 1904–05. He also captained the side. He made his debut for the Eastern Province on 17 March 1894 at Newlands Rugby Ground, Cape Town. He scored 59 (his highest first class score) and 28. Transvaal won by 149 runs. His second game came on 20 March 1894 against Griqualand West once again at the Newlands Rugby Ground, Cape Town. Cook scored 3 and 1 and caught D Lloyd off the bowling of Alfred Britton for 0. Griqualand West won by 9 wickets. On 13 February 1896 Cook was selected to play in the first Test against Lord Hawke's XI (England) at the St George's Park, Port Elizabeth. Cook batted number nine, making seven out of a total of 93 in the first innings but failing to score a run in his second, when South Africa were bowled out for a very poor 30. The famous George Lohmann took eight wickets for seven runs in South Africa's first innings. In his second innings, Cook was Lohmann's first victim in his hat trick, which ended the game. Lohmann later emigrated to South Africa for health reasons and went on to manage the South African team. He died of TB at the early age of 36 and is considered one of the finest bowlers of all time.

England won by 288 runs. He went on to play against Western Province and Natal making his final first class appearance against Western Province on 26 December 1904 at Newlands, Cape Town. Opening for the Easter Province, Cook scored 11 and 3 Western Province winning by 6 wickets.

At the outbreak of the war Cook was commissioned into the Border Regiment and was quickly promoted to captain. He went out to Gallipoli with his unit and was attached to 1/4th Bn (Queen's Edinburgh Rifles) Royal Scots. He was killed in action on 30 November 1915.

Cook is buried in Pink Farm Cemetery, Helles, Grave reference Sp. Mem 18.

His next of kin was given as his wife Mary Ames Cook, of 14A Goldfinch Street, Hillbrow, Johannesburg, South Africa.

Batting and fielding averages

	Mat	Inns	NO	Runs	HS	Ave	100	50	6s	Ct	St
Tests	1	2	0	7	7	3.50	0	0	0	0	0
First-class	6	12	2	172	59	17.20	0	1		1	0

Bowling averages

	Mat	Inns	Balls	Runs	Wkts	BBI	BBM	Ave	Econ	SR	4w	5w	10
Tests	1	-	-	-	-	-	-	-	-	-	-	-	-
First-class	6	-	-	-	-	-	-	-	-	-	-	-	-

Sapper Robert William Barry
Canterbury, New Zealand
New Zealand Engineers
Died 3 December 1915
Aged 37
Right Handed Bat

"Died twice"

Robert William Barry was born at Akaroa, Canterbury, New Zealand on 9 September 1878 to Mrs E. Barry, 4 Dilworth Terrace, Parnell, Auckland. A very good athlete, he represented Canterbury in both hockey and cricket. He made one first-class appearance for Canterbury against Hawke's Bay on 4 January 1902 at Lancaster Park, Christchurch. He scored 13 and 4 and took 1 wicket for 21 off 7 overs. Hawke's Bay winning by 6 wickets.

Affectionately known to his friends as Bob Barry, he played his club cricket for the Parnell Club and helped to introduce hockey to the city. On finishing his education he joined the clerical staff of the New Zealand Express Company in Auckland. Barry saw service during the Second Boer War. During the First World War he served with the New Zealand Field Engineers.

He died of wounds received during the fighting in Gallipoli on board HM Hospital Ship *Dongola* on 3 December 1915 and was buried at sea.

The *Auckland Star* carried the following obituary on 14 December 1915:

It will be remembered that Sapper Barry was by mistake reported killed in action in June last. A later message showed that he had been wounded. He has since recovered, and returned to the firing line, but there is reason to fear that the present message is genuine …

He is commemorated on the Lone Pine Memorial, Panel 72, in Lone Pine Cemetery, Anzac, Turkey.

Batting and fielding averages

	Mat	Inns	NO	Runs	HS	Ave	100	50	Ct	St
First-class	1	2	1	17	13*	17.00	0	0	0	0

Bowling averages

	Mat	Balls	Runs	Wkts	BBI	Ave	Econ	SR	5w	10
First-class	1	114	42	1	1/21	42.00	2.21	114.0	0	0

Sergeant Matthew Stanley McKenzie
Tasmania
1st Clearing Hospital, Australian Army Medical Corps
Died 8 December 1915
Aged 25
Right-handed Bat

'Died caring for others, the way he had lived'

Matthew Stanley McKenzie was born on 17 May 1890 in Launceston, Tasmania. The son of Mr Harry McKenzie, Warden of the Launceston Marine Board, Stan was educated at the prestigious Scotch College, where he was regarded as an average student and an outstanding sportsman. He represented both his school and his state in football, athletics and cricket. After graduating, he began a career in banking, while continuing to play football in the winter and cricket in the summer.

A right-handed opening batsman, he played five first-class matches for Tasmania between January 1910 and January 1913. He made his debut on 29 January 1910 against Victoria at the Melbourne Cricket Ground, Melbourne. He made 14 not out and 40 Victoria winning by an innings and 126 runs. He had to wait two years before he made his next first class appearance this time against the MCC in Australia at the North Tasmania Cricket Association Ground, Launceston. McKenzie made 59 and 26 and took 2 wickets for 65 off 17 overs and caught Frank Woolley off the bowling of Edward Windsor for 45. MCC won by 8 wickets. He played against the MCC again a few days later on 26 January 1912 this time at the Tasmania Cricket Association Ground Hobart. McKenzie made 0 and 29. The MCC won by an innings and 95 runs. The match was notable for the 305 not out made by Frank Woolley. He made 50 in 24 minutes, 100 in 84 minutes, beat his previous best of 184, made 200 in 154 minutes and 300 in 219 minutes. It is also worth noting that on reaching 141 he reached 8000 runs in first class cricket. The MCCs William Rhodes also made 102 and John Williams 97. On the Tasmanian side George Paton made his first century scoring 112 passing his previous best of 81. On 16 February 192 Tasmania took on Victoria at Launceston, McKenzie scoring 11 and 7. He made two catches, Edgar McDonald off the bowling of Edward Winsor for 2 and Christopher Dwyer once again off the bowling of Windsor for 0 (Windsor took 10 wickets for 196 during the match). Tasmania won by 2 runs. McKenzie made his final first class appearance a year later on 24 January 1913 again against Victoria at the Melbourne Cricket Ground, Melbourne. McKenzie made 0 and 25 and once again made 2 catches Rowland Bailey off the bowling of George Paton for 9 and Patrick Shea off the bowling of Arthur Watt for 7. Tasmania won by 54 runs.

McKenzie was also recruited by Australian rules club Carlton in 1914. Stan McKenzie, a tall, versatile player, spent just one season with Carlton Football Club during their Premiership year of 1914. He played fourteen consecutive matches for the Blues, kicking six goals before losing his place in the team on the eve of that year's Grand Final.

At the outbreak of the war Stan enlisted in the 1st Australian Imperial Force as a medical orderly. He spent some months tending to Australian casualties on the Gallipoli Peninsula, where he was promoted to sergeant. In late-1915 Stan was posted to 2/2nd Clearing Hospital at Alexandria Egypt. While serving there, he suffered a severe attack of appendicitis and was hospitalized on board the hospital ship *Gloucester Castle* where he died on 8 December 1915 in Alexandria Harbour.

A local paper later carried his obituary.

SERGEANT 'STAN' McKENZIE DEAD.

General regret will be occasioned by the news received yesterday of the death from appendicitis of Sergeant M. S. McKenzie, son of Mr Harry McKenzie, Warden of the Launceston Marine Board. The sad intelligence was conveyed to the parents by Canon de Coetlogon, who expressed the deepest regret and sympathy of their Majesties the King and Queen, and the Commonwealth Government, as well as the District Commandant, in the loss sustained by them and the army. The late Sergeant McKenzie went from Australia with the First Clearing Hospital and after a brief sojourn in England with his unit, had been several months at the Dardanelles, where the hospital was established immediately after the historic landing on April 25. His death removes a man who was amongst Tasmania's finest athletes; as a footballer he often played for Northern Tasmania, and represented the state in the big Australasian carnival, held at Adelaide some years ago. He was regarded as the most brilliant centre man of recent years, and played for a number of years with the Launceston club, from which he transferred to the Victorian League team, Carlton. His cricket prowess was equally fine, for he made many runs for Northern Tasmania, and attained to very considerable success as a bowler. The late Sergeant McKenzie, who was a bank clerk prior to enlistment, was well known in the athletic field throughout Tasmania. A younger brother, Sapper G. F. McKenzie, was awarded the DCM for conspicuous gallantry in rescuing a comrade under fire.

Stan McKenzie is buried in Alexandria (Chatby) Military and War Memorial Cemetery, Grave Reference A.61.

Batting and fielding averages

	Mat	Inns	NO	Runs	HS	Ave	100	50	Ct	St
First-class	5	10	1	211	59	23.44	0	1	5	0

Bowling averages

	Mat	Runs	Wkts	BBI	Ave	5w	10
First-class	5	255	2	2/65			

Major Gilbert George Reginald Sackville, 8th Earl de la Warr
Earl de la Warr's XI, Lord Sheffield's XI
Royal Navy, HMML California
Died 16 December 1915
Aged 46

'A man of dignity and great energy. Gone too soon.'

Gilbert George Reginald Sackville was born on 22 March 1869 at Westminster, London. He was the second but only surviving son of Reginald Sackville, 7th Earl de la Warr, and the Honourable Constance Mary Elizabeth Baillie-Cochrane, daughter of Alexander Baillie-Cochrane, 1st Baron Lamington. He became heir apparent to the earldom in 1890 when his elder brother, Lord Cantelupe, died unmarried. Sackville then took the name Lord Cantelupe.

Sackville made two first-class appearances. The first was on 25 May 1891 for Lord Sheffield's XI against the MCC, played at the Sheffield Park, Uckfield. The match was drawn with Sackville scoring one run in one innings and catching Timothy O'Brien off the bowling of George Lohmann for 28. His second appearance was on 30 July 1896 at the Manor Ground, Bexhill-on-Sea, when he turned out for Earl de la Warr's XI against the visiting Australians. Once again he scored only one run in one innings and caught Frank Iredale off the bowling of John Hearne for 10. Warr's XI going on to beat the Australians by four wickets.

He became a deputy lieutenant of Sussex in 1891 and succeeded to the earldom in 1896, aged 25. In 1891 he took a commission in the 2nd (Cinque Ports or Eastern) Division of the Royal Artillery. He was promoted to captain before resigning his commission in 1895. However, he was re-appointed in 1900 and took part in the Second Boer War and was wounded in Vryheid. He was promoted to major in 1901 but resigned his commission once again in 1902.

In 1903 and 1904 he was Mayor of Bexhill-on-Sea, Sussex; he was also a county alderman and a Justice of the Peace for Sussex. Shortly after the outbreak of the First World War he served with the Southdown Battalion of the Royal Sussex Regiment in November 1914 before resigning his commission. A life-long yachtsman, he went on to join the Royal Naval Volunteer Reserve, serving as a lieutenant. He was first employed in the Channel in command of a motor-boat. Afterwards he served on the French and Belgian canals, where he did useful work for the Admiralty. In July 1915 he was on his way to the Dardanelles when he was taken seriously ill with rheumatic fever and gastritis, and was landed at Messina.

He died ten weeks later, on 16 December 1915, from heart failure and was buried at Messina with full naval honours two days later. His body lies in the cemetery which the Italians gave Lord Nelson as a burial-ground for naval officers, Plot Section 2, Row 2, Grave 4.

Batting and fielding averages

	Mat	Inns	NO	Runs	HS	Ave	100	50	4s	6s	Ct	St
First-class	2	2	0	2	1	1.00	0	0	0	0	2	0

Bowling averages

	Mat	Balls	Runs	Wkts	BBI	BBM	Ave	Econ	SR	4w	5w	10
First-class	2	-	-	-	-	-	-	-	-	-	-	-

Lieutenant Charles Neil Newcombe
Derbyshire
7th Bn The King's Own Yorkshire Light Infantry
Died 27 December 1915
Aged 24
Right-handed Bat/Left-arm Slow Medium

'Good at all sports but never really had chance to shine'

Charles Neil Newcombe was born on 16 March 1891 in Great Yarmouth, Norfolk, the son of E. Percy G. Newcombe and Helen Ada L. Newcombe, late of Matlock, Derbyshire. He was educated at Chesterfield School where he was head boy. A handy right-handed batsman and decent left-arm slow-medium bowler, Newcombe made a single first-class appearance for Derbyshire during the 1910 County Championship playing against Yorkshire at Queen's Park, Chesterfield. Unfortunately he didn't do well. He hit his own wicket after only one run in the first innings and was bowled for a duck by Alonzo Drake in his second innings (he never bowled a first-class ball).

A good all-round athlete he also played football for several teams including Creswell, Chesterfield and Rotherham Town, Sheepbridge Works, and Tibshelf Colliery, between 1910 and 1912.

At the outbreak of the war Newcombe took a commission in the 7th Bn The King's Own Yorkshire Light Infantry. He landed with his battalion at Boulogne on 24 July 1915 and was killed in action at Fleubaix on 27 December 1915.

He was buried at Y Farm Military Cemetery, Bois-Grenier, grave reference K. 13.

Batting and fielding averages

	Mat	Inns	NO	Runs	HS	Ave	100	50	4s	6s	Ct	St
First-class	1	2	0	1	1	0.50	0	0	0	0	0	0

Bowling averages

	Mat	Balls	Runs	Wkts	BBI	BBM	Ave	Econ	SR	4w	5w	10
First-class	1	72	32	0	-	-	-	2.66	-	0	0	0

1916

Captain Sholto Douglas
Middlesex
16th Bn The Middlesex Regiment (Duke of Cambridge's Own)
Died 28 January 1916
Aged 42
Right-handed Bat

'An inspiration to all that knew him'

Sholto Douglas was born on 8 September 1873 at Norwood Green, Southall, Middlesex, the son of Sir Robert and Lady Douglas. He was educated at Dulwich College where he was in the First XI for four years between 1890 and 1894 and was captain in his final year. He was also in the First XV, captain of Fives and twice won the steeplechase. Heading the batting averages in 1891 and 1893, his best performance was against Bedford School when he scored 97 in a convincing Dulwich victory. Douglas made 1 first class appearance for Middlesex against Surry on 30 August 1906 in the County Championship at the Kennington Oval. He scored 14 and 16 and caught Thomas Hayward off the bowling of Francis Tarrant for 110. The match was drawn (all three of his brothers also played for Middlesex at one time or the other).

On leaving college he worked as a teacher in a preparatory school. In 1896 he went to Assam in India, but he found the climate too much and returned to England two years later to resume his teaching. At the outbreak of the Second Boer War he joined the Wiltshire Yeomanry and served in South Africa with them. On returning to England he continued to teach at his old school before joining his brother James in 1905 at his school in Hill Side, Godalming.

At the outbreak of the war Arnold took a commission as a second lieutenant in the 16th Bn (Public Schools) Middlesex Regiment, being promoted to captain in March 1915. He travelled to France with his battalion and landed in Boulogne on 17 November 1917 but was killed in action on 28 January 1916. An account of his death was later published in the *Lancing* magazine in a description of the actions of another officer, George Heslop, who was wounded in the same action:

> On the 26th of January 1916 the Germans attacked across the old Loos battlefield and the 16th Middlesex were called upon to re-enter the front line (they had been resting) to support a battalion of the King's Royal Rifle Corps. On the morning of the 28th of January the Company Commander of B Company, Major Way, was moving along the front line trench with Captain Sholto-Douglas and the company runner. Shortly behind them was George Heslop leading a group of men of roughly platoon strength. Suddenly a heavy barrage fell on the group killing the two officers and wounding Heslop and a number of others.

Sholto Douglas is buried in the Cambrin Churchyard Extension, grave reference L. 19.

Batting and fielding averages

	Mat	Inns	NO	Runs	HS	Ave	100	50	Ct	St
First-class	1	2	0	30	16	15.00	0	0	1	0

Bowling averages

	Mat	Balls	Runs	Wkts	BBI	BBM	Ave	Econ	SR	4w	5w	10
First-class	1	-	-	-	-	-	-	-	-	-	-	-

Captain Francis Bernard Roberts
Cambridge University/Gloucestershire
9th Bn The Prince Consort's Own (Rifle Brigade)
Died 8 February 1916
Aged 33
Right-handed Bat/Right-arm fast

'Followed his boys to war, served and died by their side'

Francis Bernard Roberts was born on 20 May 1882 at Anjini Hill, Nasik, India. The son of Canon W. A. and Mrs Roberts of Nasik, Bombay Presidency, India. He was educated at Magdalen College School (1894–1898), Oxford where he was in the XI and Rossall School, Lancashire where he represented the school XI for three years from 1898. He went up to Jesus College Cambridge where he got his Blue, both for cricket and hockey. Roberts, who always played in glasses, made 80 first class appearances between May 1903 and August 1914 mostly for Cambridge University and Gloucestershire in the County Championship. He made his debut against Warwickshire on 21 May 1903 at Fenner's. He scored a disappointment 1 and 0 but redeemed himself by taking 3 wickets for 44 off 21 overs. Cambridge University won by 21 runs. Roberts went on to play for the university against, Yorkshire, Worcestershire, Gentlemen of Philadelphia, Surrey, Sussex, MCC, Oxford University, Warwickshire and South Africa. He made his debut for Gloucestershire on 2 August 1906 against Middlesex at the Ashley Down Ground, Bristol. He made 0 and 1, took 3 wickets for 44 off 29 overs in the first innings and 1 wicket for 28 off 10 overs in the second. He also caught Francis Tarrant off the bowling of Edward Dennett for 5 and Edward Littlejohn again of the bowling of Dennett for 1. Gloucestershire won by 121 runs. He made his final first class appearance on 24 August 1914 against Yorkshire at the Ashley Down Ground, Bristol. He scored 12 and 7, Yorkshire winning by an innings and 227 runs. In addition, he played for Oxfordshire in the Minor County Championship, (1901–03) and H. Webb's XI (1913). During his first class career Roberts made 2566 runs including 5 centuries and 6 half centuries. His highest score being 157 he also took 88 wickets for 3005 runs his best figures being 5 for 69. He made 66 catches.

In the middle of all this cricket, Roberts managed to find time to become a master at Wellington College. During the First World War he served with 9 battalion The Prince Consort's Own (Rifle Brigade).

After training he landed at Boulogne on 17 November 1915 and was killed in action on 8 February 1916 at St Julien, Ypres, Belgium, having been in France for less than two months.

He is buried in Talana Farm Cemetery, grave reference I.D.1.

His brother, Mr A. W. Roberts, also played cricket for Gloucestershire.

Batting and fielding averages

	Mat	Inns	NO	Runs	HS	Ave	100	50	Ct	St
First-class	80	138	12	2566	157	20.36	5	6	66	0

Bowling averages

	Mat	Balls	Runs	Wkts	BBI	Ave	Econ	SR	5w	10
First-class	80	5835	3005	88	5/69	34.14	3.08	66.3	1	0

Captain Bernard Philip Nevile
Worcestershire/Free Foresters
7th Bn The Lincolnshire Regiment
Died 11 February 1916
Aged 27
Right-handed Bat/Right-arm Fast

'A fine cricketer from a family of cricketers'

Bernard Philip Nevile was born on 1 August 1888 at Wellingore Hall, Lincolnshire, and was educated at Trinity College Cambridge. Although Nevile didn't get his Blue for cricket he did play in the Seniors' match at Cambridge in 1912 and took four wickets for 27 runs in the second innings. He did, however, obtain his Blue for golf and also played hockey for his university. Nevile made 6 first class appearances between June 1912 and July 1913. One university match, and five in the County Championship for Worcestershire. He made his debut on 10 June 1912 for the Free Foresters against Cambridge University. He scored 4 in his only innings. Free Foresters won by 5 wickets. He made his debut for Worcestershire on 3 July 1913 against Middlesex at he County Ground, New Road, Worcester. He made 1 and 0 not out. The match was drawn. He went on to play against Hampshire and Kent. He made his final first class appearance against Surrey on 4 July 1913 at the Kennington Oval, Kennington.

He scored 4 and 7 and took 4 wickets for 53 of 22.2 overs. The match was drawn. During his first class career Roberts made 65 runs highest score being 17. He also took 7 wickets for 149 runs his best figures being 4 for 53. He made 1 catch. He also played for and captained Lincolnshire in the Minor Counties' Championship.

At the outbreak of the war he was commissioned in the 7th Bn Lincolnshire Regiment. He quickly rose to the rank of

The Cambridge team for the 23rd annual hockey match against Oxford, 28 February 1912.
W. N. Scholes (Pembroke) A.H.A Vann (Jesus, 25.5.15 KIA) K.M. Robotham (Caius) B.P.Nevile (Trinity)
Sitting Middle: B.S. Bland (Emmanuel) S.H. Saville (Trinity) H.M. Robinson (Capt Pembroke) R.P.Dalley (Pembroke) D.O Light (Pembroke)
Sitting Floor: J.M. Kendal (Corpus) R.B Lagden (Pembroke).

captain and landed in France with his battalion on 14 July 1915. Nevile was killed in action on 11 February 1916 near Ypres, Belgium.

His body was never recovered and he is commemorated on the Ypres (Menin Gate) Memorial, Panel 21.

His brother, Hugo George Nevile, South Wales Borderers, who played for the Minor Counties, was also killed in action on 21 August 1915 during the Gallipoli campaign.

Batting and fielding averages

	Mat	Inns	NO	Runs	HS	Ave	100	50	Ct	St
First-class	6	10	2	65	17*	8.12	0	0	1	0

Bowling averages

	Mat	Balls	Runs	Wkts	BBI	Ave	Econ	SR	5w	10
First-class	6	260	149	7	4/53	21.28	3.43	37.1	0	0

Lieutenant Harold Godfrey Bache
Cambridge University/Worcestershire
10th Bn Lancashire Fusiliers
Died 16 February 1916
Aged 26
Left-handed Bat/Slow Left-arm Orthodox

'The first man ever to use the double-handed backhand at
tennis, and a truly great sportsman.'

Harold Godfrey Bache was born on 20 April 1889 in Churchill, Worcestershire, the son of William and Frances Mary Bache, of West Bromwich. He was educated at King Edward VI School in Birmingham and then Caius College, Cambridge. Bache was in the XI at King Edward VI's Grammar School and, although he represented Cambridge on three occasions, he still failed to get his Blue. However, he did get his Blue for both football and tennis, winning the University Lawn Tennis Championship in 1911 and getting his name into tennis history when he was the first man to use a double-handed backhand.

Bache made 20 first-class appearances between August 1907 and July 1910, three for Cambridge University and seventeen for Worcestershire. He made his debut for Worcestershire against Surrey on 22 August 1907 in the County Championship at the County Ground, New Road, Worcester. Bache caught Albert Primrose, (Lord Dalmeny) off the bowling of John Cuff for 5 in the first innings. He scored 9 in his only innings being bowled by Lord Dalmeny (sweet revenge). He also caught Albert Baker off the bowling of John Cuff for 35 and John Crawford off the bowling of Dick Pearson for 9 in the second. The match was drawn. He made his debut for Cambridge University against the visiting Australians on 3 June 1909 at Fenner's. Bache made 0 and 4. The match was drawn. Bache made his final first class appearance for Worcestershire against Kent on 28 July 1910 at the County Ground, New Road, Worcester. It was a inglorious end, as Bache scored two ducks Kent winning by 7 wickets. During his first class career Bache made 270 runs his highest score being 36 against Middlesex on 1 July 1909 at Lords. He also took 3 wickets for 39 his best figures being 2 for 4. He made 5 catches.

Despite only being 5 feet 8 inches tall and weighing 10 stone Harold Bache was also a first-class amateur international centre forward who, had it not been for the war, was destined for major soccer honours. He joined West Bromwich Albion in 1914 and played fourteen games for them, scoring four goals. Long before he moved to the Albion, however, he had also been a good England amateur international, collecting seven caps between 1910 and 1913. In one famous game against France at Ipswich in 1910 he scored seven of England's goals in their 20–0 victory.

On the outbreak of the First World War in October 1914, Bache together with 100 men from the Staffordshire area were posted to the 10th Lincolns (Grimsby Chums) where they formed part of D Company. In the same month Bache starred in a fund-raising match at Blundell Park playing against the 5th Lincolns. In a closely fought match the 10th Lincolns finally came out on top 3–2, with Bache scoring twice. He became a corporal before being commissioned into the 10th (Service) Battalion Lancashire Fusiliers as a second Lieutenant and later promoted to Lieutenant. Bache still appeared in charity games playing for Corinthian F.C. against Aldershot Command and scoring four goals. He was later posted to France and then Belgium as a bombing officer. He was lucky to survive when the barn in which he was being billeted was hit by shell-fire killing 20 and wounding a further 27 members of his battalion. Harold was finally killed by a sniper on 16 February 1916 (some records have him being killed on the 15th however Commonwealth War Graves give the date as the 16th) just after returning from an attempt to regain a lost trench. His body was never recovered and he is commemorated on the Ypres (Menin Gate) Memorial, Panel 33.

After his death, his brother John set up the Bache Memorial Fund in his memory. The fund paid for a permanent memorial in King Edward's School, together with a cup which is still awarded every year to the best sportsman in the school.

Batting and fielding averages

	Mat	Inns	NO	Runs	HS	Ave	100	50	Ct	St
First-class	20	31	1	270	36	9.00	0	0	5	0

Bowling averages

	Mat	Balls	Runs	Wkts	BBI	Ave	Econ	SR	5w	10
First-class	20	114	39	3	2/4	13.00	2.05	38.0	0	0

Lieutenant Colonel Edward Campion
Europeans (India)
Seaforth Highlanders
Died 25 February 1916
Aged 42
Not Known

'It was corruption not the enemy that took him'

Edward Campion was born on 17 December 1873 at Danny Park, Hurstpierpoint, Sussex, the third and youngest son of Colonel William Henry Campion CB VD and Gertrude Campion, née Brand, daughter of the Right Honourable Sir Henry Bouverie William Brand, 1st Viscount Hampden. Educated at Eton before entering Sandhurst, he was commissioned in the 3rd Battalion Royal Sussex Regiment in 1893 but transferred to the Seaforth Highlanders in 1895 and in 1898 was promoted to lieutenant; in 1901 he was promoted to captain. He served in Crete in 1897 and between October 1900 and October 1901 was ADC to the Major General, Infantry Brigade, Aldershot.

Campion saw service during the Nile Expedition of 1898 and was engaged in the battles of Atbara and Khartoum. He also served in the Second Boer War and, later, in India. While in India he made his one first class appearance in a Bombay Presidency match for the Europeans against the Parsees on 21 September 1903 at the Deccan Gymkhana Ground, Poona, scoring 29 and 14. However, it wasn't enough to save the Europeans who went down by an innings and 6 runs.

He travelled to France with his battalion on 23 August 1914 and in October was promoted to major. Mentioned in Sir John French's Despatches (*London Gazette,* 17 February 1915) for valour in the field. He was promoted to temporary lieutenant colonel. A few months later his name appeared in the casualty list as suffering from gas poisoning, near Ypres, in May 1915. He was sent home to be treated and seemed to be recovering well. However, he had a relapse during his convalescence and died from the effects of the gas poison in London on 25 February 1916. He was buried with full military honours at his birthplace, Hurstpierpoint, Sussex, in the Old Cemetery, grave D 108.

The war diary for the incident in which Colonel Campion was gassed is quite telling and worth noting. It wasn't just the Germans who were causing British troops casualties:

2nd May – About 5.30pm enemy sent over cloud of asphyxiating gas – after gas had cleared enemy tried to attack but was repulsed.

4th to 6th May – five men are still suffering from the effects of the gas.

Notes for May 1915:

On 2nd May our respirators were found to be no good being made out of nothing but woollen waistbelts. We lost several men killed from gas. By 24th May the men had quite a good muslin respirator which was more efficacious.

After Major Campion was hospitalized, Captain Hopkinson took over command of the battalion.

Batting and fielding averages

	Mat	Inns	NO	Runs	HS	Ave	100	50	Ct	St
First-class	1	2	0	43	29	21.50	0	0	0	0

Bowling averages

	Mat	Runs	Wkts	BBI	BBM	Ave	SR	4w	5w	10
First-class	1	10	0	-	-	-	-	0	0	0

1093 Private Frederick Percy Hardy
Somerset/MCC
West Somerset Yeomanry
Died 9 March 1916
Aged 34
Left handed bat/Right-arm medium pace

'A sad end for a man confused in heart and mind'

Frederick Percy Hardy was born on 26 June 1881 at Blandford Forum, Dorset. The son of Frederick Hardy and Elizabeth of Blandford, he was educated at the College of Preceptors, Milton Abbas School, Blandford. A talented cricketer, he played for Dorset against Wiltshire on 26 June 1902 in a Minor Counties' Championship match scoring 8 and 2 and taking 3 wickets for 87. Wiltshire finally won by an innings and 32 runs. While little more than a schoolboy at the age of 19 he was tried for Surrey and in two memorable innings for the Surrey Colts in 1901 he scored 141 against Wandsworth, followed by 144 not out, against Mitcham Wanderers. He was on the Oval ground staff in 1900 and in 1903 began to play county cricket for Somerset.

Hardy made 100 first-class appearances, mainly for Somerset between May 1902 and May 1914. The majority were County Championship matches but he also played in University Matches, against Oxford May 1902, May 1904, against Australia in the British Isles in July 1902, June 1909 and June 1912, South Africa in July 1904 and June 1912 and India in the British Isles in July 1911. In addition he played one match for the MCC against Oxford University, on 27 June 1912. He made his first-class debut for Somerset against Oxford University on 15 May 1902 at the University Parks, Oxford and scored 44 in his only innings; he also took 2 wickets for 6, off three overs and caught William Evans off the bowling of Beaumont Cranfield for 6. The match was drawn. In his second match against Australia in the British Isles, played at the County Ground, Taunton on 17 July 1902, he scored 20 and 17 and took a remarkable slip catch to dismiss the great Australian opening batsman Victor Trumper for just 5. The match was drawn. Hardy made one appearance for the MCC on 27 June 1912 against Oxford University at Lords. Hardy made 46 and 1 not out and took 1 wicket in the first innings for 25 off 5.3 overs and a further wicket in the second innings for 16 off 3.3 overs. The match was drawn. He played his final first-class match against Kent on 18 May 1914 at the County Ground, Taunton, scoring 2 and 1, Kent won by 193 runs. During his first-class career he scored 2,743 runs, his highest score being 91 against Kent at Taunton. He also took 91 wickets for 3,216 runs, his best figures being 6 for 82. He made 41 catches. Somewhere in the middle of all this Hardy married Maude Mary Hardy and settled down at 18, Magdalene Street, Taunton. They had two children Frederick (1904) and Winifred (1906).

Hardy enlisted into the ranks of the Somerset Yeomanry on 18 September 1914. However, following an accident involving a car which ruptured his kidneys he was discharged from the Army as unfit.

Mystery has always surrounded Hardy's death. He was found dead on the floor of the public lavatories at King's Cross Station on 9 March 1916. His throat was cut and his own blood-stained knife was discovered by his side. David Frith in his moving and extraordinary book *Silence of the Heart* concludes: 'He had collapsed mentally at the terrifying prospect of returning to the fighting on the Western Front.'

The inquest was held at St Pancras Coroner's Court where the jury returned a verdict of suicide while of unsound mind.

Hardy is buried in Kensal Green (St Mary's) Roman Catholic Cemetery, grave reference 9 (Screen Wall). Worth a visit and a few flowers.

Hardy's story has been very confusing. For years his number was given as 2208 and his regiment as the City of London Yeomanry. I can find nobody of this name who served with the London Yeomanry, nor can I find anyone who served with the Yeomanry called Hardy and with the number 2208. Furthermore, there is no record of him serving in France or any other theatre of war. He also gave his next-of-kin details as his mother, Elizabeth, and not his wife, Maude. If this information is correct, and it comes from his papers lodged at Kew, then maybe his suicide wasn't so much to do with the effects of the war as the effects of a marriage break-up. The only alternative is that he served under an assumed name, as many did, and the confusion came after his death. Also why was his body not returned to Somerset, and what was he doing in London? No medal index card in his name exists, which again means he did not serve abroad.

Batting and fielding averages

	Mat	Inns	NO	Runs	HS	Ave	100	Ct	St
First-class	100	176	8	2743	91	16.32	0	41	0

Bowling averages

	Mat	Runs	Wkts	BBI	Ave	5w	10
First-class	100	3216	91	6/82	35.34	2	0

Lieutenant Gerald Howard-Smith MC
Cambridge University/MCC
6th Bn The South Staffordshire Regiment
Died 29 March 1916
Aged 36
Right-handed Bat/Right-arm Bowler

"His cricket, and general athletic gifts, which had earned him distinction
at Trinity College, Cambridge, he always put at the disposal of his men..."

Gerald Howard-Smith was born on 21 January 1880 at Earls Court, Kensington, London, the son of Judge Howard-Smith and Mrs M. B. Howard-Smith of 11 Alexandra Mansions, Chelsea, London. He was educated at Eton College from September 1893 to July 1899, where he was in the First XI from 1898 to 1899. In his matches against Harrow and Winchester he scored 67 runs in five innings, and took thirteen wickets for 17.92 runs each. In 1899 it was said of him that he 'Bowls straight and fast, and has often been most useful. A powerful hitter, and with better defence would be a dangerous batsman. Works hard in the field, and has done some brilliant things.'

Howard-Smith was also in the Field XI in 1899 and the Mixed Wall in 1898. On leaving Eton in 1899 he went up to Trinity College Cambridge. He played in the Freshmen's match in 1900 and later for the Seniors, but did not get his Blue until 1903. He made twenty first class appearances for Cambridge University and the MCC between May 1900 and July 1903. He made his debut playing for the MCC on 21 May 1900 against Cambridge University at Fenner's. He scored 19 and 18 Cambridge winning convincingly by 10 wickets. He went on to play for Cambridge University against, AJ Webbe's XI, Yorkshire, London County, Worcestershire, South African's, MCC, HD Leveson Gower's XI, Warwickshire, Gentlemen of Philadelphia, Surrey and Sussex. He made his final first class match For Cambridge University against Oxford University on 2 July 1903 at Lords. He made 11 and 0 not out, took 1 wicket for 31 off 9 overs and caught Hugh Wyld off the bowling of Francis Roberts for 19. Oxford won by 268 runs.

He made 189 runs his highest score being 23. He also took 29 wickets for 1279 runs his best figures being 6 for 23. He made 15 catches.

A fine all-round athlete, he also won the high jump against Oxford in 1903, clearing six feet, and becoming President of the Cambridge University Athletic Club. He played county cricket for Staffordshire in the Minor Counties and became a member of the MCC in 1900. He was also a member of the Free Foresters. After leaving Trinity College he was employed by Underhill, Thorneycroft & Smith and Neve & Co., Wolverhampton.

In September 1914, shortly after the outbreak of war, he received a commission as a second lieutenant in the South Staffordshire Regiment. He wrote to his commanding officer at the time, 'I am afraid you will never make a soldier of me, but I am willing to do my best.'

Howard-Smith went to the front with his battalion in March 1915 where he was promoted to lieutenant and became the battalion's bombing officer. He was also known as the Anarchist because of his left wing views. A gallant soldier, he was wounded on three occasions, Mentioned in Despatches on three occasions and awarded the Military Cross in the King's New Year's Honours list for 1916. Howard-Smith died on 29 March 1916 from shrapnel wounds he had received at Merville St Vaast, France.

A comrade later wrote of him:

No one expected Howard-Smith to die. He had been hit several times before, and he hadn't died then! Besides, not an officer or man felt that he could be spared. He was moved to hospital, and the last associations with him were of the usually merry kind. Even a few hours before the setting in of the fatal complications, the CO, on his way to 'leave in U.K.', looked in at the hospital and took a jovial message from the wounded son to his people at home.

Another observed:

His cricket, and general athletic gifts, which had earned him distinction at Trinity College, Cambridge, he always put at the disposal of his men, who eagerly seized upon them. Add to this his undeniably marked boldness and fearlessness, and it will be readily understood that he was as much missed, by all ranks, as any officer could be. In his men's eyes he lived as a loose-limbed hero, and in him they lost a very humorous and a very gallant gentleman.

He is buried in the Aubigny Communal Cemetery extension, grave reference V.A. 2. There is also a memorial plaque in St Mary's Church, Bushbury from his parents.

Batting and fielding averages

	Mat	Inns	NO	Runs	HS	Ave	100	50	Ct	St
First-class	20	33	16	189	23*	11.11	0	0	15	0

Bowling averages

	Mat	Balls	Runs	Wkts	BBI	Ave	Econ	SR	5w	10
First-class	20	2075	1279	29	6/23	44.10	3.69	71.5	1	0

Captain Alexander Gordon Cowie
1st Bn The Seaforth Highlanders (Ross-shire Buffs, The
Duke of Albany's)
Cambridge University/Hampshire/Army
Died 7 April 1916
Aged 27
Right-handed Bat/Right-arm Fast

'The rising smoke of Ruin curls, Shrieks of the wounded,
silence of the dead, A more enlightened age of lead.'

Alexander Gordon Cowie was born on 27 February 1889 at Yeatton House, Hordle, Lymington, Hampshire to Alexander Hugh Cowie, Colonel, Royal Engineers, of Burgoyne House, Stanhope Lines, Aldershot, and Katherine Elizabeth Cowie, née Ward. Cowie was educated at the Summerfields School, Oxford and Charterhouse (under Dr G. H. Rendall), where he was in the XI. He went up to Conville and Caius College Cambridge on 1 October 1909 on an Honorary Entrance Scholarship.

Cowie got his Blue and went on to make 14 first class appearances between May 1910 and June 1914 for Cambridge University, Hampshire and the Army. Cowie made his first class debut for Cambridge University against Surrey on 12 May 1910 at Fenner's. He made 0 not out in his only innings took 5 wickets for 67 off 13 overs in the first innings and 2 wickets for 40 off 12 overs in the second. Cambridge won by 2 wickets. He went on to play for Cambridge against Sussex, Yorkshire, MCC, Gentlemen of England, Oxford University, Surrey and Gloucestershire. He made one first class appearance for Oxford and Cambridge against the Army and Navy on 7 July 1910 at the Officers Club Service Ground, Aldershot. He made 6 not out and 0, took 3 wickets for 46 off 11 overs in the fist innings and 1 wicket for 16 off 6 overs in the second. The Army and Navy won by 6 wickets. He made two first class appearances for Hampshire the first against Derbyshire on 8 August 1910 at Queens Park, Chesterfield in the County Championship. Cowie scored 2 in his only innings and took 2 wickets for 59 off 15.4 overs. He also caught Richard Sale off the bowling of John Newman for 6. He made his second appearance for Hampshire against Lancashire on 11 August 1910 at the County Ground, Southampton. Cowie scored 0 and 1 and took 5 wickets for 94 off 26 overs in the first innings and 2 wickets for 85 off 18 overs in the second. Lancashire won by 5 wickets. Cowie made his final first class appearance for the Army against Cambridge University on 11 June 1914 at Fenner's. He made 27 and 5 being stumped twice by George Wood and took 1 wicket for 27 off 6 overs. Cambridge University won by an innings and 80 runs. During his first class career Cowie made 98 first class runs his highest score being 28 against the Gentlemen of England on 27 June 1910. He also took 58 wickets for 1395 runs his best figures being 6 for 87. He made 6 catches.

Cowie took a commission in the Seaforth Highlanders on the onset of war, rising to the rank of captain. He was wounded in 1915 but soon returned to duty but died of wounds received while serving in Mesopotamia on 7 April 1916.

He is buried in Amara War Cemetery, grave reference I.D.16.

Final Wicket

Before dying Cowie wrote the following poem:

Though not a different land, a different age
Is ours, a different stage:
New characters are on the scene:
Instead of peace, the bright steel's sheen
In lieu of rest, mad Rage:
The warlike clarion's shrill alarms,
The ruthless power of deadly sin:
Round humble cots, round verdant farms
The roar of beasts, the clash of arms,
And o'er the land the battle hideous din:
Thro' hill and dale a storm of discord whirls
The rising smoke of Ruin curls
Shrieks of the wounded, silence of the dead
A 'more enlightened' age – of lead!

Batting and fielding averages

	Mat	Inns	NO	Runs	HS	Ave	100	50	Ct	St
First-class	14	20	6	98	28	7.00	0	0	6	0

Bowling averages

	Mat	Balls	Runs	Wkts	BBI	Ave	Econ	SR	5w	10
First-class	14	1979	1395	58	6/87	24.05	4.22	34.1	5	0

Captain Hugo Francis Wemyss Charteris, Lord Elcho
Surrey
Royal Gloucestershire Yeomanry
Died 23 April 1916
Aged 31
Right-handed Bat

'Despite his position felt the need to do his duty'

Hugh Francis Charteris, Lord Elcho, was born on 28 December 1884 at Wilbury House, Sailsbury, Wiltshire, the son of Hugo Richard Charteris, 11th Earl of Wemyss and Mary Constance, née Wyndham. He was educated at Eton where he was in the XI and played against Winchester on 24 June 1902, but oddly not as a recognised member of the team. Eton won by four wickets. Later he was in the side that played against Liverpool in 1903, the match was drawn.

Charteris only made one first-class appearance for Gloucestershire – against Surrey at the Kennington Oval on 30 May 1910. He played at number nine and was bowled out after scoring a single run in his only innings. Gloucestershire went on to win by six wickets.

He was married to Lady Violet Catherine Manners and was the father of two sons, Francis David Charteris, 12th Earl of Wemyss, and Lieutenant Colonel Martin Michael Charles Charteris, Baron Charteris of Amisfield. He joined the MCC in 1904.

At the outbreak of the war Charteris joined the Royal Gloucestershire Hussars, rising to the rank of captain. He was killed in action at Qatian, Egypt on 23 April 1916. The action is described by Lindsay Bayl in the book *Horsemen, Pass By* (Chapter 3, Mounted in Sinai):

The Affair at el Qatiya was a small and very successful action undertaken by the Ottoman forces against the British forces scattered around el Qatiya and Bir el Dueidar on 23 April 1916. The raid created panic in the British command and highlighted the need for a greater commitment to strengthening the defences of Romani, eventually leading to a battle at that place ....

On 22 April 1916, the 5th Mounted Brigade were routed by just what they were there to prevent: a Turkish surprise attack. The survivors fell back to the canal and the next day the 2nd Light Horse Brigade were ordered to Kantara, Duedir and Romani by forced march, to retrieve the position. A long doggerel poem of my father's, much prized by his fellows and his family, says: The Yeomanry camps told their stories. There were dead men and horses, the occasional one still dying. Stragglers and wanderers, horses stampeding in at the scent of water. Small heaps of cartridge cases beside individuals who had burrowed in the sand and fought to the death. Others were bayoneted through their blankets. Too much of a good thing in beer and wine for officers' messes. Men tortured by Bedouins, garrotted with the thin baling wire used for horse fodder. The Bedouins had hung around the camps cadging food, pretending to be friendly, spying for the Turks; then they killed and stripped the soldiers, crying 'Finish British! Turks Kantara! Turks Port Said! Turks Cairo!' The 6th and 7th Regiments buried 80 Yeomanry at Katia, then eight days later another 300 corpses were found.

Charteris is commemorated on the Jerusalem War Cemetery, Yerushalayim (Jerusalem District) Israel.

His younger brother, Second Lieutenant The Honourable Yvo Alan Charteris, was killed in action in October 1915.

Batting and fielding averages

	Mat	Inns	NO	Runs	HS	Ave	100	50	4s	6s	Ct	St
First-class	1	1	0	1	1	1.00	0	0	0	0	0	0

Bowling averages

	Mat	Balls	Runs	Wkts	BBI	BBM	Ave	Econ	SR	4w	5w	10
First-class	1	-	-	-	-	-	-	-	-	-	-	-

Lieutenant Colonel Francis Henry Browning
Ireland
The Veteran Corps, General Reserve
Died 26 April 1916
Aged 47
Right-handed Bat/Wicket-keeper

'An honourable comrade and true and distinguished sportsman'

Francis Henry Browning was born on 23 June 1868 in Kingstown, Dublin. He was the son of Jeffrey Browning and Julia Mary Smart. He was educated at Marlborough where he was in the XI between 1885 and 1886 averaging 13.00 in the former year and 16.50 in the latter. He also proved himself to be a first class wicket keeper a positioned he continued in for the rest of his cricketing career. He also made an impressive 36 runs in two innings against Rugby School.

After leaving Marlborough he went up to Trinity College Dublin playing in their first XI. A first class batsman he made over 2000 runs in 1889. He was also an excellent wicket-keeper. Between May 1902 and September 1909 Browning made 9 first class appearances for Ireland and 2 the Gentlemen of Ireland. He made his debut for Ireland against London County on 19 May 1902 at Crystal Palace Park, Crystal Palace. He made 49 and 25 and caught Percy May off the bowling of William Harrington for 1 and the famous W G Grace off the bowling of Thomas Ross for 19. He also stumped Leslie Poidevin once again off the bowing of Ross for 5. He went on to play against the MCC, Oxford University, Cambridge University, Yorkshire, South Africa (1907) Gentlemen of Philadelphia (in the British Isles 1908) and Scotland. He made two first class appearances for the Gentlemen of Ireland both against the Gentlemen of Philadelphia during their North American tour of 1909. The first match took place on 17 September 1909 at the Merion Cricket Club Ground, Haverford. Browning made 1 and 0 and caught Francis White off the bowling of George Morrow for 118 and John Evans off the bowling of Oscar Andrews for 8. The Gentlemen of Philadelphia won by an innings and 168 runs. He made his final first class appearance once again for the Gentlemen of Ireland against the Gentlemen of Philadelphia on 24 September 1909 at Germantown Cricket Club Ground, Manheim, Philadelphia. Browning scored 5 and 1 not out and stumped Philip LeRoy off the bowling of William Coffey for 42. The Gentlemen of Philadelphia won by an innings and 66 runs.

During his first class career Browning made 363 first class runs his highest score being 56 against Oxford University on 26 May 1902. He also made 9 catches and 4 stumpings.

He joined the MCC in 1890 and was President of the Irish Rugby Football Union. After leaving University he became a barrister and was Examiner of Titles, Registry of Ireland. In 1912 he also became President of the Irish Football Union. He married Constance Carter, daughter of W. B. Carter and they lived together at 17 Herbert Park, Dublin, County Dublin, Ireland.

Two weeks after the declaration of war, the Irish Rugby Football Corps was established and became part of the Irish Association of Volunteer Training Corps. It was organized along similar lines to the British 'Pals Battalions" system and Browning became the driving forces behind the Corps. As a result largely of his efforts around two hundred, mostly former serviceman enlisted at Lansdowne Road, in D company of the 7th Battalion of the Dublin Fusiliers. They were then split into two groups. The older men and those not considered fir enough for the regular army were sent to Dublin to form a sort of Home Guard. While the fitter men found themselves heading for Gallipoli those that remained walked straight into the Easter Rising.

On Easter Monday 24th April 1916 the 1st VTC (Dublin) unit Browning had helped to form were on an exercise in the Dublin Mountains when they heard that the Easter Rising had started in Dublin. They headed back to Dublin and marched straight into the fighting. The Corps were in civilian clothes with only arm-bands to distinguish who they were. They carried rifles but had not been issued with any ammunition. Their return route led them across the narrow Mount Street Bridge where they came under fire from an Irish Volunteer position at 25 Northumberland Road. Seven of the volunteers were wounded, four of them, fatally. Frank Browning who had been shot on Haddington Road, (Beggers Bush) was rushed to Baggot Street Hospital but died two days after the attack on 26 April 1916. Browning was the only first class cricketer to be killed during the War for Independence and only member of the MCC to have been involved in the 1916 Easter Rising.

Browning had also been a keen rugby player, playing half back for Trinity, Wanderers and Ireland.

He was buried in Dublin's Deans Grange Cemetery South Dublin. His gravestone was erected by the IRFU. They inscribed on the stone,

"He will live in the memory of all as an honorable comrade and distinguished sportsman."

Batting and fielding averages

	Mat	Inns	NO	Runs	HS	Ave	100	Ct	St
First-class	11	22	2	363	56	18.15	0	9	4

Bowling averages

	Mat	Balls	Runs	Wkts	BBI	BBM	Ave	Econ	SR	4w	5w	10
First-class	11	-	-	-	-	-	-	-	-	-	-	-

Although it could be argued that he was not a First World War casualty, I have still decided to include him in the book.

Captain Alexander Basil Crawford
Nottinghamshire/Warwickshire
17th Bn The Prince of Wales's Own (West Yorkshire Regiment)
Died 10 May 1916
Aged 24
Right-handed Bat/Right-arm Fast-Medium

'If anything too brave'

Alex Basil Crawford was born on 24 May 1891 at Coleshill, Warwickshire to Dr Alexander and Mrs Etty Crawford. Alexander Crawford was the doctor at Healswood, Skegby, in 1912. Alex Basil was educated at Nottingham Boys' High School from 14 January 1902 until Easter 1903 and was then moved to Oundle in May 1903 (Laxton House) to complete his education. While there, he was in the cricket XI between 1906 and 1908. On leaving school he studied for the law, passing his final examinations in 1914. He had recently established a practice in Boston, Lincolnshire.

Crawford made 18 first-class appearances for Warwickshire and Nottinghamshire between June 1911 and June 1912 all but 4 in the County Championship. He made his debut for Warwickshire against India in the British Isles on 15 June 1911 at Edgbaston. Crawford made 24 not out in his only innings. He also took 6 wickets for 36 off 13.3 overs. Warwickshire won by 10 wickets. He went on to play for Warwickshire against Derbyshire, Hampshire, Surrey, Gloucestershire and Yorkshire. In 1912 he transferred his talents to Nottinghamshire making his debut for them against the MCC at Lords on 1 May 1912. Crawford made 10 and 35 and took 2 wickets for 98 off 25 overs. The MCC won by an innings and 56 runs. He went on to play for Nottinghamshire against Australia, Leicestershire, Surrey, Kent, Sussex, South Africa and Middlesex. He made his final first class appearance against Lancashire on 27 June 1912 at Old Trafford, Manchester. He made 10 and 6 and caught Reginald Spooner off the bowling of Thomas Wass for 29. The match was drawn. Crawford made 381 first class runs during his career his highest score being 51 against the Australians on 6 May 1912. He also took 21 wickets for 607 runs his best figures being 6 for 36. He also made 5 catches.

At the outbreak of the war, he enlisted into the ranks of the 5th Bn Lincolnshire Regiment. During the early months of 1915 he was commissioned into the Nottinghamshire and Derbyshire Regiment (Sherwood Foresters) before transferring into the 17th (2nd Leeds Pals) Bn West Yorkshire Regiment and being promoted to captain. The 17th was a Bantam battalion which specialised in men who were under the normal regulation minimum height of five feet three inches. After initial training, they joined 106 Brigade, 35th Division in June 1915 at Masham, North Yorkshire. They then moved to Salisbury Plain for final training in August and were initially ordered to embark for Egypt in late 1915. However, that order was rescinded and instead the battalion proceeded to France on 1 February 1916, landing at le Havre. In May the battalion was in the Neuve Chapelle-Ferme du Bois Sector and on 10 May 1916 Crawford was killed in action. On the same day the Divisional History recorded, 'A few quiet days followed, during which Captain A. B. Crawford and Captain G. S. de Williams were unfortunately killed in the line by shell burst.'

His Divisional Commander wrote to his parents:

Your boy was doing splendidly. He had been commanding his company for some time and was if anything too brave. He is a great loss to his Regiment, I might say to the Division. I wish we had more like him.

His battalion commander also wrote:

He was a most able Company Commander, a most gallant man, full of dash and pluck, and would have risen high in the army.

Crawford was buried in St Vaast Military Cemetery, Richebourg-l'Avoue, Pas de Calais, France, grave reference III.F.8.

Batting and fielding averages

	Mat	Inns	NO	Runs	HS	Ave	100	50	Ct	St
First-class	18	27	4	381	51	16.56	0	1	5	0

Bowling averages

	Mat	Balls	Runs	Wkts	BBI	Ave	Econ	SR	5w	10
First-class	18	902	607	21	6/36	28.90	4.03	42.9	1	0

Lieutenant Harry Broderick Chinnery
Surrey/Middlesex/MCC
13th Bn The King's Royal Rifle Corps
Died 28 May 1916
Aged 40
Right-handed Bat/Slow Left-arm Orthodox

'He was in the middle of his men, encouraging them in a moment of danger'

Harry Broderick Chinnery was born on 6 February 1876 at Teddington in Middlesex. He was the second son of Walter M. Chinnery of Hatchford Park, Cobham, Surrey and was educated at Eton College where he was in the Eton XI in 1894 and 1895. A first-class bat, he managed to top the averages in his final season and scored 75 and 64 in the annual match against Harrow. Chinnery made 66 first class appearances, mostly in the County Championship and mostly for Surrey and Middlesex although he did turn out for the MCC, Gentlemen (against the Players), CI Thornton's England XI, AJ Webbe's XI, HDG Leveson-Gower's XI, Oxford University Authentics and the Gentlemen of England. Chinnery made his fist class debut against Leicestershire on 3 May 1897 at the Kennington Oval, Kennington. He made 1 in his only innings. Surrey winning by an innings and 285 runs. He made his debut for the MCC against Yorkshire on 26 August 1897 at North Marine Road, Scarborough. He made 12 and 24 and caught George Hirst of the bowling of Gilbert Jessop for 11. Hirst had his revenge however catching Chinnery in his fist innings, catching and bowling him in his second. Yorkshire won by 69 runs. He made his first appearance for Middlesex in the County Championship on 8 June 1899 against Sussex at Lords. Chinnery made 46 and 13 and caught the famous C B Fry (Wisden Cricketer of the Year 1895) the Sussex opener off the bowling of John Hearne (Wisden cricketer of the year 1892) for 94. Middlesex won by 5 wickets. He made his final first class appearance on 30 June 1910 for the Gentlemen of England against Oxford University. At The Saffrons, Eastbourne. Chinnery scored 15 and 21, The Gentlemen of England winning the match by 113 runs. During his first class career Chinnery made 2536 runs, including 4 centuries his highest score being 165 for the MCC against Oxford University 20 May 1901 in his second innings. He had previously made 105 in his first. He also took 12 wickets for 554 runs his best figures being 4 for 51 and made 25 catches.

ETON XI, 1895.

R. W. Mitchell,   A. E. Lubbock,   F. R. Robertson,   A. S. Ward,
A. W. F. Reid,   H. W. Kenkwell,   C. C. Pilkington,   A. M. Hollins,   H. B. Chinnery.
A. B. Legard,   C. T. Allen.

On leaving school he became a member of the Stock Exchange (1898) and a partner in his late father's firm, Chinnery Brothers. After taking up fulltime work, Chinnery found making time for cricket difficult and he retired from the game in 1910. Wisden commented that his 'early retirement was much to be regretted, but he continued to assist the Eton Ramblers and I Zingari'.

At the outbreak of the First World War he was commissioned in the 13th Bn King's Royal Rifle Corps. He was killed in action in France on 28 May 1916. The circumstances of his death were later related by his company commander:

He was in the middle of his men, encouraging them in a moment of danger. He was killed by the last shell fired at a night working party, which was advancing our line nearer to the enemy. It was a trying night, and he did splendidly all the earlier part of it in keeping them at their work and keeping up their spirits.

His colonel also wrote:

He will be greatly missed by his brother-officers and the men of his Company, while by his death the Battalion has lost a valuable officer whom it would be difficult to replace.

His loss was clearly felt as shown by a letter sent to his family from a rifleman who sent it 'on behalf of the fellows in his Platoon and myself':

Mr Chinnery was loved and respected by all of us that he came in contact with. While in charge of the Machine Gun Section in England, and last Autumn out here, he was looked upon as something more than a good officer and a perfect gentleman; and although he had only been with No. 6 Platoon six weeks, yet no Officer was more respected and had their complete confidence.

Many are the stories told by his men of his splendid courage and coolness on Sunday night (the night of his death); always first in his area to go to a wounded man, to assist and cheer with a kindly word.

Chinnery is buried in Berles-Au-Bois Churchyard Extension, Pas de Calais, France, grave reference Sp. Mem.

His brother Esme Chinnery was also killed in action on 18 January 1915 (see earlier).

Batting and fielding averages

	Mat	Inns	NO	Runs	HS	Ave	100	Ct	St
First-class	66	108	6	2536	165	24.86	4	25	0

Bowling averages

	Mat	Runs	Wkts	BBI	Ave	5w	10
First-class	66	554	12	4/51	46.16	0	0

Lieutenant Cecil Abercrombie
Hampshire/Navy
Royal Navy, HMS *Defence*
Died 31 May 1916
Aged 29
Right-handed Bat/Right-arm Medium

'Nothing could have made him miss that fight'

Cecil Abercrombie was born on 12 April 1886 in Mozufferpore, India. The son of Walter D. Abercrombie (Indian Police) and Kate E. Abercrombie, he was educated at Allan House, Guildford, Berkhamstead School and Britannia Royal Naval College, Dartmouth. A first-class sportsman he was in both the Cricket XI and Rugby XV at his schools and Britannia.

In 1902 he was posted to HMS *Hyacinth* and was one of the brave party under the command of Captain the Honourable Horace Hood, which attacked the Mullah's stronghold at Illig, on the east coast of Somalia on 21 April 1904, finally destroying the Mullah's force once and for all.

A free hitting batsman Abercrombie made 16 first class appearances mainly for Hampshire in the County Championship but also made 2 appearances for the Navy and 1 for the Army and Navy. He made his first class debut for the Army and Navy against Oxford and Cambridge on 7 July 1910 at the Officers Club Service Ground, Aldershot. He scored 40 not out and 13 not out. The Army and Navy won by 6 wickets. He next represented the Navy against the Army on 30 May 1912 at Lords. He made 37 and 100 the first of 4 centuries he was to make during his career. He also took 3 wickets for 27 off 8.4 overs and caught Trevor Spring off the bowling of Arthur Skey for 30 in his fist innings and took 1 wicket for 86 off 19 overs and caught Francis Wyatt off the bowling of Hugh Orr for 6 in the second. Despite Abercrombie's best efforts the Army still won by 6 wickets. He made one more appearance for the Navy against the Army on 3 June 1913 at Lords. The Army won again this time by 10 wickets. He made the first of his 13 appearances for Hampshire on 30 June 1913 for Hampshire against Oxford University at the County Ground Southampton. He scored 126 and 39, took 1 wicket for 81 off 19 overs and caught Richard Twining off the bowling of Hamilton Smith for 33. The match was drawn. Abercrombie also represented Hampshire against, Worcestershire, Essex, Yorkshire, Middlesex, Gloucestershire, Sussex, Somerset and Kent. Against Essex on 24 July 1913 at the County Ground, Leyton, Hampshire followed on 317 behind in what looked like a hopeless situation. Abercrombie made 165 in his second innings stand with George Brown (140) they put on 305 for the seventh wicket. The match was eventually drawn. During his first class career Abercrombie made 1126 runs his highest score being 165 against Essex on 24 July 1913 including 4 centuries and 2 fifties. He also took 8 wickets for 329 runs his best figures being 3 for 27. He made 11 catches. Abercrombie also played rugby for Scotland on six occasions between 1910 and 1913.

At the outbreak of the First World War Abercrombie was on the Mediterranean station but returned home quickly. He was eventually transferred to HMS *Defence* and was with that ship when it sailed out to confront the German High Seas Fleet at Jutland. During the battle *Defence* was the flagship of Rear Admiral Sir Robert Arbuthnot, leading the First

Cruiser Squadron. *Defence* was hit by two salvoes from the German ships that caused the aft 9.2-inch magazine to explode. The resulting fire spread via ammunition passages to the adjacent 7.5-inch magazines, which detonated in turn. The ship exploded at 6.20pm with the loss of all hands (about 903). Abercrombie went down with her.

One of Abercrombie's former captains later wrote to his wife:

> You and I are in a position to realise to the full the loss that the country has sustained by the death of your husband. I feel perfectly sure that it was his gun that was being fired when the ship gave her final plunge – directly I heard of it, I felt it.

Cecil Halliday Abercrombie is commemorated on the Plymouth Naval Memorial, Panel 10.

Batting and fielding averages

	Mat	Inns	NO	Runs	HS	Ave	100	50	Ct	St
First-class	16	31	3	1126	165	40.21	4	2	11	0

Bowling averages

	Mat	Balls	Runs	Wkts	BBI	Ave	Econ	SR	5w	10
First-class	16	551	329	8	3/27	41.12	3.58	68.8	0	0

Lieutenant Commander John Matthew Murray
Royal Navy, HMS *Queen Mary*
Died 31 May 1916
Aged 42
Right-handed Bat/Right-arm Fast

'His love of the Navy matched only by his love of Cricket'

John Matthew Murray was born on 23 June 1873 in Aberdeen. The son of James and Christian Murray of Aberdeen, he was educated at Aberdeen Grammar School, Galashiels Academy and Heriot Watt Engineering School.

He played in one first-class match – on 3 June 1913 for the Royal Navy against the Army at Lord's. He scored 0 and 29, the Army finally winning by 10 runs.

He was appointed to superintend the construction of the battleship *King Edward VII*, joining the ship when it was commissioned in 1915. He served for a number of terms during his twenty-year career at the Dartmouth Naval College as an engineer instructor. Seconded to the battleship HMS *Queen Mary*, he was lost together with fifty-seven officers and 1,209 men when the ship blew up during the Battle of Jutland on 31 May 1916.

HMS *Queen Mary* was the last battle-cruiser built by the Royal Navy before the First World War. She was completed in 1913 and took part in the Battle of Heligoland Bight as part of the Grand fleet in 1914. She made an unsuccessful attempt to intercept the German force that bombarded the North Sea coast of England, including Scarborough, in December 1914, but failed to find them. During the Battle of Jutland HMS *Queen Mary* was hit twice by the German battle-cruiser SMS *Derfflinger* during the early part of the battle. Her magazines exploded shortly afterwards, sinking the ship. Only eighteen survivors were finally picked up. Commander John Matthew Murray wasn't among them.

Murray is commemorated on the Portsmouth Naval Memorial, Panel 11.

Batting and fielding averages

	Mat	Inns	NO	Runs	HS	Ave	100	50	Ct	St
First-class	1	2	0	29	29	14.50	0	0	0	0

Bowling averages

	Mat	Balls	Runs	Wkts	BBI	BBM	Ave	Econ	SR	4w	5w	10
First-class	1	-	-	-	-	-	-	-	-	-	-	-

Lieutenant Charles Dennis Fisher
Oxford University/Sussex/MCC
Royal Navy, HMS *Invincible*
Died 31 May 1916
Aged 38
Right-handed Bat/Right-arm Off-break

'a safe and steady batsman'

Charles Dennis Fisher was born on 19 June 1877 in Blatchington Court, Blatchington, Sussex, England, the ninth of the eleven children of Herbert William Fisher and his wife Mary Louisa (née Jackson). His father had been tutor to King Edward as Prince of Wales at Oxford. Charles and his brothers were all educated at the Dragon School and he was in the school football XV from 1889 until 1891, and the cricket XI during the same years. He sang at the school concert: 'one of the best voices'. He was first in the Westminster Challenge in 1889, was in the Westminster Cricket XI from 1893 to 1896 and was captain in the two last years; he was in the association football XI during the same time. In 1896 Fisher got a Westminster Studentship at Christ Church, Oxford, and the Slade Exhibition; he played in the Freshmen's Association match in March 1896. In cricket he turned out for the Harlequins and Sussex. In 1901 he got his Studentship at Christ Church, having obtained a First Class in Honour Moderations 1898, and Second in Greats in 1900, in which year he also got his cricket Blue.

Charles Fisher made 21 first class appearances for Oxford University, Sussex and the MCC. He made his debut for Sussex in the County Championship on 25 July 1898 at the County Ground, Hove against Middlesex. He made 6 and 2 (batting with CB Fry who made 108 and 123 passing his 4000 runs in first class cricket) He went on to play for Sussex against Kent, Gloucestershire, Somerset and Hampshire before making his debut for Oxford University against Somerset on 18 May 1899 at The University Parks, Oxford. He made 0 in his only innings however Oxford still won by 83 runs. He went on to play for Oxford against Sussex, Surrey Sussex, MCC and Cambridge University. He returned to Sussex playing against Lancashire on 13 August 1900 at the Central Recreation Ground, Hastings. He made 3 and 5, Lancashire won by 10 wickets. He also played against the MCC, Worcestershire, Gloucestershire, Somerset, Oxford University and Yorkshire. He made 1 appearance for the MCC against Oxford University on 4 June 1903 at the University Parks, Oxford. Fisher scored 0 and 24. The MCC won by 24 runs (a member in 1904). He made his final first class appearance for Sussex against Oxford University on 25 June 1903 at the County Ground, Hove. He scored 2 and 14, Sussex won by 117 runs. Fisher made 429 first call runs his highest score being 80 against Worcestershire at Hove in 1901. He also took 8 wickets for 242 runs, his best figures being 2 for 8. He made 7 catches. Deciding on an academic career, he was elected tutor in Christ Church in 1903 and served as Senior Censor from 1910 to 1914.

At the beginning of the First World War he joined the Royal Army Medical Corps Motor Ambulance and served with them on the Western Front as an orderly and interpreter, being Mentioned in Despatches. He was then transferred to the Royal Naval Volunteer Reserve with a lieutenancy and appointed to HMS *Invincible* on board which he was killed in action at the Battle of Jutland on 31 May 1916. Commander Dannreuther, one of the six survivors, wrote:

> We hit the *Derfflinger* with our first salvo, and continued to hit her entirely owing to the perfect rate Charles gave us. Everything was going splendidly at the time, and it was entirely due to Charles' cool head and excellent judgement that our firing was so effective. I saw him only a few minutes before the end – a smile on his face and his eyes sparkling. He was by my side and in the highest spirits, when there was a great explosion and shock, and when I recovered consciousness I found myself in the water. Ship and crew had disappeared.'

A writer to the *Morning Post* commented:

> Charles Fisher towered a very prince among his fellows. He was of huge stature and splendid in bearing. The formidable shoulders, the active hands, the swinging gait, the characteristic toss of the foot, above all the noble face and head, and the mobile piercing eye made his an unforgettable figure. He loved games and the men who played them, and cricket and cricketers above the rest. A Blue in 1900, he also played occasionally for Sussex, his native county. He was the life of many a team on tour and of innumerable matches, never happier or more likely to win than in an uphill fight, for, besides strength and skill, he brought a peculiar personal power to the game, so that he could stampede a losing side into victory, and he was a great cricketer partly because he was a great man. His special study was Tacitus, on whom he did much valuable work as editor for the Oxford Press.

Charles Fisher's body was never recovered and he is commemorated on the Portsmouth Naval Memorial, Panel 24.

Batting and fielding averages

	Mat	Inns	NO	Runs	HS	Ave	100	50	Ct	St
First-class	21	33	1	429	80	13.40	0	1	7	0

Bowling averages

	Mat	Balls	Runs	Wkts	BBI	Ave	Econ	SR	5w	10
First-class	21	436	242	8	2/8	30.25	3.33	54.5	0	0

678 Corporal William Henry de Rockstro Malraison
Transvaal
1st South African Horse
Died 31 May 1916
Aged 39
Not Known

'Always ready for a fight'

William Henry de Rockstro Malraison was born on 4 December 1876 at Wepner in the Orange Free State, South Africa, the son of Bernard de Rockstro Malraison and Annie Georgina Malraison of 10/11 Adelaide Buildings, Johannesburg.

Malraison made 2 first class appearances for the Transvaal both in the Currie Cup in 1904. He made his debut for the Transvaal on 25 November 1904 against Natal at Albert Park, Durban. He scored 13 in his only innings and caught John Budgen off the bowling of Richard Norden for 27. Transvaal won by 15 runs. He made his second appearance on 30 December 1904, once again in the Currie Cup, against Griqualand West at the Old Wanderers' Ground in Johannesburg. Malraison scored 28 in his only innings. Transvaal won by 67 runs. He had also umpired two first-class matches in 1895, again in the Currie cup.

Malraison died of fever in East Africa on 31 May 1916 while serving with the 1st South African Horse, which was part of the 2nd East African Division under Major General J. van Deventer. He is buried in the Dar Es Salaam Cemetery, Joint Grave 5, L. 12.

Batting and fielding averages

	Mat	Inns	NO	Runs	HS	Ave	100	50	Ct	St
First-class	2	2	0	41	28	20.50	0	0	1	0

Bowling averages

	Mat	Balls	Runs	Wkts	BBI	BBM	Ave	Econ	SR	4w	5w	10
First-class	2	-	-	-	-	-	-	-	-	-	-	-

109632 Lance Sergeant Leonard Cecil Leicester Sutton
Somerset
C Squadron 4th Canadian Mounted Rifles Battalion
Died 3 June 1916
Aged 26
Left-handed Bat/Left-arm Slow-Medium

'Leicester Sutton was most attractive both as boy and man. Straight, capable, fearless and good-humoured, he was a fine type of Brutonian and Englishman'

Leonard Cecil Leicester Sutton, known as Leicester to his friends, was born on 14 April 1890 at Half Way Tree, Kingston, Jamaica. He was the second of four children, two boys and two girls, born to Leonard Sutton JP, who ran a plantation at Mandeville, Jamaica, and Kathleen Mary Sullivan Sutton. Leicester returned to England in 1904 to attend the King's School, Bruton, Somerset. A first-class sportsman, he was in the cricket, football and hockey XIs, captaining the football team in his last term. He was in the cricket XI for five consecutive years and was described in the school magazine as:

a good hard-hitting bat with plenty of strokes, notably an excellent off-drive, a magnificent shot just behind point, a good late cut and a fine powerful pull.

He always opened the bowling for the school team and was a left-arm slow-medium pace bowler. Sutton made 17 first class appearances between 17 May 1909 and 15 July 1912 all for Somerset, fifteen in the County Championship, one against South Africa in the British Isles and one against the Australians in the British Isles. He made his debut for Somerset against Hampshire on 17 May 1909 at the County Ground, Southampton, while he was still at school. He scored 3 and 30, which was to be his highest score in first-class cricket, Hampshire winning by six wickets.

Leicester left King's School in December 1910 and commenced work as an estate agent, working for Lord Hylton's Estate Agent at Kilmersdon, Somerset. He continued to appear for Somerset playing against Worcestershire, Lancashire, Middlesex, Surrey, Sussex, Hampshire, Kent, Gloucestershire, Yorkshire, Derbyshire, South Africa, Australia and Northamptonshire. His final first-class match was on 15 July 1912 against Derbyshire at the County Ground, Derby in which he scored zero and 1. He also caught Charles Root off the bowling of Ernest Robson for 3 and Thomas Forrester off the bowling of Norman Hardy for 23. Of his total of 171 first-class runs, his highest score was 30 against Hampshire on 30 May 1909. He made 10 catches.

Shortly before the outbreak of war, Leicester moved to Canada where he continued to work in the real estate business, this time in Toronto. He enlisted in the ranks of the Central Ontario Regiment as Private 109632 on 30 December 1914. The battalion moved into the trenches in November 1915 near St Yves, south of Messines, before moving to a position near Hill 63, Ploegsteert.

On 2 June 1916 there was a short notice visit by Major General Malcolm Smith Mercer, GOC of 3rd Canadian Division, who was making a personal reconnaissance of the front line. He was accompanied by Brigadier General Victor Arthur Seymour Williams, commander of 8 Canadian Brigade. They were met at battalion headquarters by Lieutenant Colonel Ussher who was to guide them through their reconnaissance.

Around 8.30am the enemy commenced a very heavy bombardment; it was to be the opening shots in the Battle of Mount Sorrel (2nd to 13th June, 1916). A shell exploded near the visiting party, deafening Major General Mercer and slightly wounding Brigadier General Williams. The war diary records 'The bombardment increased and we were bombarded in the front line, support and reserves by thousands of shells of every description.'

The bombardment continued for four and a half hours, finally ceasing about 1.00pm. The Germans then detonated three mines, followed by a massed infantry attack. The war diary describes the attack:

> an order came down the line to withdraw. At this time the whole front line was flattened out and there were no trenches of any description, and very few of the battalion that were able to carry on.

Major General Mercer was wounded again and died from his wounds while they tried to evacuate him. Brigadier General Williams and Lieutenant Colonel Ussher were taken prisoner with over 100 of their men. As a result of the attack, the Germans gained between 300 to 700 yards along the Canadian front. The following day only three officers and seventy-three men could be accounted for. Unfortunately, Leicester was not amongst them. At first he was reported missing, however as time passed it was assumed that he had been killed on the day of the attack, 3 June 1916. It wasn't until after the war that the exact circumstances of Leicester's death were revealed by a returning comrade. The school magazine, *The Dolphin*, reported his words:

> he was very severely wounded by shrapnel at Zillebeke, a singularly desolate and forbidding locality not far from Ypres. Carried to a German dug-out he was as well treated as circumstances would allow, and remained conscious and cheerful for a time. Next morning he died in the presence of Corporal White of his regiment, through whom this information is obtained. He was very popular with all ranks.

In 1919 *The Dolphin* wrote of him again:

> Leicester Sutton was most attractive both as boy and man. Straight, capable, fearless and good-humoured, he was a fine type of Brutonian and Englishman. The best form of sympathy with his relatives in their long anxiety and grievous loss is the assurance that his memory is honoured here and his example remembered.

Leicester's body was never recovered and he is commemorated on the Ypres (Mein Gate) Memorial, Panels 30–32

Batting and fielding averages

	Mat	Inns	NO	Runs	HS	Ave	100	50	Ct	St
First-class	17	29	5	171	30	7.12	0	0	10	0

Bowling averages

	Mat	Balls	Runs	Wkts	BBI	BBM	Ave	Econ	SR	4w	5w	10
First-class	17	6	6	0	-	-	-	6.00	-	0	0	0

Captain Francis Sydney Gillespie
Surrey
13th Bn (3rd South Downs) The Royal Sussex Regiment
Died 18 June 1916
Aged 26
Left-handed Bat

'a model of energy and cheerfulness in the performance of his duty,
and was always ready to help anyone who was in trouble'

Francis Sydney Gillespie was born on 26 March 1889 in Upper Norwood, Surrey. He was the son of John and Eleanor A. Gillespie of 102 West Hill, Sydenham, London and was educated at Dulwich between 1902 and 1904, but only made the second XI. He did, however, play for London County, Surrey and the Wanderers. In 1912, playing for Surrey's Second XI, he made 105 against Wiltshire at the Oval and averaged more than 60 overall. In the same season he made a remarkable 217 not out for Wanderers. He made 6 first class appearances for Surrey in 1913 and played six first-class matches for them during the 1913, 5 in the County Championships one against Scotland in England. He made his debut against Gloucestershire on 19 May 1913 at the Kennington Oval. He made 14 and 72 and caught Cyril Sewell off the bowling of John Hitch for 16. Surrey won by 260 runs. He went on to play against Essex, Warwickshire and Hampshire. He made his final first class appearance against Scotland on 13 June 1913 once again at the Kennington Oval. Gillespie scored 30 and 33 and caught James Sorrie off the bowling of Gilbert Reay for 36. Surrey won by 7 wickets. Gillespie made a total of 249 first class runs his highest score being 72 against Gloucester on 19 May 1913. He made 2 catches.

Gillespie didn't pursue his cricketing career but chose instead to go into the city with his father. On 11 August 1914, at the outbreak of the war, Gillespie joined the Honourable Artillery Company as a private before taking a commission in the 13th Bn Royal Sussex Regiment. With 200 others he went through the School of Musketry at Hythe and passed out top with a certificate of distinction. Francis Gillespie was promoted to captain in July 1915 and went to the front in March 1916. Badly wounded when out on patrol in no man's land on 18 June 1916, he died from his injuries a few hours later.

The war diary explains the feelings of the battalion over his death:

17 June: With the exception of dropping a few 'minnies' on the head of Plum Street at 6.30pm, the enemy was very quiet. Usual machine-gun and rifle fire at night. Our trench mortars registered in the afternoon. Usual patrols reconnoitred at night. Captain Gillespie and Lieutenant Ripley wounded during patrol, the former seriously.

18 June: Enemy very quiet except for machine-gun and rifle fire at night. Our rifle grenades were active both during the day and night. Captain Gillespie reported died of wounds. This was a great blow to the Battalion and one very much felt by all ranks. This officer was a model of energy and cheerfulness in the performance of his duty, and was always ready to help anyone who was in trouble. His funeral took place at Merville and was attended by Second Lieutenants Jones and M. Sparks.

He is buried at the Merville Communal Cemetery, Grave Reference VII, A. 19.

Batting and fielding averages

	Mat	Inns	NO	Runs	HS	Ave	100	50	Ct	St
First-class	6	11	0	249	72	22.63	0	1	2	0

Bowling averages

	Mat	Balls	Runs	Wkts	BBI	BBM	Ave	Econ	SR	4w	5w	10
First-class	6	-	-	-	-	-	-	-	-	-	-	-

Second Lieutenant Major William Booth
England/Yorkshire/MCC
15th Bn The Prince of Wale's Own (West Yorkshire
Regiment)
Died 1 July 1916
Aged 29
Right-handed Bat/Right-arm medium-fast

'England lost one of the most promising and charming young
cricketers it was ever my lot to meet.'

Major William Booth was born on 10 December 1886 at Pudsey, Yorkshire, the son of James and Louise Booth, of Town End House, Pudsey. He was educated at Fulneck and played his early cricket for them. He was then associated with Pudsey St. Lawrence and the Wath Athletic Club, which played in the Mexborough League, which he captained. He appeared regularly for the Yorkshire Second Eleven in 1907 and the two following seasons, and in 1908 received his first trial for the county against Somerset at Dewsbury but failed to impress. He did not, however, secure a regular place in the team until two years later. Booth played in 162 first-class matches and appeared in two tests for England between June 1908 and August 1914. He played most of matches for Yorkshire in the County Championship but also turned out for the MCC, Lord Londesborough's XI, Players (against the Gentlemen) and GL Jessops XI. He made his debut in the County Championship on 29 June 1908 against Somerset at Savile Ground, Dewsbury. Booth scored 1 in his only innings, and caught Albert Lewis off the bowling of John Newstead for 20. Yorkshire won by eight wickets. His most memorable match probably came against Worcestershire on 22 May 1911 at the County Ground, New Road, Worcester when he scored a remarkable 210 runs, including twenty-three 4s, in his first and only innings. The match was also well known for the nine wickets for 41 off fifteen overs taken by George Hirst in the first innings, all but two of the Worcestershire line-up; the exceptions were Ernest Bale, bowled by John Newstead for 2, and Frederick Hunt not out, zero. He also caught William Burns, (killed in action on 7 July 1916), off the bowling of George Hirst for 28.

One Yorkshire newspaper described his performance: 'the ease with which he made his runs was astonishing. Few finer examples of off-driving and square cutting can have been seen ...'

He also played in two Tests for England, his first being against the South Africans on 13 December 1913 at Lord's, Durban. Booth scored 14 in his only innings and took two wickets for 38 off ten overs. England won by an innings and 157 runs. His second Test appearance came on 27 February 1914 at St George's Park, Port Elizabeth, once again against South Africa. He scored 32 in his only innings and took one wicket for 43 in the first innings and four wickets for 49 in the second. England won by ten wickets.

His bowling was also later described in a newspaper as possessing 'a free, natural action and his height enabled him to extract considerable bounce as many county sides found to their cost.'

On his return from South Africa, Booth discovered he had been selected as one of *Wisden*'s five cricketers of the year (1914 edition).

In total he scored 1,125 runs for Yorkshire and took seventy-four wickets during the 1911 season. During the 1913 season he made over 1,000 runs and took 167 wickets. However, his 1914 season wasn't as successful, only taking 141 wickets for 18 runs per wicket.

During the latter part of the 1914 season, Booth formed a deadly partnership with his fellow Yorkshire bowler Alonzo Drake (1884–1919). Together they bowled without a break against Gloucestershire at Bristol, Booth taking twelve wickets for 89. Against Somerset at Weston-Super-Mare, Booth took five wickets for 77. The 1914 season ended prematurely due to the war; by that time Booth had taken 157 first-class wickets at an average of 17.85. He made his final first class appearance on 31 August 1914 for Yorkshire against Sussex at the County Ground, Hove. He scored 1 and 9 and took 2 wickets for 104 off 28 overs. The match was drawn.

At the outbreak of the First World War, Major Booth enlisted in the ranks of the 15th Battalion West Yorkshire Regiment (Leeds Pals) and was quickly promoted to sergeant. On 16 July 1915 he was commissioned second lieutenant. He served in Egypt before being sent to the Western Front. He was sent to the Somme and went 'over the top' with his battalion on 1 July 1916, the first day of the Battle of the Somme, at la Cigny and was lost to sight and sound. An account of his death was later related by another cricketer, Abe Waddington (Yorkshire and England, 1893–1959). Abe who had been in the second wave of the attack was hit and fell into a shell hole where he found Booth badly wounded and dying. He held him in his arms until he expired. Although stretcher-bearers were able to rescue Waddington later in the day, Booth's body remained in no man's land until the spring, when he was finally recovered and buried at Serre Road No. 1 Cemetery, grave reference I.G.14.

Yorkshire's President, Lord Hawke, summed up the loss of Booth: 'England lost one of the most promising and charming young cricketers it was ever my lot to meet.'

Batting and fielding averages

	Mat	Inns	NO	Runs	HS	Ave	100	50	6s	Ct	St
Tests	2	2	0	46	32	23.00	0	0	0	0	0
First-class	162	243	39	4753	210	23.29	2	21		120	0

Bowling averages

	Mat	Inns	Balls	Runs	Wkts	BBI	BBM	Ave	Econ	SR	4w	5w	10
Tests	2	3	312	130	7	4/49	5/92	18.57	2.50	44.5	1	0	0
First-class	162		25189	11953	603	8/47		19.82	2.84	41.7		43	9

Lieutenant William Magee Crozier
Dublin University
9th Bn (Tyrone Volunteers) The Royal Inniskilling Fusiliers
Died 1 July 1916
Aged 42
Right-handed Bat

'The most caring officer I ever served with'

William Magee Crozier was born on 5 December 1873 at Roebuck Hall, Dundrum, County Dublin. He was the second of three sons of Francis Crozier, a solicitor, and Catherine, née Magee. In September 1886 he was sent to Repton School in Derbyshire to be educated. A first-class athlete, he was in both the football and cricket XIs in 1892. While at Repton he made 113 runs with an average of 7.53. *Lillywhite's Cricketers' Annual* commented that William Crozier 'Played respectably once or twice, but, on the whole, was most disappointing.'

In November 1892 William went up to Trinity College Dublin and did well academically, becoming a Scholar of the College. He played in three matches against county opposition for his university. The first was against Gloucestershire on 21 June 1894 when he scored 0 and 3, Gloucestershire winning by nine wickets. He played against them again on 14 June 1897, William not doing too well once again with 5–1. The match is better remembered for WG Graces' ill-tempered outburst against the umpires (although he did score 121 in his only innings in the match). Gloucestershire won by an innings and 92 runs. None of these, unfortunately, were first-class matches. However, the situation changed in 1895 when Crozier was selected to play for the University in his debut first-class match against Leicestershire. The match was played on 13 June 1895 and Crozier scored four before being run out in his first innings and three before being out lbw to the bowling of Hillyard in the second. Leicester won by 126 runs.

Crozier graduated in 1897 and shortly afterwards was called to the Bar, becoming a successful barrister in Dublin. At the beginning of the First World War, Crozier took a commission as a second lieutenant in the 9th Bn (Tyrone Volunteers) Royal Inniskilling Fusiliers, which was part of 36th (Ulster) Division. He was killed in action on 1 July 1916 during the first day of the Battle of the Somme. For their attempts to capture the Schwaben Redoubt, to the north of the German fortress village of Thiepval, the 36th (Ulster) Division was awarded four Victoria Crosses, one of which went posthumously to Captain Eric Norman Frankland Bell, another officer of 9th Inniskillings.

William Crozier's body was never recovered or identified and he is commemorated on the Thiepval Memorial, Pier and Face 4 D and 5 B.

Final Wicket

Batting and fielding averages

	Mat	Inns	NO	Runs	HS	Ave	100	50	Ct	St
First-class	1	2	0	7	4	3.50	0	0	0	0

Bowling averages

	Mat	Runs	Wkts	BBI	BBM	Ave	SR	4w	5w	10
First-class	1	42	0	-	-	-	-	0	0	0

Sergeant David Kennedy
Scotland
17th Bn The Highland Light Infantry (Glasgow Commercials)
Died 1 July 1916
Aged 25
Right-handed Bat

'Loved his children and men with equal zeal'

David Kennedy was born on 10 July 1890 at Uddingstone, Lanarkshire and educated at Uddingston Grammar School and Jordanhill Teacher Training College before becoming a teacher at Townhead School, Glasgow.

Kennedy played one first-class match for Scotland against Ireland on 16 July 1914 at the Observatory Lane, Rathmines, Dublin. He scored 1 and 10. Despite Kennedy's poor showing Scotland still won by 11 runs.

At the outbreak of the war he enlisted into the ranks of the 17th Battalion, the Glasgow Commercials, Highland Light Infantry (HLI) part of 97 Brigade in 32nd Division. A natural leader he was soon promoted to sergeant and sent to France with his battalion and prepared for the battle of the Somme. The battalion spent the night before the battle of the Somme in huts at Bouzincourt before making their way to the front line via trenches between Aveluy and Authuille and taking up their battle positions at 6.25am. Their objective was to seize and hold a position called the Leipzig Salient, which was part of the German front line. The regimental history takes up the story:

> At 7.30am the 17th HLI on the right and the 16th HLI on the left crept out of their trenches and moved close up to the German wire under cover of the barrage … When they rose up they immediately came under heavy enfilade fire from the ruins of Thiepval; the wire was intact but for the occasional gaps which were covered … They had with them sappers, carrying Bangalore torpedoes, for it had been realized that the barrage had not been effective on the wire in this sector, but they were all shot down on the wire … The 17th HLI pushed on towards the second line, but the failure on their left exposed their flank and the leading companies were all shot down. The remainder consolidated the first line – the Leipzig Redoubt and held it.

James Turnbull of the 17th Battalion earned a posthumous Victoria Cross for this action. The HLI casualties were twenty-two officers and 447 other ranks. Amongst those killed was the schoolteacher and sergeant, David Kennedy. His body was later recovered and he is commemorated at Lonsdale Cemetery, Authuille, Grave Reference III. D. I.

Batting and fielding averages

	Mat	Inns	NO	Runs	HS	Ave	100	50	Ct	St
First-class	1	2	0	11	10	5.50	0	0	0	0

Bowling averages

	Mat	Balls	Runs	Wkts	BBI	BBM	Ave	Econ	SR	4w	5w	10
First-class	1	-	-	-	-	-	-	-	-	-	-	-

Second Lieutenant John Alexander Hellard
Somerset
3rd (attd 1st) Bn Prince Albert's (Somerset Light Infantry)
Died 2 July 1916 (1 July 1916)
Aged 34
Right-hand bat/Right-arm Fast-Medium

'He travelled halfway around the world to protect his mother country'

John Alexander Hellard was born on 20 March 1882 at Stogumber, Somerset, the second son of Edwin Hellard, a solicitor, and Alice Jane of The Knoll, Stogumber, Somerset. He was educated at the King's School, Canterbury, from January 1896 to July 1900, where he won a Junior Scholarship in July 1896 and a Senior Scholarship in July 1900. He was in the

1900

Fraser H. I. Wilson L. R. Cooper E. L. Massey J. A. Hellard E. C. Green
    E. Finn   R. C. Paris   B. C. Covell   H. E. Green F. A. Husbands

rugby XV in 1899 and the cricket XI in 1900, playing against Merchant Taylors School and scoring 3 in his only innings and taking one wicket (he also caught G. J. Langley); the match was drawn. On 4 July 1900 he played against Felsted School, taking two wickets but not scoring in his single innings. Once again the match was drawn. Hellard was also a member of the Officers Training Corps (OTC).

John Hellard played two first-class matches for Somerset in the County Championship in June 1907 and June 1910. He made his debut for Somerset on 10 June 1907 at the Recreation Ground, Bath, against Worcestershire he scored 0 and 15. Worcester won by six wickets. In his second match, played on 23 June 1910, at the Country Ground, New Road, Worcester – once again against Worcester – he scored 3 in his only innings. The match was drawn.

On leaving school he became a solicitor's clerk, being admitted as a solicitor in June 1906 and practising in Colombo, Ceylon. While he was there he served with the Town Guard Artillery from 1914 to 1915. Later in 1915 he returned to England and was commissioned as a second lieutenant in the Somerset Light Infantry on 27 April 1915. He landed in France with his battalion on 21 May 1915.

On the morning of 1 July 1916 the 1st Battalion was part of 11 Brigade and at 7.30am left its trenches to the south-east of the village of Serre in support of the 1st Battalion The Rifle Brigade. The scene was later described by a brother officer:

> The sight was magnificent, line after line of men advancing at a slow trot towards the German line with hundreds of shells, ours for the most part, bursting behind the German lines.

Heavy machine-gun fire forced them off to the left and they found themselves in the German trenches in the position known as the Quadrilateral. Those men who continued advancing were shot down from behind by German troops emerging from their deep dugouts. Very early on there were only two officers still unwounded and by 1.30pm they too had been struck down.

By the end of the day twenty-six officers and 438 other ranks were listed as casualties. Unfortunately, among the casualties was second lieutenant John Hellard. His official date of death is 2 July 1916 but it is almost certain that he was killed on the 1st.

He is buried in the Serre Road, Cemetery No. 2, Grave Reference II. A. 1.

Batting and fielding averages

	Mat	Inns	NO	Runs	HS	Ave	100	50	Ct	St
First-class	2	3	0	18	15	6.00	0	0	0	0

Bowling averages

	Mat	Balls	Runs	Wkts	BBI	BBM	Ave	Econ	SR	4w	5w	10
First-class	2	-	-	-	-	-	-	-	-	-	-	-

Final Wicket

Lieutenant Cecil Argo Gold
Middlesex
5th Bn Princess Charlotte of Wales's (Royal Berkshire Regiment)
Died 3 July 1916
Aged 29
Right-handed Bat

'He was a splendid example of an officer, keen hard working and
always had the battalion's comfort and welfare in his mind'

Cecil Argo Gold was born on 3 June 1887 at St Pancras, London. The son of Argo and Mary Gold, of 31 Gloucester Square, Hyde Park, London, he was educated at Eton College where he was in the XI in 1905 and 1906. He had a batting average of 26.60 in his first season and 21.50 in his second. In his matches against Winchester and Harrow he made 186 runs, averaging 23.25. In 1906 he made his highest score of 57 against the old enemy, Harrow. After leaving Eton, he went up to Magdalen College Oxford to read History, where he played in the Freshmen's match, scoring zero and 35 but failed to get a Blue. On leaving Oxford he became a solicitor.

Gold made one first-class appearance on 29 July 1907 for Middlesex against Hampshire at the County Ground, Southampton. He didn't bowl and made 2 ducks. Hampshire won by 161 runs. He also played for Berkshire in the Minor Counties in 1906 and G. N. Foster's XI in 1907. Gold, joined the MCC in 1907, was also a very keen amateur golfer.

On the outbreak of the war Gold took a commission in the 5th Royal Berkshire Regiment where he was promoted to lieutenant and became the adjutant. He was mentioned in General Haig's Despatches for bravery and distinguished conduct in the field (30 April 1916) before being killed in action on 3 July 1916. His death was explained by a brother officer in a letter to his family:

> The battalion was ordered to attack and capture a certain village just before it got light. As soon as the companies had gone I went forward to the German trenches with Cecil and my orderly, who was I believe also killed. Cecil was killed on the road and instantaneously, as he was shot through the brain. I cannot tell you what a blow his death is to all of us and how much we will miss him. He was a splendid example of an officer, keen, hardworking and always had the battalion's comfort and welfare in his mind. I never saw him depressed and his unselfishness knew no bounds. As an adjutant he was splendid and cannot be replaced and we will all miss very much him I know. Cecil fagged for my brother at Austen-Leigh's. His body lies buried in Aveluy Cemetery just north of Albert. I will have a cross erected.

He is buried in Aveluy Communal Cemetery Extension, Somme, France, Grave reference H. 38.

Batting and fielding averages

	Mat	Inns	NO	Runs	HS	Ave	100	50	4s	6s	Ct	St
First-class	1	2	1	0	0*	0.00	0	0	0	0	0	0

Bowling averages

	Mat	Balls	Runs	Wkts	BBI	BBM	Ave	Econ	SR	4w	5w	10
First-class	1	-	-	-	-	-	-	-	-	-	-	-

Second Lieutenant Alban Charles Phidias Arnold
Cambridge University/Hampshire
11th (attd 8th) Bn The Royal Fusiliers (City of London Regiment)
Died 7 July 1916
Aged 23
Right-handed Bat/Wicket-keeper

'He would probably have developed into a cricketer of very high class'

Alban Charles Phidias Arnold was born on 19 November 1892 at Tattenhall, Cheshire. The son of the Reverend Charles Lowther Arnold and Mary Delamere Arnold, of Holy Trinity Vicarage, Fareham, Hampshire, he was educated at Twyford School near Winchester where he was in the First XI. From Twyford he went to Malvern, playing for the College in 1909 and 1910 when he topped the averages with 44.33.

He went up to Magdalene College Cambridge in 1911 and played in the Freshmen's match in 1912 and in the Seniors' in 1913. However, he did not obtain his Blue until 1914 when he scored a disappointing 22 and 0 against Oxford. Arnold made 22 first class appearances between June 1912 and August 1914 mainly for Hampshire and Cambridge University but also turned out for the Free Foresters. He made his début first-class appearance against South Africa on 3 June 1912 at F. P. Fenner's Ground, Cambridge. He scored 10 and 11 and stumped Louis Tancred off the bowling of Norman Holloway for 94. South Africa won by ten wickets. He went on to represent Cambridge University against Hampshire, Middlesex, MCC and Oxford University, The following month on 1 July 1912 he made his debut for Hampshire against Surrey at the Kennington Oval in the County Championship. He made 2 in his only innings, the match was drawn due to the weather. He went on to play for Hampshire on a further 15 occasions against Surrey, Oxford University, Worcestershire, Sussex, Cambridge University, Essex, Middlesex, Nottinghamshire, Lancashire, Derbyshire, Somerset and Warwickshire. He made his final first class appearance for Hampshire against Kent on 31 August 1914 at Dean Park, Bournemouth in the County Championship. He scored 54 in his only innings. Hampshire won by an innings and 83 runs. He made 836 first class runs, including seven 50s, his highest score being 89 for Cambridge University against the MCC on 2 July 1914. He made 13 catches. Wisden said of him 'He would probably have developed into a cricketer of very high class'.

At the outbreak of the First World War Arnold enlisted into the 11th Battalion Royal Fusiliers, later transferring to the 8th. He was commissioned as a second lieutenant and was killed in action at Ovillers-la-Boisselle during the Battle of the Somme on 7 July 1916.

His body was never recovered and he is commemorated on the Thiepval Memorial, Pier and Faces 8C, 9A and 16A.

His brother, Edward Gladwin Arnold, a lieutenant in the Royal Field Artillery, was also killed in action on 21 March 1918.

Batting and fielding averages

	Mat	Inns	NO	Runs	HS	Ave	100	50	Ct	St
First-class	22	35	2	836	89	25.33	0	7	13	2

Bowling averages

	Mat	Balls	Runs	Wkts	BBI	BBM	Ave	Econ	SR	4w	5w	10
First-class	22	6	0	0	-	-	-	0.00	-	0	0	0

Second Lieutenant William Beaumont Burns
Worcestershire/MCC
1st Bn The Worcestershire Regiment
Died 7 July 1916
Aged 32
Right-handed Bat/Right-arm fast

'dashing, hard-hitting batsman'

William Beaumont Burns was born on 29 August 1883 at Rugeley, Staffordshire, and was educated at the King's School, Ely, where he played in the XI. William had a natural flair for cricket and, at the tender age of sixteen, played for Staffordshire in the Minor Counties' Championship. He made a remarkable 217 first class appearances between May 1903 and August 1913 mostly for Worcestershire in the County Championship but he also turned out for the MCC, HK Foster's XI, Gentlemen (against Players), The Rest (against England) and Lord Londesborough's XI. He made his debut for Worcestershire against Oxford University on 8 May 1903 at the University Parks, Oxford. He scored 3 and 35 and caught Robert Darling off the bowling of Albert Bird for 23. Oxford University won by 59 runs. He went on to play against Cambridge University at Fenner's and the Gentlemen of Philadelphia at the County Ground, Worcester during the 1903 season. However, he was unable to play in the Country Championships because he had yet to qualify.

In 1904 Burns appeared for Worcestershire on nineteen occasions. He scored 834 runs at 26.00, his best scoring coming against Oxford University when he made a free-hitting 165 in 180 minutes. He had a poor 1905 however, but in 1906 he returned to form, hitting 1,206 first-class runs at 43.07, with another innings of 165 against Oxford among the three centuries he scored that season.

His form quickly came to notice and he travelled with the MCC on their New Zealand Tour the following winter. His form with the bat was poor, only twice passing 50 during his eleven innings. He did, however, take his maiden wicket when he dismissed the Wellington player Harold Monaghan, caught Percy May for 17.

As with his 1905 season, 1907 was a poor one for Burns. The following four seasons, however, saw his form return once again. He hit over 1,000 first-class runs in 1908, making three centuries along the way. In 1909 he scored over 500 runs in five matches, making his career best score of 196 against Warwickshire. Together with Ted Arnold, Burns shared a remarkable fifth-wicket stand of 393, which remains a Worcestershire record for this wicket.

Wisden described Burns as a 'dashing, hard-hitting batsman'. However, they were not quite so complimentary about his bowling which they thought had to be considered suspect: 'the fairness of his delivery was often questioned – and not without good reason'.

In fact 1908 saw Burns develop as a bowler. He made 633 deliveries claiming sixteen wickets at 28.50 which included 6 for 110 against Hampshire. During the next three seasons he made around 2,000 deliveries per season taking 145 first-class wickets while recording his career best figures of 7 for 58 for the Gentlemen against the Players at the Oval in July 1910. Although 1912 had been another poor season, scoring a poor (for Burns) 599 and only taking six wickets in twenty-two matches, the following season he recovered, taking forty-two first-class wickets at 30.81, as well as scoring a creditable 866 runs at 27.06 and made over a century (102) not out against Gloucestershire. Burns also claimed six wickets in an innings against both Hampshire and Somerset. He made his final first class appearance for Worcestershire against Somerset on 28 August 1913 at the County Ground Taunton. He scored 4 in his only innings, took 6 wickets for 41 off 12.4 overs in the first innings and 1 for 26 off 9 overs in the second. He also caught the Somerset openers John Daniell off the bowling of Robert Burrows for 26 and William Hyman again off the bowling of Burrows for 14. Worcestershire won by an innings and 35 runs. Some people considered Burns to be faster than the great Harold Larwood, but this was tempered by the fact that many were suspicious of his style. He joined the MCC in 1911.

At the conclusion of the 1913 season he settled in Canada. In 1914 he enlisted in the ranks of the Canadian Infantry at Valcartier, Quebec, as private 25916, later being promoted to corporal. Returning to England he received a commission as a second lieutenant in the 1st Bn Worcestershire Regiment. He was killed in action at Contalmaison on 7 July 1916 during the Battle of the Somme together with his Worcestershire team-mate Arthur Isaac (Killed in action 7 July 1916). The regimental history gives an account of the action:

At about 2pm the enemy were heavily reinforced and commenced a powerful attack. The German artillery pounded the ruins held by the Worcestershires, a fierce machine-gun fire was directed onto the village from the untaken trenches on both flanks, and strong bombing parties of the enemy worked down from the higher ground. Fighting stubbornly from house to house, the survivors of the three companies were forced back. The position was clearly untenable but there was no thought of surrender. A desperate struggle raged round the ruins of the church, where a party of the Worcestershire, inspired by two brave subalterns, 2nd Lt A. W. Isaac and 2nd Lt W. B Burns, fought on till all were overwhelmed.

He has no known grave and is commemorated on the Thiepval Memorial, Pier and Face A5, 6C.

His next of kin was given as Mrs Edwards, sister, Fernbank, Merthyr, Vale Farm, South Wales.

Batting and fielding averages

	Mat	Inns	NO	Runs	HS	Ave	100	Ct	St
First-class	217	374	23	9479	196	27.00	12	147	0

Bowling averages

	Mat	Runs	Wkts	BBI	Ave	5w	10
First-class	217	6334	214	7/58	29.59	8	1

Second Lieutenant Arthur Whitmore Isaac
Worcestershire
5th (attd 1st) Bn The Worcestershire Regiment
Died 7 July 1916
Aged 42
Right-handed Bat

A wonderful man to know

Arthur Whitmore Isaac was born 4 October 1873 at Powick Court, Worcestershire. The son of John Swinton Isaac of Boughton Park and Mrs Isaac, he was educated at Harrow and Oriel College Oxford but failed to represent the XI. In 1889 Isaac became a partner in the firm of Berwick Ledmore & Co. and when it amalgamated with the Capital and Counties Bank, he was appointed one of the local directors.

He played for Worcestershire in the Minor Counties before making his first class debut. He made a total of 52 first class appearances between May 1899 and May 1913 almost all for Worcestershire in the County Championship. He made his debut on 25 May 1899 for Worcestershire against Oxford University at the University Parks, Oxford. He made 1 in his only innings. Worcestershire won by 7 wickets. He only played for Worcestershire occasionally until 1903 when he played for the county on fourteen occasions, making 279 runs at an average of 13.28; it was the only time he made 200 runs in a season. Isaac never made a century but did make three half-centuries, his highest score being 60 against Hampshire in 1904. He also played in 2 matches against the visiting South Africans on 15 July 1901 (drawn) and 2 June 1904 (Worcestershire won by 137 runs) and twice against the Gentlemen of Philadelphia 13 July 1903 (Worcestershire won by 215 runs) and 9 July 1908 (Gentlemen of Philadelphia won by 95 runs). He made his final first class appearance for HK Foster's XI against Oxford University on 15 May 1913 at the University Parks, Oxford. Isaac scored 6 and 43. Oxford University won by 157 runs. During his first class career he made 1136 runs his highest score being 60 against Hampshire on 9 June 1904. He made 9 catches.

He was also a member of the Worcestershire Hunt but was prone to 'Rider's Cramp'. A sidesman at St John's Church, he took a great deal of interest in church affairs in the parish and was President of St John's Working Men's Club. He gave useful service as a member of the Royal Albert Orphanage, assisted other philanthropic institutions and identified himself also with the works of the Conservative Party in St John's, becoming chairman of the party's ward committee. Isaac also wrote a history of the Worcester Old Bank. In 1899 he married Lucy, only daughter of the Reverend Foley Vernon, Rector of Shrawley, Worcestershire.

Arthur Isaac received a commission as a second lieutenant in the 5th Bn Worcestershire Regiment in July 1915 before transferring to the 1st Battalion and become their bombing officer. He was killed in action on 7 July 1916 together with another Worcestershire County Cricket Club player, William Burns (Killed in action 7 July 1916).

His body was never recovered and he is commemorated on the Thiepval Memorial, Pier and Face 5A and 6C.

He left a widow and two sons. His brother, Captain John Isaac, and his brother in law, Colonel Woodhouse, were also killed during the war.

Batting and fielding averages

	Mat	Inns	NO	Runs	HS	Ave	100	Ct	St
First-class	52	87	5	1136	60	13.85	0	9	0

Bowling averages

	Mat	Balls	Runs	Wkts	BBI	BBM	Ave	Econ	SR	4w	5w	10
First-class	52	-	-	-	-	-	-	-	-	-	-	-

Lieutenant Frank Street
Essex
9th Bn Royal Fusiliers (City of London Regiment)
Died 7 July 1916
Aged 46
Right-handed Bat/Right-arm Medium

'A good bat, with an extremely pretty style, and a steady Bowler'

Frank Street was born on 31 May 1870 in Randolph Crescent, Maida Vale, London, the second son of John Bamfield Street, a barrister, and Eliza Martha Ellen, née Wren. Educated at Westminster School and Christ Church College Oxford, where he was a Scholar, he was in the Westminster XI in 1888 and 1889. In 1888 he was top of the batting averages and second in bowling and, in 1889, became captain of the XI and was second in batting and third in bowling averages. It was said of him at school that he was 'A good bat, with an extremely pretty style, and a steady bowler'.

At Oxford he failed to get his Blue for cricket but did get it for association football. He made 9 first class appearances between May 1898 and August 1899, all for Essex in the County Championship. He made his debut against Surrey on 16 May 1898 at the County Ground, Leyton. Street scored 26 in his only innings and caught Henry Wood off the bowling of Frederick Bull for 14. Essex won by 6 wickets. Essex won by six wickets. He went to play against Sussex, Leicestershire, Warwickshire, Derbyshire, Hampshire, Kent and Gloucestershire. He made his final first class appearance against Leicestershire on 7 August 1899 at Grace Road, Leicester. He scored 76 in his only innings and caught Charles Trafford off the bowling of Frederick Bull for 37. Essex won by 223 runs. He made a total of 246 first class runs his highest score being 76 against Leicestershire on 7 August 1899. He made 4 catches.

On leaving Oxford he became a schoolteacher at the Forest School before becoming a house master for Fircroft House, Uppingham School. During that time he also found time to marry Marie Willoughby. At the outbreak of the war, and despite being over age, Street enlisted in the ranks and served as a sergeant before being commissioned in the 9th Bn Royal Fusiliers.

Street went out to France with his battalion on 14 November 1915. On 7 July 1916, during the Battle of the Somme, the battalion attacked in the area of Mash Valley. The 9th Fusiliers succeeded in capturing and holding the first and second lines close to Ovillers, but suffered heavy casualties. One of the casualties was Lieutenant Frank Street who was shot dead by a sniper while clearing some woods.

His body was never recovered and he is commemorated on the Thiepval Memorial, Pier and Face 8 C 9 A and 16 A.

Probate was granted to his brother, John Gwynne Street, a chartered accountant, on 26 September 1916. Street left £3,932-14s-7d.

Batting and fielding averages

	Mat	Inns	NO	Runs	HS	Ave	100	Ct	St
First-class	9	11	0	246	76	22.36	0	4	0

Bowling averages

	Mat	Balls	Runs	Wkts	BBI	BBM	Ave	Econ	SR	4w	5w	10
First-class	9	10	14	0	-	-	-	8.40	-	0	0	0

Captain Oswald Eric Wreford-Brown
Gloucestershire
9 Bt Northumberland Fusiliers
Died 7 July 1916
Aged 38
Right-handed Bat

'The captain had a heart like a lion'

Oswald Eric Wreford-Brown was born on 21 July 1877 at Clifton, Bristol, the sixth son of William and Clara Jane Wreford-Brown of 5 Litfield Place, Clifton. Educated at Waynflete, Durdham Down and Charterhouse School between 1891 and 1896, he was in both the cricket and association football XIs. After leaving school he became a member of the Stock Exchange in 1902. A keen cricketer, he made one first-class appearance for Gloucestershire County Cricket Club against Middlesex on 14 June 1900 at Lord's, scoring five runs in his first innings; Gloucestershire won by 7 wickets. Wreford-Brown also played for the Old Carthusians.

He emigrated to Canada where he remained for four years. Shortly before the outbreak of the war he returned to England and trained with the Inns of Court Regiment. He was then commissioned into the 9th Bn Northumberland Fusiliers on 8 November 1914 and subsequently became a captain. He was wounded by a shell in the Quadrangle Trench, near Fricourt, on 5 July 1916 and died in a casualty clearing station two days later. Wreford-Brown was buried in Corbie Communal Cemetery, near Amiens, the following day.

His commanding officer later wrote:

None gave his life with greater gallantry or showed greater contempt for danger. No one was more solicitous for the welfare of his men who loved him so well.

A former colonel with whom Oswald had served also took the trouble to write to his family:

Nobody could possibly be more unselfish or so unsparing of himself. He treated his company like his children. All our men, who spent two years nearly with him, will be the better for it, for he gave them such a splendid example of always playing the game.

One of his sergeants also wrote:

A stouter heart I never knew. He was a Britisher absolutely, and never flinched. He was everyone's favourite.

One of his men wrote, 'The captain had a heart like a lion'.
A Charterhouse master put his feelings into words:

To some of us older ones here … this is the worst knock we have had, and that's saying a good deal. We shall never forget the keenest and cheeriest of Carthusians.

Oswald Wreford-Brown's grave is in Corbie Communal Cemetery Extension, grave reference Plot 1, Row B, Grave 48.

His brother, Captain Claude Wreford-Brown DSO, also serving in the Northumberland Fusiliers, had been killed on 25 May 1915.

Batting and fielding averages

	Mat	Inns	NO	Runs	HS	Ave	100	50	Ct	St
First-class	1	1	0	5	5	5.00	0	0	0	0

Bowling averages

	Mat	Balls	Runs	Wkts	BBI	BBM	Ave	Econ	SR	4w	5w	10
First-class	1	-	-	-	-	-	-	-	-	-	-	-

Major Sir Foster Hugh Egerton Cunliffe, 6th Baronet
Middlesex/Oxford University
13th Bn The Prince Consort's Own (Rifle Brigade)
Died 10 July 1916
Aged 40
Left-handed Bat/Left-arm Medium

'As a batsman he had a fine, free style ...'

Foster Hugh Egerton Cunliffe was born on 17 August 1875 in Belgravia, Westminster, London, the son of Sir Robert Cunliffe, 5th Baronet, of Acton Park, Denbighshire, and his wife, the former Eleanor Sophia Egerton Leigh, daughter of Egerton Leigh. Educated at Eton College and New College Oxford, Cunliffe was in the Eton XI in 1893 and 1894, and in his four Public School matches obtained thirty-five wickets for 10.17 runs each; he also took eleven for 74 against Winchester in 1893 and thirteen for 94 against Harrow in 1894. Cunliffe made 56 first class appearances between March 1895 and June 1904 mostly for Oxford University and Middlesex but he also turned out for, Gentlemen (against Players) Oxford University Past and Present (against Australia), The MCC, AJ Webb's XI, and I Zingari. He played cricket for Oxford between 1895 and 1898, obtained his Blue as a Freshman and was made captain in 1898. He made his debut for Oxford University on 20 May 1895 against Somerset at the University Parks, Oxford. He scored 13 and 3 and took 2 wickets for 31 off 12 overs. Oxford won by 1 wicket.

Wisden said of him:

As a batsman he had a fine, free style, and he excelled as a left-handed medium-pace bowler, having a good length and sending down a difficult ball that came with his arm.

He made his debut for Middlesex against Surrey on 15 July 1897 at Lords. He scored 2 and 4 and took 4 wickets for 144 runs off 54 overs.

Surrey won by 8 wickets. He made his final first class appearance for I Zingari against the Gentlemen of England on 6 June 1904 at Lord's. He scored 12 in his only innings and took 2 wickets for 58 runs off 16 overs.

I Zingari won by 6 wickets. During his first class career he made 1053 runs his highest score being 70. He also took 235 wickets for 5120 runs his best figures being 8 for 26. He made 25 catches.

He played for Middlesex between 1897 and 1903 and for the MCC from 1899 to 1903. Cunliffe was a fine left-handed batsman and a left-arm medium pace bowler. In 1895 he became a member of the MCC and served on the committee from 1903 until 1906.

Cunliffe became a Fellow of All Souls Oxford and a lecturer in history at Oxford University, writing *The History of the Boer War.* He inherited the baronetcy on the death of his father in 1905.

During the First World War he served in the 13th Bn The Rifle Brigade reaching the rank of major and died of wounds at Ovilliers-la-Boiselle on 10 July 1916.

He was buried at Bapaume Post Military Cemetery, Albert, Somme, France, Grave Reference Plot I, Row G, Grave 3.

Final Wicket

Batting and fielding averages

	Mat	Inns	NO	Runs	HS	Ave	100	Ct	St
First-class	56	85	16	1053	70	15.26	0	25	0

Bowling averages

	Mat	Balls	Runs	Wkts	BBI	Ave	Econ	SR	5w	10
First-class	56	11304	5120	235	8/26	21.78	2.71	48.1	15	5

Private Joseph Williams
Marylebone Cricket Club
10th Bn The Cheshire Regiment
Died 10 July 1916
Aged 24
Left-handed Bat

'A Great Lover of the Game, just liked to be near it'

Joseph Williams was born in 1892 at Bromborough Pool, Cheshire, and began his cricketing career with the Bromborough Pool Cricket Club. He went on to play for two seasons in the Liverpool and District league in which, at the tender age of eighteen, he took almost 200 wickets. His talents came to notice and he went on to play for Cheshire in the Minor Counties' Championship, making his debut during the 1909 season. During the 1912 season he began to play for the MCC (in non-first-class matches) while working as a groundsman at Lord's.

Williams played in one first-class match for the MCC against Kent on 9 May 1914 at Lords. He scored 11 which included a partnership of 39 for the ninth wicket with former Test player Jack Hearne. He was dismissed by another test player Colin Blythe for 8 in his second. Kent won by an innings and 19 runs. His bowling wasn't too impressive, conceding 26 runs from his three overs.

During the war Williams served as a private in the 10th Bn Cheshire Regiment and was killed in action at Thiepval on 10 July 1916 during the Battle of the Somme.

His body, like those of thousands of others, was never recovered and he is commemorated on the Thiepval Memorial, Pier and Face 3 C and 4 A.

Batting and fielding averages

	Mat	Inns	NO	Runs	HS	Ave	100	50	Ct	St
First-class	1	2	1	19	11*	19.00	0	0	0	0

Bowling averages

	Mat	Balls	Runs	Wkts	BBI	BBM	Ave	Econ	SR	4w	5w	10
First-class	1	18	26	0	-	-	-	8.66	-	0	0	0

Lieutenant Claude Ludovic Hickman Mulcahy
Natal and South Africa
2nd South African Infantry (B Company)
Died 11 July 1916
Aged 30

'Here lies a splendid soldier, a devoted son'

Claude Ludovic Hickman Mulcahy was born on 26 June 1886 at Little Headington, Oxfordshire, the son of Captain Henry Hickman Mulcahy, late King's Own Scottish Borderers, and Annie Margaret Mulcahy, of Estcourt, Natal, South Africa.

He played in one first-class match in the Currie Cup on 15 March 1911 for Natal against the Orange Free State at Lord's No. 4 Durban, scoring 2 not out in his first innings. He didn't bat in the second. Natal won by five wickets.

Mulcahy also played for Northern Natal against the MCC at Settlers Park, Ladysmith, on 4 February 1914. He scored 17 during his first innings and did not bat in the second. The match was drawn. This wasn't a first class match.

He was killed in action at Bernafay Wood on the Somme on 11 July 1916 and is commemorated at the Corbie Communal Cemetery Extension, Plot 1, Row C, Grave 47.

On his grave his parents have had inscribed: 'Here lies a splendid soldier, a devoted son'.

NATAL.
Winners of Currie Cup Tournament, 1911.

[Photo by The Bower Studio, Durban.
G. C. Anderson, L. D. Dalton, H. Morley, L. R. Tuckett, J. L. Cox, C. D. Savile, D. K. Pearse.
C. N. Mulcahy, H. W. Taylor, Rev. C. D. Robinson, W. K. Thomson, S. V. Samuelson.
D. J. Nicol, E. B. Morris.

Batting and fielding averages

	Mat	Inns	NO	Runs	HS	Ave	100	50	4s	6s	Ct	St
First-class	1	1	1	2	2*	-	0	0	0	0	0	0

Bowling averages

	Mat	Runs	Wkts	BBI	BBM	Ave	SR	4w	5w	10
First-class	1	17	0	-	-	-	-	0	0	0

11225 Private Lachlan Donald Mcintosh Sinclair
Transvaal
1st Bn The Black Watch (Royal Highlanders)
Died Between 11 July and 13 July 1916
Aged 37
Right-handed Bat/Right-arm Medium Pace

'He played the game to the very end'

TRANSVAAL.
Winners Currie Cup Tournament, 1904-5.

[Photo by Alf. F Hosking, Capetown.

F. Smith (umpire), E. G. McDonald, G. A. Faulkner, R. O. Schwarz, W. Hazelhurst, W. A. Shalders, R. W. Norden, D. Sinclair, F. Hearne (umpire).
J. J. Slatem, J. H. Sinclair, P. W. Sherwell, L. J. Tancred, T. T. Cradock.
J. H. Piton (manager).

Lachlan Donald Mcintosh Sinclair (some sources have his name as just Donald Mcintosh Sinclair) was born on 3 September 1878 at Cape Town, Cape Province, South Africa.

He made two first-class appearances for Transvaal in January 1904 and March 1905 both in the Currie Cup. He made his debut against the Orange Free State on 1 January 1904 at the Ramblers Cricket Club Ground, Bloemfontein. Playing alongside his more famous brother, James Hugh Sinclair.[1] He scored 26 in his one innings and took 2 wickets for 10 runs off 11

1. James Hugh Sinclair did more than anyone to put South African cricket on the map. Between 1896 and 1911 he played in twenty-five tests for South Africa. In 1898–99 he scored 86 (as an opener) at Johannesburg and followed with a brilliant 106 at Cape Town (South Africa's first Test hundred) against the all-conquering England side led by Lord Hawke. At Cape Town he also took six for 26 and three for 63. In 1901 he toured England. Sinclair not only excelled at cricket; he also played rugby for South Africa and England, and was a skilled hockey and football player.

overs in the first innings and 2 wickets for 35 runs off 7 overs in the second. He also caught Richard Worsley (killed in action 4 May 1917) the Orange Free State opener off the bowling of Gordon White (killed in action 17 October 1918) for 2. Transvaal won by an innings and 327 runs. Sinclair made his second appearance on 16 March 1905, against Rhodesia at the Old Wanderers Ground in Johannesburg. Sinclair was out for a duck in his first and only innings and, although he took no wickets, he did catch Frederick Brooks off the bowling of Richard Norden for 61. Transvaal won by an innings and 170 runs.

Returning to Britain at the outbreak of war, he enlisted in the ranks of The Black Watch (Royal Highlanders). After training he travelled with his regiment to France on 22 December 1915. Sinclair was killed in action at Glatz Redoubt, Trones Wood between 11 and 13 July 1916.

He has no known grave and is commemorated with thousands of others on the Thiepval Memorial, Pier and Face 10A.

Batting and fielding averages

	Mat	Inns	NO	Runs	HS	Ave	100	50	Ct	St
First-class	2	2	0	26	26	13.00	0	0	2	0

Bowling averages

	Mat	Balls	Runs	Wkts	BBI	Ave	Econ	SR	5w	10
First-class	2	108	57	5	3/22	11.40	3.16	21.6	0	0

Private William Eric Carlsson
Western Province
1st Regiment South African Infantry
Died 14 July 1916
Aged 24
Not Known

'A true South African'

William Eric Carlsson was born in January 1892 in Cape Town, Cape Province, South Africa and was the son of Oscar and Margaret Carlsson of 5 Howglen Villa, Albert Road, Tamboers Kloof, Cape Town.

Carlsson played four first-class matches for Western Provinces all in the Currie Cup during the 1911 season. He made his debut on 13 March 1911 at Lord's No. 4, Durban, against Eastern Province. He scored 3 and 24, and caught Frederick Hippert off the bowling of Frank Bond for 0 and William Glisson off the bowling of Frank Bond for 35. Eastern Province won by 5 wickets. He went on to play against Border on 15 March, Western Province won by 40 runs, Natal on 17 March, Natal won by 4 wickets. He made his final first class appearance against Griqualand West on 24 March 1911. He scored 1 in his only innings, Western Province winning by an innings and 116 runs. During his first class career he scored 54 runs his highest score being 24 against Eastern Province on 13 March 1911. He also made 4 catches.

Carlsson was killed in the fighting in and around Delville Wood while serving with D Company 1st South African Infantry on 14 July 1916.

His remains were never recovered and he is commemorated on the Thiepval Memorial, Pier and Face 4C.

CURRIE CUP TOURNAMENT, AT DURBAN, 1911.

[Photo by The Bower Studio, Durban.

Batting and fielding averages

	Mat	Inns	NO	Runs	HS	Ave	100	50	Ct	St
First-class	4	9	0	54	24	6.00	0	0	4	0

Bowling averages

	Mat	Balls	Runs	Wkts	BBI	BBM	Ave	Econ	SR	4w	5w	10
First-class	4	-	-	-	-	-						

Captain George Bruce Gilroy MC
Oxford University
8th Bn The Black Watch (Royal Highland Regiment)
Died 15 July 1916
Aged 26
Right-handed Bat/Wicket-keeper

'As brave a Scot as there has ever been'

George Bruce Gilroy was born on 16 September 1889 at Clatto House, Cupar, Fife, the son of George, a jute spinner and manufacturer, and Annie Gilroy of Clatto. He was educated at Ardvreck School, Winchester College and Magdalen College Oxford. At Winchester he was Head of House, a Commoner Prefect and Captain of the Commoner VI. A first-class wicket-keeper and decent bat, he was in the Winchester XI in 1908, scoring 10 and 12 against Eton and making two catches. Against Pennsylvania University he scored 0 (run out) and 2.

He made one first-class appearance for Oxford University against the MCC on 28 June 1909 at Lord's. Gilroy wasn't given a chance to do much with his bat, scoring 2 in his only innings. The match was drawn. He also played for the Grange Cricket Club, Edinburgh, and the Forfarshire Cricket club, Broghty Ferry, Dundee.

After leaving Magdalen College, Gilroy moved into his father's business at Dundee. At the outbreak of the war he enlisted immediately, later being commissioned in the 8th Bn Black Watch. He went to France with his battalion in May 1915, earning the Military Cross (MC) at the Battle of Loos.

Captain Gilroy was mortally wounded at Longueval on 14 July 1916 during the Battle of the Somme and died the following day.

He is buried in Corbie Communal Cemetery Extension, Plot 1, Row D, Grave 26.

His brother, Lieutenant Kenneth Reid Gilroy, who also served with the Black Watch, was killed in action on 12 March 1915 as was his brother-in-law Captain Robert Edgar Forrester who was killed in action on 5 June 1915.

Batting and fielding averages

	Mat	Inns	NO	Runs	HS	Ave	100	50	4s	6s	Ct	St
First-class	1	1	1	2	2*	-	0	0	0	0	0	0

Bowling averages

	Mat	Balls	Runs	Wkts	BBI	BBM	Ave	Econ	SR	4w	5w	10
First-class	1	-	-	-	-	-	-	-	-	-	-	-

Lance Corporal William Greive
Scotland
Lothians and Border Horse Yeomanry
Died 18 July 1916
Aged 28
Right-handed Bat

'Lived like a Scot, died like a Scot'

William Greive was born on 1 March 1916 at Howden, Selkirkshire, to James and Margaret Greive, of Howden. Educated at Selkirk High School, he was a member of Selkirk Cricket Club and considered one of the best cricketers in the Borders.

Greive played one first-class match for Scotland against Ireland on 21 July 1910 at College Park, Dublin. He scored 6 and 0 and bowled twenty-one overs without success. Ireland won by 208 runs.

He served with the Lothians and Border Horse during the war and died of wounds on 18 July 1916. The regimental war diary explains his death a little more fully:

Preparations were now being made for the attack on the Messines Ridge, and every man who was in the area was at once put on to dig, and much time was spent on the Kemmel defences. Our observers, some 28 of them at Siege Farm, were particularly busy at this time, the whole system of observation on the Corps front being organized by Captain Nelson. At 5.30 on the 17th July a high explosive shell struck and set fire to the observers' building at Siege Farm. Fortunately, only half of the party were in the position at the time. Trooper Wickharn was killed on the spot, and Sergeant Inglis and Lance Corporal Greive died of wounds next day, and Lance Corporal Palfrey in October. Two other men were also wounded. Very brave work was done in getting the wounded from the burning building, which was kept under heavy shell fire and in which much SAA was exploded. Sergeant Jack and Lance Corporals Riddell and Young received the Military Medal for gallantry.

The following obituary appeared in the local paper:

Scottish Internationalist Cricketer Killed in Action.

Official intimation has now been made that Mr Walter Greive, Highland Light Infantry, missing since April 1917, is presumed to have been killed in action on that date. Mr Greive, who was the youngest son of Mr James Greive, farmer, Howden, Selkirkshire, was a well-known member of Selkirk Cricket Club, a batsman of great ability and force, and a good change bowler. After taking part in many representative engagements in the Border district he was selected to play for Scotland against the Australians, and other recognition of international rank was conferred on him. Prior to enlistment Mr Greive was associated with his father in the management of the farm at Howden. An elder brother, Mr William Greive, a former captain of Selkirk Cricket Club, was killed in action some time ago.

William Greive is buried in Bailleul Communal Cemetery Extension, Nord, Grave Reference II, E. 4.

Batting and fielding averages

	Mat	Inns	NO	Runs	HS	Ave	100	50	Ct	St
First-class	1	2	0	6	6	3.00	0	0	0	0

Bowling averages

	Mat	Balls	Runs	Wkts	BBI	BBM	Ave	Econ	SR	4w	5w	10
First-class	1	24	21	0	-	-	-	5.25	-	0	0	0

Second Lieutenant Albert Ernest Pratt
Auckland
53rd Bn Australian Imperial Force
Died 19 July 1916
Aged 23
Unknown

'One of the missing of Fromelles finally at Rest'

Albert Ernest Pratt was born on 16 April 1893 in Auckland, New Zealand. The son of Henry and Matilda Pratt, Bega Road, Northbridge, North Sydney, New South Wales, he served in grammar school cadets and in college rifles and was a member of the North Sydney Rugby Rifle Club.

He made one first-class appearance for Auckland against Hawke's Bay at the Recreation Ground, Napier, on 22 March 1913. He made 2 runs in his only innings. He took 3 wickets for 34 runs off 16 overs in the first innings and 2 wickets for 21 runs off 8 overs in the second. Auckland won by 343 runs.

Pratt enlisted on 6 June 1915 in Liverpool, New South Wales, as 3099 Private Pratt, 1st Bn 10th Reinforcement. He embarked from Sydney, New South Wales on board HMAT A69 *Warilda* on 8 October 1915, bound for Egypt. Promoted to corporal on 11 January 1916, he transferred to 53rd Bn Australian Imperial Force on 14 February 1916. He was appointed as a temporary sergeant on 16 March before being commissioned as a second lieutenant on 26 April. Pratt embarked from Alexandria to join the British Expeditionary Force in France on 19 June 1916, arriving in Marseilles on 25 June.

He was killed in action on 19 July 1916 at Fromelles during the Battle of the Somme. A letter sent home to his parents explains his death in more detail:

> Lieut Pratt was killed about midnight 19/20 July in the 2nd enemy line in front of Fromelles. He was shot through the heart and died instantly. The position was retaken by the enemy next morning and the body was not recovered.

Another letter was received from 3169 Private J. H. Dean, B Company, 53rd Battalion, dated 24 August 1916:

> I knew Mr Pratt; he was a 2 Lt in B. VII., and I saw him fall in the 2nd line of German trenches at Fleurbaix, on 19.7.16, and he only lived a few minutes and I stayed with him until he died. We laid him at the back of the trench. I think he was hit in the upper part of the chest. He did not speak, nor did he seem to suffer. I think he was unconscious. I am quite sure he was dead and that it was he. He was my platoon commander. We retired from this trench at 10.30 the next morning but there was no chance of recovering his body … .

A third statement came from 4869 Private J. J. Pritchard of B Company, 53rd Battalion, dated 28 August 1916:

I knew Mr Pratt; he was in No. 9 Section of B. VII and he was shot through the chest on the night of 19th July at Fleurbaix in a German trench. I carried him from where he was shot into a trench that I thought would be safe. I was with him until he died. He only lived about ½ hour and was unconscious all the time and I covered his body with a bomber's apron. We were driven out about 2 hours later and as we were being surrounded I had to leave his body there. He did not suffer nor did he regain consciousness.

His body was recovered from a mass grave in 2009 and identified by DNA testing. A new cemetery, the first for some fifty years, was dedicated exactly ninety-four years after the battle of Fromelles. Second Lieutenant Albert Pratt was finally laid to rest at Fromelles (Pheasant Wood) Military Cemetery, Grave Reference I. E. 10.

Batting and fielding averages

	Mat	Inns	NO	Runs	HS	Ave	100	50	4s	6s	Ct	St
First-class	1	1	0	2	2	2.00	0	0	0	0	0	0

Bowling averages

	Mat	Balls	Runs	Wkts	BBI	Ave	Econ	SR	5w	10
First-class	1	144	55	5	3/34	11.00	2.29	28.8	0	0

2929A Private Andrew Moncrieff Given
Otago
60th Bn Australian Imperial Force
Died 19 July 1916
Aged 30
Unknown

'His body was lost but his memory will always remain close'

Andrew Moncrieff Given was born on 30 January 1886 at Dunedin, Otago, New Zealand, the only son of Andrew M. and Isabella Given.

He played in one first-class match for Otago against Southland at Carisbrook, Dunedin on 2 April 1915. He scored 4 in his only innings and took 3 wickets for 32 off 12 innings. The match was drawn.

Leaving New Zealand, he moved to Melbourne, Australia.

During the war he served with the 60th Battalion of the Australian Imperial Force, embarking from Melbourne on the SS *Makarini* on 15 September 1915. He lasted less than a year.

He was reported wounded and missing on 19 July 1916 and for some time there was hope he might have survived. However, the awful truth soon emerged and it was established that he had died from his wounds on that date. A fellow soldier, 2397 Thomas Killy, later gave an account of his death:

On July 19th at Armentières, Given was killed alongside where I was wounded. He was already wounded and was crawling back like me when a shell killed him. It was in no man's land. His body was picked up after lying out for 36 hours.

Despite his body being recovered from the battlefield it was later lost like thousands of others and he is commemorated at V.C. Corner Australian Cemetery and Memorial, Fromelles, Panel reference 20.

Batting and fielding averages

	Mat	Inns	NO	Runs	HS	Ave	100	50	Ct	St
First-class	1	1	1	4	4*	-	0	0	0	0

Bowling averages

	Mat	Runs	Wkts	BBI	Ave	5w	10
First-class	1	59	3	3/32	19.66	0	0

Sergeant Ernest Shorrocks
Somerset
20th Bn Royal Fusiliers (City of London Regiment)
Died 20 July 1916
Aged 41

'Chaps like me ought to go'

Ernest Shorrocks was born on 12 March 1875 at Rhodes, Middleton, Lancashire, and educated at William Hulme's Grammar School, Manchester, on a foundation scholarship between 1887 and 1892. He was the head of the School in both work and games and captain of cricket and football, before entering Manchester University with a County Council Scholarship in science. Shorrocks took his degree of BSc in 1896 with first-class honours in chemistry, and afterwards achieved a Master's. He returned to William Hulme's for a year as assistant master, before moving on to Knaresborough Grammar School and then heading south to Taunton as science master at Queen's College. After ten years at Queen's he went to London University for further study, before becoming science master of Taunton Grammar School. He was an old member of the Chorlton-cum-Hardy Cricket and Golf Clubs and showed his continued interest in the old school by giving an annual prize for cricket, which was awarded for excellence in fielding.

He made one first-class appearance for Somerset against Lancashire on 19 June 1905 at the County Ground, Taunton. He scored 0 and 16 not out and took two wickets (Reggie Spooner and James Halloes) for 60 off 20 overs. Lancashire won the match by 79 runs.

Shorrocks was on holiday with his parents when war was declared and despite their objections made it clear that he was enlisting by stating that 'Chaps like me ought to go'.

He enlisted in the ranks of the 20th Bn Royal Fusiliers and was killed with them on 20 July 1916 during the Battle of the Somme. Captain Templer later wrote to his parents, 'Sergeant Shorrocks died fighting splendidly. He did wonderful work re-organising the men.'

With thousands of others, Shorrocks' body was never recovered and he is commemorated on the Thiepval Memorial, Pier and Face 8 C 9 A and 16 A.

Batting and fielding averages

	Mat	Inns	NO	Runs	HS	Ave	100	50	Ct	St
First-class	1	2	1	16	16*	16.00	0	0	0	0

Bowling averages

	Mat	Balls	Runs	Wkts	BBI	Ave	Econ	SR	5w	10
First-class	1	120	60	2	2/60	30.00	3.00	60.0	0	0

611 Private Percy Jeeves
Warwick
15th Royal Warwickshire Regiment
Died 22 July 1916
Aged 28
Right-Handed Bat / Right-Arm Medium-Fast

"The Real Jeeves"

Percy Jeeves was born on 5 March 1888, at Earlsheaton, Dewsbury, Yorkshire. He was the son of Edwin and Nancy Jeeves, of 1A, Craven St., Ravensthorpt, Dewsbury, Yorks. He played club cricket at Goole Cricket Club, before finally becoming a professional player with Hawes Cricket Club. Although he trialed for Yorkshire in 1910 he failed to impress and his efforts went no further.

A persistent man Jeeves persevered and in 1912 joined Warwickshire County Cricket Club as a fast-medium bowler. He made fifty first class appearances between May 1912 and August 1914, all but one played for Warwickshire mostly in the County Championship. He made his debut for Warwickshire on 30 May 1912 against the visiting Australians at Edgbaston, Birmingham. Jeeves was run out in the first innings for 1 and 0 in the second. He also took 2 wickets for 35 off 14 overs. The match was drawn. He played his second match against the visiting South Africans on 4 July 1912, once again at Edgbaston, Birmingham. Jeeves scored 9 and 15 and took 1 wicket for 12 off 4 overs. South Africa won by 6 wickets. He played one match for the Players against the Gentlemen on 9 July 1914 at the Kennington Oval. He scored 11 in his one innings and took 1 wicket for 24 off 13.2 overs in the first innings and 4 for 44 off 15 overs in the second. Players won by 241. Plum Warner was so impressed by Jeeves bowling that he saw him as a future England player. He made his final first class appearance against Surrey on 27 August 1914 at Edgbaston in the County Championship. Jeeves scored 7 and 18 and took 5 wickets for 52 off 19 overs in the first innings and 2 for 36 off 21 overs in the second. Warwickshire won by 80 runs. During his first class career Jeeves scored 1204 runs including 4 fifties his highest score being 86. He also took 199 wickets for 3987 runs, his best figures being 7 for 34. He made 49 catches.

A few months after the outbreak of the war Jeeves enlisted as a private into the 15th Battalion Royal Warwickshire regiment and was killed with them at High Wood near Montauban on 22 July 1916 during the battle of the Somme.

His body was never recovered and he is commemorated with thousands of others on the Thiepval Memorail Pier and Face 9 A 9 B and 10 B.

The writer P. G. Wodehouse got the name of Bertie Wooster's manservant Jeeves from Percy. Wodehouse was having a short holiday in Wensleydale, and happened to come across a cricket match at Hawes where Percy Jeeves was playing. Wodehouse, like his friend and mentor Sir Arthur Conan Doyle, had a passion for cricket.

Fifty years later Wodehouse commented,

'I suppose Jeeves's bowling must have impressed me. I remembered him in 1916 when I was in New York and starting the Jeeves and Bertie saga, and it was just the name I wanted. I remember admiring his action very much.'

Batting and fielding averages

	Mat	Inns	NO	Runs	HS	Ave	100	50	Ct	St
First-class	50	81	6	1204	86*	16.05	0	4	49	0

Bowling averages

	Mat	Balls	Runs	Wkts	BBI	Ave	Econ	SR	5w	10
First-class	50	8952	3987	199	7/34	20.03	2.67	44.9	12	1

Captain William Gerald Knox Boswell
Oxford University
5th (attd 2nd) Bn The Prince Consort's Own (Rifle Brigade)
Died 28 July 1916
Aged 24
Right-hand Bat

'Play up Play up and play the game'

William Gerald Knox Boswell was born on 24 June 1892 in Chelsea. The son of Mr and Mrs W Albert Boswell, of Hornton Cottage, Kensington, he was educated at Eton College where he was in the XI in both 1910 and 1911. Going up to New College Oxford he played in the Freshmen's match where he scored 75 and 20 and took four wickets for 47. Despite his Freshmen's performance it wasn't until 1913 that he obtained his Blue.

Boswell made fourteen first-class appearances between June 1912 and July 1914, all for Oxford University. Boswell made his debut for Oxford on 13 June 1912 against the Free Foresters at the University Parks, Oxford. He scored 21 and 0 and caught Eliot Druce off the bowling of John Fraser fir 1. The Free Foresters finally came out on top by 260 runs. Boswell went on to play against Scotland, Sussex, H. D. G. Leveson-Gower's XI, Hampshire, MCC, Cambridge University, Middlesex, G. J. V. Weigall's XI and L. G. Robinson's XI. He made his final first-class appearance against Cambridge University on 6 July 1914 at Lord's, scoring 5 and 36, and taking 1 wicket for 17 off 6 overs. He also caught Edward Baker off the bowling of Frank Naumann for 3. During his first-class career Boswell made 756 first class runs, his highest score being 101 against Hampshire. He also took fourteen wickets for 343 runs, his best figures being four for 22. He made 2 catches.

During the war he served with the 5th Battalion and then became attached to the 2nd Battalion of the Rifle Brigade. He rose to the rank of captain before dying from wounds received in action on 28 July 1916 on the Somme.

Boswell is commemorated in the Abbeville Communal Cemetery, grave reference VI. E. 16.

Batting and fielding averages

	Mat	Inns	NO	Runs	HS	Ave	100	Ct	St
First-class	14	26	1	756	101*	30.24	1	2	0

Bowling averages

	Mat	Balls	Runs	Wkts	BBI	Ave	Econ	SR	5w	10
First-class	14	563	343	14	4/22	24.50	3.65	40.2	0	0

Lance Corporal Frank Leslie Lugton
Victoria
24th Bn Australian Imperial Force
Died 29 July 1916
Aged 22
Right-handed Bat/Right-arm fast medium.

'of a modest and retiring disposition, and was extremely well liked by all'

Frank Leslie Lugton was born on 4 November 1893 at Northcote, Victoria, Australia. He was one of ten children born to Charles Edward and Jane Ann Lugton of Hillburn, Prospect Grove, Northcote. After leaving school he became an electrical engineer and played his cricket for Northcote Cricket Club where his ability with both bat and ball soon came to notice. He made five first-class appearances in Australia between January and March 1914, all for Victoria. He made his debut against New Zealand in Australia at the Melbourne Cricket Ground, Melbourne on 9 January 1914. He made 36 in his one innings and took 1 wicket for 21 off 5 overs in the first innings and 1 wicket for 21 off 8 overs in the second. Victoria won by an innings and 110 runs. He went on to play against New South Wales, South Australia and Tasmania twice. He made his final first class appearance against Tasmania on 6 March 1914 at the North Tasmania Cricket Association Ground, Launceston. He scored 94 not out (his highest first class score) and 20. Victoria won by 550 runs. During his career he made 218 runs his highest score being 94. He also took 9 wickets for 306 runs his best figures being 3 for 45. He made 1 catch.

Frank was known as being 'of a modest and retiring disposition, and was extremely well liked by all'.

Lugton enlisted as private 447 into the 24th Battalion Australian Imperial Force on 22 March 1915, and proceeded to Alexandria as part of the 1st Australian Imperial Force. One of the first to volunteer, he signed up as soon as the cricket season finished. While serving in Gallipoli in charge of a grenade party he was buried alive for six hours by a shell explosion. He had previously been lucky to escape with his life when a Turkish sniper shot the bolt out of his rifle. Suffering from shell-shock and a 'defective right eye', he spent some months in hospital in Malta.

After serving at Gallipoli, Lugton was promoted to lance corporal and sent to fight in France. However a note on his records shows that, on 13 May 1916, while serving at l'Hallobean in France, he requested to revert to the ranks, a sign perhaps of what the war was doing to him. He was killed in action at Pozières on 29 July 1916. A local paper, *The Argus*, reported his death:

Frank Lugton is another of the leading Victorian cricketers who has made the supreme sacrifice. He lost his life fighting in France. Lugton was considered by good judges to have been one of Victoria's coming cricketers. He was selected by Mr J. Worrall for several of the interstate colts' matches, wherein he performed well, and he was a member of the last Victorian team to visit Tasmania, where his work with bat and ball was pleasing. He was one of the leading players of the Melbourne Football Club, his work on the half-back line being of a high order. His comrades of the Northcote Baseball Club wore armbands in their match against Williamstown on Saturday as a mark of respect to his memory. He was of a modest and retiring disposition, and was well liked by all.

It was recorded at the time that he was 'Buried in the vicinity of Pozières'. However, his remains were never recovered and he is commemorated on the Villers-Bretonneux Memorial.

Black armbands were respectfully worn when Frank's sporting teams played. Tragically his brother, Archibald, another Northcote cricketer, was wounded on the battlefield and subsequently died of his wounds in August 1918. Lugton Street in Alphington was named as a local tribute to the Lugtons' contribution to Northcote. Frank was also a member of the Northcote Baseball Club and a player in the half-back line for the Melbourne Football Club when war broke out.

Batting and fielding averages

	Mat	Inns	NO	Runs	HS	Ave	100	50	Ct	St
First-class	5	8	1	218	94*	31.14	0	1	1	0

Bowling averages

	Mat	Runs	Wkts	BBI	Ave	5w	10
First-class	5	306	9	3/45	34.00	0	0

Lance Corporal Arthur Marsden
Derbyshire
12th Bn The Manchester Regiment
Died 31 July 1916
Aged 35
Right-handed Bat

'His father's child, England's Son'

Arthur Marsden was born on 28 October 1880 at Fairfield, Buxton, Derbyshire, the son of William E. Marsden, a railway driver, and his wife Eliza. Arthur was captain of the Chetham's School XI in Manchester and played his club cricket for Longsight and Levenshulme cricket clubs.

Arthur made one first-class appearance for Derbyshire against Kent on 2 June 1910. He opened the first innings but was out for a duck and in the second innings, playing lower down the order was run out for 6. He also caught Frank Woolley of the bowling of Arthur Morton for 20. Derbyshire lost by 304. It wasn't as bad as first appeared, as it was only the second innings stand between James Seymour (124) and Kenneth Hutchings (killed in action 3 September 1916) 122 that made the difference.

Marsden enlisted in the ranks of the 12th Bn Manchester Regiment, later being promoted to lance corporal. He was seriously wounded on the Western Front and died from his wounds in St Pancras, London, on 31 July 1916.

He is buried in Gorton (Brookfield) Unitarian Churchyard, Manchester. Worth a visit, lets not forget them.

Batting and fielding averages

	Mat	Inns	NO	Runs	HS	Ave	100	50	Ct	St
First-class	1	2	0	6	6	3.00	0	0	1	0

Bowling averages

	Mat	Balls	Runs	Wkts	BBI	BBM	Ave	Econ	SR	4w	5w	10
First-class	1	-	-	-	-	-	-	-	-	-	-	-

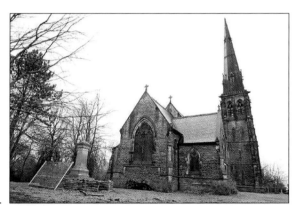

Gorton church.

7425 Private Claude Newberry
South Africa, Transvaal
3rd Regiment South African Infantry
Died 1 August 1916
Aged 27
Right-handed Bat/Right-arm Fast, Leg-break

Claude Newberry (sometimes known as Newbury) was born on 1 January 1889 at Port Elizabeth, Cape Province. He was the nephew of Mrs E. Roberts, of Bertrams, Johannesburg. For a Test player very little seems to be known about him.

Newberry played in four Tests and made twelve first-class appearances for the Transvaal between October 1910 and February 1914. He made his debut for the Transvaal against the, South Africa to Australia Touring team on 1 October 1910, at Old Wanderers Ground, Johannesburg. He took 3 wickets for 103 runs off 18.4 overs and failed to bat. The match was abandoned and the result declared a draw. His next match was played on 13 March 1911 in the Currie Cup, at Lord's No 3, Durban, against the Orange Free State. He was run out for 0 in his first innings and scored 20 in the second. He also took 3 wickets for 23 off 12.2 overs in the first innings and a further 2 wickets for 2 off 2.1 overs in the second. He also caught Reginald Stanton off the bowling of Raymond Thompson for O. Transvaal won by 188 runs. He went on to play against Eastern Province, Griqualand West, Border, Natal, Western Province, The Rest, PW Sherwell's XI and the MCC.

Newberry played in four of the five Tests against England during the MCC tour of South Africa in 1913–14. The second Test was played on 26 December 1913 at the Old Wanderers, Johannesburg against England. He scored 1 and 5 and took 3 wickets for 93 off 26 overs. England won by an innings and 12 runs. The third Test was played on 1 January 1914 once again at the Old Wanderers, Johannesburg. Newberry scored 15 and 13 and took 4 wickets for 72 off 22 overs; England won by 91 runs. The fourth Test was played on 14 February 1914 at Lord's, Durban. Newberry scored 0 and 16 and took 2 wickets for 18 off 11 overs in the first innings and 1 wicket for 22 off 10 overs in the second. The match was drawn. He played in his final test on 27 March 1914 at St George's Park, Port Elizabeth, making 11 and 1 and taking one wicket for 34 off 14 overs. England won by ten wickets. This was also Newberry's final first class appearance. It was said that if Newberry had a fault it was that he tried to bowl too fast thereby reducing his effectiveness.

During the war Newberry enlisted into the ranks of the 3rd Regiment South African Infantry and went out to France with them. He served on the Somme at Delville Wood. The name like so many others held a dread for thousands. The conditions were later described by a survivor,

'Every semblance of a trench seemed full of dead-sodden, squelchy, swollen bodies. Fortunately the blackening faces were invisible except when Verey lights lit up the indescribable scene. Not a tree stood whole in that wood…

We stood and lay on putrefying bodies and the wonder was that the disease (dysentery) did not finish off what the shells of the enemy had started.

There was hand-to-hand fighting with knives, bombs, and bayonets; cursing and brutality on both sides such as men can be responsible for when it is a question of "your life or mine…"'

Newberry was killed in Action at Delville Wood on 1 August 1916 and is buried in Delville Wood Cemetery, Longueval, grave reference III. L. 10

Batting and fielding averages

	Mat	Inns	NO	Runs	HS	Ave	100	50	6s	Ct	St
Tests	4	8	0	62	16	7.75	0	0	0	3	0
First-class	16	24	3	251	42	11.95	0	0		21	0

Bowling averages

	Mat	Inns	Balls	Runs	Wkts	BBI	BBM	Ave	Econ	SR	4w	5w	10
Tests	4	6	558	268	11	4/72	4/101	24.36	2.88	50.7	1	0	0
First-class	16		2123	1213	49	6/28		24.75	3.42	43.3		1	0

Captain William Manstead Benton
Middlesex
12th Bn The Manchester Regiment
Died 17 August 1916
Aged 43
Right-handed Bat

'Thine Eyes Shall See The King In His Beauty'

William Manstead Benton was born 11 July 1873 in Chelsea, London, the son of Thomas Manstead Benton, a stockbroker. His parents lived at Herne Bay in Kent. William was educated at Framlingham College but he was headstrong and didn't take to discipline easily. As if to emphasize this, he ran away constantly and had to be brought back. On the third occasion his parents all but gave up. He achieved little academically but did well at sports. A prefect, he won the Gooch Medal for Elocution in 1887 and 1888 and the Mantle Essay Prize 1890 and was in the Cricket XI in 1888, 1889 and 1890 and the Football XI in the 1888–9 and 1889–90 seasons.

When William was seventeen his father died and left him a small fortune. Like his father he became a stockbroker but, given his background and temperament, he couldn't have chosen a worse profession. He ran away, taking all his money with him and enlisted in the Royal Marine Artillery. Once again he made a bad decision and, after a fight with a corporal, whom he knocked unconscious, he deserted.

William made his way to Australia under the name of Richard White (this was the name under which he joined the army). He was employed in various ways until joining the Australian Artillery as a gunner and serving throughout during the Second Boer War. When the war ended he was on the verge of being commissioned. However, he remained in South Africa and enlisted in the Cape Mounted Police. While in Cape Town, he learned that there was a job going in the Leper Colony on Robben Island (later to be Nelson Mandela's 'home' for over twenty-five years) as a cook. He got the job and worked not only as a cook but also as a painter, laundryman, and general dogsbody. His work on Robben Island had a profound effect on him.

As a result of this, Benton gave himself up to the authorities. He was tried by court martial and served a prison sentence but received a royal pardon and was released early, going on to spend two years at Lichfield Theological College before being ordained deacon in 1907 and priest in 1909. He became curate of St Peter's, Walsall, where he was known as 'The Fighting Parson'. However, his experiences at Robben Island called him back and he became chaplain on the Island. He eventually returned to England and became curate of Bearsted.

Always a fine cricketer, he played whenever he could.

He made two first-class appearances for Middlesex in 1913, the first on 7 May 1913 against Cambridge University, at F. P. Fenner's Ground, Cambridge. Benton scored 1 and 5, Middlesex losing by nine wickets. This was also the match that saw R. B. Langden score 100 in 130 minutes (total 142), passing his 500 runs in first-class cricket when he reached

43. He played his second 1ˢᵗ class match on 10 May 1913 against Hampshire in the County Championship at Lord's. He scored 19 not out, in his one innings. Middlesex won by an innings and 36 runs.

On the outbreak of the war he became a military chaplain and went to France. His experiences of German 'frightfulness' and the use of gas affected him profoundly. Giving up his role as a chaplain he became an infantry lieutenant, joining the 12th Battalion Manchester Regiment, later being promoted captain. He was later put in charge of the brigade snipers.

Writing home on 3 April 1916, he commented:

> I am still with the 51st Brigade and like them very much. General Pilcher sent for me the other day and told me he thought that great credit was due for the way in which we had got under the evening sniping on our front. They had the best of it to begin with, but we have only had two men hit by snipers since we came in (though we have had many hit by shells and shrapnel-fire), and they were both on the first day, and we have knocked over thirteen of them. There is a lot of shelling going on. I am at present working under Lord Dunmore. We have a man coming out to stay with us who will have some money to spend on the men for games and things. We shall be glad of his help. Yesterday the Editor of the *Westminster Gazette* and his wife came out to visit our camp. He was very much struck with all our arrangements, and he is starting a fund in his paper for providing amusements and games for our men. Did I tell you that General Maxwell called me out and thanked me personally for the assistance which the Major told him I had given him? I was rather bucked, though I don't know that I have done anything particular here... . General Woodhouse has been round to inspect the Company. He congratulated the Major and the staff on the 'splendid work done in camp and the tone of the men' (his own words), so we feel rather pleased about it. One of the doctors and I are digging in our spare time a 6 x 6 x 6ft sunk pit for an officers' bath-tent. The ground is gravel and flint, so it takes some getting through.

On 8 August 1916, Major Magnay, 12th Bn Manchester Regiment wrote to Mrs Benton:

> Dear Mrs Benton,
> Just a short note to tell you that your husband was wounded the other day. He asked me to write to you if things went wrong. I am afraid he has gone through most of the torments of Hell, but I consider him the most gallant gentleman in the world. He knew absolutely no fear. On my orders he went forward to try and reorganize after an attack which had failed. Whilst on the front line he saw a wounded man trying to crawl back from near the German trenches. He at once went out to help him. He got him back some way when both were hit by snipers, your husband in the right leg below the knee. He got into a shell-hole. He was wounded about 5 a.m. I sent four parties out to try and get him in, and two other battalions sent out patrols at my request to bring him in, but they could not find him, and when they shouted they drew bombs and machine-gun fire and several men were hit. Next morning your husband showed himself, and two officers went out at about twelve noon, and brought him in. I cannot tell you what a relief it was to me to see him again. I have known him only for three or four weeks, but in that time I have come almost to worship him for what he is, and that is the finest and manliest man I have ever known. I am desperately sorry to have to tell you that he is wounded, but I am sure that you will be relieved to have him

safe at home under any conditions. I am very sorry to lose his services and only wish I had him with me when we go back into the fight.

With kindest regards,
Yours sincerely,
P. W. Magnay (Major)

Just over a week later the following letter was sent by the chaplain, 36 CCS, BEF, France. 17 August, 1916.

Dear Mrs Benton,

It is with the deepest regret I write to let you know that your dear husband, Capt. W. Benton, passed away about 2 o'clock this morning. I have been in close touch with him since he was admitted here on the 6th, and he was always so grateful for my ministrations. He received Holy Communion two or three times, and I read and prayed with him almost every day. I was with him till twelve o'clock last night, and he was then sinking fast, and the night nurse tells me he passed peacefully away about 2 a.m. During the first few days after being admitted we had such pleasant conversations. He told me of his ministerial work and his chaplaincy before he took a combative commission. It is a comfort to know he died not only a good and brave soldier of the King, but as a good soldier of the King of Kings.

Please accept my sincere sympathy in your very sad loss, and I pray God may comfort and sustain you.

Yours sincerely,
C. A. Adderley CF

He is buried in Heilly Station Cemetery, Mericourt-l'abbe, grave reference II. F. 12.

Batting and fielding averages

	Mat	Inns	NO	Runs	HS	Ave	100	50	Ct	St
First-class	2	3	1	25	19*	12.50	0	0	0	0

Bowling averages

	Mat	Balls	Runs	Wkts	BBI	BBM	Ave	Econ	SR	4w	5w	10
First-class	2	-	-	-	-	-	-	-	-	-	-	-

Second Lieutenant George Frederick Macnamara
Ireland
8th Bn Royal Dublin Fusiliers
Died 17 August 1916
Aged 23
Right-handed Bat/Medium-pace Bowler

'The Minstrel Boy'

George Frederick Macnamara was born in June 1893 in Dublin. One of six children born to Richard A. (a prosperous solicitor) and Mary Macnamara of 10 Fitzwilliam Place, Dublin, he was educated at The Oratory School, one of Britain's leading Catholic public schools, which was then situated at Edgbaston, Birmingham (now in Oxfordshire). A fine all-round sportsman, he was in the First XI, represented the school at football and was a keen tennis player.

He played against the school's old rivals, Beaumont College, on 3 July 1908 at the Queen's College Ground, Oxford, scoring 9 in his only innings and being bowled out by William Thomson (one of Thomson's three victims that day). Quick in the field, Macnamara also managed to catch Derek Fitzgerald off the bowling of George French, (killed in action on 9 May 1915), for 17 and Arthur McGrath, also off the bowling of French, for 2. The match was drawn. He next played against Beaumont College on 16 June 1910 at the Jesus College Ground, Oxford. This time he scored 7, being caught by V. Perez off the bowling of H. J. Churchill (one of six wickets he took during the first innings). The Oratory School went on to win the game by 16 runs. The 1911 season saw Macnamara in fine form, scoring 118 against King Edward's School, Birmingham. In the match against Beaumont, once again at the Jesus College Ground, Oxford, played on 13 June 1911, he opened the batting and scored 108 not out in his only innings. He also took two wickets for 39 runs off twenty, the Oratory School winning by nine wickets. Macnamara was also a first-class footballer, playing in the school XI and being their leading goal scorer; on one occasion he put five past the City of Birmingham Police.

On leaving school he went up to New College Oxford. Although he played cricket for his college he wasn't selected for the university team but he did win a half-Blue for football for the match against Cambridge University. He was also a member of the University OTC. His sporting life having taken up his academic time, he graduated in 1914 with a fourth class in history,

Macnamara, who also turned out for Leinster during his university vacations, made one first-class appearance for Ireland against Scotland on 10 July 1913 at the Raeburn Place Ground, Edinburgh. Macnamara scored 30 before being bowled by Frazer in his first innings, and 24 not out in his second. He failed to take a wicket in his thirteen overs in a match that was eventually drawn.

In August 1915 Macnamara was commissioned into the 4th Battalion Royal Dublin Fusiliers as a second lieutenant, later transferring to the 8th Battalion. The battalion was heavily engaged during the battle of the Somme and it was during this battle that George Macnamara was killed near Loos on 18 August 1916 while defending the salient.

He is commemorated in the Philosophe British Cemetery, Mazingasbe, Pas de Calais, grave reference I.K. 1.

First-class statistics

Macnamara has previously and incorrectly been identified as S. F. Macnamara (1880–1913) but thanks to some first-class research by better men than me, he has now been correctly identified.

THE XI. 1910.

ROBERTSON.   HOWETT.   KERR.   GRANT.   CASE.   EGERTON.

FRENCH.   DE TRAFFORD.   ST. LAWRENCE.   MACNAMARA.   HEFFERNAN.

Lieutenant The Honourable Brian Danvers Butler
Marylebone Cricket Club
13th (attd 7th) Bn King's Royal Rifle Corps
Died 18 August 1916
Aged 40
Not Known

'A natural leader, always at the head of his men'

Brian Danvers Butler was born on 18 April 1876 at Swithland Hall, Leicestershire, the fourth son John Butler, 6th Earl of Lanesborough, and Annie.

He made two first-class appearances, both for the MCC, between May 1913 and May 1914. Butler made his debut for the MCC on 22 May 1913 against Hampshire at Lord's, scoring 29 and 3, the MCC winning by 208 runs. His second and final first-class appearance came on 23 May 1914, once again against Hampshire at Lord's. He scored 2 and 8 the MCC winning by 73 runs. Butler also played for I Zingari in 1909.

During the war he served with the 13th Battalion Kings Royal Rifle Corps but was attached to the 7th Battalion when he was killed in action on 18 August 1916 during the fighting in and around Delville Wood.

His body was never recovered and he is commemorated on the Thiepval Memorial, Pier and Face 13 A and 13 B.

Batting and fielding averages

	Mat	Inns	NO	Runs	HS	Ave	100	50	Ct	St
First-class	2	4	0	42	29	10.50	0	0	0	0

Bowling averages

	Mat	Balls	Runs	Wkts	BBI	BBM	Ave	Econ	SR	4w	5w	10
First-class	2	-	-	-	-	-	-	-	-	-	-	-

Lieutenant Charles George Edgar Farmer
MCC
7th Bn King's Royal Rifle Corps
Died 18 August 1916
Aged 30
Not known

'Never to see his daughter born'

Charles George Edgar Farmer was born in Chelsea, London on 28 November 1885. The son of Charles and Emily Farmer, he was educated at Eton College where, in his final year, he was one of the two keepers of the fives. He was in the First XI in 1904 when he made 360 runs with an average of 30.00; he scored 26 and 5 against Winchester and 21 against Harrow. Showing early promise, he was also selected to play for the MCC, becoming a member in 1905. He made two first class appearances the first in July 1905 and the second in June 1906, both played at Lords. He made his debut for the MCC on 17 July 1905 against Derbyshire. Farmer scored 9 in his only innings and caught Frederick Hunter off the bowling of Albert Trott for 45. MCC won by 252 runs. He made his second appearance on 21 June 1906 against Worcestershire. Farmer scored 14 and 55. Worcestershire won by 5 wickets.

On leaving Eton he went up to New College Oxford to study chemistry. At Oxford he appeared in trial games but did not obtain his Blue. In 1906 he was elected as a Fellow of the Chemical Society. Interestingly one of the counter-signatories of his application was Andrea Angel, who was also to die during the Great War trying to save lives during a factory fire on 19 January 1917, his bravery earning him the Edward Medal.

On obtaining his degree, Farmer entered Inner Temple before moving to Lincoln's Inn. Six months later he went into patent work and became involved in some very important cases. In 1914 he married Angela Mary Cicely Ewart, daughter of Herbert Brisbane Ewart and Lady Napier Gore. They had one daughter, Pamela, born shortly before he was killed in 1916.

Despite having a promising career in front of him he felt the need, like thousands of other young men, to join up. In 1915 he took a commission in the 7th Bn King's Royal Rifle Corps and was promoted to the rank of lieutenant. Going to the front in April 1916 he became the battalion's bombing officer and was killed in action at the Battle of Delville Wood during the Somme Offensive on 18 August 1916.

His body was never recovered or identified and he is commemorated on Thiepval Memorial, Somme, France. Pier and Faces 13 A and 13 B.

He also played for I. Zingari, Free Foresters and Eton Ramblers, being Secretary of the Ramblers for six years.

Batting and fielding averages

	Mat	Inns	NO	Runs	HS	Ave	100	50	Ct	St
First-class	2	3	0	78	55	26.00	0	1	1	0

Bowling averages

	Mat	Balls	Runs	Wkts	BBI	BBM	Ave	Econ	SR	4w	5w	10
First-class	2	-	-	-	-	-	-	-	-	-	-	-

Second Lieutenant Sydney Thomas (Tommy) Askham
Northamptonshire
9th Bn The Suffolk Regiment
Died 21 August 1916
Aged 19
Right-handed Bat/Right-arm Fast-Medium

Sydney Thomas (Tommy) Askham was born on 9 September 1896, at the Crown, Market Street, Wellingborough, Northamptonshire. The son of Thomas and Ada Askham, of 38, Castle St., Wellingborough, he was educated at Wellingborough where, according to *Wisden*, E. B. Noel said of him, in his review of public school cricket, that he was 'an exceptional boy cricketer who met with astonishing success as a bowler and is a fine batsman too'.

He was in the school XI for four years, heading the bowling in his last season at the school and also made three centuries with the bat, 112, 108 and 149.

Askham played in five first-class matches in August 1914, all for Northamptonshire and all in the County Championship. He made his debut for Northamptonshire on 3 August 1914 at the County Ground, Northampton against Leicestershire. Askham scored 11 not out, and 3, Northampton won by 4 runs. He went on to play against Kent and Essex. He

The First Cricket Club, 1914.
C. T. Rudd, A. Walker, C. S. Colman, H. W. Tait, J. Hill, M. E. Hancock, W. Sewell, H. Pink
G. T. Carter, K. White, P. A. Fryer, W. W. Robinson, A. D. Denton, S. T. Askham
C. E. Brown, M. Robinson, B. Wright, S. Vergette, A. Johnson, J. T. Badham

made his final first class appearance on 28 August 1914 against Lancashire at Old Trafford, Manchester. He scored 18 in his only innings and took 2 wickets for 68 off 13 overs. The match was drawn. During his first class career Askham scored 83 runs his highest score being 28 against Essex on 22 August 1914.

He won a scholarship to Cambridge University but before having the chance to take it up the First World War erupted and he took a commission in the 9th Bn Suffolk Regiment in October 1915. He was sent to France in 1916 and was killed during the Battle of the Somme while leading his company in an attack on 21 August 1916. He was only 19 years old.

His body was never recovered and he is commemorated on the Thiepval Memorial, Pier and Face 1 C and 2 A.

His older brother, William Askham (born 1894), was also killed in action on 11 April 1918.

Batting and fielding averages

	Mat	Inns	NO	Runs	HS	Ave	100	50	Ct	St
First-class	5	9	3	83	28*	13.83	0	0	0	0

Bowling averages

	Mat	Balls	Runs	Wkts	BBI	Ave	Econ	SR	5w	10
First-class	5	114	86	2	2/68	43.00	4.52	57.0	0	0

Private Frank William P. Dredge
Wellington
1st Bn The Wiltshire Regiment (Duke of Edinburgh's)
Died 22 August 1916
Aged 36
Left-handed Bat

Thiepval memorial.

'Returned home when the bugle called'

Frank William Dredge was born during the March quarter 1880 at Alderbury, Wiltshire. During the December quarter of 1910 he married. At some point during his life he moved to New Zealand and it was there that he played his one and only first-class game for Wellington against Hawke's Bay at Basin Reserve, Wellington, on 9 March 1906. He scored 16 runs in his only innings, Wellington winning by an innings and 322 runs.

Dredge served with the 1st Bn Wiltshire Regiment during the First World War and was killed in action on 22 August 1916 in an attack on the Leipzig Salient. The Wiltshires' war diary explains:

Our artillery was active all day. B Coy moved up from OBAN AVE to NO MAN'S ALLEY. The attack was made at 1 minute past 6p.m. The objective was the line from (R.31.C.40.65) – (R.31.C.9.0.) The attack was done by C Coy on the left and D Coy on the right. These two Coys went over together with the Gloucester Regt (4th) on the right. The British guns were putting a very heavy barrage on our objective; our men very nearly reached our barrage when it lifted Eastwards. The objective was gained. A block was established about 50 yards up the trench from R.31.C.0 – R.31.D.2.6. Consolidated. The enemy shelled our trenches throughout the night, heavily. Casualties amounted to roughly 90.

Dredge's body, like those of thousands of others, was never recovered and he is commemorated on the Thiepval Memorial, Pier and Face 13A.

Batting and fielding averages

	Mat	Inns	NO	Runs	HS	Ave	100	50	Ct	St
First-class	1	1	0	16	16	16.00	0	0	0	0

Bowling averages

	Mat	Balls	Runs	Wkts	BBI	BBM	Ave	Econ	SR	4w	5w	10
First-class	1	-	-	-	-	-	-	-	-	-	-	-

Second Lieutenant Edward Lionel Austin Butler
Tasmania
12th Bn Australian Imperial Force
Died 23 August 1916
Aged 33
Right-handed Bat

'Loved cricket as much as his country'

Edward Lionel Austin Butler, better known as Leo, was born on 10 April 1883 at Hobart, Tasmania, the son of Mr E. H. Butler of Sandy Bay, Hobart and Fanny Amy Butler, née Clerk. Educated at Hutchins School, Hobart before going up to the University of Tasmania to read law, after university he began work as a solicitor in Hobart. He was the fourth generation in the family law firm, Butler, MacIntyre and Butler.

He played his club cricket for the South Hobart District Cricket Club. During the 1914–15 season, the last he took part in, he not only captained the club but also headed the batting averages with 32.0 as well as making a 119 stand against West Hobart. He played two first-classes matches for Tasmania, for whom his father had also played. He made his debut for Tasmania on 6 February 1914 against New South Wales at the Sydney Cricket Ground. Butler scored 13 and 4, Tasmania losing by an innings and 180 runs. He played his second and final first class match on 29 January 1915 against Victoria at the Melbourne Cricket Ground where he scored 7 and 0, Tasmania losing once again this time by an innings and 130 runs. He never represented Tasmania again but he did represent the South against the North on four occasions, his best score being 76 (30–46).

He was commissioned into the 12th Battalion (16th Reinforcement) Australian Imperial Force on 2 August 1915. He sailed for France from Melbourne, Victoria, on board the RMS *Orontes* on 29 March 1916. He had been at the front less than six months when he was seriously wounded in action at Mouquet Farm, Pozières on 22 August, dying from his wounds the following day.

He is buried at Puchevillers British Cemetery, grave reference III. A.

On the 16 August 1917 a memorial window was erected at St David's Cathedral, Hobart, dedicated to Butler's memory.

Batting and fielding averages

	Mat	Inns	NO	Runs	HS	Ave	100	50	Ct	St
First-class	2	4	0	24	13	6.00	0	0	0	0

Bowling averages

	Mat	Balls	Runs	Wkts	BBI	BBM	Ave	Econ	SR	4w	5w	10
First-class	2	-	-	-	-	-	-	-	-	-	-	-

690 Staff Sergeant Christopher George Arthur Collier
Worcestershire
Army Ordnance Corps
Died 25 August 1916
Aged 30
Right-handed Bat/Right-Arm Slow

'the best at everything he did'

Christopher George Arthur Collier was born on 23 August 1886 at Banff, Scotland. He played in fifty-three first-class matches between May 1910 and August 1914, mostly in the County Championship but he also played two university matches and one against the touring South Africans.

Collier made his first-class debut for Worcestershire against Warwickshire on 16 May 1910 at the County Ground, New Road, Worcester, making 10 and 2 in the drawn match. Against Oxford University on the 25 May 1911 at the University Parks, Oxford, Collier got his debut first-class wicket when he bowled the Oxford University opener Richard Twining for 57, going on to the the wickets of Robert Bardsley for 37, John Vidler twice for 12 in the first innings and 2 in the second and finally Robert Burton for 0. He made 16 and 6 with the bat, Worcestershire wining by 6 wickets. He played against South Africa in the British Isles on 23 May 1912 at the County Ground, New Road, Worcester, hitting 3 and 9, South Africa winning by an innings and 42 runs. Playing for H. K. Foster's XI against Oxford University on 30 May 1912 at the University Parks, Oxford, Collier scored 29 and 10 and achieved a career best bowling 3/28 in the first innings.

Also during the 1912 season, Collier made his first and only half-century, hitting 72 for Worcestershire against Hampshire on 15 July at the United Service Ground, Portsmouth. Despite Colliers best efforts however Hampshire still won by 8 wickets. Collier played his final first-class match on 6 August 1914 against Surrey at the County Ground, New Road, Worcester. He scored 25 in his only innings. The match was eventually drawn. He made a total of 1,021 first-class runs, his highest score being 72 against Hampshire. He took 10 wickets for 369 runs, his best figures being 3 for 28 and made 13 catches.

At the outbreak of the war Collier enlisted in the ranks of the Army Ordnance Corps and quickly rose to the rank of staff sergeant. Collier was killed in action near Mametz during the Battle of the Somme on 25 August 1916.

He is buried in the Flatiron Copse Cemetery, Mametz, grave reference X. H. 6

Batting and fielding averages

	Mat	Inns	NO	Runs	HS	Ave	100	50	Ct	St
First-class	53	87	8	1021	72	12.92	0	1	13	0

Bowling averages

	Mat	Balls	Runs	Wkts	BBI	Ave	Econ	SR	5w	10
First-class	53	521	369	10	3/28	36.90	4.24	52.1	0	0

617 Sergeant Samuel Harold Bates
Warwickshire
15th Bn The Royal Warwickshire Regiment
Died 28 August 1916
Aged 26
Right-handed Bat/Slow Left-arm Orthodox

'Born to play cricket'

Samuel Harold Bates was born on 16 June 1890 at the Edgbaston Cricket Ground, Birmingham, the son of John Bates of 22 Station Road Ainsdale, Southport, who was a groundsman at Edgbaston. Bates followed his father's example and became a groundsman at Lord's.

Bates was a useful all-round player, being a left-handed bowler and right-handed bat. He made five first-class appearances, all for Warwickshire in the County Championship between July 1910 and July 1912. He made his debut for Warwickshire on 23 July 1910 against Leicestershire at Aylestone Road, Leicester, scoring 0 and 2 and taking 1 wicket for 53 off 14 overs. Leicestershire won the game by an innings and 79 runs. He went on to play against Surrey, Worcestershire and Northamptonshire, making his final first-class appearance against Middlesex on 25 July 1912 at Edgbaston, scoring 13 and 0. Warwickshire won by 118 runs. Bates made a total of 24 first-class runs, his highest score being 13 against Middlesex. He also took six wickets for 182, his best figures being 3 for 56.

Bates was killed in action on 28 August 1916 near Hardecourt, France. His body was never recovered and he is commemorated on the Thiepval Memorial, Pier and Face 9 A 9 B and 10 B.

Batting and fielding averages

	Mat	Inns	NO	Runs	HS	Ave	100	50	Ct	St
First-class	5	9	1	24	13	3.00	0	0	0	0

Bowling averages

	Mat	Balls	Runs	Wkts	BBI	Ave	Econ	SR	5w	10
First-class	5	348	182	6	3/56	30.33	3.13	58.0	0	0

Lieutenant Kenneth Lotherington Hutchings
England and Kent
4th Bn (attd 12th Bn) The King's (Liverpool Regiment) attd
Welsh Regiment
Died 3 September 1916
Aged 33
Right-handed Bat/ Right-arm fast.

'Of all the cricketers who have fallen in the War he may
fairly be described as the most famous'

Kenneth Lotherington Hutchings was born on 7 September 1882 in Southborough, Kent and educated at Tonbridge School where he excelled at cricket, was in the XI for five years and headed the batting for three successive seasons.

Hutchings was regarded by many as the most graceful English batsman of the so-called 'Golden Age' of English cricket, before the First World War. Hutchings played in 207 first-class matches and seven tests between August 1902 and September 1912, mostly for Kent and mostly in the County Championship. His made his first class debut for Kent on 8 August 1902, (the year he left school), against Worcestershire at the Angel Ground, Tionbridge. He made 10 and 1, and hung onto catches from Henry Foster off the bowling of Blyth, (killed in action 8 November 1917), for 7 and William Lowe, again off the bowling of Blythe for 0. Blyth took eleven wickets during the match and reached his hundredth wicket in County Championship games. Kent won by nine wickets.

Hutchings' made his Test debut (first Test) against Australia on 13 December 1907, during the MCC's tour of Australia in 1907/08, at the Sydney Cricket Ground. He scored 42 and 17 and caught Peter McAlister off the bowling of Sydney Barnes for 3. Australia won by 2 wickets. He played in a further four tests during the tour, making his highest Test score of 126 during the second Test. Further games against Australia followed in England during the Australia tour in 1909, where he played at Old Trafford and at the Kennington Oval. From a total of 341 Test runs, his highest score was 126 against Australia during the second test.

Hutchings was a member of the Kent team that won the County Championship in 1906, 1909 and 1910 and in 1907 was named *Wisden* Cricketer of the year. His final first-class match for the MCC was against Yorkshire on 2 September 1912 at North Marine Road, Scarborough in which he scored 5 and 0 and caught Archibald White off the bowling of John Douglas for 12; the match was drawn. Major Booth (killed in action on 1 July 1916) reached his hundredth first-class wicket for the season during this match.

His health deteriorating, Hutchings lost form after the 1910 championship season and dropped out of first-class cricket in 1912. During his first-class career he scored 10,054 runs at an average 33.62, with a top score of 176, including twenty-one centuries and fifty-six fifties. He took 179 catches and, with his occasional bowling, managed twenty-four wickets for 938 runs, his best figures being 4 for 15.

A. A. Thomson wrote of him:

Though a crabbed unemotional Northerner, I sometimes think that if one last fragment of cricket had to be preserved, as though in amber, it should be a glimpse of K. L. Hutchings cover-driving under a summer heaven.

When the First World War broke out, he was in business in Liverpool, living at 71 London Road, Southborough, and immediately volunteered for service. He was gazetted into the Special Reserve of The King's (Liverpool Regiment) on 24 September 1914, going to France on 26 April 1915, attached to the 2nd Battalion Welsh Regiment. He was gazetted lieutenant on 17 December 1915 and in July 1916 returned to the King's, being attached to the 12th Battalion. He was constantly in action until being killed by a shell at Ginchy on 3 September 1916. *The Daily Telegraph* included the following obituary:

By his death on the field of battle one of the greatest cricketers has been taken from us. A typical man of Kent, in that his cricket was splendid characteristics of his country – bright, free, sparkling – Hutchings at his best was the most engaging batsman of his day. So long as he was at the wicket he brought out all that was best in a glorious game. On any wicket, against any bowling – circumstances did not matter – he was magnificent. His dash, his vigour, his quick eye, his indifference to care, as we understand care among crack batsmen, made him unlike any other cricketer, not in this generation have we seen his equal …

His body was never recovered and he is commemorated on the Thiepval Memorial, Pier and Face 1D 8B and 8 C.

Batting and fielding averages

	Mat	Inns	NO	Runs	HS	Ave	100	50	6s	Ct	St
Tests	7	12	0	341	126	28.41	1	1	1	9	0
First-class	207	311	12	10054	176	33.62	22	56		179	0

Bowling averages

	Mat	Inns	Balls	Runs	Wkts	BBI	BBM	Ave	Econ	SR	4w	5w	10
Tests	7	4	90	81	1	1/5	1/39	81.00	5.40	90.0	0	0	0
First-class	207		1439	938	24	4/15		39.08	3.91	59.9		0	0

Lieutenant Garnet Edwin Driver
Griqualand West
8th South African Horse
Died 7 September 1916
Aged 32
Not Known

'A Soldier and a Man'

Garnet Edwin Driver was born on 26 May 1883 in Maritzburg, South Africa. The son of Edwin James Driver, a broker, of Maritzburg, he was educated at Hilton and Maritzburg College, Natal. A good all-round sportsman, he played rugby for the Wasps and his cricket for the Standard Cricket Club. Driver played in one first-class match for Griqualand West on 26 November 1903 against Western Provinces at the Eclectics Cricket Club Ground, Kimberley in the Currie Cup. Driver scored 37 and 62. He also caught Charles Fock off the bowling of Gustave Verheyew for 6. Despite Driver's best efforts, Western Provinces still won by 48 runs.

Driver became a solicitor and conveyancer and later married Ruby Adelaide Driver. They had one child, Sylvia Margaret Driver, who died in 1991. On 1 November 1914 he was commissioned into the 8th South African Horse and embarked for East Africa on 22 May 1916. During the various actions in which he was involved he was Mentioned in Despatches 'For meritorious service in the field in East Africa' for his actions at Kissaki (*London Gazette*, 8 February 1917). It was during this action, on 7 September 1916, that Driver was seriously wounded and captured at Kissaki, dying the same day from his wounds still in enemy hands.

He is buried in Morogoro Cemetery, grave reference IV. E. 13.

Batting and fielding averages

	Mat	Inns	NO	Runs	HS	Ave	100	50	Ct	St
First-class	1	2	0	99	62	49.50	0	1	1	0

Bowling averages

	Mat	Balls	Runs	Wkts	BBI	BBM	Ave	Econ	SR	4w	5w	10
First-class	1	-	-	-	-	-	-	-	-	-	-	-

2259 Corporal Edwin Bertram Myers
Surrey
21st London Regiment (First Surrey Rifles)
Died 15 September 1916
Aged 28
Right-hand Bat/Slow Left-arm Orthodox

'Good at Every Sport'

Edwin Bertram Myers was born on 5 July 1888 in Blackheath, Kent, the son of Edwin A. Myers. an electrical engineer of 12 St George's Road, Greenwich.

Between May 1910 and June 1914 he played eleven first-class matches for Surrey, all but one in the County Championship, making his debut against Derbyshire on 5 May 1910 at the Kennington Oval and scoring 13 in his only innings. The match was drawn. He went on to play against Leicestershire, Hampshire, Kent, Northamptonshire, Lancashire and Nottinghamshire and made his final first-class appearance against Hampshire on 18 June 1914 at the Kennington Oval. He scored 30 not out and took a wicket in both innings for 56 runs off 17 over; the match was drawn. Although the majority of his matches were in the County Championship he did play against the visiting Australians on 17 June 1912 at the Oval, scoring 2 and 40. Surrey won by 21 runs.

During his first-class career with Surrey he scored 217 runs, his best score of 40 being against the visiting Australians. He also took three wickets for 211 runs, his best figures being 1 for 10. A good all-round athlete, Myers also played professional football for Crystal Palace.

During the war Myers served with the 21st Battalion London Regiment (First Surrey Rifles) and was killed on 15 September 1916 near Adanac.

He is commemorated in the Adanac Military Cemetery, Miraumont, grave Reference VII.F.28.

Batting and fielding averages

	Mat	Inns	NO	Runs	HS	Ave	100	50	Ct	St
First-class	11	17	1	217	40	13.56	0	0	3	0

Bowling averages

	Mat	Balls	Runs	Wkts	BBI	Ave	Econ	SR	5w	10
First-class	11	405	211	3	1/10	70.33	3.12	135.0	0	0

6/3961 Second Lieutenant Rupert George Hickmott
Canterbury
2nd Bn The Canterbury Regiment, New Zealand
Expeditionary Force
Died 16 September 1916
Aged 22
Right-handed Bat

'The most promising young cricketer in New Zealand'

Rupert George Hickmott was born on 19 March 1894 in Christchurch, Canterbury, New Zealand, the son of George and Martha Hickmott of 41 Ranfurly Street, St Albans, Christchurch. Educated at Christchurch High School where he was in the school XI for five seasons and captain for three, he played his club cricket for St Albans Cricket Club. In November 1911 he scored 235 for XV Colts against the Canterbury XI on the Christchurch ground. During the same year he was tried for Canterbury. Hickmott worked as a clerk.

He made 17 first-class appearances between December 1911 and January 1915. Seven were played in the Plunket Shield, four for New Zealand in Australia and three against Australia in New Zealand. He made his first-class debut on 30 December 1911 for Canterbury against Wellington at the Basin Reserve, Wellington; he made 30 and 39 and took catches from William Gibbes off the bowling of Daniel Reese for 76 and John Findlay off the bowling of Joseph Bennett for 1. Canterbury won by 5 wickets.

He took part in New Zealand's tour of Australia between December 1913 and January 1914, his opening appearance taking place on 19 December 1913, against Queensland at Brisbane Cricket Ground, Woolloongabba, Brisbane. He scored 19 and 1 and caught William Evans off the bowling of Daniel Reese for 30 and Charles Barstow off the bowling of Joseph Bennett for 0. New Zealand won by 12 runs. As well as playing against New South Wales, Victoria and South Australia, he turned out three times against Australia in New Zealand, twice for Canterbury and once for New Zealand. He made his final first class appearance on 9 January 1915, in the Plunket Shield against Wellington at the Basin Reserve, Wellington. He scored 13 and 28, Canterbury winning by 92 runs. During his first-class career Hickmott scored 778 runs, his highest score being 109 against Hawke's Bay. He also took 11 wickets for 300 runs, his best figures being 4 for 5. He made 7 catches.

He served with C Company of 2nd Canterbury Infantry during the war, embarking for the Western Front on board the *Willochra* on 4 March 1916. During the fighting on the Somme on 16 September 1916 he was killed in action.

Hickmott's remains were never recovered and he is commemorated on the Caterpillar Valley (New Zealand) Memorial.

Batting and fielding averages

	Mat	Inns	NO	Runs	HS	Ave	100	50	Ct	St
First-class	17	31	0	778	109	25.09	1	4	7	0

Bowling averages

	Mat	Runs	Wkts	BBI	Ave	5w	10
First-class	17	300	11	4/5	27.27	0	0

Second Lieutenant John Henry Sneyd Carew Hunt
Middlesex
23rd Bn London Regiment
Died 16 September 1916
Aged 41
Right-hand Bat/Right-arm Fast-Medium

'He was a very plucky punishing bat, a useful bowler, right-hand fast,
and a brilliant fieldsman, wherever he was placed'

John Henry Sneyd Hunt was born on 24 November 1874 at Kensington, London. The son of Robert Ponsonby Carew Hunt and Ada Hunt, née Sneyd, he was educated at Ascham House, Bournemouth, before going to Winchester College (1888–1893, House E). He played cricket for Winchester and took part in their annual meeting against Eton College on 23 June 1893, scoring 16 and zero and taking two wickets. Eton College won by five wickets. He went up to Oxford University but failed to get his Blue. On leaving Oxford he became a clerk in the Probate and Divorce Registry, Somerset House.

Between May 1902 and May 1912, Hunt made 46 first-class appearances, almost exclusively for Middlesex in the County Championship. A good all-round cricketer, he was a punishing bat, and a useful right-hand fast bowler as well as being brilliant in the field with large hands. He made his debut for Middlesex was on 19 May 1902 against Somerset at Lord's, he scored 8 and 60 and took two wickets for 4 off 1.4 overs. In fact, he took a wicket with his first ball in a first-class match during Somerset's first innings. Somerset won by one wicket. In 1903, when Middlesex won the County Championship, he scored an average of 27, with 57 being his highest score. He headed the bowling in 1908, taking 13 wickets in 5 matches with an average of 19 runs a wicket. He made 1393 runs during his first class career, his highest score being 128 for the Gentlemen against the Players at the Oval on 7 July 1904. He also took 80 wickets for 2137 runs his best figures being 5 for 60. He made 29 catches.

At the outbreak of war he enlisted into the ranks of the 15th Battalion London Regiment before being commissioned into the 23rd Battalion. Hunt was killed in action on the Somme on 16 September 1916 during the battle to capture High Wood.

His obituary in *Wisden* in 1917 recorded that:

He was a very good all-round cricketer, and so keen and enthusiastic that he was more valuable on a side than many players of greater natural gifts. He was a very plucky punishing bat, a useful bowler, right-hand fast, and a brilliant fieldsman, wherever he was placed.

Like thousands of others, his body was never recovered and he is commemorated on the Thiepval Memorial, Pier and Face 9D, 9C, 13C and 12C.

John Hunt also played hockey for Surrey.

Batting and fielding averages

	Mat	Inns	NO	Runs	HS	Ave	100	50	Ct	St
First-class	46	71	6	1393	128	21.43	1	5	29	0

Bowling averages

	Mat	Balls	Runs	Wkts	BBI	Ave	Econ	SR	5w	10
First-class	46	4295	2137	80	5/60	26.71	2.98	53.6	2	0

Second Lieutenant Henry David Keigwin
Scotland, Essex, Gentlemen of England
3rd Bn Lancashire Fusiliers,
attd 19th Bn, attd 29th Divisional Salvage Company
Died 20 September 1916
Aged 35
Right-hand Bat/Left-arm Medium

'Returned from Africa to die in France'

Henry David Keigwin was born on 14 May 1881 at Lexden Colchester, Essex. He was the son of Charles David and Louisa Keigwin of Parson's Hill, Lexden and was educated at St Paul's School where he was in the XI between 1899 and 1900. On leaving school he went up to Peterhouse College Cambridge. Although he did not obtain his Blue he played brilliantly for his college, making over 1,000 runs in both 1901 and 1904. On 26 April 1904 Henry scored 140 not out for Peterhouse against Fitzwilliam Hall, together with his brother, R. P. Keigwin, who scored 120 in the same match, making 318 runs between them.

Keigwin made 11 first-class appearances between June 1905 and June 1909, 4 for Essex, against Sussex, Derbyshire, Surrey, and South Africa, 4 for the Gentlemen of England against Cambridge University, Oxford University and Surrey (twice) and three for Scotland against South Africa, Nottinghamshire and Australia. He made his first class debut for the Gentlemen of England against Cambridge University on 19 June 1905 at Crystal Palace Park, when he scored 0 and 5 and took five wickets for 83 off 23 overs; Cambridge University won by 9 wickets. He made his debut for Essex against Sussex on 9 August 1906 at the County Ground, Leyton, scoring 16 in his one innings and taking 1 wicket for 54 off 17 overs. Essex won by 10 wickets. His first match for Scotland was against South Africa on 22 July 1907 at Raeburn Place, Edinburgh. Keigwin scored 36 and 41 and took 2 wickets for 46 off 12 overs in the first innings and 1 wicket for 9 off 3 overs in the second; South Africa won by 8 wickets. He also played for the Gentlemen of England against Surrey on 20 April 1908 in W. G. Grace's final first-class match. During his first class career Keigwin scored 351 runs his highest score being 77 against Surrey on 16 April 1906. He also took 15 wickets for 472 runs his best figures being 5 for 83. He made 3 catches.

Keigwin became an organ scholar at Trinity College Cambridge and later became director of music at Trinity College, Glenalmond. He eventually decided to settle in Bulowayo.

In January 1916 Keigwin returned from Africa and was commissioned into the 3rd Battalion Lancashire Fusiliers, and posted to the 19th Battalion and attached to 29th Divisional Salvage Company. He was killed on 20 September 1916 while serving on the Somme.

He is buried in Bouzincourt Communal Cemetery Extension, grave reference I. H. 7.

Batting and fielding averages

	Mat	Inns	NO	Runs	HS	Ave	100	50	Ct	St
First-class	11	18	0	351	77	19.50	0	1	3	0

Bowling averages

	Mat	Balls	Runs	Wkts	BBI	Ave	Econ	SR	5w	10
First-class	11	816	472	15	5/83	31.46	3.47	54.4	1	0

Captain Arthur Franklin Willmer
Oxford University
9th Bn The Prince Consort's Own (Rifle Brigade)
Died 20 September 1916
Aged 26
Right-arm Fast

'His death is one of the greatest tragedies the college has had to face'

Arthur Franklin Willmer was born on 10 January 1890 at Claughton, Birkenhead, Cheshire, the first son of Arthur Washington Willmer JP of Oakhurst, Grosvenor Road, Birkenhead, a cotton broker, and Janet Mary Willmer, née Cooper. Educated at the Birkenhead School where he was in the XI for four years and captain in his last two, he went up to Brasenose College Oxford on an open scholarship to read law. While at Oxford he played one first-class match for Oxford University against the Free Foresters on 13 June 1912. He scored 5 not out and 7 not out and took no wickets for 36. In 1914 he played two minor county games for Cheshire.

He passed both his intermediate and final examinations for the Bar. He joined the Inns of Court Officer Cadet Corps (OTC) in October 1914, after which on the 24 December he was commissioned as a second lieutenant into the 9th Battalion The Rifle Brigade. Promoted to lieutenant in April 1916 and temporary captain the following June, he had gone to France during the early part of 1915 and was severely wounded in the jaw by shrapnel in June 1915.

After convalescing for some months he returned to the front, only to be wounded again by shrapnel on 18 September 1916 while fighting on the Somme, dying two days later. The *Oxford Magazine* carried the following obituary in November 1916:

> His death is one of the greatest tragedies the College has had to face, his devotion to duty, high principles and crystal-clear intellect had justified us in predicting for him a distinguished career.

He is buried in St Sever Cemetery, Rouen, Officers A. 10. 6.

Batting and fielding averages

	Mat	Inns	NO	Runs	HS	Ave	100	50	Ct	St
First-class	1	2	2	12	7*	-	0	0	0	0

Bowling averages

	Mat	Balls	Runs	Wkts	BBI	BBM	Ave	Econ	SR	4w	5w	10
First-class	1	60	36	0	-	-	-	3.60	-	0	0	0

Lieutenant Colonel William Drysdale DSO
Europeans (India)
2nd Bn Royal Scots (The Lothian Regiment)
Commanding Officer 7th The Leicestershire Regiment
Died 29 September 1916
Aged 39
Right-handed Bat

'He was the best man I knew for making other men fight'

William Drysdale was born on 4 November 1876 at Piteadie, Kirkcaldy, Fife, the son of William Drysdale, of Kilrie, Fife. Educated at Loretto School between 1890 and 1894, he was in the both the school XI and XV, as well as being a school prizeman. On leaving school he decided on a career in the Army and entered Sandhurst in 1894. He was in the Sandhurst XI as well as playing in a number of other military matches and winning First Prize for riding. He was gazetted in the 2nd Royal Scots on 5 September 1896 and saw service in Burma and India. Between September 1900 and September 1902 Drysdale played four first-class matches, all Bombay Presidency Matches for the Europeans. He made his debut on 13 September 1900 against the Parsees at the Deccan Gymkhana Ground, Poona. He scored 2 and 55 in a drawn match. He had to wait almost a year to make his second appearance, turning out again against the Parsees on 29 August 1901, this time at the Gymkhana Ground, Bombay. He scored 5 and 0, Parsees winning by eight wickets. He next played on 12 September 1901 at the Deccan Gymkhana Ground, Poona, he scored 16 and 0, and caught Dinshaw Kanga off the bowling of Archibald Douglas for 5. The Europeans winning by 192 runs. His final first-class match came on 11 September 1902, again at Poona; he scored 2 and 12, the Europeans winning by four wickets.

Wisden commented on his play, 'A very useful all-round player – he could hit hard, field brilliantly at cover point and bowl lobs and fast …'

On 19 January 1904 he married Mary Louisa, daughter of Sir J. Muir Mackenzie. He attended Staff College in 1908 and 1909, becoming captain of their cricket and hockey teams and won the College point to point, golf and tennis. Drysdale was awarded a medal for attempting to save a comrade from drowning on 24 November 1902.

In August 1914 at the outbreak of war he went to France as a brigade major. He was wounded in 1914 at Ypres where he also earned the DSO:

Captain Drysdale showed an unsurpassed example of fearlessness and cheerful courage, refusing to quite his brigade when wounded. (*London Gazette*, 18 February 1915)

On 1 October 1915 he was given command of the 7th Battalion Leicestershire Regiment, and was brevetted lieutenant colonel in spring 1916. He was wounded at the storming of Bazentinle-Petit on 14 July 1916 and had only just returned to his battalion when he was killed in action on 29 September. A comrade described seeing a stretcher with a body on it, covered by a blanket. When he pulled the blanket back he saw it was his commanding officer, Colonel William Drysdale: a hole had been drilled through his head. He had been looking over the edge of a trench around Guedecourt which the Leicesters had just captured when he was shot by a German sniper.

His general wrote, 'He was a splendid officer, fearless and always cheery. He was the best man I knew for making other men fight.'

He is buried in Caterpillar Valley Cemetery, Longueval, grave reference VI. E. 11.

Batting and fielding averages

	Mat	Inns	NO	Runs	HS	Ave	100	50	Ct	St
First-class	4	8	0	92	55	11.50	0	1	1	0

Bowling averages

	Mat	Balls	Runs	Wkts	BBI	BBM	Ave	Econ	SR	4w	5w	10
First-class	4	-	-	-	-	-	-	-	-	-	-	-

Captain Edward Alfred Shaw
Oxford University
6th Bn The Oxfordshire and Buckinghamshire Light Infantry
Died 7 October 1916
Aged 24
Right-handed Bat/Wicket-keeper

'If ever a family suffered through the First War, it was the Shaws'

Edward Alfred Shaw was born on 16 May 1892 at Bishop's Stortford, Hertfordshire. He was the son of Edward Domett Shaw, the first Bishop of Buckingham (Oxford Cricket Blue 1882), and Agnes Shaw and was educated at Marlborough College, where he was in the school XI for five years, captaining the side in the last three. In 1911 he made 485 runs and was second in the averages with 40.41, his highest score being 144 against H. Plunket Green's XI. In his five matches at Lord's against Rugby he made 161 runs in ten innings, taking two catches and stumping two in an innings in the 1910 game. He made his debut for Buckinghamshire in the Minor Counties Championship in 1908, playing against Wiltshire. After leaving Marlborough he went up to Brasenose College Oxford where he achieved his Blue.

He made thirteen first-class appearances for Oxford University between June 1912 and July 1914. He made his first class debut on 13 June 1912 against the Free Foresters at the University Parks, Oxford. He scored 30 and 31 and stumped Noel Phillips off the bowling of John Fraser for 8 and caught Edmond Foljambe, once again off the bowling of Fraser, for 15. The Free Foresters won by 260 runs. He also appeared against H. D. G. Leveson-Gower's XI, Hampshire, Cambridge University, H. K. Foster's XI, Kent, MCC, Scotland, G. J. V. Weigall's XI, and L. G. Robinson's XI. He made his final first-class appearance against Cambridge University on 6 July 1914 at Lord's. He made 57 not out and 15, Oxford winning by 194 runs. During his first-class career Shaw made 424 runs, his highest score being 57 against Cambridge University and Free Foresters. He also made 12 catches and 8 stumping.

He made a further sixteen appearances for Buckinghamshire in the Minor Counties, his highest score being 117 against Dorset in 1914 during his final match at Aylesbury. Interestingly Edward Shaw always played in glasses, which seemed to have no effect on his batting or wicket-keeping.

Shaw served as a lieutenant with the 6th Battalion Oxfordshire and Buckinghamshire Light Infantry during the war, being promoted to captain on 19 November 1915. He was killed in action near le Sars in France on the 7 October 1916 during the Battle of the Somme. He was the third son of the Bishop of Buckinghamshire to fall. His body was never recovered and he is commemorated on the Thiepval Memorial, Pier and Face 10 A and 10 D.

There is a stained-glass window in High Wycombe parish church dedicated to the three Shaw brothers. The bells of the church were tolled for over three hours to commemorate each of the brother's deaths.

Edward Shaw's brothers: Bernard Henry Gilbert, killed 18 December 1914, aged 21, and Arthur Gilbey, killed 24 December 1915, aged 19. Another brother, Robert John, served in the Navy and was at Jutland; he also played cricket for the Royal Navy and Combined Services. I met him shortly before he died in 1995, a wonderful man full of stories.

Batting and fielding averages

	Mat	Inns	NO	Runs	HS	Ave	100	Ct	St
First-class	13	22	2	424	57*	21.20	0	12	8

Bowling averages

	Mat	Balls	Runs	Wkts	BBI	BBM	Ave	Econ	SR	4w	5w	10
First-class	13	-	-	-	-	-	-	-	-	-	-	-

S/11889 Lance Corporal Herbert James Rogers
Hampshire
7th Bn The Seaforth Highlanders (Ross-Shire Buffs, The
Duke of Albany's)
Died 12 October 1916
Aged 23
Left-handed Bat/Right-arm Off-break

'He didn't have to fight, he wanted to'

Herbert James Rogers was born on 6 March 1893 at Camberley Surrey. The son of Peter and Ellen Rogers, née Wyeth, of St John's Ground, 211 Woodstock Road, Oxford, he was educated at Bedford House School where he was in the cricket XI. He later became a professional cricketer, a middle-order left-hand bat and off-break bowler. Although eligible to play for Worcestershire County Cricket Club he found himself turning out for Hampshire.

He made seven first-class appearances between May 1912 and August 1914, all for Hampshire in the County Championship. He made his debut against Yorkshire on 13 May 1912 at Bramall Lane where he scored 10 in his only innings and took one wicket for 26. He went on to play against Gloucestershire, Middlesex, Nottinghamshire and Lancashire, making his final first-class appearance against Derbyshire on 13 August 1914 at Queen's Park, Chesterfield, scoring 0 and 7. Hampshire won by 15 runs. During his first-class career Rogers made 69 first class runs, his highest score being 18 against Gloucestershire. He also took 1 wicket for 62, his best figures being 1 for 26. He made 12 catches. Rogers played for Hampshire in Ireland and the North Oxford Cricket Club.

In October 1914, shortly after the outbreak of war, he enlisted in the ranks of the Oxfordshire and Buckinghamshire Light Infantry before being gazetted in the 15th Battalion Middlesex Regiment as a second lieutenant in June 1915. Invalided out in October 1915, he re-enlisted into the ranks of the 7th Battalion Seaforth Highlanders the following November, rising to the rank of lance corporal. He went to France with his battalion in August 1916 and was killed in action during the Battle of the Somme on 12 October 1916.

His death was reported in the local Oxford Paper:

The death in action of 'Bert' Rogers, adds another to the growing list of the North Oxford Cricket Club who have made the great sacrifice in the war. Young Rogers could not very well help being a decent cricketer. His father Peter Rogers has been one of the mainstays of Oxford cricket for something over 20 years. And if the son's prowess had not fully developed, he yet afforded some evidence that he would not allow the family reputation to suffer. It was some 6 or 8 years ago when he first came to the front as a right-hand leg-break bowler. In local cricket he played havoc with all sorts of batsmen, and on his day was almost unplayable. On such occasions his length and break were remarkable. He attracted the attention of Mr F. H. Bacon, the Hants county secretary, and after being attached for a short time to the county ground staff he qualified for the southern County, and played for three matches for them in 1912. He afterwards qualified for Worcestershire, and in 1914, his last cricket season, he accomplished many excellent performances both with bat and ball. Indeed it has been said, that his batting showed remarkable improvement he bode fair to become an all-round cricketer of merit. A young fellow of splendid physique, quiet habits, and unassuming manner, he was a credit to the profession he had adopted, and genuine regrets will be felt at his early death, though the manner of it is, perhaps, such as he would have desired.

His body was never recovered and he is commemorated on the Thiepval Memorial, Pier and Face 15 C.

Batting and fielding averages

	Mat	Inns	NO	Runs	HS	Ave	100	50	Ct	St
First-class	7	12	0	69	18	5.75	0	0	0	0

Bowling averages

	Mat	Balls	Runs	Wkts	BBI	Ave	Econ	SR	5w	10
First-class	7	66	62	1	1/26	62.00	5.63	66.0	0	0

22625 Private Charles Henry Yaldren
Hampshire
1st Bn The Hampshire Regiment
Died 23 October 1916
Aged 24
Right-handed Bat

'A career cut so short'

Charles Henry Yaldren was born on 8 December 1891 at Southampton, Hampshire, the son of Charles Henry and Alice M. Yaldren of 3, Russell Court, King Street, Southampton. Charles was described as a useful bowler and tail-end bat.

He made one first-class appearance for Hampshire against Cambridge University at the County Ground, Southampton on 24 June 1912. Yaldren scored 8 in his only innings, and took the wicket of Geoffrey Hopley, (who died of wounds on 12 May 1915) caught by James Stone for 36; the match was drawn due to rain.

During the war Yaldren enlisted in the ranks of the 1st Battalion Hampshire Regiment (G Company) and was killed on action on 23 October 1916.

His body was never recovered and he is commemorated on the Thiepval Memorial, Pier and Face 7 C and 7 B.

Batting and fielding averages

	Mat	Inns	NO	Runs	HS	Ave	100	50	Ct	St
First-class	1	1	0	8	8	8.00	0	0	0	0

Bowling averages

	Mat	Balls	Runs	Wkts	BBI	Ave	Econ	SR	5w	10
First-class	1	66	60	1	1/52	60.00	5.45	66.0	0	0

50353 Private Arthur Edward Davis
Leicestershire
11th Bn The Royal Fusiliers (City of London Regiment)
Died 4 November 1916
Aged 34
Right-handed Bat/Wicket-keeper

'Nothing was ever too difficult for him'

Arthur Edward Davis was born on 4 August 1882 in Victoria Park, Leicester to Samuel Davis and Mary E. Davis and was educated at Mill Hill School (1897) where he was in the school XI in both 1898 and 1899.

He played his club cricket for the Leicester Ivanhoe Cricket Club and made 21 first-class appearances for Leicestershire between July 1901 and July 1908. Eighteen were in the County Championship, one against the County of London, one against the MCC, and one against the Gentlemen of Philadelphia. He made his debut against Yorkshire on 4 July 1901 at North Marine Road, Scarborough; he made 6 and 10 and caught George Hirst off the bowling of Samuel Coe for 61. Davis played against Derbyshire, Surrey, Hampshire, Warwickshire, Nottinghamshire, Worcestershire, Sussex and Essex. He played his final first-class match against Nottinghamshire on 27 July 1908 at Aylestone Road, Leicester, scoring 7 in his only innings. He also stumped George Gunn off the bowling of John King for 33 and caught Thomas Wass off the bowling of William Odell, (killed in action on 4 October 1917). During his first-class career he scored 334 runs, his highest score being 55 against Sussex. He also took 37 catches and made 10 stumpings.

He married Hettie Louise Davis and moved to 63 Knighton Drive, Leicester. During the war he served with the 11th Battalion Royal Fusiliers as private 50353. He was killed in action with his battalion on 4 November 1916, his body was never recovered and he is commemorated on the Thiepval Memorial, Pier and Face 8 C 9 A and 16 A.

Batting and fielding averages

	Mat	Inns	NO	Runs	HS	Ave	100	50	Ct	St
First-class	21	31	4	334	55	12.37	0	1	37	10

Bowling averages

	Mat	Balls	Runs	Wkts	BBI	BBM	Ave	Econ	SR	4w	5w	10
First-class	21	-	-	-	-	-	-	-	-	-	-	-

Captain Cyril Stanley Rattigan
Cambridge University
7th Bn The Royal Fusiliers (City of London Regiment)
Died 13 November 1916
Aged 32
Right-handed Bat/Right-arm medium

'could not leave his regiment and the men he loved'

Cyril Stanley Rattigan was born on 5 August 1884 in Camberwell, London, the youngest son of Sir William Rattigan KC, MP for Lanarkshire, and of Lady Rattigan of Lanarkslea, Cornwall Gardens, London. Educated at Harrow School, he was in the cricket XI in 1903 and 1904 and also won the 200 yards on three occasions, the 100 yards twice, and the quarter mile once as well as being runner-up for the School Rackets for two years in succession. On leaving Harrow he went up to Trinity College Cambridge where he became a member of Butterflies and was a keen golfer.

Although he didn't win his Blue for cricket, he made six first-class appearances, five for Cambridge University between May 1906 and June 1907 and one for the MCC against Cambridge University in 1908. He made his debut for Cambridge against Yorkshire on 14 May 1906 at Fenner's, Rattigan made 42 and 2, Cambridge University winning by 305 runs. Rattigan also played against Northamptonshire, W. G. Grace's XI, Lancaster and Surrey and made his final first-class appearance for the MCC against Cambridge University on 25 June 1908 at Lord's. He scored 3 and 34 not out; Cambridge won by 2 wickets. He scored 183 first-class runs with his highest score 42 against Yorkshire and took 5 wickets for 217, his best figures being 3 for 61. In addition he took 3 catches.

In 1909 he was appointed Honorary Attaché in His Majesty's Diplomatic Service, being sent to Fez with the Sir Reginald Lister mission. Gazetted in the 7th Battalion Royal Fusiliers, he was on the staff of the garrison commander at Falmouth from September 1914. However, he resigned this 'safe job', writing that he could not leave his regiment and the men he loved 'all of whom are such fine fellows'. Rattigan went to the front with D Company 7th Royal Fusiliers in July 1916 and was killed by a sniper a few months later on 13 November. A brother officer, Lieutenant Downing, wrote the following to his brother:

Your brother was slightly wounded in the mouth sometime before he was killed, but the bullet only cut his lip and he refused to go away. When he discovered that the company was held up, he decided to remain where we were, namely in a shell-hole in 'No Man's Land' until receiving orders. He and I lay in a shell hole about 30 yards from the Hun for about five hours, until we discovered a mine-shaft running back to our own front line. It was very difficult to move as there was a sniper within a few yards, and when we did look up I got a bullet through the hat, so your brother decided to lie low for a bit and then make a rush for the shaft. When he was just going to make a rush, he saw a wounded man a few yards away and he said, "I'm going to have a shot at getting him in." He sat bolt upright in the shell hole and was looking towards the man, when the same sniper hit him in the head through his hat…He was buried two days afterwards in the same shell-hole he was killed in … By his death I have lost one of the finest friends I ever had.

His body could not be recovered and he is commemorated on the Thiepval Memorial, Pier and Face 8 C 9 A and 16 A.

The famous playwright Terence Rattigan was his nephew.

Batting and fielding averages

	Mat	Inns	NO	Runs	HS	Ave	100	50	Ct	St
First-class	7	11	2	183	42	20.33	0	0	3	0

Bowling averages

	Mat	Balls	Runs	Wkts	BBI	Ave	Econ	SR	5w	10
First-class	7	444	217	5	3/61	43.40	2.93	88.8	0	0

Second Lieutenant Charles William Rorich Minnaar
Western Province (South Africa)
3rd (attd 8th) Bn The East Lancashire Regiment
Died 16 November 1916
Aged 34
Unknown

'A South African that came to serve the mother land and died defending it'

Charles William Rorich Minnaar was born in August 1882 at Wepner, Orange Free State, South Africa. The son of Mr S. T. and Mrs M. Minnaar, of Cape Province, he played in one first-class game on 7 March 1914 for the Western Provinces against the MCC at Newlands, Cape Town, scoring 0 and 4 not out. Minnaar took 4 wickets for 95 off 43 overs in the first innings and 1 wicket for 74 off 17 overs in the second innings. He also managed to hang on to two catches, both from Lionel Tennyson off the bowling of Edward Budgen, in the first innings for 9 and James Blanckenberg for 42 in the second.

WESTERN PROVINCE CRICKET CLUB.
Winners of Senior Championship, 1913-14.

[Photo by W. Duffus, Capetown.

P. T. Lewis, W. H. Mars, P. A. M. Hands, R. A. Rail.
C. W. R. Minnaar, R. H. M. Hands, A. V. C. Bisset (captain), R. de Smidt, A. Kennedy.
C. Jackson, F. Reid.

His cricket career was cut short by the beginning of the war. Initially he enlisted as a trooper in the South African Mounted Rifles before coming to England and being commissioned as a second lieutenant into the 3rd Battalion East Lancashire Regiment, attached to the 8th Battalion.

He was killed in action on 16 November 1916, during an unsuccessful attack on Munich Trench and Frankfurt Trench by D and A Companies of the 8th East Lancashire Regiment.

He is buried in Wagon Road, Cemetery, Beaumont-Hamel, grave reference A. 10.

Batting and fielding averages

	Mat	Inns	NO	Runs	HS	Ave	100	50	Ct	St
First-class	1	2	2	4	4*	-	0	0	2	0

Bowling averages

	Mat	Runs	Wkts	BBI	Ave	5w	10
First-class	1	169	5	4/95	33.80	0	0

54 Troop Sergeant James Stewart Swallow
Border (South Africa)
South African Horse
Died 17 November 1916
Aged 38
Not Known

'A more decent fellow I never met'

James Stewart Swallow was born at Uitenhage, Cape Province in 1878. The son of. James Stuart Swallow, who lived and worked in India, and Mrs E. L. Swallow of 'Charlton', Cheltenham Road, Mowbray, Cape Province, formerly of 'Hernidale', Chaucer Road, Bedford.

He was sent to England to be educated and attended Bedford Grammar School where he played in the First XI against Kensington Park on 6 June 1896, scoring 65. Bedford School won by 73 runs.

Returning to South Africa, Swallow played in three first-class matches for Border between March 1907 and March 1909, the first against Transvaal on 30 March 1907 at the Jan Smuts Ground, East London. He scored 8 in his only innings; the match was drawn. His second match was against Western Province on 19 March 1909 in the Currie Cup, played at Newlands Rugby Ground, Cape Town. He scored 7 and 0, Western Province winning by two wickets. His final first-class match was played on 26 March 1909, against Eastern Province, once again in the Currie Cup at the Newlands Rugby Ground. He scored 0 in his only innings and took 2 catches, Aidan Lyons for 11 off the bowling of Arthur Sprenger and Charles Fock for 51 off the bowling of Sibley Snooke. Border won by 8 wickets.

He served during the Second Boer War and re-enlisted in December 1915, joining D Squadron 4th South African Horse, and being promoted to troop sergeant. The troop was absorbed into 1 South African Mounted Brigade on 1 September 1916; 1st and 9th Troops were also absorbed on 24th November 1916.

Swallow died at Morogoro, German East Africa on 17 November 1916 from blackwater fever.

He is commemorated in the Morogoro Cemetery Tanzania, Grave reference VI. D. 7.

Batting and fielding averages

	Mat	Inns	NO	Runs	HS	Ave	100	50	Ct	St
First-class	3	4	0	25	10	6.25	0	0	2	0

Bowling averages

	Mat	Balls	Runs	Wkts	BBI	BBM	Ave	Econ	SR	4w	5w	10
First-class	3	-	-	-	-	-	-	-	-	-	-	-

Second Lieutenant Leonard James Moon
England/Cambridge University/Middlesex/MCC
Devonshire Regiment
Died 23 November 1916
Aged 38
Right-handed Bat/Wicket-keeper

'The finest cricketer ever to die for his country'

Leonard James Moon was born on 9 February 1878 in Kensington London and educated at Westminster School and Pembroke College Cambridge. He was in the Westminster XI in 1894 and the two following seasons, heading the averages with 25.71 in 1895 and being second in 1896 with 46.69. During his last season at the school he scored an impressive 57 against Charterhouse. Going up to Pembroke College Cambridge he obtained his Blue for cricket against Oxford in both 1899 and 1900; he also got a Blue for football, later playing for the Corinthians.

He made 96 first-class appearances and played in 4 Tests between 20 May 1897 and 1 September 1913, playing for Cambridge University, Middlesex and England. He made his debut for Cambridge University against A. J. Webbe's XI on 20 May 1897 at F. P. Fenner's Ground, Cambridge. He scored 12 and 14 and caught Hugh Bromley-Davenport off the bowling of Eustace Shine for 13. Cambridge University won by 9 wickets. He travelled with the MCC on their tour of North America between July and August 1905 and playing against the Gentlemen of Philadelphia twice, wining the first by 7 wickets and loosing the second by 61 runs. He followed this up by travelling with the MCC on their tour of South Africa between December 1905 and March 1906. He played against Western Province, Transvaal, South African Army, Natal and Eastern Province. He also played in 4 Test against South Africa. Missing the first Test he played in the second on 6 March 1906 at the Old Wanderers Ground, Johannesburg. He scored 30 and 0. South Africa winning by 9 wickets. In the third Test on 10 March 1906 also played at the Old Wanderers Ground Moon scored 36 and 15 and caught Arthur Nourse off the bowling of Albert Relf for 61. South Africa won by 243 runs. Keeping faith with him Moon was selected for the forth Test played on the 24 March 1906 at Newlands, Cape Town. He scored 33 and 28 and caught Reginald Schwarz (died of wounds 18 November 1918) off the bowling of Albert Relf for 33. England won by 4 wickets. He made his final Test appearance in the fifth test on 30 April 1906 once again at Newlands, South Africa. Moon scored 7 and 33 and caught Louis Tancred the South African opener off the bowling of John Crawford for 26 and George Faulkner off the bowling of Albert Relf for 43. South Africa won by an innings and 16 runs. He made his final first-class appearance on 1 September 1913 for L. G. Robinson's XI against J. R. Mason's XI at Buckingham Hall, Attleborough; he scored 3 and 12 and made two catches hanging onto a ball from Harold Hardinge off the bowling of Sydney Barnes for 0 and Lionel Troughton, once again off the bowling of Barnes, for 26. He also stumped Gerald Weigall off the bowling of Barnes for 10. The match was drawn. Moon made one appearance for the Gentlemen of England in 1904.

He became a member of the MCC in 1898. During his career he made 182 runs in Test matches, his highest score being 36. He made 4 catches. He scored 4,166 first-class runs, his highest score being 162 and took 1 wicket for 55 runs, his best figures being 1 for 5. He took 72 catches and made 13 stumpings.

On leaving university he became a teacher. He died of wounds while serving as a second lieutenant with the 10th Battalion Devonshire Regiment near Karasouli in Salonika, Greece.

He is buried in Karasouli Military Cemetery, Greece, grave reference A 189.

His brother William (Billy) Moon was also a cricketer and represented England at football.

Batting and fielding averages

	Mat	Inns	NO	Runs	HS	Ave	100	50	4s	6s	Ct	St
Tests	4	8	0	182	36	22.75	0	0	19	1	4	0
First-class	96	163	8	4166	162	26.87	7				72	13

Bowling averages

	Mat	Inns	Balls	Runs	Wkts	BBI	BBM	Ave	Econ	SR	4w	5w	10
Tests	4	-	-	-	-	-	-	-	-	-	-	-	-
First-class	96		90	55	1	1/5		55.00	3.66	90.0		0	0

Major Attwood Alfred Torrens
Marylebone Cricket Club/Free Foresters
Royal Artillery
Died 8 December 1916
42 Years
Right-handed Bat/Right-arm Medium

'He had a real genius for friendship'

Attwood Alfred Torrens was born on 13 February 1874 at Baston Manor, Hayes, Kent, the son of Captain Alfred and Mrs Torrens. Educated at Harrow between 1888 and 1892, he was in the cricket XI in 1892 and played against Eton College on 8 July 1892 at Lord's, scoring 10 (not out) and 14 (not out). He also took one wicket for 13 off six overs. On leaving school he went to work at the Stock Exchange.

Torrens made 9 first-class appearances between December 1906 and June 1913, 8 for the MCC and 1 for the Free Foresters. He made his debut on 25 December 1906 for the MCC against Wellington in the MCC's 1906–7 tour of New Zealand at the Basin Reserve, Wellington. He scored 8 and 3; the match was drawn. Torrens went on to play against Auckland, Hawke's Bay and New Zealand and, in June 1907, played for the MCC against both Oxford and Cambridge University. He made his final first-class appearance for the Free Foresters against Cambridge University on 9 June 1913 at F. P. Fenner's Ground. He scored 9 in his only innings. He also took 3 wickets for 41 off 17 overs in the first innings and 2 for 35 off 6 overs in the second. Free Foresters won by 8 wickets. Torrens scored 183 first-class runs, his highest score being 87 against Hawke's Bay on 22 February 1907 and took 11 wickets for 335, runs his best figures being 3 for 41.

At the outbreak of war, Torrens enlisted in the ranks of the Public Schools' Battalion before obtaining a commission in the Royal Artillery in 1915 and left for the front with his battery in May 1916. He was killed instantaneously by a shell fragment on 8 December 1916 while running across the open to move his men to safety. His loss was keenly felt. Brigadier General R. C. Coates wrote:

> I and the whole of the Artillery of the Division much feel his loss. He was an exceptionally popular Officer, both with his brother-officers and also with his men. He was a keen soldier.

Lieutenant Colonel H. A. Roebel, commanding 307th Brigade RFA, wrote: 'He met his death like a soldier. He was an excellent Officer and very popular in the Brigade. We all deplore his loss.'

Lieutenant Kobel wrote:

> His battery was being shelled and being uneasy about the safety of his men he went out to move them and was struck and killed instantaneously by a piece of shell. He was an excellent officer and very popular in the brigade. We all deplore his loss.

One of his subalterns wrote:

> He was such a favourite with us all. I feel his loss very deeply. I have only been in his battery three months but they have been quite the happiest three months of my army life.

The following was written by a well-known man who preferred to sign himself 'Chaplain':

> Not a soldier by profession, or perhaps by inclination, he made himself into a most efficient Officer. He had a real genius for friendship, and his knowledge of and care for the Officers and men of his Battery were quite out of the common. I was closely and constantly associated with him for many weeks during the period of training, and I can say without exaggeration that his influence was immense, and that it was always exerted for good.

Torrens is commemorated in the Pozières British Cemetery, Ovillers-la-Boisselle, grave reference II.F.4.

His name also appears on the Roll of Honor at Lord's Cricket Ground.

Batting and fielding averages

	Mat	Inns	NO	Runs	HS	Ave	100	Ct	St
First-class	9	13	0	183	87	14.07	0	2	0

Bowling averages

	Mat	Runs	Wkts	BBI	Ave	5w	10
First-class	9	335	11	3/41	30.45	0	0

Captain/Flight Commander John William Washington Nason
Cambridge University/Gloucestershire/Sussex
Royal Sussex Regiment/Royal Flying Corps
Died 26 December 1916
27 Years
Right-handed-Bat/Right-arm Slow

'Brilliant at every sport'

John William Washington Nason was born on 4 August 1889 at Corse Grange, Tewkesbury, Gloucestershire, the son of Dr Charles Richard Nason, late of 23 Grosvenor Crescent, St Leonard on Sea. Educated at the University School, Hastings and Queen's College Cambridge, he obtained his Blue in 1909 and was regarded as a player of great promise. Nason also played football for his university and was a good amateur golfer who found time to fall in love with and marry his wife, Fredrica Nason.

He played in 57 first-class matches between August 1906 and June 1914, 40 in the County Championship for Sussex and, later in 1913, for Gloucestershire, fourteen university matches for Cambridge University, one for South Africa in the British Isles, one for Australia in the British Isles and one for the Gentlemen of the South against the Players of the South. He made his debut first-class match on 23 August 1906 for Sussex against Warwickshire at the Central Recreation Ground, Hastings. He scored 4 and 53 not out; Warwickshire won by 10 wickets. In 1913 he began to turn out for Gloucestershire and on 26 May 1913, in a match against Nottinghamshire at the Spa Ground, Gloucestershire, he made his highest-ever first-class score of 139 in his one innings, eventually being out lbw to John Gunn. He also caught Garnet Lee off the bowling of Edward Dennett for 39. He played his final first-class match for Gloucestershire against Kent on 29 June 1914 at the Spa Ground, Gloucester; he scored 8 and 0, and caught Charles Hatfeild off the bowling of Charles Parker for 13. Kent won by 7 wickets. During his first-class career, Nason scored 1,649 runs, his highest score being 139 against Nottinghamshire and took ten wickets for 395 runs, his best figures being 2 for 24. He made 35 catches.

He was commissioned in the Royal Sussex Regiment in August 1914 and promoted to captain the following November. In January 1916 he transferred to the Royal Flying Corps (RFC) and became a pilot with No.46 Squadron. He was promoted to flight commander in November 1916 and was killed while flying a Nieuport 12 together with his observer, Lieutenant C. A. F. Brown, over Railway Wood on 26 December 1916, almost certainly a victim of Vzfw A. Ulmer of *Jasta* 8. They were the first casualties of No.46 squadron.

His Commanding Officer later wrote:

He was an extremely useful pilot, and his loss will be very keenly felt. Not only as regards duty, but as to his friends in the squadron.

He is commemorated in the Vlamertinghe Military Cemetery, grave reference: V. B. 11.

Batting and fielding averages

	Mat	Inns	NO	Runs	HS	Ave	100	Ct	St
First-class	57	98	6	1649	139	17.92	1	35	0

Bowling averages

	Mat	Balls	Runs	Wkts	BBI	Ave	Econ	SR	5w	10
First-class	57	533	395	10	2/24	39.50	4.44	53.3	0	0

Lieutenant William Keith Eltham
Tasmania
9 Battery, Australian Field Artillery
Died 31 December 1916
Aged 30
Right-handed Bat/Right-arm Medium

'A gifted man with so few years'

William Keith Eltham was born on 11 October 1886 in Hobart, Tasmania. He was the son of William Cooper and Jane Colville Eltham, née Lynch. His father was a clerk in the City Engineer's Department, of 156 Park Street, Hobart. William displayed an artistic streak from an early age, going on to be a gifted painter, writer and cartoonist while also displaying a strong talent for cricket.

He played in 11 first-class matches between January 1910 and February 1914, all for Tasmania, making his debut on 29 January 1910 against Victoria at the Melbourne Cricket Ground; he scored 20 and 21, Victoria winning by 126 runs. Eltham also played against New South Wales, South Africa (in Australia), MCC (MCC in Australia) and made his final first-class appearance on 27 February 1914 against Victoria at the Tasmania Cricket Association Ground, Hobart. He scored 10 and 5, Victoria winning by eight wickets. Eltham made 429 runs, including three fifties, with his highest score being 78 against New South Wales and took six wickets for 221 runs, his best figures being two for 39. He made 1 catch.

At the outbreak of war Keith enlisted and was assigned to 9 Battery, Australian Field Artillery. He left Tasmania with the first contingent embarking from Hobart on 20 October 1914 on board the HMAT *Geelong*.

While serving in Gallipoli he was hit in the mouth by a piece of shrapnel and badly wounded. From Gallipoli he was sent to France where, on 19 April 1916, he was promoted to corporal and, a year later, on 17 May 1916, received a commission. Shortly after his commission he was again wounded in action and evacuated to London for treatment but returned to the front line, spending Christmas with his men. However on 31 December, while he was resting in his dugout, the position took a direct hit from a German shell which buried him. Although he was dug out quickly he was found to be dead and was buried later that night at a nearby cemetery at Flers.

Later his remains were re-interred at Guards' Cemetery, Lesboeufs., Peronne, Picardie, France, Grave reference VIII.N.10.

Batting and fielding averages

	Mat	Inns	NO	Runs	HS	Ave	100	50	Ct	St
First-class	11	22	1	429	78	20.42	0	3	1	0

Bowling averages

	Mat	Runs	Wkts	BBI	Ave	5w	10
First-class	11	221	6	2/39	36.83	0	0

1917

Rifleman Roland George Blinko
Hawke's Bay
1st Bn New Zealand Rifle Brigade
6 January 1917
Aged 31
Left-handed Bat

'A fine cricketer overlooked by many'

Roland George Blinko was born on 1 May 1886 at Birmingham, Warwickshire. He emigrated to New Zealand in 1911, initially establishing himself as a cabinetmaker at Marlborough before moving to Hastings. In both 1913 and 1914 he played cricket for Hastings Cricket club, where his talent was quickly recognised and he was selected to play for Hawke's Bay against the visiting Australians. The match was played at Hastings on 18 February 1914. Blinko scored 10 and 21 in his second. These scores were better than they seemed as he was batting against the great Australian spinner Arthur Mailey (1886–1967) who took eight wickets for 51. Blinko also took a difficult catch, dismissing Victor Trumper who had, only a month before, scored 293 (including forty-four 4s) against Canterbury. Although Hawke's Bay lost the match by nine wickets, had it not been for Blinko's catch it could have been a lot worse.

Much to many people's surprise, Blinko didn't play for Hawke's Bay again. In his *History of Hawke's Bay Cricket*, Frank Cane refers to Blinko as a 'versatile run-getter with all the strokes … [who] … also specialized very effectively in the close-in positions in the field'. It is another of those strange decisions, the reason for which has been lost to history. Blinko next came to note as a member of the Hastings' championship-winning side of 1914–15, after which he appears to have retired from the game.

Blinko joined the New Zealand Rifle Brigade on 8 January 1916. On 19 April of that year, and while still in training, he married Annie Christina Manson at Wanganui and they moved to 512W Lyndon Road, Hastings. The following month, on the 27th, he was sent to the front as part of the 7th Reinforcements, F Company, 2nd Battalion. A few months later, at the end of August, he was at the front facing all the horrors that it had to offer. On 18 September he was seriously wounded in the head and cheek during the attack on Fiers. His wounds were so severe that he was evacuated to England and he was treated at No. 2 New Zealand General Hospital at Mount Felix in Walton-on-Thames. However, despite the best efforts of the doctors, he contracted meningitis and died on 6 January 1917.

He is commemorated at Walton and Weybridge Cemetery adjoining St Mary's Churchyard, Walton, Screen Wall 407. He's not alone, as a further nineteen New Zealanders are buried in the same churchyard. If passing pop in and pay your respects. They're a long way from home.

Batting and fielding averages

	Mat	Inns	NO	Runs	HS	Ave	100	50	Ct	St
First-class	1	2	0	31	21	15.50	0	0	1	0

Bowling averages

	Mat	Balls	Runs	Wkts	BBI	BBM	Ave	Econ	SR	4w	5w	10
First-class	1	-	-	-	-	-	-	-	-	-	-	-

Second Lieutenant Gilbert (Gillie) Howe
Wellington
9 Battery, New Zealand Field Artillery
Died 10 January 1917
Aged 25
Left-handed Bat/Wicket-keeper

'The game well played, the life too short'

Gilbert (Gillie) Howe was born on 6 August 1891 at Wellington, New Zealand. The son of Robert and Eliza Howe, of Wellington, he attended Berhampore School before going up to Kilbirnie School where he remained between 1899 and 1902. On leaving school Howe became a clerk.

Gillie Howe played his club cricket for The Rivals, Wellington East and University. Between January and April 1914 he played 5 first-class matches for Wellington, including two against Australia. He made his debut against Auckland on 29 January 1914 at the Basin Reserve, Wellington. Howe scored 31 in both innings and caught Evan

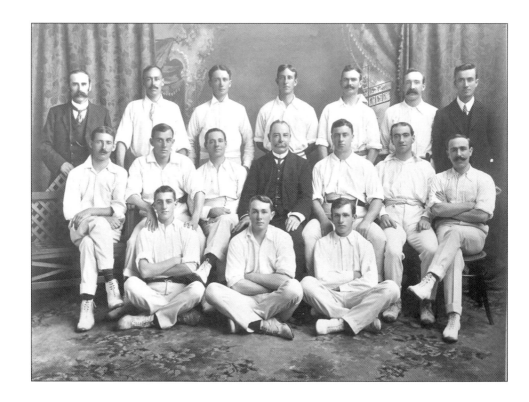

MacCormick off the bowling of John Hiddleston for 4. Auckland won by 33 runs. He went on to play against Hawke's Bay, Australia twice on the 13 February and 20 March both played at the Basin Reserve. Australia won the first match by 7 wickets the second match was drawn. He made his final first class appearance against D Reese's Canterbury XI on 10 April 1914 once against at the Basin Reserve, Wellington. Howe scored 20 and 7, Stumped Carl Beal of the bowling of Thomas Southall for 14, caught Donald Sandman off the bowling of John Saunders for 0 and then stumped Joseph Bennett off the bowling of Thomas Southall for 7 in the first innings and caught Ernest Crawshaw (killed in action 9 October 1918) off the bowling of Charles Robinson for 5. Wellington won by 117 runs. During his fist class career he made 139 runs his highest score being 31 against Auckland on29 January 1914. He also displayed a pair of safe hands as a wicket-keeper, taking five catches and making four stumpings. One newspaper commented that 'He stood up well to the wicket'.

At the outbreak of the war Howe was sent to German Samoa as part of the New Zealand Expeditionary Force, quickly being promoted to sergeant with the New Zealand Field Artillery. On his return to New Zealand he discharged himself from the Army but in 1916 thought better of it and once again joined the New Zealand Field Artillery.

He trained like thousands before him at Trentham Camp and must have impressed since he was given a commission as a second lieutenant. Arriving in France with his battery on 21 November 1916 he was killed in action two months later on 10 January 1917 near Messines, Belgium.

He is commemorated at the Cite Bonjean Military Cemetery, Armentières, Grave Reference IV.C.48.

After his death, and in memory of her son, Gilbert Howe's mother presented The Gilbert Howe Memorial Trophy to be awarded to the most improved cricket player in Wellington. The award continued for more than twenty years after his death.

Batting and fielding averages

	Mat	Inns	NO	Runs	HS	Ave	100	50	Ct	St
First-class	5	9	0	139	31	15.44	0	0	5	4

Bowling averages

	Mat	Balls	Runs	Wkts	BBI	BBM	Ave	Econ	SR	4w	5w	10
First-class	5	-	-	-	-	-	-	-	-	-	-	-

72/421 Sergeant Laurence Frank Gatenby
Tasmania
40th Bn Australian Imperial Force
Died 14 January 1917
Aged 28
Right-handed Bat

'A dedicated cricketer a dedicated Tasmanian'

Laurence Frank Gatenby was born on 10 April 1889 at Epping Forest, Tasmania. The son of Robert Corney Gatenby and Harriette Mary Gatenby, of 6 Berean St., Launceston, Tasmania, he was educated at the Launceston Church Grammar School, Tasmania.

He played two first-class matches for Tasmania in 1914. The first, against Victoria, was on 27 February 1914 at Tasmania Cricket Association Ground, Hobart. Gatenby scored 1 and 13, Victoria winning by eight wickets. His second appearance took place on 6 March 1914, once again against Victoria, at the North Tasmania Cricket Association Ground, Launceston. This time Gatenby scored 11 and 10, took one wicket for 58 and caught Benjamin Sheppard off the bowling of Thomas Elliott for 13. Tasmania went down once again, this time by 550 runs. He also represented the North against the South on four occasions and holds the record score for the North Tasmania Cricket Association with a remarkable innings of 367.

Gatenby joined the 40th Infantry Battalion of the Australian Imperial Force on 30 August 1914 and was assigned to the machine-gun section. Despite his early enlistment, it wasn't until 1 July 1916 that he embarked for the Western Front with his unit on board the *Berrima* from Hobart.

He was seriously wounded at the front and died on 14 January 1917 at the 2nd Australian Casualty Clearing Station, France.

He is commemorated at Trois Arbres Cemetery, Steemwerck, grave reference I.D. 16

Batting and fielding averages

	Mat	Inns	NO	Runs	HS	Ave	100	50	Ct	St
First-class	2	4	0	35	13	8.75	0	0	1	0

Bowling averages

	Mat	Runs	Wkts	BBI	Ave	5w	10
First-class	2	58	1	1/58	58.00	0	0

Private George Augustus Poeppel
Queensland
15th Bn Australian Imperial Force
Died 2 February 1917
Aged 23
Right-handed Bat

'An Aussie through and through'

George Augustus Poeppel was born on 6 November 1893 in Bundaberg, Queensland, the son of Frederick and Eva Poeppel of Nundah, Brisbane, Queensland. A warehouseman by profession, he made one first-class appearance for Queensland against New South Wales on 19 February 1915 at the Sydney Ground when he scored 3 and 13; Queensland lost by an innings and 231 runs. This was also the match where Callaway scored his double century on his debut (killed in action 3 May 1917).

Poeppel enlisted into the 15th Bn Australian Imperial Force on 7 September 1915 and, after training, embarked for the front on 31 January 1916 on the HMAT *Wandilla*. He was badly wounded by a shell and taken prisoner of war on 1 February 1917, dying from his wounds in German hands the following day. An account of the action in which he was wounded was later given by two privates from his battalion.

> a party of about 70 were sent to take a German advance post at Guidecourt. We held it for a time but our bombs ran out and the Germans came at us in large numbers taking many of us prisoner before we could get away and they recovered the position. The operation lasted from 7pm on 1st Feb until 4am the following morning. I got away. I am almost certain that these men were taken prisoner. I saw Jones and Lenman lying badly wounded and of course they may have died. They were all from Brisbane where I come from and from A Company except Poeppel of whose company I am not sure ...
>
> (Private A. D. Edwards, 4495, B Company, 26 March 1917)

> I last saw Pte George Poeppel lying badly wounded in a trench at Chalk Cliff behind Flers on Feb 2nd. He had been lying there all night. The Germans took the trench but we got it back two days later.
>
> (Private 4773 William Downey)

Poeppel was originally buried at Hermer (Hermies) but was later re-interred in Achiet-le-Grand Communal Cemetery Extension, Plot II, Row M, Grave 4.

Batting and fielding averages

	Mat	Inns	NO	Runs	HS	Ave	100	50	Ct	St
First-class	1	2	0	16	13	8.00	0	0	0	0

Bowling averages

	Mat	Balls	Runs	Wkts	BBI	BBM	Ave	Econ	SR	4w	5w	10
First-class	1	-	-	-	-	-	-	-	-	-	-	-

Conductor Henry Bernard Stricker
Transvaal
South African Service Corps
(Animal Transport)
Died 15 February 1917
Aged 29
Right-handed Bat

'Gone far too soon before his potential could be fulfilled'

Henry Bernard Stricker was born in 1888, in Johannesburg, Transvaal, South Africa. He was the son of Louis Stricker and the husband of Maude Blanche Stricker, of 49 Wyndcliff Road, Johannesburg, Transvaal.

He played in three first-class matches for the Transvaal, one in 1913 and two in 1914. He made his debut against Griqualand West at the Old Wanderers' Ground, Johannesburg, on 20 March 1913. He scored 2 and 66 not out and took one wicket for 23 off 5 overs. Transvaal lost by eight wickets. He made his second appearance against the touring MCC side on 14 January 1914 at the East Rand Proprietary Mines' ground in Boksburg, Stricker scored 2 runs in his one innings, and caught Lionel Tennyson off the bowling of Claud Newberry (killed in action 1 August 1916) for 21. The match was drawn. The third match was once again against the MCC at the Old Wanderers' Ground, Johannesburg, on 30 January 1914. Stricker scored 0 in his one innings, took 1 wicket for 33 off 8 overs and caught John Hobb the MCC opener off the bowling of Frederick Roux for 10 and John Hearne off the bowling of Claud Newberry for 136. The match was once again drawn.

During the war he served with the South African Service Corps, Animal Transport, and died of Blackwater Fever on 15 February 1917. He is commemorated in the Dodoma Cemetery, Tanzania, Grave Reference I. H. 9.

His brother, L. A. Sticker, was also a first-class cricketer.

Batting and fielding averages

	Mat	Inns	NO	Runs	HS	Ave	100	50	Ct	St
First-class	3	4	1	70	66*	23.33	0	1	3	0

Bowling averages

	Mat	Balls	Runs	Wkts	BBI	Ave	Econ	SR	5w	10
First-class	3	198	161	2	1/23	80.50	4.87	99.0	0	0

Major Robert Wilfred Fairey Jesson
Hampshire/Oxford University
5 Duke of Edinburgh's (Wiltshire) Regiment
Died 22 February 1917
Aged 30
Right-Handed Bat/Leg Break Bowler

"There was never a more lion-hearted cricketer than he"

Robert Wilfred Fairey Jesson was born on 17 June 1886, the son of Robert William and Annie Randall (nee Fairey) Jesson of 10 Archers Road, Southampton. He was educated at Handel College, Southampton, and Sherborne School where he was in the first XI 1903-04-05. On leaving school he went up to Merton College Oxford, where he played in the Freshmen's match in 1907 and the seniors' match in 1908–09 (but didn't get his Blue). After university he worked as a Managing Clerk with Hepherd & Winstanley, of Southampton.

Between July 1907 and May 1910 Jesson made 15 first class appearances, 14 in the County Championship for Hampshire and one University match for Oxford University against the MCC. He made his debut for Hampshire against Warwickshire on 8 July 1907 at the County Ground, Southampton. Jesson scored 23 not out and 4. More impressively he took 5 wickets for 42 runs off 10.4 overs in the first innings. He took a further wicket in the second innings for 7 off 9 overs. He also caught William Quaife off the bowling of John Badcock for 2. Warwickshire won by 5 wickets. He went on to play against Leicestershire, Worcestershire, Surrey, Middlesex, Derbyshire, Gloucestershire, Somerset, Yorkshire, the MCC, Northamptonshire, and Sussex. He made one first class appearance for Oxford University against the MCC at Lord's on 29 June 1908 when he scored 3 and 4 and took no wickets. The MCC won by 6 wickets. He made his final first class appearance for Hampshire against Sussex on 16 May 1910 at the County Ground, Hove. He scored 0 and 5, Sussex winning by an innings and 52 runs. During his first class career he scored 198 runs his best score being 38 against Surrey. He also took 21 wickets and made 8 catches. A good all round sportsman he played rugby for the Trojans and Rosslyn Park.

With war looming he join the Inns of Court Officer Training Corps on 6th August 1914, being later gazetted as a second lieutenant into the 5th (Service) Battalion, Wiltshire Regiment. He was promoted to lieutenant in October 1914, and six months later in March 1915 became a Captain and later Major. He served during the Gallipoli campaign and was wounded in action on 9th August 1915. After recovering from his wounds in October he returned to his Regiment. However he wasn't there long when in December of that year he was once again evacuated, this time with Shellshock (although officially listed as frost bite).

On recovering in July 1916 he was sent back to his regiment now serving in Mesopotamia. He was killed by a Turkish sniper on 22 February 1917, whilst in action outside the Kut, near Basra now in modern day Iraq. He was also mentioned in Dispatches.

His obituary in the Sherborne School magazine said of him:

There was never a more lion-hearted cricketer than he; and to have him on our side went a long way towards victory. But it was not in the field only that he played so great a part. Which of us will ever forget his cheerfulness, his modesty, his tact, his sympathy and his intense love of all that had to do with Sherborne?

His body was never recovered and he is commemorated on the Basra Memorial panel 30 and 64.

Batting and fielding averages

	Mat	Inns	NO	Runs	HS	Ave	100	50	Ct	St
First-class	15	28	4	198	38	8.25	0	0	8	0

Bowling averages

	Mat	Balls	Runs	Wkts	BBI	Ave	Econ	SR	5w	10
First-class	15	882	528	21	5/42	25.14	3.59	42.0	1	0

Lieutenant Charles Frearson Younger
Scotland and Oxford University
Lothians and Border Horse Yeomanry
Died 21 March 1917
Aged 31
Right-handed Bat/Left-arm Medium

'he ruled cheerfully and firmly, he met with ready obedience, and his influence was deeply felt'

Charles Younger was born on 9 September 1885 at Tillicoultry, Clackmannanshire. He was the third and youngest son of Sir George Younger, 1st Baronet and 1st Viscount Younger of Leckie, MP (for Ayr Burghs) JP DL of Leckie, Stirlingshire. His mother was Lucy Younger, daughter of Edward Smith MD FRS of Heanor Fall, Derbyshire. Younger was educated at the Cheam School and Winchester College (Hawkin's House) and became Head of House. As a fine left-hand bowler he was a prominent member of the First XI in both 1903 and 1904. It was his bowling that made the difference in the match against Eton in 1904 when he took eight wickets for 97, the match ending in a Winchester victory.

He went up to New College Oxford and played in the Freshmen's in 1904 and Seniors in 1906–07. Younger made 2 first class appearances in June 1907 and June 1912. He made his debut for Oxford University against the MCC at the Parks in on 6 June 1907. He failed to appear in the first innings due to an injury and made 27 in his second. Took 2 wickets for 18 off 11 overs and caught Leonard Braund off the bowling of Humphrey Gilbert for 8 in the first innings and caught him again in the second this time of the bowling of Trevor Bowring for 38. The MCC went on to win by two wickets. He made his second appearance for Scotland against the visiting South Africans on 24 June1912 at the Hamilton Crescent, Glasgow. He made 14 not out and 1. He also took 2 wickets for 56 off 22 overs. The South Africans won by an innings and 97 runs. Younger played his club cricket for The Grange.

After leaving Oxford he entered his father's brewery business in Alloa, becoming managing director but occasionally returned to Winchester to play cricket for the Old Wykehamist team. In 1913 he married Marjory Caroline Murray of Gartur, Stirling.

Younger was commissioned in the Lothians and Border Horse in 1909 (some records give this date as 29August 1914). Seriously wounded in action at St Leger, near Albert on 20 March 1917, he died the following day at Aveluy. He was, as a letter from a brother officer, remarked, 'unconscious and free from pain'.

The school magazine, *The Wykehamist*, of April 1917 said of him:

It was here that his character came out, his healthy tastes, his simple straightforwardness, his good judgement, his strength of will. As many have testified, he ruled cheerfully and firmly, he met with ready obedience, and his influence was deeply felt.

He is commemorated in the Aveluy Communal Cemetery Extension, grave reference M.8.

His older brother, Second Lieutenant Edward John Younger, 16th Lancers was killed during the Boer War.

Batting and fielding averages

	Mat	Inns	NO	Runs	HS	Ave	100	50	Ct	St
First-class	2	3	1	42	27	21.00	0	0	3	0

Bowling averages

	Mat	Runs	Wkts	BBI	Ave	5w	10
First-class	2	80	4	2/18	20.00	0	0

30180 Private Walter Greive
Scotland
17th (Glasgow Chamber of Commerce) Bn The Highland
Light Infantry
Died 1 April 1917
Aged 26
Right-handed Bat/Right-arm Medium

'I lang hae thought, my youthfu' friend'

Walter Greive was born on 10 February 1891 in Selkirk, Scotland. The youngest son of James Grieve, a farmer at Howden, Selkirk, he attended Selkirk High School where he played in the XI.

He made two first-class appearances in July 1912 and July 1914. He made his debut on the 8 July 1912 for Scotland against the visiting Australians at Raeburn Place, Edinburgh. Greive scored 18 and 6; Australia won by 296 runs. His second first-class appearance came on 16 July 1914 when, once again, he played for Scotland, this time against Ireland, scoring 1 and 0, Scotland finally winning by 11 runs. He also played for the Border League.

During the war he served with the 17th Battalion Highland Light Infantry (Glasgow Chamber of Commerce Battalion) and was killed in action on 1 April 1917. The following obituary appeared in the April 1918 edition of the *Highland Light Infantry Chronicle*:

> Scottish Internationalist Cricketer Killed in Action. – official intimation has now been made that Mr Walter Greive, Highland Light Infantry, missing since April 1917, is presumed to have been killed in action on that date. Mr Grieve, who was the youngest son of Mr James Grieve, farmer, Howden, Selkirkshire, was a well-known member of Selkirk Cricket Club, a batsman of great ability and force, and a good change bowler. After taking part in many representative engagements in the Border district he was selected to play for Scotland against the Australians, and other recognition of international rank was conferred on him. Prior to enlistment Mr Grieve was associated with his father in the management of the farm at Howden. An elder brother, Mr William Grieve, a former captain of Selkirk Cricket Club, was killed in action some time ago.

His body was never recovered or identified and he is commemorated on the Thiepval Memorial, Pier and Face 15C.

Batting and fielding averages

	Mat	Inns	NO	Runs	HS	Ave	100	50	Ct	St
First-class	2	4	0	28	18	7.00	0	0	0	0

Bowling averages

	Mat	Balls	Runs	Wkts	BBI	BBM	Ave	Econ	SR	4w	5w	10
First-class	2	90	73	0	-	-	-	4.86	-	0	0	0

Lieutenant Edward Charles Coleman
Essex
Royal Field Artillery
Died 2 April 1917
Aged 25
Left-handed Bat/Wicket-keeper

'A safe pair of hands'

Edward Charles Coleman was born on 5 September 1891. He was the son of E. H. and R. L. Coleman of 'Whitefield', De la Warr Road, Bexhill-on-Sea. Educated at Dulwich College, he was in the cricket XI in 1907, 1908, 1909 and 1910, captaining the team in 1910. Winning the prize for fielding in 1909 and 1910, he also won the Challenge Cup for Fives in the same two years.

After leaving Dulwich he went up to Pembroke College Cambridge, and although he played in the Varsity trial match for Etceteras versus Perambulators in 1911 he never had the opportunity of playing for Cambridge and failed to get his Blue. In 1910 he played for Essex County Second XI, and in 1912 represented the County First XI on two occasions, being a very fine wicket-keeper.

He played in three first-class matches In July 1911 and June 1912. He made his debut for Oxford and Cambridge Universities against the Army and Navy on 6 July 1911 when he scored 0 and 4 and caught George Lyon off the bowling of Norman Holloway for 90. Oxford and Cambridge loosing 6 wickets. He then made two first-class appearances for Essex, firstly against Yorkshire on 6 June 1912 in which he made 0 in his only innings and stumped Benjamin Wilson off the bowling of Walter Mead for 31. The match was drawn. His second and final first class match came against Surrey on 13 June 1912. Coleman scored 6 and 4 and caught John Hobbs off the bowling of John Douglas for 72. Surrey won by 287 runs.

Prior to the war Coleman held a commission in the Reserve of Officers, Royal Field Artillery, and volunteered for active service at the outbreak of war. He was posted to the 4th East Anglian Brigade Royal Field Artillery (TF) attached to 114 Brigade Trench Mortar Battery, 26th Division on the Macedonian Front. He was promoted to lieutenant in January 1915 and, before being sent abroad, married Miss Dorothy Gwendoline Petchell of Eastbourne, Sussex.

He was killed in action in the trenches at Salonika on 2 April 1917. He is commemorated in the Doiran Military Cemetery, Greece, Grave Reference Gr. 5.

His brother, Herbert Edward Evatt, aged 23 years, had been killed in action seven months before on 9 September 1916.

Batting and fielding averages

	Mat	Inns	NO	Runs	HS	Ave	100	50	Ct	St
First-class	3	5	1	14	6	3.50	0	0	2	1

Bowling averages

	Mat	Balls	Runs	Wkts	BBI	BBM	Ave	Econ	SR	4w	5w	10
First-class	3	-	-	-	-	-	-	-	-	-	-	-

Captain Geoffrey Laird Jackson
Derbyshire/Oxford University
1st Bn The Prince Consort's Own (Rifle Brigade)
Died 9 April 1917
Aged 23
Right-handed Bat/Right-arm Medium

'He was thought an admirable soldier'

Geoffrey Laird Jackson was born on 10 January 1894 at Birkenhead, Cheshire. He was the eldest son of Brigadier General Geoffrey M. Jackson, former commanding officer of the Sherwood Foresters (The Nottinghamshire and Derbyshire Regiment) and managing director of the Clay Cross Colliery Company, and his wife Jessie C. C. Jackson. Jackson was educated at Harrow School where he was Head of House, represented the school at racquets in 1912 and 1913, played football and was in the Cricket XI in 1911–12 and 1913, captaining the side in his final year. He also won the English Essay prize in 1913.

Jackson made 7 first class matches between August 1912 and June 1914, four in the County Championship and three University Matches for Derbyshire and Oxford University. He made his debut while still at Harrow on 26 August 1912 for Derbyshire against Nottinghamshire at the Miners Welfare Ground, Blackwell. He scored 2 in his only innings, took the wicket of the celebrated George Gunn for 29 off 1 over and caught William Whysall off the bowling of Thomas Forrester for 18. The match was eventually drawn. He went on to play for Derbyshire against Northamptonshire and, Nottinghamshire again. On leaving Harrow Jackson went up to Balliol College Oxford where he began to play for the University. He turned out against the MCC, the Free Foresters and GJK Weigall's XI. He made his final first class appearance for Derbyshire against Somerset on 27 June 1914 at Queens Park, Chesterfield. He made 7 and 9 and although he failed to bowl he did catch the Somerset opener, Albert Rippon, for 0 off the bowling of James Horsley. Derbyshire won by 167 runs.

Jackson made 150 first class runs his top score being 50, against Weigall's XI, and took 10 first-class wickets for 238 runs off 7 overs. He made 4 catches.

At the outbreak of war Jackson was given a commission in the Rifle Brigade, going to France with his battalion in October 1914. He was gassed and invalided home after the Second Battle of Ypres, and spent several months in England recovering. He returned to France, as Adjutant of the 1st Battalion, in December 1915, and was Mentioned in Despatches on 1 January 1916 for gallantry. He received his captaincy in 1917 and was mortally wounded later that year by a piece of shell after advancing about 6,000 yards, during the Battle of Arras. He died at Fampoux, Arras, France before reaching the dressing station on 9 April 1917.

Balliol College later said of him:

It need hardly be said that he was throughout an admirable soldier, popular with everyone, a keen and capable officer who had the best company in the Battalion.

He is commemorated in the Highland Cemetery, Roclincourt, Grave Reference I.B.37.
His brother Guy and cousin Anthony also played cricket for Derbyshire.

Batting and fielding averages

	Mat	Inns	NO	Runs	HS	Ave	100	Ct	St
First-class	7	12	0	150	50	12.50	0	4	0

Bowling averages

	Mat	Runs	Wkts	BBI	Ave	5w	10
First-class	7	238	10	3/52	23.80	0	0

Captain Cecil Herbert Wyndham Bodington
Hampshire
Household Battalion
Died 11 April 1917
Aged 37
Right-handed Bat

'Outstanding at Everything'

Cecil Herbert Wyndham Bodington was born on 20 November 1880 at the Rectory, Suffield in Norfolk. He was the second son of the Reverend Herbert James Bodington, Vicar of Upton Grey, and Louisa Augusta (née Mares-Cecil) of The Vicarage, Upton Grey, Winchfield in Hampshire. Educated at the National School at Overstrand, Cromer, Norfolk before going to Charterhouse School in September 1893 as a Junior Scholar, in January 1896 he went on to the King's School Canterbury, having gained a Junior Scholarship in December 1895. A Senior Scholarship followed in July 1897 and he was appointed as a school monitor in September 1897. He played rugby for the first XV, was in the Fives Pair in 1897–98, and played First XI cricket from 1896 to 1898, being captain for his last two years.

On leaving King's he went up to Peterhouse College Cambridge on an Open Classical Scholarship and represented the college at cricket. He played in the Freshmen's match of 1899 and varsity cricket in 1901 and 1902. Having achieved a BA in 1902, he left university and, after a short time in the Cape, became the tutor to the three children of the Maharaja of Kapurthala for two years. On his return he became an assistant schoolmaster at Elstree and Stanmore Park Preparatory Schools.

Between May 1901 and August 1902 Bodington represented Hampshire in 10 first-class matches, 9 in the County Championship and 1 against Australia in the British Isles. He made his debut against Surrey on 9 May 1901 at the Kennington Oval. He made 3 and 1 and took 2 wickets for 54 runs off 18 overs. He also caught Vivian Crawford the Surrey opener off the bowling of Victor Barton for 44. The match was drawn. He went on to play against Leicestershire, Worcestershire, Warwickshire, Sussex, Somerset, Kent and Derbyshire. He made his final first class match against the Australians on 7 August 1902 at the County Ground, Southampton. Bodington made 0 and 1 and failed to take a wicket. Australia won by an innings and 79 runs. During his first class career Bodington made 154 runs at an average of 11.00, with a high score of 36 against Sussex. He also took 9 wickets for 287 runs his best figures being 3 for 19. He made 4 catches. He also played for the Household Brigade XI.

Shortly after the war commenced on 10 November 1914 he was commissioned as a second lieutenant in the Royal Horse Guards. On 9 September 1916 he was promoted captain and posted to the newly-formed Household Battalion. The Household Battalion had been formed on 1 September from a surplus of men who had joined the Household Cavalry and were formed into an infantry battalion. Captain Bodington was given command of Number 4 Company. On 25 July 1916, while waiting to be posted to France, he found the time to fall in love with and marry Lillian May (née Somerville) at St Peter's Church, Bayswater. The battalion arrived in France on 8 and 9 November 1916.

On 11 April 1917, during the Battle of Arras, the Household Battalion was ordered to attack in support of the 2nd Seaforth Highlanders at Roeux. The Seaforth advanced at midday, having endured a German artillery barrage while waiting to go over the top. A quarter of an hour later the Household Battalion followed, Number 4 Company forming up on the left of the battalion. As they advanced from the Hyderabad Redoubt, Captain Bodington was killed by machine-gun fire and the two leading platoons of his company were all but wiped out.

His body was never recovered and he is commemorated on the Arras Memorial, Bay 1. He is also commemorated on the war memorial at Upton Grey and on the memorial at Charterhouse School.

Batting and fielding averages

	Mat	Inns	NO	Runs	HS	Ave	100	50	Ct	St
First-class	10	18	4	154	36	11.00	0	0	4	0

Bowling averages

	Mat	Balls	Runs	Wkts	BBI	Ave	Econ	SR	5w	10
First-class	10	375	287	9	3/19	31.88	4.59	41.6	0	0

Captain William Grant Spruell Stuart MC
Scotland
7th Bn The Queen's Own Cameron Highlanders
Died 23 April 1917
Aged 27
Right-handed Bat

'The second of two brave sons to fall'

William Grant Spruell Stuart was born on 8 June 1889 at Gartly, Aberdeen, the son of the Reverend W. Stuart MA, of Burnshill, Cape Colony, South Africa. He was educated at the George Watson School Edinburgh from 1901 to 1908 where he was captain of school in 1907 and of the first XV. He was also in the cricket XI and was a sergeant in the OTC. From Watson's School Stuart went up to Edinburgh University where he read Classics. William made one first-class appearance on 16 July 1914 for Scotland against Ireland, played at the Observatory Lane, Rathmines, Dublin. Stuart scored 17 and 10, and caught Robert Lambert off the bowling of Maurice Dickson for 68 and Frederick Shaw off the bowling of Thomas Watt for 65. Scotland won by 11 runs. He also played cricket for Watsonians as well as East and West Scotland.

OFFICERS OF THE 7th BATTALION CAMERON HIGHLANDERS.

Back row (l. to r.)—Lt. Macdonald, Capt. Bateman, M.C., Lt. Murchison, Capt. Findlay, M.C., Lt. R. R. Anderson, M.C., Lt. Cameron.
Middle row—Capt (now Major) Russell, C.F., Capt. McCrae, Lt. (now Capt. and Adjt.) Lumsden, M.C., Lt. Mackay, Lt. Hardman, Capt. Johnston, Lt. Martin, D.S.O., Lt. McCracken, M.C.
Front row—Capt. Hamilton, Capt. (later Lt.-Col.) Norman Macleod, C.M.G., D.S.O., Major Cunningham, D.S.O., Lt.-Col. Marsh, D.S.O., Capt. and Adjt. Chapman, M.C., Capt. W. G. Stewart, M.C., Capt. Rollo, Staff.
On ground—Lt. (now Capt.) Mauchlin, M.C., Lt. McNiven.

He was about to join the civil service when the war broke out. In September 1914, together with his brother Robert Alexander, he took a commission in the 7th Bn Cameron Highlanders and was sent to France in May 1915, landing at Boulogne.

On 9 September 1915 Stuart was wounded together with two other officers by a trench mortar. On 25 September William Stuart's brother, Robert, was killed in action (he is commemorated on the Loos Memorial). William was promoted to captain in the same month. Always in the thick of the fighting, Stuart was awarded the Military Cross in December 1916 for his outstanding work over many months (*London Gazette*, 1 January 1917), including a major trench raid for which he received the personal thanks of his commanding officer. Stuart was killed in action at Arras during an attack on Cavalry Farm and the German trenches to the east of it on 23 May 1917. It was later written of him:

> better known as 'W.G.' he came out with the Battalion in 1915, and had taken part in all the fighting in which the Division had been engaged. A quiet, unassuming man, with a strong personality, he was known and loved not only by the officers and men of his own battalion, but throughout the Brigade. I have seldom had a man of his Company before the CO. In fact, the apparent pain which it gave to 'W.G.'to think that a man had done anything to bring disgrace on his beloved Company was the greatest punishment that man could have. The men would have done anything for him, and discipline was maintained out of love and regard for their Captain. If the Battalion on our left had succeeded in obtaining their objective, or had at least silenced the enemy, the attack on the farm would probably have proved a success.

William Stuart is commemorated at the Faubourg d'Amiens Cemetery, Arras, Grave Reference IV. C. 15.

Batting and fielding averages

	Mat	Inns	NO	Runs	HS	Ave	100	50	Ct	St
First-class	1	2	0	27	17	13.50	0	0	2	0

Bowling averages

	Mat	Balls	Runs	Wkts	BBI	BBM	Ave	Econ	SR	4w	5w	10
First-class	1	-	-	-	-	-	-	-	-	-	-	-

Second Lieutenant Harold James Goodwin
Cambridge University/Warwickshire
135 Battery Royal Garrison Artillery
Died 24 April 1917
Aged 31
Right-handed Bat/Leg Break

'Whenever he appeared, the side played up with a dash and vigour'

Harold James Goodwin was born on 31 January 1886 at Edgbaston, Birmingham. He was the son of Frederick Sidney Goodwin of Diddington Hall, Meriden, Warwickshire and Agnes Louisa (née Chance) and was educated at Marlborough College where he was in the First XI from 1903 to 1905, scoring 193 and 40 for Marlborough against the Free Foresters in his final year. From Marlborough he went up to Jesus College Cambridge, where he read Mathematics. While there he took Blues in both cricket and hockey. On leaving Cambridge he became a solicitor in Birmingham.

Goodwin played in 39 first-class matches between May 1906 and July 1912. Twenty for Cambridge University and nineteen for Warwickshire all in the County Championship. He made his debut for Cambridge on 28 May 1906 against Northamptonshire at Fenner's. He made 11 in his only innings and took 2 wickets for 45 off 17.1 overs. He also caught William East off the bowling of Alfred Morcom for 0 and Edmund Crosse of the bowling of Morcom once more for 20. Cambridge University won by an innings and 78 runs. He went on to play against Surrey, WG Grace's XI, Middlesex, Lancashire, South Africa (in the British Isles), Yorkshire, Gentlemen of England, MCC, HDG Leveson Gower's XI, Oxford University and GJV Weigall's XI. He made his debut for Warwickshire on 12 August 1907 at the Town Ground, Peterborough in the County Championship. He scored 2 and 16 and caught Harold Pretty off the bowling of Sydney Santall for 22. Warwickshire won by 4 wickets. He made his final first class match on 25 July 1912 in the County Championship at Edgbaston, Birmingham. He made 9 and 8 and took 1 wicket (that of the Middlesex opener Francis Tarrant) for 35 off 9 overs. Warwickshire won by 118 runs. He captained Warwickshire in 1910.

During his career he scored 1,255 runs with his highest score being 101. He also took 86 wickets for 2092 runs, his best figures being 7 for 33. He made 33 catches.

Wisden said of him:

It was a thousand pities that he could not find time to play more regularly. Whenever he appeared, the side played up with a dash and vigour worthy of all praise for Goodwin.

Goodwin also played hockey for England against Scotland.

He married, on 28 January 1913, Jessie Forbes of Edinburgh and they had two children, Harold Anthony, born 25 February 1916, and Pamela Forbes, born 11 August 1917.

In December 1916 Harold Goodwin was commissioned in the Royal Garrison Artillery and was killed while serving at Arras on 24 April 1917.

He is commemorated at Faubourg d'Amiens Cemetery, Arras, Grave Reference V. C. 1.

Batting and fielding averages

	Mat	Inns	NO	Runs	HS	Ave	100	50	Ct	St
First-class	39	67	4	1255	101	19.92	1	3	33	0

Bowling averages

	Mat	Balls	Runs	Wkts	BBI	Ave	Econ	SR	5w	10
First-class	39	3577	2092	86	7/33	24.32	3.50	41.5	5	1

Lieutenant Colonel Meredith Magniac DSO
Army/South Africa
1st Bn The Lancashire Fusiliers
Died 25 April 1917
Aged 36

'he was a very gallant gentleman'

Meredith Magniac was born on 27 June 1880 at Hitchin in Hertfordshire, England, the third son of Major General F. L. Magniac of Coombe Cot, Abbotsham, Devon. Meredith was educated at Clifton College, Bristol, where he was in the First XI. Deciding to make a career in the Army, he entered Sandhurst in 1898 where he was once again in the XI. He was gazetted in the Lancashire Fusiliers, joining the 4th Battalion. Having been assistant adjutant for some years, he was subsequently transferred to the 3rd Battalion, then in South Africa. On the disbandment of the 4th Battalion, he was sent to the 1st Battalion, with which he served in Malta and India. He became adjutant of the 1st Battalion, and on the expiry of his term as adjutant he passed a course at the Staff College at Quetta and was appointed brigade major to a brigade at Fermoy in Ireland.

Magniac made one first-class appearance, playing for the South African Army against Pelham Warner's MCC team at Thara, Tswane, Pretoria on 12 January 1906. He scored 1 and 14 and took 2 wickets for 81 off 14 overs. The MCC won by an innings and 218 runs.

On the outbreak of the war he returned to England and landed with his battalion in Gallipoli on 25 April 1915, where the Lancashire Fusiliers won six VCs before breakfast. He remained with the battalion throughout the campaign and rendered valuable service during the evacuation of the peninsula in December 1915, for which he was awarded the DSO (*London Gazette*, 3 June 1916). He was also given command of the 1st Battalion while still at Cape Helles. He travelled to France with the battalion in that capacity and was wounded during the attack on 1 July 1916, the first day of the Somme campaign. Lieutenant Colonel Magniac DSO was killed in action on 25 April 1917 at Monchy-le-Preux, near Arras, France. An account of his death was later forwarded by a brother officer:

> He was of course in the front line with his men and the shell that killed him killed his Bombing Officer as well and wounded Mr Bloodworth, his Adjutant. He died instantly, and the doctor is sure, quite painlessly. I am thankful to say we were able to bring him down from the line and we buried him early this morning in the Military Cemetery at Ronville, in Arras. One of the Brigade Chaplains read the service. We are having a cross made to mark the grave, which will be railed round as well. I do not think there was an Officer in the Division who did not admire and respect the Colonel, and not an Officer or man in the Battalion who did not love him. He was the finest soldier ever met, a strong man and a born leader. As Colonel Fuller said to me this morning, he was a very gallant gentleman. All ranks in the Regiment join with me now in offering you our most sincere and heartfelt sympathy.
>
> Yours sincerely,
> T. UTTERSOX, Second-in-Command. B.

Magniac is commemorated at the Beaurains Road Cemetery, Beaurains, Pas de Calais, France, Grave Reference B.4. His next of kin was given as his wife, Winifred E. Magniac, of The Austen, Rye, Sussex. His brother, Lieutenant Colonel Erskine Magniac, was killed in action three days later on 28 April 1917.

Batting and fielding averages

	Mat	Inns	NO	Runs	HS	Ave	100	50	Ct	St
First-class	1	2	0	15	14	7.50	0	0	0	0

Bowling averages

	Mat	Runs	Wkts	BBI	Ave	5w	10
First-class	1	81	2	2/81	40.50	0	0

Major Maurice Edward Coxhead
Oxford University/Middlesex
9th Bn The Royal Fusiliers (City of London Regiment)
Died 3 May 1917
Aged 27
Right-handed Bat/Right-arm Fast

'Loved by all, the bravest of the brave'

Maurice Edward Coxhead was born on 24 May 1889 in Kensington, London. He was the eldest son of Frederick Charles Coxhead and Amy Bruce (née (Gribble) of 7 Essex Villas, Kensington, and was educated at Wootton Court, Canterbury, Eastbourne College, where he captained the First XI, and Brasenose College, Oxford where he received his cricket Blue.

He made 6 first-class appearances between May 1909 and June 1911, 4 for Oxford University and 2 for Middlesex in the County Championship. He made his debut for Oxford University against Kent on 27 May 1909 at the University Parks, Oxford. He made 9 and 5 and took 5 wickets for 53 off 18 overs. Kent won by an innings and 4 runs. He also turned out for Oxford against the MCC, Worcestershire and the Gentlemen of England. On the 19 June 1911 he made his debut for Middlesex against Gloucestershire at Lord's. He scored 6 in his only innings, took 1 wicket for 9 off 3 overs and caught Alan Imlay off the bowling of Francis Tarrant for 1 and Gilbert Jessop off the bowling of Tarrant once again, for 0. Middlesex won by 7 wickets. He made his final first class appearance for Middlesex against Gloucestershire on 29 June 1911 at the Spa Ground, Gloucester. He failed to make a run or take a wicket but did mange to catch Thomas Langdon (the Gloucestershire opener) off the bowling of Edward Mignon for 4. Middlesex won by an innings and 63 runs.

He made 29 first class runs his highest score being 9 against ?????? He also took 13 wickets for 300 runs his best figures being 5 for 53. He made 4 catches. He also played for Aldershot Command and was a member of the Free Foresters and Oxford Harlequins.

Coxhead married Dorothea Allan at St Mary Abbots Church, Kensington on 8 August 1914. They had one daughter, Diana, who was born on 9 July 1915.

On 13 February 1912 he was gazetted as a second lieutenant in the Royal Fusiliers and was promoted to lieutenant on 5 September 1914, being posted to the 9th Battalion on its formation. He was promoted to captain on 18 October 1915 and achieved his majority on 7 July 1916. Coxhead served as Brigade Musketry Officer between April and May 1915 before going out to France with his battalion that month. Appointed adjutant the following August, he became second in command of his battalion in July 1916. He took part in the Battle of the Somme before being killed in action near Monchy, during the fighting around Arras on 3 May 1917 while in command of his battalion. A letter from a brother officer described his death:

> the Germans were counter-attacking, bombing our men out of the newly-won position. Seeing how things were going, Major Coxhead went out into the open to re-organise and rally the men, and was killed instantaneously by machine-gun fire while standing in an exposed position.

The commanding officer of another battalion wrote:

> I feel sure that but for him our two battalions would not only have had far heavier losses, but I doubt if the trench would have been taken at all. His arrangements beforehand were splendid, and his power of command and decision were magnificent. I think this account will show what a fine death he died. I believe his presence, even the short time he was there (out in the open), saved a large number of lives.

He was Mentioned in Despatches (*London Gazette*, 22 May 1917) by General Sir Douglas Haig, for gallant and distinguished service in the field.

He is commemorated at Faubourg d'Amiens cemetery Arras. Plot: IV. G. 14.

Batting and fielding averages

	Mat	Inns	NO	Runs	HS	Ave	100	50	Ct	St
First-class	6	8	0	29	9	3.62	0	0	4	0

Bowling averages

	Mat	Balls	Runs	Wkts	BBI	Ave	Econ	SR	5w	10
First-class	6	480	300	13	5/53	23.07	3.75	36.9	1	0

Private Norman Frank Callaway
New South Wales
19th (NSW) Bn, Australian Imperial Force
Died 3 May 1917
Aged 22
Right-handed Bat

'He certainly should rise to great heights'

Norman Frank Callaway was born on 5 April 1896 in Hay, New South Wales, Australia, to Thomas and Emily Callaway of 22 Eblery Street, Waverley, New South Wales. Callaway appeared for Paddington in Sydney Grade Cricket in the 1913–14 season. On his first appearance at the tender age of 17 he was the top scorer with 41 against Balmain, followed by 16 and 26 (top scorer again) against University, and 137 not out with 24 boundaries against Middle Harbour. He scored 578 runs in the season for Paddington at an average of 41.28 and took three wickets. In January 1914 Callaway scored an impressive 129, and a duck in the second innings, in a New South Wales Colts versus Victorian Colts match at the Melbourne Cricket Ground. At the beginning of the 1914–15 season, Callaway moved to Waverley. His ability with the bat continued to impress and he quickly found himself being called up to play for the New South Wales Colts at the age of 18.

He made one first-class appearance for New South Wales against Queensland at the Sydney Cricket Ground on 19 February 1915. Batting in the middle order, when he took the wicket things were not going New South Wales' way and they were 17 for 3. He knocked up 50 within the first hour and made his century half an hour later, ending the day on 125. The following day his quick scoring continued and he became the first man in first-class cricket to score a double century on his debut, scoring a total of 207 runs before being caught by Sydney Ayres off the bowling of John McLaren. He also made two catches, Sydney Ayres off the bowling of William Cullen for 7 and William Thompson off the bowling of Cullen once again for 1. New South Wales won the match by an innings and 231 runs. Callaway reached this total in 214 minutes, hitting twenty-six 4s, and was dropped 5 times. The *Sydney Morning Herald* said of him 'He certainly should rise to great heights, all going well with him.'

He played one more summer for Waverley but before he had a chance to appear in another first-class he match enlisted in the 19th New South Wales Battalion, Australian Imperial Force. Leaving Sydney in October he was in France late in December. He was reported missing during the Second Battle of Bullecourt on 3 May 1917. By September 1917 it was confirmed that Callaway had died on that day.

His body was never recovered or identified and he is commemorated on the Villers-Bretonneux Memorial.

Batting and fielding averages

	Mat	Inns	NO	Runs	HS	Ave	100	50	Ct	St
First-class	1	1	0	207	207	207.00	1	0	2	0

Bowling averages

	Mat	Balls	Runs	Wkts	BBI	BBM	Ave	Econ	SR	4w	5w	10
First-class	1	-	-	-	-	-	-	-	-	-	-	-

Lieutenant Colonel Richard Stanley Worsley DSO
Orange Free State
Army Service Corps
Died 4 May 1917
Aged 37
Right-handed Bat

'Selfless to the end'

Richard Stanley Worsley was born on 7 September 1879 at Harrington Hall, Spilsby, Lincolnshire. The son of Major General Richard Worlsey, Indian Army, and Edith Meaburn Worsley, née Staniland, he was educated at Wellington College and the Royal Military College Sandhurst. Gazetted as a second lieutenant in the Army Service Corps on 21 February 1900. He was promoted to lieutenant on 1 April 1901. On 9 June 1904 he became a captain and achieved his majority on 7 October 1914. Worsley was promoted to lieutenant colonel on 25 October 1916.

He made one first-class appearance on 1 January 1904 during the Currie Cup at the Ramblers' Cricket Club Ground, Bloemfontein, playing for the Orange Free State against Transvaal. Worsley scored 2 and 10, Orange Free State going down by an innings and 327 runs.

Worsley took part in the Second Boer War from 1900 1902. He was a staff officer to the East Lancashire Territorial Division from January 1908 to April 1912 and in 1913 was attached to the Egyptian Army. On 25 April 1915 he landed in Gallipoli attached to the Australian and New Zealand Army Corps (ANZAC). During the fighting he was Mentioned in Despatches three times for his gallantry before being awarded the DSO (*London Gazette*, 2 May 1916).

Leaving Gallipoli in September 1915, he was sent to Darfur in the Sudan and, while there, was Mentioned in Despatches on a further two occasions, as well as being awarded his brevet lieutenant colonelcy. He drowned on 4 May 1917 when the SS *Transylvania* was torpedoed and sunk off the coast of Genoa en route to Salonika. He has no known grave and is commemorated by name on the Savona Memorial, Italy.

The following is extracted from *Dictionary of Disasters at Sea*, by Charles Hocking:

The liner *Transylvania* was designed to accommodate 1,379 passengers but the Admiralty fixed her capacity at 200 officers and 2,860 men, besides crew. She was carrying nearly this number when she left Marseilles for Alexandria on 3 May 1917, with an escort of two Japanese destroyers, the *Matsu* and the *Sakaki*. At 10a.m. on the 4th the *Transylvania* was struck in the port engine room by a torpedo from a submarine.

At the time the ship was on a zig-zag course at a speed of 14 knots, being two and a half miles S. of Cape Vado, Gulf of Genoa. She at once headed for the land two miles distant, while the *Matsu* came alongside to take off the troops, the *Sakaki* meanwhile steaming around to keep the submarine submerged. Twenty minutes later a torpedo was seen coming straight for the destroyer alongside, which saved herself by going astern at full speed. The torpedo then struck the *Transylvania* and she sank very quickly, less than an hour having elapsed since she was first hit.

Lieutenant Brennell (the ship's captain), one other officer and ten men of the crew, together with twenty-nine military officers and 373 other ranks were killed.

One of the survivors later said that he last saw Worsley helping to get people off the ship before jumping into the sea himself. It was the last anyone saw of him. His body was never recovered and he is commemorated at Savona cemetery, Italy. An organ was also presented to St Mary's church, Somersby, Lincolnshire in his memory.

Batting and fielding averages

	Mat	Inns	NO	Runs	HS	Ave	100	50	Ct	St
First-class	1	2	0	12	10	6.00	0	0	0	0

Bowling averages

	Mat	Balls	Runs	Wkts	BBI	BBM	Ave	Econ	SR	4w	5w	10
First-class	1	-	-	-	-	-	-	-	-	-	-	-

Staff Sergeant Henry (Harry) George Blacklidge
Surrey
5th Bn The Hampshire Regiment
Died 23 May 1917
Aged 33
Left-handed Bat/Left-arm fast-medium, Slow left-arm
orthodox

'Always willing to lend a hand. A wonderful Coach'

Henry (Harry) George Blacklidge was born on 14 July 1884 in Stoughton, Surrey, the son of John and Jean Blacklidge, of 2 Rosamond Villas, Church Path, East Sheen.

He played in seven matches for Surrey between July 1908 and May 1913 all but one in the County Championship. He made his debut for Surrey against the Gentlemen of Philadelphia on 30 July 1908 at the Kennington Oval. He scored 14 and 12 and took 1 wicket for 49 off 18 overs in the first innings and 4 for 26 off 7.7 overs in the second. He also caught Herbert Hordern off the bowling of Walter Less for 14. Surrey won by 122 runs. He went on to play against Essex, Gloucestershire, Somerset, and Nottinghamshire. He made his final first class appearance against Warwickshire on 29 May 1913 at the Kennington Oval. He made 6 in his only innings took 1 wicket for 46 off 11 overs. He also caught Frank Foster off the bowling of William Spring for 24 and Percy Jeeves (killed in action 22 July 1916) off the bowling of Morice Bird for 39. The match was eventually drawn.

In 1914 he was appointed coach to Derbyshire's newly-formed cricket nursery. He was to play for the county when qualified, but the outbreak of war put an end to this.

Blacklidge died from dysentery serving with Army Gymnastic Staff at Amara in Mesopotamia on 23 May 1917.

He is commemorated at the Amara War Cemetery, Grave Reference XIII. G. 11.

Batting and fielding averages

	Mat	Inns	NO	Runs	HS	Ave	100	50	Ct	St
First-class	7	9	2	100	45	14.28	0	0	8	0

Bowling averages

	Mat	Balls	Runs	Wkts	BBI	Ave	Econ	SR	5w	10
First-class	7	645	334	10	4/26	33.40	3.10	64.5	0	0

Captain Hubert George Selwyn-Smith
Queensland
49th Bn Australian Imperial Force
Died 7 June 1917
Aged 26
Unknown

'A fine example of a Queenslander'

Hubert George Selwyn Smith was born on 9 October 1891 at Beaudesert, Queensland. The youngest son of Montagu Selwyn-Smith, of Beaudesert, Queensland, and Diamantina Emma Selwyn-Smith, he trained as a solicitor before being articled to Mr W. Hamilton Hart of Messrs Flower and Hart, solicitors.

A good all-round athlete, Smith excelled at cricket and made three first-class appearances for Queensland between March 1912 and January 1913, playing against New South Wales twice and Victoria once. He made his debut for Queensland on 8 March 1912 against New South Wales at the Brisbane Cricket Ground, Woolloongabba. Although he failed to score in either innings, he took 3 wickets for 50 off 19 overs. New South Wales won by 10 wickets. He made his second first-class appearance was on 22 November 1912, also against New South Wales at the same venue. He scored 2 and 7 and took 2 wickets for 25 off 8 overs. New South Wales won again, this time by 8 wickets. Smith played his final first-class match against Victoria on 13 January 1913 at Woolloongabba, Brisbane. He scored 15 and 5 and took two wickets for 22 off 7.1 overs. Victoria won by 6 wickets.

A few months before his final law examinations he enlisted as a private into the 49th Infantry Battalion and travelled with them to France on 1 September 1915 on board HMAT *A33 Ayrshire* from Sydney, New South Wales. He qualified for his commission at the Instruction School in Egypt, where he was offered, but declined, a position on the staff. Returning to France in 1916 he was promoted in the field to the rank of captain. Wounded at Mouquet Farm on 8 September 1916 he was invalided home but returned to France on 25 October.

He was killed in action eight months later on 7 June 1917 at Messines, Belgium. His body was never recovered or identified and he is commemorated on the Ypres (Menin Gate) Memorial, Panels 7, 17, 23, 25, 27, 29, 31.

Batting and fielding averages

	Mat	Inns	NO	Runs	HS	Ave	100	50	Ct	St
First-class	3	6	0	29	15	4.83	0	0	0	0

Bowling averages

	Mat	Runs	Wkts	BBI	Ave	5w	10
First-class	3	186	7	3/50	26.57	0	0

Lieutenant John Edward Raphael
Surrey/Oxford University/London County
18th Bn The King's Royal Rifle Corps
Died 11 June 1917
Aged 35
Right-handed Bat/Right-arm Slow Medium

'If character be destiny then his is assured'

John Edward Raphael was born on 30 April 1882 in Brussels, Belgium. Jewish by faith, he was the only child of Albert and Harriette Raphael of 5 Wild Hatch, Hendon, London. Educated at Merchant Taylors' School before going up to St John's College, Oxford, while at school he was in the XI for the five years from 1897 to 1901 and, in 1898, headed the batting with an average of 23; he also managed to take thirty-two wickets at a cost of less than 9 runs each. He read History at Oxford and played cricket for the university. At Lord's, during his debut in 1903, he scored 130, following that up in 1905 with a very decent 99. He was also president of the university swimming club and gained his Blue for water polo in 1902 and 1904.

Between 1902 and 1904 he was also selected to play rugby for the University XV against Cambridge on four occasions, playing centre-three-quarter and only once failing to score a try. While at Oxford he earned fourteen Blues, four for rugby, three for cricket, three for swimming, and four for water polo. Between 1902 and 1906 he also played rugby for England on nine occasions and captained the 1910 British Lions' tour of Argentina, which included the South America nations inaugural Test match. As if that wasn't achievement enough, he also played first-class cricket. He made 77 first class appearances between August 1901 and August 1913. He played for numerous sides, London County, Surrey, Oxford University, MCC, Gentlemen of England, South of England, Gentlemen of the South, HDG Leveson Gower's XI. And England XI. He made his first class debut on 5 August 1901 for London County against Leicestershire at the Aylestone Road, Leicester. He made 8 and 35 took 1 wicket for 107 off 35 overs and caught Ralph Joyce off the bowling of James Gilman for 42. Leicestershire won by 45 runs.

Between 1903 and 1906 he played cricket for Surrey, captaining the side in 1904. He also played for Oxford and Surrey against the South Africans in 1904 and for Oxford University against the Australians in the British Isles in 1905. He made his final first class appearance for an England XI against Yorkshire on 21 August 1913 at St George's Rd, Harrogate. He scored 1 and 22 not out, the match was drawn. During his first class career Raphael scored 3,717 runs including five centuries, four for Oxford University, one of which was his career best score of 201, which he made against Yorkshire. It remains the only double hundred to be made by an Oxford cricketer against Yorkshire. His only century for Surrey came against Worcestershire in 1904 during the County Championship, when he scored 111. He also took three first-class wickets, those of Samuel Coe, Lord Dalmeny and the well-known test cricketer John King. He made 36 catches.

Raphael entered Lincoln's Inn in 1905 and was called to the Bar in 1908. Having already been president of the Palmerston Club in 1904/05, he unsuccessfully stood for parliament as the Liberal candidate in Croydon in 1909, being defeated by Sir Robert Trotter Hermon-Hodge Bt, the Unionist candidate. Despite being a pacifist, he joined up in August 1914, joining the Honourable Artillery Company. In December 1914 he was gazetted into the West Riding Regiment, before finally transferring to the 18th Bn King's Royal Rifle Corps, which had been raised by his cousin, Sir Herbert Raphael, MP for West Derby. Raphael was appointed to the General Staff as Aide de Camp to the General Officer Commanding, 41st Division.

John Raphael died at 10 Casualty Clearing Station on 11 June 1917 from wounds received on 7 June 1917 during the Battle of Messines. An account of his death later appeared in the book *Sapper Martin: The Secret Great War Diary of Jack Martin*. In the entry dated 7th June 1917 concerning the Messines Ridge:

> Lieut Raphael, the Surrey Cricketer, was up here this morning for no earthly reason as far as I can make out, other than that of souvenir hunting. He brought his batman with him and both were killed by a shell in a dugout which he was exploring.

A brother officer who was with him when he was wounded later wrote:

> I have seen gallant men in many parts of the world, under all sorts of conditions, but never in my experience have I been so impressed by such a magnificent display of sheer pluck and unselfishness as was shown by Lieut J. E. Raphael.

Raphael is commemorated in Lijessenthoek Military Cemetery, Poperinghe, West-Vlaanderen, Belgium, Grave Reference XIII, A. 30.

A memorial service was held for Raphael at St Jude's church on 21 June 1917. His mother had a memorial erected to her dead son in 1919. The monument, which sits on the north wall of the church near the organ, was designed by the sculptor Charles Sykes who also designed the Spirit of Ecstasy mascot for Rolls Royce cars. It was unveiled on 26 October 1919 by Dr Nairn, the headmaster of Merchant Taylors' school.

Batting and fielding averages

	Mat	Inns	NO	Runs	HS	Ave	100	Ct	St
First-class	77	128	8	3717	201	30.97	5	36	0

Bowling averages

	Mat	Balls	Runs	Wkts	BBI	Ave	Econ	SR	5w	10
First-class	77	690	411	3	1/34	137.00	3.57	230.0	0	0

Lieutenant Colonel Percy Macclesfield Heath
Europeans (India)
Mahratta Light Infantry
Died 14 July 1917
Aged 40
Not Known

'He died a hero's death in conditions no man should ever suffer in'

Percy Macclesfield Heath was born on 16 June 1877 at Poona (now Pune), Maharashtra, India to Percy Charles, a captain with the Staff Corps (who died in1880) and Isabella Caroline, née Burrows. Educated at Wellington College where he was in the XI in 1895, he entered Sandhurst in 1895 and was gazetted to the Unattached List of the Indian Army in 1897. Percy beame a lieutenant in 1901 and a captain in 1906. He served with the 110th Mahratta Light Infantry, rising to the rank of lieutenant colonel and married Pear St John Richardson at St Mary's Church, Poona in 1906; they had one son, Peter.

Between August 1901 and September 1909 Heath made 7 first-class appearances for the Europeans, six against the Parsees and one against Hindus. All the matches were either

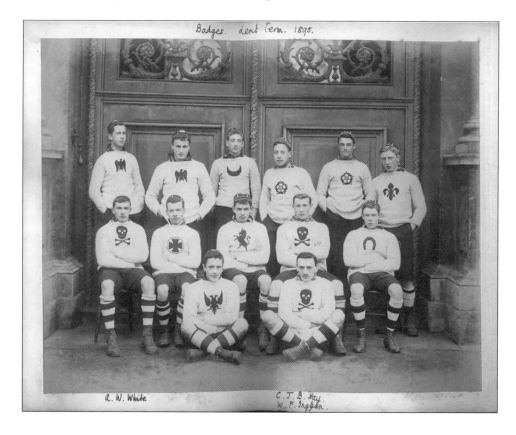

in the Bombay Triangular Tournament or a Bombay Presidency match, played at either the Gymkhana Ground, Bombay or the Deccan Gymkhana Ground, Poona. Heath made his debut for the Europeans on 29 August 1901 in a Bombay Presidency match played at the Gymkhana Ground, Bombay. He scored 0 and 35, and caught Dinshaw Kanga off the bowling of Lionel Milman for 17. The Parsees won by 8 wickets. His final first-class match also against the Parsees on 21 September 1909 at the same venue, in the final of the Bombay Triangular, Tournament. He scored 9 in his only innings. The match was drawn. During his first-class-career he scored 162 runs, his highest score being 46 against Parsees on 10 September 1908. He also took 7 catches.

During the war 110th Mahrattas were attached to 6th (Poona) Division during the Mesopotamian Campaign, in the course of which Heath was awarded the Order of Karageorge, 4th Class (with Swords), (*London Gazette*, 15 February 1917). This decoration was established in Serbia on 1 January 1904 by King Peter I (1844–1921) and was awarded in four degrees.

After initially doing well the 6th Division was forced to pull back after the Battle of Ctesiphon. Instead of continuing the march downriver towards Basra, Major General Charles Townsend established a defence position at Kut Al Amara in December 1915, commencing a lengthy siege. Although not a bad defensive position, the Allies had trouble resupplying Kut and after 147 days and many attempts to break the siege, both militarily and diplomatically, Townsend surrendered his army and the town on 29 April 1916. Around 13,000 Allied soldiers survived to be made prisoners; 70 per cent of the British and 50 per cent of the Indian troops died of disease or at the hands of their Ottoman guards during captivity.

One of these prisoners was Lieutenant Colonel Percy Heath who was transported to Baghdad, where he would have been kept in the most appalling conditions. Heath died of heatstroke on 14 July 1917 while still a prisoner.

A brother officer later wrote:

He was rightly in the Bombay Presidency. I should say he had one of the largest circles of friends of any Indian Army officer, due to his high reputation as a soldier, sportsman, and real good fellow in every way. When I stayed with him at Belgaum I shall never forget noticing at once how his men loved him and how his regiment depended on him.

In June 1917 a dinner was held to raise money for a Baghdad Exhibition, the idea being to pay for the education of the children of fallen officers in this particular theatre of war. The catch phrase 'The Turks may bag dad, but we mean to pay for the son' became popular at the time.

Heath is commemorated in Baghdad (North gate) War Cemetery, grave reference XV. D. 13.

Batting and fielding averages

	Mat	Inns	NO	Runs	HS	Ave	100	50	Ct	St
First-class	7	12	1	162	46	14.72	0	0	7	0

Bowling averages

	Mat	Runs	Wkts	BBI	BBM	Ave	SR	4w	5w	10
First-class	7	5	0	-	-	-	-	0	0	0

Lieutenant Edward Hedley Cuthbertson
Cambridge University
9th Bn The Royal Warwickshire Regiment
Died 24 July 1917
Aged 29
Left-handed Bat/Wicket-keeper

'He lived a life so strong he will be remembered forever'

Edward Hedley Cuthbertson was born on 15 December 1888 at Hackney in London. The oldest son of Edward Hedley and Alice Cuthbertson of Bushey House, Bushey, Hertfordshire, he was educated at Malvern College, where he was in the XI, and Clare College, Cambridge. Although he did play for his university, he failed to get his Blue. He did, however, get a Blue for football. On leaving university he became a member of the Stock Exchange in 1911.

Cuthbertson made 3 first-class appearances between June 1908 and July 1914. He made his debut for Cambridge University against Sussex on 4 June 1908 at Fenner's. He made 3 and 8 and caught George Cox off the bowling of Kenneth MacLeod for 81. Sussex won by 9 wickets. His second match was once again against Sussex played on 9 June 1910, once again at Fenner's. Although he scored a duck in both innings he did manage to catch Joseph Vine off the bowling of Alexander Cowie for 3. Sussex came out on top again this time by 138 runs. He made his final first-class appearance for the MCC, this time against Cambridge University. The game was played on 2 July 1914 at Lord's Cricket Ground. He scored 3 and 18 and caught John Morrison off the bowling of William Astill for 45, and Stanley Saville off the bowling of Gilbert Jessop for 1. He also made three stumpings, all off the bowling of Eric Kidd – George Wood for 20, Stanley Saville for 2 and Edward Baker for 1. Cambridge University went on to win the match by 28 runs. Between 1906 and 1913 Cuthbertson also played twenty-five matches for Hertfordshire in the Minor Counties. On 15 August 1910, playing against the MCC at Lord's, Cuthbertson made a remarkable 151 in his first innings. Hertfordshire won by an innings and 41 runs. He joined the MCC in 1909.

In August 1914 at the outbreak of the war and keen to get 'stuck in', he enlisted as a private into the Public Schools' Battalion of the Royal Fusiliers. He was eventually given his commission in the 9th Bn Royal Warwickshire Regiment and went with them to France in March 1915. Wounded at Ypres a few weeks later, he was invalided home. On returning to France he was once again wounded in July 1916 and sent home once more to recover. Together with his battalion he was posted to Mesopotamia, where he died in hospital at Amara on 24 July1917. Cuthbertson is commemorated at Amara War Cemetery, Grave Reference XIII, L. 6.

His next of kin was given as his wife, Mary Constance Follett (formerly Cuthbertson) of 72 Onslow Gardens, South Kensington, London. Hugh Cuthbertson, his younger brother, was killed in action with the Royal Field Artillery in France nine months later on 14 April 1918. Another brother, Geoffrey Bourke Cuthbertson, who died on 9 August 1993, aged 92, was captain of Northamptonshire in 1936 and 1937. He had been a member of the

Malvern XI, played for Cambridge, although like his brother he failed to get a Blue, Sussex and Middlesex. When he died he was joint-senior member of MCC, having been elected in 1919.

Batting and fielding averages

	Mat	Inns	NO	Runs	HS	Ave	100	50	Ct	St
First-class	3	6	1	32	18	6.40	0	0	4	3

Bowling averages

	Mat	Balls	Runs	Wkts	BBI	BBM	Ave	Econ	SR	4w	5w	10
First-class	3	-	-	-	-	-	-	-	-	-	-	-

Second Lieutenant Herbert Packer Bailey MC
Barbados
12th Bn The East Surrey Regiment
Died 31 July 1917
Aged 27

'His love and cricket were equally matched'

Herbert Packer Bailey was born on 5 December 1889 at River Road, St Michael, Barbados. His parents were Edward Shepherd and Ethel Clarke Bailey, of Glindale, 7 Avenue, Belleville, Barbados.

Bailey played in three first-class matches between January 1909 and September 1910, all in the Inter-Colonial Tournament. He made his debut for Barbados against British Guiana on 13 January 1909 at the Kensington Oval, Bridgetown. He scored 13 runs in his one innings. Barbados won by 9 wickets. His second first-class match was played on 19 September 1910 at Bourda, Georgetown, once again against British Guiana. Although Bailey only scored 1 run in his only innings he took 8 wickets for 28 runs off 16 overs and caught Jonathan Nurse off the bowling of Cyril Browne for 0. Largely thanks to Bailey, Barbados won by 8 wickets. His final first-class appearance came against Trinidad on 26 September 1910 played at the Bourda, Georgetown. Bailey scored 12 runs in his own innings and failed to bowl. Barbados came out on top by an innings and 48 runs.

During the First War Bailey first enlisted with the 28th London Regiment (Artists Rifles) as private 6746 and on 4 September 1916 commissioned into the East Surrey Regiment becoming attached to a trench mortar battery. On 7 June 1917 he won the Military Cross for bravery near St Éloi. The citation read:

> He displayed the greatest gallantry in handling a Stokes gun [the standard equipment of a trench mortar battery], following the first line infantry up to the final objective, where he consolidated later in the day. He showed great judgement, and was instrumental in repelling an enemy counter-attack by the skilful use of his gun.

He was killed a few weeks later on 31 July 1917. His body was never recovered or identified and he is commemorated on the Ypres (Menin Gate) Memorial, Panel 34.

Batting and fielding averages

	Mat	Inns	NO	Runs	HS	Ave	100	50	Ct	St
First-class	3	3	0	26	13	8.66	0	0	1	0

Bowling averages

	Mat	Runs	Wkts	BBI	Ave	5w	10
First-class	3	66	8	6/12	8.25	1	0

Second Lieutenant James Gordon Kinvig
Wellington
Wellington Regiment
Died 31 July 1917
Aged 29
Left-arm Medium Pace

'A true son of New Zealand. So much promise not realised'

James Gordon Kinvig, better known as 'J. G.', 'Kinny' or simply Gordon, was born on 19 July 1888 at Christchurch, Canterbury, New Zealand, the son of Richard C. and Annie M. Kinvig of 47 Bidwell Street, Wellington. Educated at Christchurch Boys' High School, he quickly established himself as a good all-round athlete and showed particular promise at cricket, being considered one of the best players in the school.

On leaving Wellington, he became a warehouseman but continued to play cricket, representing clubs such as Wellington East, Central, Rivals and Trentham Army Camp, as well as making numerous one-off appearances. Also a fine rugby player, he represented Oriental Rugby Club as a five-eighth or utility back. His ability at both games led to him being selected to play for Wellington at both cricket and rugby in the same year.

He made two first-class appearances for Wellington in February and March 1910. He made his debut for Wellington on 11 February 1910 against the Australians in New Zealand at Basin Reserve, Wellington. He scored 8 and 17 and took 3 wickets for 36 off 7.4 overs. Despite Kinvig's best efforts, Australia won by 6 wickets. His second appearance for Wellington came against Hawke's Bay on 26 March 1910 at the Recreation Ground. Kinvig scored 0 and 15 and took 1 wicket for 4 during off 1 over. The match was eventually drawn.

He enlisted in the ranks of the Wellington Regiment in September 1915, becoming 11774 Private Kinvig. Because of previous reservist experience, he was quickly promoted to sergeant and later, after service in France, was commissioned as a second lieutenant with the same regiment. He embarked for Suez on 1 May 1916 from Wellington on the *Ulimaroa* as part of the 12th Reinforcements, Wellington Infantry Battalion, B Company.

After officer training he returned to his regiment to take up his duties and was killed in action during the early morning of 31 July 1917 during an attack on la Basse Ville.

Gordon Kinvig is buried in Mud Cemetery, on the northern edge of Ploegstreet Wood, alongside eighty-four others. Grave reference II, D. 5.

Batting and fielding averages

	Mat	Inns	NO	Runs	HS	Ave	100	50	Ct	St
First-class	2	4	0	40	17	10.00	0	0	0	0

Bowling averages

	Mat	Runs	Wkts	BBI	Ave	5w	10
First-class	2	70	4	3/36	17.50	0	0

Second Lieutenant Logie Colin Leggatt
Cambridge University
2nd Bn Coldstream Guards
Died 31 July 1917
Aged 22
Right-handed Bat/Legbreak

'Beloved by all'

Logie Colin Leggatt was born on 24 September 1894 at St John's Hill, Bangalore, India. The son of William Chades Foster Leggatt and Alice Leggatt, of 25/3 Cleveland Square, Paddington, London, he was educated at Eton College where he was in the XI in 1912 and 1913. A good bat, he averaged 33 in 1912 and 26 in 1913, scoring 74 against Winchester in 1913.

Going up to King's College Cambridge he was in the Freshmen's match in 1914. He made 116 and 12, and in a trial match scored 160 not out, carrying his bat throughout the innings. Despite his best efforts, however, he failed to get his Blue. Leggatt also played an impressive innings of 76 for Old Etonians against Old Harrovians at Lord's in 1914.

He played one first-class match on 28 May 1914 at F. P. Fenner's Ground, Cambridge, against Yorkshire, scoring 3 and 6. Yorkshire won by an innings and 6 runs.

Leggatt with the 2nd Battalion Coldstream Guards during the war and was killed in action at Pilckem Ridge with his regiment on 31 July 1917, the day that saw the opening of the Third Battle of Ypres (better known as the Battle of Passchendaele). The attack had been well planned and was preceded by several days of artillery barrage. The Guards brigades would attack from the village of Boesinghe, to the north of Ypres, towards the enemy positions on Pilckem Ridge. Zero hour was set for 3.50am and, exactly on schedule, the men left their trenches. The Coldstreams were not in the first wave of the attack but used to mop up behind the main attack. By 6.00am, the Coldstreams had reached their first main objective, perhaps 1000 yards away.

Half an hour later, they had moved forward another 700 yards to the second objective, marked on operational maps as the Black Line. Here they halted for an hour to regroup while, 200 yards in front of them, the British artillery bombardment continued to destroy enemy positions. The barrage then started to roll forward at a rate of 100 yards every four minutes and the Coldstreams kept close behind it for protection as they advanced another 1,000 yards towards their final objective marked as the Green Line. It was during this action that Private Thomas Witham of the Coldstream Guards earned the Victoria Cross.

His citation read:

On 31 July 1917 at Pilckem near Ypres, Belgium, during an attack an enemy machine gun was seen to be enfilading the battalion on the right. Private Whitham on his own initiative immediately worked his way from shell-hole to shell-hole through our own barrage, reached the machine gun and, although under very heavy fire, captured it, together with an officer and two other ranks. This bold action was of great assistance to the battalion and undoubtedly saved many lives.

Leggatt is commemorated in Artillery Wood Cemetery, grave reference V. B. 17.

The famous female racing driver Muriel Thompson was badly affected by her nephew Logie's death and never fully recovered from it.

Batting and fielding averages

	Mat	Inns	NO	Runs	HS	Ave	100	50	Ct	St
First-class	1	2	0	9	6	4.50	0	0	0	0

Bowling averages

	Mat	Balls	Runs	Wkts	BBI	BBM	Ave	Econ	SR	4w	5w	10
First-class	1	-	-	-	-	-	-	-	-	-	-	-

77439 Gunner William Riley
Nottinghamshire
133 Siege Battery Royal Garrison Artillery
Died 9 August 1917
Aged 28
Left-handed Bat/Left-arm Slow Medium

'Never did a man love his county, city or club more'

William Riley was born on 11 August 1888 at Newstead Colliery, Nottinghamshire, to John and Catherine Riley of 109 Newstead Colliery Village. Riley played in 80 first-class matches for Nottinghamshire between May 1909 and August 1914 mostly in the County Championship but he also played against the MCC on three occasions as well as playing against Australia in the British Isles in May 1912 and South Africa in the British Isles in June 1912. He made his debut for Nottinghamshire on 13 May 1909 against Sussex at the County Ground, Hove. He scored 2 and 5 and took 4 wickets for 104 off 31 overs. Sussex won by an innings and 107 runs. Riley made his final first class appearance on 17 August 1914 against Middlesex at Lords. He made 1 and 7 not out and took 3 wickets for 41 off 23 overs. Middlesex won by 239 runs. During his first class career he scored 740 runs his highest score being 48. He also took 235 wickets for 5497 runs his best figures being 7 for 80. He made 69 catches.

In 1914 Riley played professional cricket for Oldfield Cricket Club, Staffordshire

Riley served with 133 Siege Bty Royal Garrison Artillery during the war as Gunner 77439. He was hit by a shell splinter and killed on 9 August 1917 while serving as a gunner with 133 Siege Battery near Coxyde, Belgium. Amongst items returned to his parents after his death were letters, photographs, two reference books, a safety razor with strap in a case, hair brush, money bag and a farthing.

He is commemorated in Coxyde Military Cemetery, Grave Reference II, E. 30.

Batting and fielding averages

	Mat	Inns	NO	Runs	HS	Ave	100	50	Ct	St
First-class	80	110	24	740	48	8.60	0	0	69	0

Bowling averages

	Mat	Balls	Runs	Wkts	BBI	Ave	Econ	SR	5w	10
First-class	80	13675	5497	235	7/80	23.39	2.41	58.1	10	2

Lance Sergeant Vivian Claude Kavanagh
Auckland
2nd Bn New Zealand Rifle Brigade
Died 9 August 1917
Aged 35
Right-handed Bat

'Never shirked his duty'

Vivian Claude Kavanagh was born on 2 June 1882 in Mauku, Auckland, New Zealand. He was the son of Mr Charles and Mrs Charlotte Kavanagh of 140 Crummer Road, Grey Lynn, Auckland, and, on leaving school, trained as a carpenter. Kavanagh later became a master builder and formed a company with a Mr Williams. He served with B Squadron of A Company, 10th Contingent, New Zealand Mounted Rifles during the Second Boer War of 1899 to 1902, embarking for Durban, South Africa, on 14 April 1902.

Vivian played in one first-class match for Auckland against Canterbury, in the Plunket Shield, on 29 January 1913 at the Auckland Domain. He scored 12 and 6, Auckland going down by 8 wickets.

During the First World War Kavanagh served with the 2nd Bn New Zealand Rifle Brigade, leaving New Zealand on 17 November 1915. He was killed in action with his battalion on 9 August 1917.

He is commemorated at Prowse Point Military Cemetery, Grave Reference III, A. 24.

Batting and fielding averages

	Mat	Inns	NO	Runs	HS	Ave	100	50	Ct	St
First-class	1	2	0	18	12	9.00	0	0	0	0

Bowling averages

	Mat	Balls	Runs	Wkts	BBI	BBM	Ave	Econ	SR	4w	5w	10
First-class	1	78	55	0	-	-	-	4.23	-	0	0	0

Second Lieutenant Harry Ernest Charles Biedermann
Argentina
Queen's Own Oxfordshire Hussars/No. 57 Squadron Royal
Flying Corps
Died 10 August 1917
Aged 28
Right-handed Bat

'Returned without fail as soon as he knew his country was in peril'

Harry Ernest Charles Biedermann was born on 4 September 1887 in Eton, Buckinghamshire, the son of A. H. Biedermann of 23 Down Street, London. He was educated at Harrow School where he was in the XI in 1906, playing against Eton on 13 July 1906, scoring 32 and 14 and taking two wickets for 48 off sixteen overs. Eton finally won the game by four wickets. He also played racquets in 1906 and 1907. On leaving school in 1907 he took up ranging in Argentina.

While in Argentina he played two first-class matches in February and March 1912. He made his debut on 18 February 1912, at the Hurlington Club Ground when he turned out for Argentina against the visiting MCC, scoring 2 and 8 not out. He also took three catches, Charles Hatfeild off the bowling of Philip Foy for 39, Morice Bird off the bowling of Foy once again for 29, and Arthur Hill off the bowling of Evelyn Toulmin for 34. Argentina won by 4 wickets. He made his second first class appearance once again against the MCC on 2 March 1912 at Lomas Athletic, Buenos Aires. This time Biedermann scored 4 and 14 and took a further catch, that of Charles de Trafford off the bowling of Philip Foy for 13. On this occasion the MCC took the match by 2 wickets.

In September 1914, shortly after the outbreak of the war, he returned from Argentina and joined the 3rd County of London Yeomanry as a trooper. He was sent to Egypt in April 1915, and from there to Gallipoli, where he served throughout that campaign. On coming to England on leave his commanding officer recommended him highly for a commission, which he was given in the Queen's Own Oxfordshire Hussars. After serving for three months with this regiment, he transferred to the Royal Flying Corps, and, having obtained his pilot's certificate, was sent out to France in July 1917. He was a good pilot and shot down at least one German aircraft, on 28 July 1917. An RFC communiqué for 28 July states:

When returning from bombing Heule and Bissinghem aerodrome 5 machines of 57 Squadron encountered 30 enemy scouts, of which one was seen to break up in the air and at least 6 others were claimed as shot down out of control

Later it states:

When returning from a bombing raid de Havilland 4s of 57 Squadron met a formation of Albatross scouts. Lt Biedermann shot down one in flames, Major Joy shot down 2 others while Capt Harker shot down one out of control.

Final Wicket

Just a few weeks later, on l0 August 1917, flying from his base at Boisdinghem, Biedermann was reported missing while flying as a pilot with 57 Squadron Royal Flying Corps over Houthulst Forest in a DH4. His observer at the time was Lieutenant A. Calder who died with him. It is possible that he was shot down by the German ace Leutnant M. Muller (twenty-one victories) who claimed the only DH4 shot down on that day, although the timings do not agree.

Biedermann's body was never recovered or identified and he is commemorated on the Arras Flying Service Memorial.

Batting and fielding averages

	Mat	Inns	NO	Runs	HS	Ave	100	50	Ct	St
First-class	2	4	1	28	14	9.33	0	0	4	0

Bowling averages

	Mat	Balls	Runs	Wkts	BBI	BBM	Ave	Econ	SR	4w	5w	10
First-class	2	-	-	-	-	-	-	-	-	-	-	-

Private John Asquith Atkinson Nelson
Lancashire
11th Bn The Cheshire Regiment
Died 12 August 1917
Aged 28

'Stood at his wicket and his trench with equal vigour'

John Asquith Atkinson Nelson was born on 28 October 1891 at Marton, Blackpool, Lancashire, the son of Joseph Lauckland and Margaret Nelson of 12 Cranford Avenue, Sale, Cheshire.

He made one first class appearance for Lancashire against Warwickshire in the County Championship on 28 July 1913 at Old Trafford. Nelson scored 5 and 2; despite this poor showing, Lancashire still went on to win by 7 wickets. He also played 6 matches for the Lancashire seconds, his highest score being 66 against Yorkshire seconds.

He was killed in action serving with the 11th Bn Cheshire Regiment near Pilckem, France on 12 August 1917 and is commemorated in the Tyne Cot Cemetery, Grave Reference XLVIII, B. 11.

Batting and fielding averages

	Mat	Inns	NO	Runs	HS	Ave	100	50	Ct	St
First-class	1	2	0	7	5	3.50	0	0	0	0

Bowling averages

	Mat	Balls	Runs	Wkts	BBI	BBM	Ave	Econ	SR	4w	5w	10
First-class	1	-	-	-	-	-	-	-	-	-	-	-

Second Lieutenant Ralf Hubert Robinson
Essex
10th Bn The Royal Fusiliers (City of London Regiment) &
2nd Bn The Prince Consort's Own (Rifle Brigade)
Died 23 August 1917
Aged 32
Wicket-keeper

'Like father, like son'

Ralf Hubert Robinson was born on 28 June 1885 in Stratford to Matthew and Celia Robinson of Inglenook, New Wanstead, Wanstead, Essex. On leaving school he became a stockbroker's clerk and in 1915 married Daisy Gertrude Marion Bailey at St Mary the Virgin with Christ Church, Wanstead. They moved to Rowlands (37 Fernlea Road, Benfleet) and had two children, Sybil, born in 1916, and Ralf Hubert Reginald, born in 1917.

Robinson, who was considered to be one of the finest amateur wicket-keepers in the country. He made four first-class matches for Essex all in the County Championship during the 1912 season. He made his debut for Essex against Northamptonshire at the County Ground, Northampton on 17 June 1912. He scored 2 runs in his only innings and stumped John Denton off the bowling of Charles McGahey for 52 and John Seymour again off the bowling of McGahey for 5. Northamptonshire winning by an innings and 137 runs. He went on to play against Middlesex and Kent before making his final first class appearance against Sussex at the County Ground, Leyton on 4 July 1912. He scored 11 not out in his only innings and caught Albert Relf off the bowling of Walter Mead for 29. The match was eventually drawn.

During his first class career he made 25 runs with a high score of 11 against Sussex. He took 9 catches and made 4 stumpings. Robinson also played for Wanstead Cricket Club.

During the war he enlisted in the ranks of the 10th (Stockbrokers) Bn Royal Fusiliers and went to France with them on 31 July 1915. He was promoted to sergeant and awarded the Military Medal for bravery (*London Gazette*, 19 February 1917) for gallantry and devotion to duty under fire.

His ability quickly came to attention and he was commissioned as a second lieutenant in the 2nd Bn Rifle Brigade on 25 April 1917. A few months later, on 23 August 1917, Robinson died of wounds at Westhoek Ridge, Ypres during the Third Battle of Ypres, commonly known as Passchendaele.

He is commemorated at the Lijssenthoek Military Cemetery, Grave Reference XVI, A. 8.

After his death his widow asked if she could have his county cap for her son, which was agreed. His son, born after Ralf's death, a lieutenant with the Royal Ulster Rifles, was killed in action in Libya on 8 June 1942, aged 24, while attached to 8th Durham Light Infantry.

Batting and fielding averages

	Mat	Inns	NO	Runs	HS	Ave	100	50	Ct	St
First-class	4	7	2	25	11*	5.00	0	0	9	4

Bowling averages

	Mat	Balls	Runs	Wkts	BBI	BBM	Ave	Econ	SR	4w	5w	10
First-class	4	-	-	-	-	-	-	-	-	-	-	-

Second Lieutenant Ernest Ewart Gladstone Alderwick
Gloucestershire
11th Bn The Suffolk Regiment
Died 26 August 1917
Aged 31
Right-handed Bat

'Could strike a ball better than any man I have ever seen'

Ernest Ewart Gladstone Alderwick was born on 14 April 1886 at Montpelier, Barton Regis, near Bristol, the son of Francis and Emily Alderwick, of Bristol.

Ernest played two first-class games for Gloucestershire both in the County Championship during the 1908 season. He made his debut for Gloucestershire against Worcestershire on 13 July 1908 at the County Ground, New Road, Worcester. He scored 2 and 5, Worcestershire going on to win by 225 runs. He made his second first class appearance against Northamptonshire on 16 July 1908 at the County Ground, Northampton. He was out for a duck in his only innings. The match was drawn. Alderwick also made two appearances for Suffolk in the minor counties.

He married Florence A. Alderwick of 4 Harcourt Road, Redland, Bristol. During the war he enlisted into the ranks of the Gloucestershire Regiment in August 1916 (number 30580), arriving in France on 19 June 1917. He was then posted to 93rd Training Reserve Battalion before being transferred to the Dorsetshire Regiment and being promoted to lance corporal. He must have impressed because he was quickly commissioned into the 11th Bn Suffolk Regiment. While serving with his battalion he was killed in action on 26 August 1917.

He is commemorated at the Hargicourt Communal Cemetery Extension, Grave Reference A. 2.

Batting and fielding averages

	Mat	Inns	NO	Runs	HS	Ave	100	50	Ct	St
First-class	2	3	0	7	5	2.33	0	0	0	0

Bowling averages

	Mat	Balls	Runs	Wkts	BBI	BBM	Ave	Econ	SR	4w	5w	10
First-class	2	-	-	-	-	-	-	-	-	-	-	

Lieutenant Colonel Richard Percy Lewis
Oxford University
Devonshire Regiment, attd Manchester Regiment
Died 7 September 1917
Aged 43
Right-handed Bat/Wicket-keeper

'His one object in life was to kill Germans'

Richard Percy Lewis was born on 10 March 1874 at Kensington, London, the son of Richard Lewis, a barrister, of Wimbledon, and Secretary of the Royal National Lifeboat Institution. He was educated by the Reverend C. Fendall at Windlesham and Winchester College and was in the Winchester XI of 1891–2, including the XI that played Eton on 3 June 1891 at Upper Club, Eton College. He scored 2 in his one innings, but also took three catches and made a stumping. Winchester won by five wickets. Lewis was in the Winchester side against Eton again in 1892, Winchester once more taking the honours by 84 runs, Lewis making 2 not out in his one innings and making a single catch. During this time he also represented the Surrey and Marlborough Blue.

After leaving school Lewis went up to University College, Oxford in 1892, keeping wicket for the University XI from 1894 to 1896. He made a total of 36 first-class appearances for Oxford University, A. Priestley's XI, during their tour of the West Indies, MCC (a member since 1893), Middlesex and A. J. Webbe's XI. He made his debut for Oxford University against AJ Webbe's XI at the University Parks, Oxford on 21 May 1894. He made 2 in his only innings and caught Cyril Foley off the bowling of Dudley Forbes for 28. The match was drawn. He made his final first class appearance for the MCC against Leicestershire at Lords on the 30 June 1907. He scored 0 and 3 and caught Cecil Wood off the bowling of Claude Buckenham for 9, John King off the bowling of Buckenham again for 21 and Samuel Coe off the bowling of William Reeves for 100. He also stumped Thomas Jayes off the bowling of William Overton for 0. The match was drawn. During his first class career Lewis made 134 runs his highest score being 27. He also made 55 catches and made 21 stumpings.

After leaving Oxford he acted for a short time as editor of *The London Review*. On the outbreak of the Second Boer War he joined the City Imperial Volunteers and, after serving with them for some time in the Orange Free State, in October 1901 he received a commission in the Devonshire Regiment. In 1904 he was appointed to the Central Africa Battalion of the King's African Rifles and took part in the Nandi Expedition of 1905–06, being Mentioned in Despatches. In 1908 he was appointed to the Egyptian Army and was detained in Egypt for some time after war broke out as an intelligence officer at Cairo. Early in 1917, after a period of service as a brigade major, he was appointed to command the 1/9th (some records say 10th) Bn Manchester Regiment.

Lewis died of wounds at Ypres on 9 September 1917 during a heavy bombardment between the villages of Frezenberg and Westhoek. He was hit by a splinter from a shell and died shortly afterwards. K. W. Mitchinson, in his book *Amateur Soldier*, describes his death in more detail:

It was during one such bombardment that Lt-Colonel Lewis was killed. Battalion HQ was housed in a cellar of a ruined farmhouse known as Kit and Kat. The position lay on what in more peaceful times had been the minor road running between Frezenberg and Westhoek. Lewis was hit by a shell splinter when giving orders to a runner and died shortly afterwards. His body was taken back to Ypres and buried in the burgeoning cemetery near to the tumbled central square. Significant though it might have been to the officers, the death of the colonel probably had little effect upon the general morale of the battalion. Having only recently joined the unit, most of the men would have recognised him but would have had little to do with him. Wynne thought initially Lewis' methods had seemed harsh but later considered that he was a 'thoroughly efficient soldier' who had been 'very much misunderstood'. Bradbury believed that Lewis' one object in life was to kill Germans and that he expected everyone else to hold a similar creed.

He is commemorated at Ypres Reservoir Cemetery, Grave Reference I. A. 57.

Batting and fielding averages

	Mat	Inns	NO	Runs	HS	Ave	100	50	Ct	St
First-class	36	58	21	134	27*	3.62	0	0	55	21

Bowling averages

	Mat	Balls	Runs	Wkts	BBI	BBM	Ave	Econ	SR	4w	5w	10
First-class	36	-	-	-	-	-	-	-	-	-	-	-

**Second Lieutenant Eric Balfour 'Bill' Lundie
South Africa/Eastern Province/Transvaal/ Western
Province
3rd Bn Coldstream Guards
Died 12 September 1917
Aged 29
Right-handed Bat/Right-arm Fast**

'A Man of Many talents'

Eric Balfour Lundie was born on 15 March 1888 at Willowvale, Cape Province, now Transkei, and educated at St Andrew's College, Grahamstow, South Africa. He married his long-time girlfriend Emily Lundie and they resided at Queenstown, Cape Province. Between March 1909 and February 1914 he played in 1 Test and 9 first-class matches, making his first-class debut for Eastern Province against Transvaal on 19 March 1909 in the Currie Cup at Newlands, Cape Town. Lundie scored 9 and 8 and took one wickets for 58 off 23 overs. He also managed to catch Frederick Louis le Roux off the bowling of Charles Allison for 19. Transvaal won by an innings and 123 runs. He made his final first class match for Transvaal against the MCC on 30 January 1914 at the Old Wanderers, Johannesburg. He made 3 in his only innings and took 4 wickets for 73 off 26.3 overs. The match was drawn.

He appeared in one Test against England on 27 February 1914 at St George's Park, Port Elizabeth, South Africa, scoring 0 not out and 1; he also took four wickets for 101 runs off 46.3 overs. England won by 10 wickets. Lundie made a total of 126 first-class runs, his highest score being 29 and took 26 wickets for 659 runs, his best figures being 6 for 52. He made 7 catches.

During the war he first served with the South African Service Corps before being commissioned as a second lieutenant in the 3rd Battalion Coldstream Guards. He was killed by a shell while the 3rd Battalion was being relieved by the 2nd Battalion Irish Guards on 12 September 1917.

His body was never recovered or identified and he is commemorated on the Tyne Cot Memorial, Panel 9 to 10.

Batting and fielding averages

	Mat	Inns	NO	Runs	HS	Ave	100	50	4s	6s	Ct	St
Tests	1	2	1	1	1	1.00	0	0	0	0	0	0
First-class	9	16	1	126	29	8.40	0	0			7	0

Bowling averages

	Mat	Inns	Balls	Runs	Wkts	BBI	BBM	Ave	Econ	SR	4w	5w	10
Tests	1	2	286	107	4	4/101	4/107	26.75	2.24	71.5	1	0	0
First-class	9		1510	659	26	6/52		25.34	2.61	58.0		1	0

Sergeant Charles Pepper
Nottinghamshire
16th Bn The Sherwood Foresters (Nottinghamshire and
Derbyshire Regiment)
Died 13 September 1917
Aged 42
Right-handed Bat/Right-arm Medium

'If he wasn't playing cricket he was talking about it.
A love of the game second to none'

Charles Pepper was born on 6 June 1875 at Youghal, County Cork, Ireland, but moved to England with his parents when he was still a young boy and quickly proved himself a fine athlete, showing a special aptitude for cricket. His talent was appreciated by Rye Cricket Club, Sussex and he was employed as a professional by them while still a teenager. Later he also played for Brechin in Scotland. As an all-round sportsman, he also represented Bedford Town FC and Notts County FC. He married and had four boys.

Pepper made 7 first-class appearances for Nottinghamshire between June 1900 and August 1901, having been noticed in the match between Nottinghamshire Colts and Yorkshire Colts where he scored 57 not out, carrying his bat throughout the innings, although Yorkshire Colts went on to win by an innings and 8 runs. His first appearance for Nottinghamshire was against Middlesex at Lord's in the County Championship on 11 June 1900, when he scored 17 and a duck and caught Bernard Bosanquet off the bowling of Percy Mason for 19. Nottinghamshire winning by six wickets. He went on to play against, Kent, Gloucestershire, Essex and Derbyshire. He made his final first class appearance against Lancashire at Old Trafford, Manchester on 22 August 1901. He scored 40 not out and 26. Lancashire won by 7 wickets. During his first class career he made 162 runs his highest score being 40 against Lancashire. He also took 3 wickets for 72 and made 2 catches. He also played five times for Bedfordshire in the minor counties and represented Nottinghamshire against the West Indies on 9 July 1900 at Trent Bridge Nottinghamshire, scoring 14 in his one innings and taking two wickets. Nottinghamshire won by an innings and 27 runs. After leaving Nottinghamshire he joined Darlington, playing with them as a professional between 1902 and 1904.

At the outbreak of the war Charles enlisted in the ranks of the 16th Bn Sherwood Foresters (Nottinghamshire and Derbyshire Regiment) (Chatsworth Rifles) as private 32476. His abilities quickly came to notice and he was promoted to sergeant.

He travelled out to France with his battalion in April 1916 and was killed by a shell whilst standing outside battalion headquarters on 13 September 1917, together with his Commanding Officer, Lieutenant Colonel Noel Houghton. Charles's brother, Regimental Sergeant Major John Pepper, informed Charles's wife of his death. She had already lost a brother and eight cousins during the war. He was buried together with his Colonel with full military honours; they are still side by side to this day. Over 200 officers and men attended and the last post was played.

Two officers later wrote to his widow. The first recalled:

When I joined the battalion last December your husband was my platoon sergeant and I always found him brave and cheery soldier that could be relied on.

Another who had played cricket against him during peacetime said:

we never missed a suitable opportunity of chatting about our cricket experience during the good old days …

He is commemorated at the la Clytte Military Cemetery, Grave reference II, D. 3 (Lieutenant Colonel Noel Houghton is II,D.2)

Batting and fielding averages

	Mat	Inns	NO	Runs	HS	Ave	100	50	Ct	St
First-class	7	12	3	162	40*	18.00	0	0	2	0

Bowling averages

	Mat	Balls	Runs	Wkts	BBI	Ave	Econ	SR	5w	10
First-class	7	114	72	3	3/23	24.00	3.78	38.0	0	0

Lieutenant John Congreve Murray
Scotland
8th Bn The Royal Scots (The Lothian Regiment)
Died 23 September 1917
Aged 35
Right-handed Bat

'Lived as a Scot, died as a Scot'

John Congreve Murray was born on 21 August 1882 in Edinburgh, the son of Patrick Murray, Writer to the Signet, and Agnes Evelyn, née Congreve, of Edinburgh. Educated at the Edinburgh Academy between 1889 and 1901, he represented the school on the first XI. After leaving the Academy he became a stockbroker and was employed by Messers Guild, Lawson and Murray. He married Muriel Grace 'Betty' Murray, née Wingate, and they resided at 8 Great King Street, Edinburgh.

He played in 3 first-class matches between July 1909 and July 1913. The first was for Scotland against Ireland on 22 July 1909 at North Inch, Perth. Murray scored 34 not out in his first and only innings. Scotland won by an innings and 132 runs. He next represented Scotland against the visiting Australian team on 8 July 1912 at Raeburn Place, Edinburgh. Murray scored 18 and a duck with Australia taking the honours by 296 runs. He made his final first-class match against Ireland on 10 July 1913, once again at Raeburn Place. Murray scored 15 and 29 and caught Arthur Blair-White the Irish opener off the bowling of William Fraser for 23 and Robert Lambert off the bowling of Charles Paterson for 2. The match was eventually drawn. He also represented the Grange Cricket Club against the MCC.

He was commissioned as a second lieutenant into 1/8th Bn The Royal Scots in July 1915, being promoted to lieutenant later the same year. He landed in France on 2 June 1917 and, a few months later, on 20 September 1917 during the Third Battle of Ypres, commonly known as Passchendaele, he was seriously wounded. Lieutenant Murray died of his wounds a few days later on the 23rd.

He is commemorated at the Dozinghem Military Cemetery, West-Vlaanderen, Belgium, grave reference VIII, D.1.

Batting and fielding averages

	Mat	Inns	NO	Runs	HS	Ave	100	50	Ct	St
First-class	3	5	0	78	34	15.60	0	0	2	0

Bowling averages

	Mat	Balls	Runs	Wkts	BBI	BBM	Ave	Econ	SR	4w	5w	10
First-class	3	-	-	-	-	-	-	-	-	-	-	-

Second Lieutenant Ernest Herbert Simpson
Kent
G Anti-Aircraft Battery, ANZAC
Royal Garrison Artillery
Died 2 October 1917
Aged 41
Right handed Bat

'Never shirked his duty'

Ernest Herbert Simpson was born on 17 December 1875 in Clapton, London, the second son of F. H. Simpson of Beckenham, a member of the Stock Exchange. Ernest was educated at Malvern College where he was in the school XI for three years from 1893 to 1895, captaining the side in 1895. On leaving Malvern he, like his father, became a member of the Stock Exchange and subsequently started as a dealer in the American market.

He made 7 first-class appearances for Kent between May and June 1896. He made his debut first class appearance in the county championship on 18 May 1896 against Gloucestershire at the Bat and Ball Ground, Gravesend. Playing against the legendary W. G. Grace, who took 6 wickets and scored 44 runs in one innings, Simpson scored a duck and 17. He was playing on the same side as Charles Osborn Cooper, who was later to become his brother-in-law. Gloucestershire won the match by 9 wickets. He went on to play against Yorkshire, Warwickshire. Middlesex and the MCC. He made his final first class appearance against Sussex, once again in the County Championship, on 18 June 1896 at the Angel Ground, Tonbridge. He scored 13 and 0, Sussex winning by 4 wickets. During his first class career he made 219 runs his highest score being 94 against Lancashire on 25 May 1896. He also made 1 catch.

During the war he obtained a commission in the 29th Anti-Aircraft Section, Royal Garrison Artillery in June 1916 and served in France with them. While attached to G Anti-Aircraft Battery (Anzac Section) he was mortally wounded on 27 September 1917 near Vlamertinghe by a bomb dropped by an attacking aircraft. Simpson died from his wounds five days later on 2 October 1917 at St Omer.

He is commemorated at Longuenesse (St Omer) Souvenir Cemetery, Longuenesse, Nord Pas de Calais, France, Grave Reference Plot IV, Row E, Grave 21.

Batting and fielding averages

	Mat	Inns	NO	Runs	HS	Ave	100	Ct	St
First-class	7	14	0	219	94	15.64	0	1	0

Bowling averages

	Mat	Balls	Runs	Wkts	BBI	BBM	Ave	Econ	SR	4w	5w	10
First-class	7	-	-	-	-	-	-	-	-	-	-	-

Second Lieutenant William Ward Odell MC
Leicestershire/London County
9th Bn The Sherwood Foresters (Nottinghamshire and
Derbyshire Regiment)
Died 4 October 1917
Aged 36
Right-arm Bat/Right-arm Medium

'As outstanding an officer as he was a cricket player'

William Ward Odell was born on 5 November 1881, in Leicester, the son of the Reverend Joseph Odell, a Primitive Methodist minister. William was educated at the King Edward VI Camp Hill School for Boys where he played for the first XI.

Odell made a total of 193 first-class appearances between July 1901 and August 1914, scoring 3,368 runs including nine half centuries, his highest score being 75. Odell also took 737 wickets for 17,416 runs his best figures being 8 for 20. He made 88 catches. He made his first class debut for Leicestershire against London County Cricket Club on the 22 July 1901 at the Crystal Palace Park, Crystal Palace. Odell scored 16 in his only innings. Remarkably, the first wicket he ever took, in what was to be a long and impressive career was that of the famous W. G. Grace, who was caught on the long on boundary by John King for 83. He also caught and bowled William Murch for 44. The match was drawn. As if to add insult to injury, in the return match two weeks on 5 August 1901 at the Aylestone Road, Leicester, Odell not only took 9 wickets for 73, but once again took the wicket of W. G. Grace of the bowling of Harold Marriott for 0. His next match was against Warwickshire this time he took ten wickets for 103. A leading wicket taker between 1902 and 1908, in 1902 he took no fewer than 89 wickets, including 7 Hampshire wickets for 33. In his first match for London County against the MCC in 1902 he took 6 second-innings wickets, including that of the author of Sherlock Holmes, Arthur Conan Doyle, for 0. He took over a hundred wickets between 1903 and 1905. Although he failed to take a hundred wickets in 1906 he did take eight for 20 against the MCC while representing Leicestershire which turned out to be the best figure of his career. Back on form in 1907 he took over 100 wickets falling to 74 during the 1908 season. It was, however, to be his last full season with Leicestershire. *The Times* announced that 'Owing to business engagements Mr W. W. Odell will not be able to play for Leicestershire next season except during holidays.' The announcement proved to be true and he appeared only occasionally for Leicestershire until the outbreak of war in 1914. Odell made his final first class appearance on 29 August 1914 against Nottinghamshire at Aylestone Road, Leicester. He made 10 and 2 and took 1 wicket for 24 off 10 overs. Nottinghamshire won by 208 runs.

Odell not only represented Leicestershire and London County but also the Gentlemen of the South (1903) The Gentleman (1903–07) Gentlemen of England (1905–1906) W. G. Grace's XI (1907) and Rest of England (1903).

Final Wicket

He later married Alice Odell, whose last known address was given as 83 Audrey Road, Small Heath, Birmingham.

Odell joined the Inns of Court Officers' Training Corps as private 6424 before being commissioned in the 9th Bn Sherwood Foresters (Nottinghamshire and Derbyshire Regiment). An outstanding officer, he was awarded the Military Cross for bravery a few weeks before he died in 1917. His citation is an impressive one:

> For conspicuous gallantry and devotion to duty in taking out a patrol at a critical moment and gaining very valuable information, which resulted in bodies of the enemy who were massing for attack being dispersed by our artillery fire. Throughout all operations he has consistently displayed the utmost courage and coolness. (*London Gazette*, 14 September 1917)

Second Lieutenant William Ward Odell was killed in action on 4 October 1917 at Poelcapelle, east of Ypres, Belgium. It was during this action that Corporal Fred Greaves was to win the Victoria Cross.

> On 4 October 1917 when the platoon was held up by machine-gun fire from a concrete stronghold and the platoon commander and sergeant were casualties, Corporal Greaves, followed by another NCO, rushed forward, reached the rear of the building and bombed the occupants, killing or capturing the garrison and the machine-gun. Later, at a most critical period of the battle, during a heavy counter-attack, all the officers of the company became casualties and Corporal Greaves collected his men, threw out extra posts on the threatened flank and opened up rifle and machine-gun fire to enfilade the advance.

Odell's body was never recovered or identified and he is commemorated on the Tyne Cot Memorial, Panels 99 to 102 and 162 to 162A.

Batting and fielding averages

	Mat	Inns	NO	Runs	HS	Ave	100	50	Ct	St
First-class	193	299	53	3368	75	13.69	0	9	88	0

Bowling averages

	Mat	Runs	Wkts	BBI	Ave	5w	10
First-class	193	17416	737	8/20	23.63	45	6

Leicestershire's Eleven

Lieutenant Frederick Bisset Collins
Victoria
21st Bn Australian Imperial Force
Died 4 October 1917
Aged 36
Right-handed Bat/Right-arm fast Medium

'There never was a better cricketer or a better loved man'

F. COLLINS,
East Melbourne.

Frederick Bisset Collins was born on 25 February 1881 in Richmond, Melbourne, Victoria, Australia. One of four children born to Fred and Ann Jane Collins of 155 Princess Street, Kew, Melbourne, he was educated at the Scotch College, Melbourne, where he played in the XI. His club cricket was played for East Melbourne Cricket Club where he scored 5,896 runs and took 422 wickets. He married Gertrude Steenholdt in 1907, and the couple had two children.

He made 37 first-class appearances 36 for Victoria and 1 for 'The Rest' against Australia. He made his debut for Victoria against South Australia on 24 November 1899 in the Sheffield Shield at the Adelaide Oval. He made 0 and 9 and took 6 wickets for 81 runs off 42.3 overs in the first innings and 2 wickets for 105 runs off 30.1 overs in the second. Victoria won by 246 runs. He went on to play against, New South Wales, AC MacLaren's XI, Queensland, Lord Hawke's XI MCC and Tasmania. He made his final first class match on 19 February 1909 against Tasmania at the North Tasmania Cricket Association ground, Launceston. Collins scored 10 and took one wicket for 30. Victoria won by an innings and 287 runs. In total, Collins scored 390 first-class runs, his highest score being 37. He also took 146 wickets for 3,812 runs, taking 5 wickets in an innings on 11 occasions, and 7 for 61 against Lord Hawkes' team. He made 36 catches. Injury forced young Collins to retire from the game at the tender age of 28.

He became an agent and assistant secretary for the Amateur Sports Club. During the war he enlisted in the ranks of the 24th Bn Australian Imperial Force, 11th Reinforcement as private 4386 and underwent training at Royal Park and Broadmeadows Camp. Because of his cadet experience he was given the rank of temporary sergeant. He left Australia in March 1916 with the 11th reinforcements for the 24th Battalion on board the RMS *Malwa*. destined for the training camps in England.

After training he was sent to France in August and was transferred to the 21st Battalion, which was recovering in Belgium after heavy fighting at Pozières on the Somme. On joining the battalion on the 18 October 1916 Frank was commissioned as a second lieutenant and was made a platoon commander. He was later commissioned to lieutenant. Throughout

September 1917 the Australians had made successful attacks at Menin Road and Polygon Wood. On 4 October 1917 the 21st Battalion attacked the German positions on Broodseinde Ridge in a highly successful operation.

However casualties were high and Lieutenant Frederick Collins was among the officers reported missing. Later it was assumed he was killed on that date.

The Referee newspaper in Melbourne described Fred as being 'well liked' everywhere, adding that, 'Of the Australian cricketers who have met their deaths in the war,' Fred Collins 'had left the greatest mark on the cricket of the Commonwealth'.

His remains were never recovered or indentified and his name is commemorated on the Ypres Menin Gate Memorial, panel 7-17-23-25-27-29-31.

Batting and fielding averages

	Mat	Inns	NO	Runs	HS	Ave	100	50	Ct	St
First-class	37	62	13	390	37*	7.95	0	0	36	0

Bowling averages

	Mat	Runs	Wkts	BBI	Ave	5w	10
First-class	37	3812	146	7/61	26.10	11	0

Lieutenant Allan Ivo Steel
Middlesex
2nd Bn Coldstream Guards
Died 8 October 1917
Aged 25
Right-handed Bat/Right-arm Slow

'The son of a cricketer, the soul of his nation'

Allan Ivo Steel was born on 27 September 1892 at Toxteth, Liverpool, the son of the famous cricketer Alan Gibson Steel of Lancashire and England. His mother Georgina Dorothy (née Thomas) was descended from the family who included Commander William George Henry Skyring, who was on HMS *Beagle* surveying South America, and who, while surveying the west coast of Africa, was murdered at Cape Roxo on 23 December 1833.

Allan was educated at Eton College and played in the Fowler's match in July 1910. He matched Fowler's bowling during the first innings taking four wickets. However, in the second innings Fowler took eight wickets to Steel's two. His record at Eton was impressive and to many his style resembled that of his famous father; he took forty-two wickets in 1910 (average of 12.71) and forty-seven wickets in 1911 (average of 14.53).

He played in 5 first-class matches, three for the MCC and two for Middlesex. He made his debut for MCC was on 6 May 1912 against Yorkshire at Lord's. He scored 6 and 23, Yorkshire winning by 2 wickets. He first played for Middlesex against Sussex in the County Championship on 27 May 1912, once again at Lord's, scoring 14 in his only innings, and catching Ernest Killick off the bowling of Francis Tarrant for 22. Middlesex won by an innings and 48 runs. He went on to play for Middlesex against Essex and the MCC against Oxford University. He made his final first class appearance for the MCC against Cambridge University on 4 July 1912 at Lords. He made 21 and 7 and caught John Morrison off the bowling of George Thompson for 30. Cambridge University won by 2 wickets.

Steel made a total of 116 first-class runs with his highest score being 26 against Oxford University. He made 2 catches. He also played for Public Schools, Calcutta and Ballygunge Cricket Club and was elected a member of the MCC in 1912.

Many thought it a great loss to cricket when Steel, instead of going up to Cambridge, decided to take up business interests in India. During the war he served with the 2nd Bn Coldstream Guards and was killed in action with the battalion on 8 October 1917. His body was never recovered and he is commemorated on the Tyne Cot Memorial, Zonnebeke, West Vlaanderen, Belgium, Panels 9 to 10.

His brother, John 'Jack' Steel, who served as a lieutenant in the Royal Navy during the war, was swept overboard and drowned in heavy seas while en route to take command of HMS *Munster* on 18 April 1918.

Batting and fielding averages

	Mat	Inns	NO	Runs	HS	Ave	100	50	Ct	St
First-class	5	8	0	116	26	14.50	0	0	2	0

Bowling averages

	Mat	Balls	Runs	Wkts	BBI	BBM	Ave	Econ	SR	4w	5w	10
First-class	5	66	39	0	-	-	-	3.54	-	0	0	0

Lieutenant Richard Angwin Rail
Western Province
3rd Bn Coldstream Guards
Died 9 October 1917
Aged 29

'A fine cricketer and soldier over two continents'

Richard Angwin Rail was born in 1888 in Sydney New South Wales, Australia. The son of John Whitburn Rail and Celia Roberts Rail, née Angwin, of 'Wycroft', Kenilworth, Cape Town, South Africa. He was educated at the South African College, now the University of Cape Town, where he was in the XI.

Richard Rail made 1 first-class appearance on 7 March 1914 for Western Province against the Marylebone Cricket Club in South Africa. The match was played at Newlands, Cape Town. He scored 8 and 5 and the match was drawn. He also turned out for the Household Brigade and the Coldstream Guards.

Rail served with the 3rd Bn Coldstream Guards during the war and was killed in action on 9 October 1917 during the battalion's attack north of the Belgian town of Ypres (now Ieper), towards the Houthhoulst Forest. Although they came under heavy fire, the Coldstreams secured their objective and dug in to form a defensive flank for the whole brigade. During this time the battalion suffered 130 casualties, with six officers and fifty-seven other ranks being killed, one of these being Lieutenant Rail.

His body was never recovered and he is commemorated on the Tyne Cot Memorial, Panels 9 to 10.

Batting and fielding averages

	Mat	Inns	NO	Runs	HS	Ave	100	50	Ct	St
First-class	1	2	0	13	8	6.50	0	0	0	0

Bowling averages

	Mat	Balls	Runs	Wkts	BBI	BBM	Ave	Econ	SR	4w	5w	10
First-class	1	-	-	-	-	-	-	-	-	-	-	-

Corporal Thomas James (Jim) Bryden
Otago
4th Bn New Zealand Rifle Brigade
Died 12 October 1917
Aged 40

'A brave heart and a simple soul'

Thomas James Bryden was born on 1 June 1877 in Invercargill, Southland, New Zealand. Of Scottish descent, he was the eldest son of Thomas and Barbara Bryden and, after finishing his education, he was apprenticed as a joiner and chairmaker.

He played his club cricket for the Grange and later for Dunedin Cricket Clubs. During the 1913–14 season he had the highest batting average for Dunedin at 20.40. He was also a half decent bowler with the second best figures for Dunedin during the 1912–13 season, an average of 11 runs per wicket.

Bryden played in two first-class matches in March 1913 and February 1914 for Otago, both in the Plunket Shield. He made his debut against Canterbury at Lancaster Park, Christchurch on 22 March 1913. He scored 15 and 14, Canterbury winning by an innings and 51 runs. In made his second appearance on 13 February 1914, once again against Canterbury, this time at Carisbrook, Dunedin, Bryden came on as a last-minute replacement for Otago's captain who had been injured. He was out for a duck in both innings. Canterbury once again came out on top, this time by an innings and 32 runs.

Bryden enlisted in the New Zealand Rifle Brigade on 17 January 1917, being attached to G Company of the 4th Battalion. He embarked from Wellington on 26 April 1917 on the *Turakina* for Plymouth, England. After training at Sling Camp in England he travelled with his battalion to France, arriving at the front on 18 September 1917. He was promoted to corporal but the responsibility didn't seem to suit him and he was returned to the ranks at his own request.

Thomas Bryden was killed in action on the morning of 12 October 1917 in an attack at Passchendaele. During this attack New Zealand troops suffered their highest casualties of any single day of the war. Alas, Jim Bryden was one of them. At first he was reported missing but then it was confirmed that he had been killed.

His body was never recovered and he is commemorated on the Tyne Cot Memorial, New Zealand Apse, Panel 7.

Batting and fielding averages

	Mat	Inns	NO	Runs	HS	Ave	100	50	Ct	St
First-class	2	4	0	29	15	7.25	0	0	0	0

Bowling averages

	Mat	Balls	Runs	Wkts	BBI	BBM	Ave	Econ	SR	4w	5w	10
First-class	2	-	-	-	-	-	-	-	-	-	-	-

Major Gother Robert Carlisle Clarke
New South Wales
34th Bn AIF, attached 9th Field Ambulance
Died 12 October 1917
Aged 42
Left-handed Bat/Legbreak

'Died as he had lived, saving others'

Gother Robert Carlisle Clarke was born on 27 April 1875 in North Sydney, New South Wales, Australia, the son of Mordaunt William Shipley Clarke and Georgina Alice Branthwaite of Bay Road, North Sydney. Educated at Sydney Church of England Grammar School and the University of Sydney, he studied to become a doctor and became a Bachelor of Medicine. He later became a Master of Surgery.

He made 7 first-class appearances for New South Wales between December 1899 and Match 1902. He made his debut on 30 December 1899 against Tasmania at the Tasmania Cricket Association Ground, Hobart. He scored 4 runs in his one innings and took 1 wicket for 113 off 37 overs during the first innings, and 4 wickets for 30 off 15 overs in the second. He also caught George Gatehouse off the bowling of Arthur McBeath for 105. New South Wales won by 4 wickets. He went on to play against AC MacLaren's XI, Victoria and South Australia. He made his final first class appearance on 29 March 1902, against Queensland at the Brisbane Cricket Ground, Woolloogabba, Brisbane. He scored 7 and 4 and took 1 wicket for 36 off 8 overs in the first innings and 3 wickets for 42 off 7 overs in the second, he also caught James Carew off the bowing of Jack Marsh for 7.

During his first class career Clarke made 140 runs, his highest score being 25 against AC Maclaren's XI on 31 January 1902. He took 28 wickets for 874 runs. His best bowling figures being 6 for 133. He made 13 catches. Clarke also played for Australian Universities (non first class) against A. E. Stoddart's XI on 12 February 1898, taking four for 98, including the wickets of Ranjitsinhji and Hayward, at the University Oval, Sydney. Clarke failed to bat and the match was drawn.

He enlisted in the 34th Bn Australian Imperial Force in 1915 and was appointed Regimental Medical Officer (RMO) on 1 March 1916. He crossed to France on 2 May 1916 and saw service at Armentières, Messines and Ypres. He was promoted to major on 20 June 1917 and was killed in action dressing a wounded soldier at Passchendaele on 12 October 1917. An account of his death was later reported by one of the soldiers wounded in the same incident:

> I saw him killed at a Pill Box just in front of Passchendaele at about 9pm on the 12.10.17. A shell burst outside the Pill Box where he was working, fragments of which killed him and wounded several others. He was attending to some wounded men at the time. I was sent away a few days later, he was lying on the parapet so I do not know his place of burial … .

From other accounts he appears to have left the Pill Box to attend some of the wounded lying outside, as the Pill Box had become full. A shell landed close by and killed him. He fell dead across an officer of the 37th Battalion, whose wounds he was dressing. For his actions on that day he was Mentioned in Despatches:

> For conspicuous bravery and devotion to duty. Battle of YPRES (phase 5) 12th October 1917. This Officer established his Regimental Aid Post about 300 yards behind the jumping off line, a position which unfortunately came in for very heavy shelling in the counter barrage. He and his personnel worked throughout this, and absolutely disregarding all danger he attended to the wounded out in the open, exposed as he was to this bombardment. His personnel soon became reduced and with the utmost disregard of danger he continued to treat the increasing number of cases brought to the Regimental Aid Post. He continued with this gallant work until he himself at about 9:00am was killed outright by a High Explosive shell.

Clarke was originally buried where he was killed outside the Pill Box at Hamburg House, Zonnebeke. Later his body was moved to Buttes New British Cemetery, Polygon Wood, Zonnebeke, Grave Reference III, A. 5.

Major Clarke is also commemorated by a bell in the War Memorial Carillon at the University of Sydney.

Batting and fielding averages

	Mat	Inns	NO	Runs	HS	Ave	100	50	Ct	St
First-class	7	12	1	140	25	12.72	0	0	13	0

Bowling averages

	Mat	Balls	Runs	Wkts	BBI	Ave	Econ	SR	5w	10
First-class	7	1726	874	28	6/133	31.21	3.03	61.6	1	1

Captain Theodore Arthur Tapp MC & Bar
London County
1st Bn Coldstream Guards/3 Company Guards Machine Gun
Battalion
Died 21 October 1917
Aged 34
Right-handed Bat/Right-arm Fast

'The bravest man I ever saw with a bat a ball or his battalion'

Theodore Arthur Tapp was born on 5 April 1883 in Shortlands, Bromley, Kent, the first son of Charles James and Olga M. H. Tapp. He was educated at Rugby School where he was in the first XI and, on leaving school, went up to Caius College Cambridge. Although playing cricket for the college, he failed to obtain his Blue. On leaving Cambridge he intended entering the diplomatic service, but poor health made him give up that idea and he joined the Stock Exchange in 1905 becoming a partner in the firm of C. Andreae and Company. He married Margret Flagg, whom he had met in New York, during a trip to America.

He played in one first-class match for London County against Cambridge University on 26 May 1904, played at the Fenner's Ground, Cambridge. London County were captained by the legendary W. G. Grace, who also opened the batting. Tapp scored 5 and 4 but his real success came in the bowling. He took 5 wickets for 99 off 35.4 overs. Despite his best efforts however London County still lost by 36 runs. He was also a fine golfer, playing off scratch.

Soon after the outbreak of war Tapp was given a commission in the 1st Bn Coldstream Guards. He went to the front in November 1914 and was wounded at Cuinchy. A brief account of this can be found in the battalion war diary:

07.30 25 January 1915.
2nd Lieutenant T. A. Tapp did great execution with a machine gun, firing more than 7,500 rounds into the swarming German masses and effectually cooling their enthusiasm. At 1 p.m. a counter-attack was organised under Colonel Stewart, Black Watch, and ultimately the enemy was forced back, while the British held a somewhat broken line from the canal to the keep and thence to the main road … . 2nd Lieutenant T. A. Tapp, who having gone to the dressing-station to get his wound bound up, returned to the machine gun until the end of the action.

Five officers and eighty other ranks were killed in this action.

After a period at home recovering, Tapp returned to France in March 1915 and remained in the trenches until January 1916, when he was invalided home once again. On his return to the front he was attached to the Guards' Machine Gun Battalion. Seriously wounded at the Battle of Flanders on 11 October 1917, he died from his wounds at a casualty clearing station on 21 October.

He received two Military Crosses for bravery during the war. The first was gazetted on 26 September 1917. His Bar was gazetted on 8 January 1918.

Lt (A/Capt) Theodore Arthur Tapp, CL Gds., Spec. Res., attd. M.G. Gds.

For conspicuous gallantry and devotion to duty in getting his guns into position previous to an attack, in spite of heavy casualties, and in leading his men in the attack with great coolness, courage and resource, his fine personal example he helped a great deal towards the success of the operations.

He is commemorated in the Dozinghem Military Cemetery, Poperinge West Vlaanderen, Belgium, Grave Reference X, E. 6.

Batting and fielding averages

	Mat	Inns	NO	Runs	HS	Ave	100	50	Ct	St
First-class	1	2	0	9	5	4.50	0	0	0	0

Bowling averages

	Mat	Balls	Runs	Wkts	BBI	Ave	Econ	SR	5w	10
First-class	1	214	99	5	5/99	19.80	2.77	42.8	1	0

Lieutenant James Valiant
Essex
28th Bn The London Regiment/7th Bn The Royal Welsh
Fusiliers
Died 28 October 1917
Aged 33
Right-handed bat

'And those who were seen dancing were thought to be
insane by those who could not hear the music'

James Valiant was born on 17 July 1884 at Wavertree, Liverpool. His father was a butcher from the city. James was a keen Morris Dancer in Scarisbrick and played his club cricket for Ormskirk Cricket Club.

He played for the Lancashire Second XI against Lincolnshire on 20 July 1908 (North Division) at the Black Swan Ground, Spalding. Valiant scored 4 and 15 in a close match, Lincolnshire finally coming out on top by 4 runs. Moving to Essex he made his one and only first-class appearance for that county. The match, in the County Championship, was played on 17 June 1912 against Northamptonshire at the County Ground, Northampton; Valiant made 0 not out and 3. Northamptonshire won convincingly by an innings and 137 runs.

In February 1915 Valiant enlisted into the ranks of the 28th Bn The London Regiment (Artists Rifles), before being commissioned as a second lieutenant in the 7th Bn Royal Welsh Fusiliers the following July. He saw service in Gallipoli and Egypt before being sent to Gaza and promoted to lieutenant. He died of wounds on 28 October 1917 received during the battle of El Buggar Ridge the previous day.

He is commemorated in the Beersheba War Cemetery (modern day Israel), Grave Reference 0. 23.

Batting and fielding averages

	Mat	Inns	NO	Runs	HS	Ave	100	50	4s	6s	Ct	St
First-class	1	2	1	3	3	3.00	0	0	0	0	0	0

Bowling averages

	Mat	Balls	Runs	Wkts	BBI	BBM	Ave	Econ	SR	4w	5w	10
First-class	1	24	20	0	-	-	-	5.00	-	0	0	0

Lance Corporal Donald Lacy Priestley
Gloucestershire
1/28th Bn The London Regiment (Artists' Rifles)
Died 30 October 1917
Aged 30
Right-handed bat/Right-arm Medium

'Nothing can ever make up for his loss'

Donald Lacy Priestley was born on 28 July 1887 in Gloucestershire, the son of Joseph Edward, headmaster of Tewkesbury Grammar School, and Henrietta, née Rice, of Tewkesbury. One of four brothers and two sisters, he was educated at Tewkesbury Grammar School where he was in the First XI. Priestley played his club cricket for Tewkesbury together with his brother Stanley; his father Joseph was club secretary. Donald scored 1,141 runs in the 1907 season and in 1909, playing for the club's A team, took all ten of the opponents' wickets in their first innings, followed by three further wickets in their second.

He made 7 first-class appearances for Gloucestershire, all in the County Championship between May 1909 and July 1910. He made his debut against Sussex in the County Ground, Hove. He scored 3 and 3, and caught Joseph Vine off the bowling of Charles Parker for 0. Sussex winning by an innings and 48 runs. He went on to play against Somerset, Sussex, Nottinghamshire, Hampshire and Warwickshire.

He made his final first class appearance against Worcestershire at the War Memorial Ground, Amblecote. He scored 13 and 7. Gloucestershire won by 94 runs. During his first class career he made 154 runs his highest score being 51 against Hampshire. He made 2 catches.

Priestley married Edith Louie Boughton of Tewkesbury and they resided at Club Chambers, 25 Gower Street, Bedford Square, London.

Donald was called up in 1916 and joined the 1/28th Bn The London Regiment (Artists Rifles). He was killed in action on 30 October 1917 during the Third Battle of Ypres. His body was never recovered and he is commemorated on the Tyne Cot Memorial, Panel 153.

Donald's brother Stanley, another fine cricketer, was killed in action while serving as a lieutenant with the 8th Bn Gloucestershire Regiment on 23 July 1916, aged 28. He was first reported missing and then death was assumed on 24 February 1917. His body was eventually discovered in November 1917 and his identity disc returned to the family. Of the two surviving sons, the elder, Joseph, became a professor of biology at Leeds University and Raymond became Sir Raymond, finding fame as a member of two Antarctic expeditions between 1907 and 1913.

Batting and fielding averages

	Mat	Inns	NO	Runs	HS	Ave	100	50	Ct	St
First-class	7	13	1	154	51	12.83	0	1	2	0

Bowling averages

	Mat	Balls	Runs	Wkts	BBI	BBM	Ave	Econ	SR	4w	5w	10
First-class	7	-	-	-	-	-	-	-	-	-	-	-

924 Trooper Albert 'Tibby' Cotter
Australia /New South Wales
12th Australian Light Horse
Died 31 October 1917
Aged 33
Right-handed Bat/Right-arm fast

'His happy nature and comportment on the field
endeared him to all lovers of the game'

Albert 'Tibby' Cotter was born on 3 December 1883 at 132 Phillip Street, Sydney, sixth and youngest son of John Henry Cotter, butcher, and his wife Margaret Hay, née Pattison. When he was 6 years old his family moved to Glebe and he was educated at the Forest Lodge Public School, and Sydney Grammar School (between 1899 and 1900). In the annual matches between the Sydney and Melbourne Grammar schools in Melbourne in 1899 he took 6 for 53, and the following year in Sydney took 7 for 57. He played his club cricket for the Glebe District Cricket Club. Among his best performances for Glebe were four wickets in four balls and his highest score of 156 which included 16 sixes. He was also a very fine rugby three-quarter for Glebe, the 'Dirty Reds'. Cotter was employed as a bookkeeper by the Riverstone Meat Company.

Tibby's cricketing career was impressive. He played in 113 first-class matches and twenty-one test matches between January 1902 and January 1914. He made his debut first-class match on 25 January 1902 in the Sheffield Shield when he turned out for New South Wales against Victoria at the Sydney Cricket ground. However his two ducks and failure to take any wickets was not an impressive beginning. Despite this, New South Wales went on to win by 49 runs. It took two years before they allowed him to play again. By then he had improved and, playing once again for New South Wales against Victoria on 25 January 1904 at the Sydney Cricket Ground, although he only scored 3 in his one innings, he took 4 wickets for 50 off 13 overs in the first innings. He followed that up by taking 2 wickets for 75 off 20 overs in the second, New South Wales winning again this time by 10 wickets. On 12 February 1904, against the MCC touring side, he took 5 wickets for 44 runs in the first innings, taking a further 3 wickets for 56 in the second. He also managed to score 16 and 3 along the way. Despite Tibby's best efforts the MCC still came out on top by 278 runs. He was called up to play against England in the fourth test played at the Sydney Cricket Ground on 26 February 1904. Although he didn't do too well in the first innings, scoring 0 and taking no wickets, he made up for this in the second innings by scoring 34 runs and taking 3 English wickets for 41. England finally won by 157 runs.

He toured England with Joe Darling's team in 1905 where he took 124 wickets including 12 for 34 against Worcestershire and managed a batting average of 17.6. During the 1909 tour of England Cotter took 64 wickets at 24.09 runs each, including 5 for 38 and 6 for 95 in the third and fifth Tests.

Although considered an outstanding fast bowler with a reputation for breaking stumps, his action was considered suspect and caused controversy, especially in England, earning him the nickname 'Terror Cotter'. W. G. Grace was to feel his wrath when Cotter hit him with a full toss during his first tour of England.

Tibby took 22 wickets at 28.77 against the touring South Africans in 1910–11. However, he missed the tri-nations tour to England in 1912, when he was among six players who refused to tour as a result of a dispute with the Australian board of control. He was never to play for Australia again. During his test career Tibby, took 89 wickets, including 5 in an innings on seven occasions. He made 457 runs in Test Matches his highest score being 45 and took 89 wickets for 2549 runs and made 8 catches. He also scored 2484 first class runs his highest score being 82 and took 442 wickets for 10730 runs. Brilliant in the field he made 61 catches.

He made his final first class appearance on 9 January 1914 in the Sheffield Shield at the Adelaide Oval, Adelaide. He made 29 in his only innings, took 1 wicket for 17 off 5 overs in the first innings and 2 for 24 off 5.2 overs in the second. He also caught Donald Steel off the bowling of Robert Nassie for 42. New South Wales won by 9 wickets.

Cotter joined the Australian Imperial Force (AIF) in April 1915 and applied for and was accepted into the 1st Australian Light Horse Regiment with which he took part in the Gallipoli campaign. He later transferred to the 12th Light Horse and was commended for his 'fine work under heavy fire' during the second battle of Gaza. The official history remarked that 'he behaved in action as a man without fear'.

On 31 October 1917 while with the 4th Light Horse which captured Beersheba during a brilliant cavalry charge, Cotter was serving as a stretcher-bearer. At the end of the charge, as troops dismounted to engage the enemy, a Turk shot Cotter dead at close range. He died almost at once and cricket lost one of its favourite sons.

He is commemorated in the Beersheba War Cemetery, Grave Reference D. 50.

Batting and fielding averages

	Mat	Inns	NO	Runs	HS	Ave	100	50	6s	Ct	St
Tests	21	37	2	457	45	13.05	0	0	5	8	0
First-class	113	157	10	2484	82	16.89	0	4		61	0

Bowling averages

	Mat	Inns	Balls	Runs	Wkts	BBI	BBM	Ave	Econ	SR	4w	5w	10
Tests	21	38	4633	2549	89	7/148	9/221	28.64	3.30	52.0	4	7	0
First-class	113		19565	10730	442	7/15		24.27	3.29	44.2		31	4

Gunner Fairfax Gill
Yorkshire
21 Trench Mortar Battery, Royal Field Artillery
Died 1 November 1917
Aged 34
Right-handed Bat

'A Yorkshire man through and through'

Fairfax Gill was born on 3 September 1883 at Wakefield, Yorkshire, the son of Thomas and Susannah Gill of 21 Johnston Street, Wakefield. He married Ada Gill of 3 Thornville Marsland Terrace, Wakefield.

Gill played for the Cricket Council in the Yorkshire versus Yorkshire Cricket Council match. He scored 30 and 1, Yorkshire winning by an innings and 8 runs. In both 1905 and 1906 he played in the Yorkshire Second XI against Nottinghamshire (1905) and Mexborough (1906).

He played in two first-class matches both in June 1906. He made his debut against Derbyshire at Queen's Park, Chesterfield, in the County Championship on 7 June 1906. He scored 1, run out and 3 bowled William Bestwick, Yorkshire won by 33 runs. He played his second match against Nottinghamshire at Trent Bridge, on 21 June 1906. This time Gill scored 11, bowled by John Gunn, and 3, bowled by Albert Hallam. The match was drawn. It was to be Gill's final first-class appearance. The match was noted however for David Denton's twin century. 107 in the first innings 109 not out in the second.

During the war Gill served with the Royal Field Artillery attached to 21 Trench Mortar Battery. He died of wounds on 1 November 1917 at Wimereux, near Boulogne-sur-Mer, France, and is commemorated in the Wimereux Communal Cemetery, Grave Reference VI, F. 24A.

Batting and fielding averages

	Mat	Inns	NO	Runs	HS	Ave	100	50	Ct	St
First-class	2	4	0	18	11	4.50	0	0	0	0

Bowling averages

	Mat	Balls	Runs	Wkts	BBI	BBM	Ave	Econ	SR	4w	5w	10
First-class	2	-	-	-	-	-	-	-	-	-	-	-

Sergeant Colin Blythe
England/Kent
12th Bn The King's Own Yorkshire Light Infantry
Died 8 November 1917
Aged 38
Right-handed bat/Slow left-arm orthodox

'A quiet and sensitive man who overcame much to become one of
England finest cricketers and who died doing his duty'

Colin Blythe was born on 30 May 1879 in Deptford, Kent, one of twelve children born to Walter and Elizabeth, née Dready, of 78 Evelyn Street, Deptford. He was educated at the Alverton Street School before being apprenticed as an engineer fitter at the Woolwich Arsenal. Not in the best of health (he suffered from epilepsy which affected his career) his doctors advised that he got as much outside exercise as he could. He began his cricketing career playing for clubs like St Luke's, Blackheath Boys' and the Royal Arsenal, where undoubtedly he learned his trade and improved his skills. Oddly, it was during a match between Kent and Somerset in July 1897, which Blythe was attending as a spectator, that the well-known Kent all-rounder Walter Wright offered Blythe the opportunity to bowl at him while he was practising in the nets. Blythe took his opportunity with both hands. As a result he was offered a trial at Tonbridge. Once again he did well and was offered a place on the playing staff at Kent in 1898.

Blythe went on to make 439 first-class appearances between August 1899 and August 1914 mostly for Kent but he also represented the MCC, MCC in Australia, A. C. MacLaren's XI, South of England, J. Bamford's XI, J. R. Mason's XI and Rest of England. He made his debut against Yorkshire on 21 August 1899 at the Angel Ground, Tonbridge. He made 0 in his only innings, took 1 wicket for 25 of 4 overs in the first innings and 1 wicket for 41 off 14.1 in the second innings. Kent won by 8 wickets.

Blyth also played in 19 tests against both the Australians and the South Africans in England, Australia and South Africa. He made 183 runs his highest score being 27. He also took 100 wickets for 1863 runs. He made 6 catches.

In every season between 1902 and 1914, except for 1906, Colin took over 100 wickets. Blyth made his final first class appearance on 27 August 1914 against Middlesex at Lords. Me scored 5 and 0 and took 5 wickets for 77 off 33 overs in the first innings and 2 wickets for 48 off 17 overs in the second. Middlesex won by 298 runs.

In 1907 he met Janet Gertrude Brown and, although she was ten years younger, they married. They settled down in St Mary's Road, Tonbridge. An artistic and sensitive man, Blythe was also a fine violinist who could turn his hand to any style and play as well as any professional.

Despite his epilepsy he still insisted on joining up. In August 1914 he enlisted into the ranks of No. 1 Reserve Company of the Kent Fortress Royal Engineers together with his friend and fellow player Claude Wooley. Around this time he was also offered the job as chief coach at Eton College after the war ended. On 2 August 1917, Blyth, now a sergeant, found himself attached to the 12th King's Own Yorkshire Light Infantry (the miners' battalion).

Working mainly on light railway construction, he was constantly in the thick of the fighting and suffered several narrow escapes. His luck ran out, however, on 8 November 1917. While working on the Forest Hall, Bedlington, Gravenstafel and Pommern Castle lines, a random shrapnel shell exploded over his head. A piece of shrapnel pierced his tunic, a leather wallet in his breast pocket and a photograph of his wife, fatally wounding him. He died together with four colleagues and they were buried together in the Oxford Road Military Cemetery. Colin's grave reference is I. L. 2.

In 2009, when the England cricket team visited the Flanders war graves, they placed a 'stone cricket ball on Blyth's grave'. Andrew Strauss, the England captain, said that 'It was a deeply moving and humbling experience.'

Batting and fielding averages

	Mat	Inns	NO	Runs	HS	Ave	100	50	6s	Ct	St
Tests	19	31	12	183	27	9.63	0	0	0	6	0
First-class	439	587	137	4443	82*	9.87	0	5		206	0

Bowling averages

	Mat	Inns	Balls	Runs	Wkts	BBI	BBM	Ave	Econ	SR	4w	5w	10
Tests	19	37	4546	1863	100	8/59	15/99	18.63	2.45	45.4	2	9	4
First-class	439		103546	42094	2503	10/30		16.81	2.43	41.3		218	71

Captain Clifford Allen Saville
Middlesex
11th Bn The East Yorkshire Regiment
Died 8 November 1917
Aged 25
Right-handed bat

'He endeared himself to all who served with him'

Clifford Allen Saville was born on 5 February 1892 at Bruce Grove, Tottenham, Middlesex to Walter and Emma Saville of 17 Wadham Gardens, Hampstead. He was educated at Marlborough College from 1906 to 1909 and, in 1909, was racquet representative, and in the Hockey XI. After leaving Marlborough he studied medicine.

Saville made three first-class appearances in August 1914, all in the County Championship for Middlesex. He made his debut against Yorkshire on 10 August 1914 at Bramall Lane, Sheffield. Playing alongside his brother Stanley Herbert Saville, he scored 32 and 5, Yorkshire won by 2 wickets. He made his second first-class match three days later on 13 August, this time against Lancashire at Old Trafford, Manchester. Playing with his brother once again, Saville scored 1 in his only innings, Middlesex won by 10 wickets. His final first-class appearance came on 17 August against Nottinghamshire at Lord's. Saville scored 10 and 9, Middlesex winning by 239 runs.

He served with the 11th Battalion The East Yorkshire Regiment (Hull Tradesmen) during the war and was one of the battalion's original officers. Given command of No. 6 Platoon, he later became the battalion's bombing officer and between May and November 1917 commanded A Company. He was also responsible for organizing all the battalion's sports. Saville was promoted to captain in 1917.

In the same year the battalion was in action in the Battle of Arras. Saville was killed while leading a daylight raid on German trenches on 8 November 1917. A brother officer later wrote to his family:

> He endeared himself to all who served with him by his gift of apologetic satire when times were bad and his unfailing readiness to help on each and every occasion.

His body was never recovered and he is commemorated on the Arras Memorial, Bay 4 and 5. His next-of-kin was given as his wife, Melville Saville, of 5 Derby Road, Southport.

Batting and fielding averages

	Mat	Inns	NO	Runs	HS	Ave	100	50	Ct	St
First-class	3	5	0	57	32	11.40	0	0	0	0

Bowling averages

	Mat	Balls	Runs	Wkts	BBI	BBM	Ave	Econ	SR	4w	5w	10
First-class	3	-	-	-	-	-	-	-	-	-	-	-

Captain Guy Denis Wilson
Derbyshire
Royal Field Artillery
Died 30 November 1917
Aged 35

'A credit to his country, county, and regiment'

Guy Denis Wilson was born on 30 November 1882 at Melbourne, Derbyshire. The son of Arthur Wilson MA JP of 30 Ashbourne Road, Derby, he was educated at the Derby School, now Derby Grammar School, between 1892 and 1901. A good all-round athlete, he was captain of the cricket and football XIs as well as being a captain in the cadet corps. He also won the throwing the cricket ball competition on a number of occasions.

He made two first-class appearances in June 1902 and July 1905. He made his debut for Derbyshire against London County (captained by WG Grace) on 26 June 1902 at the County Ground, Derbyshire. Wilson scored 7 in the first innings before being stumped by John Board off the bowling of Charles Llewellyn. In fact, Llewellyn and Grace took five wickets each in the first innings, Llewellyn going on to take a further six wickets in the second. Wilson made 9 in the second innings before being bowled by Percy May. London County won by six wickets. His second appearance for Derbyshire came on 17 July 1905 at Lord's, this time against the MCC. He didn't have a good match, scoring 2 and 1, MCC going on to win by an innings and 252 runs.

On 6 August 1908 Wilson was commissioned into 1 Derbyshire Howitzer Battery, 4th North Midlands Howitzer Brigade, as a second lieutenant. However during the war he served with the Royal Field Artillery and was promoted to captain. He was killed in action on 30 November 1917 during the Battle of Cambrai, on his thirty-fifth birthday.

His body was never recovered or identified and he is commemorated on the Cambrai Memorial, Louverval, Nord, France, Panel 1.

Batting and fielding averages

	Mat	Inns	NO	Runs	HS	Ave	100	50	Ct	St
First-class	2	4	0	19	9	4.75	0	0	0	0

Bowling averages

	Mat	Balls	Runs	Wkts	BBI	BBM	Ave	Econ	SR	4w	5w	10
First-class	2	35	15	0	-	-	-	2.57	-	0	0	0

Lieutenant John Argentine Campbell
Argentina
6th (Inniskilling) Dragoons
Died 2 December 1917
Aged 40

'the most magnificent specimen of mankind'

John Argentine Campbell was born on 20 October 1877 at Las Flores, Argentina, and educated at Fettes College between 1887 and 1897 where he was in the cricket XI and rugby XV, as well as playing fives and hockey. In 1897 he went up to Trinity College Cambridge. Although he didn't win his Blue for cricket he did for rugby, playing against Oxford on three occasions and becoming captain in his final year. He also won an athletic Blue in 1898 for putting the weight. On 3 February 1906 he was selected to play for Scotland against Ireland at Lansdowne Road, Dublin. Unusually the match was drawn 0–0. It was to be his only cap.

CAMBRIDGE XV., 1897.

L. B. Hopper. J. A. Campbell. M. A. Black.
N. C. Fletcher. A. S. Pringle. D. Johnston. R. W. Bell. R. F. Cumberlege.
A. J. L. Darby, W. N. Pilkington. O. G. Mackie. A. F. C. Luxmoore. A. Balfour.
G. M. Bennett. F. H. Fasson.

378

After teaching at the Loretto School, he moved to Argentina where he became a rancher. Keeping up his sporting interests he also became a top-class polo player. He married Mary Rosary Robson in Buenos Aires on 24 December 1873 and they had four children.

Campbell played in one first-class match against the MCC in Argentina, on 18 February 1912 at the Hurlingham Club Ground, Buenos Aires. He was out for a duck in his first innings and 4 in the second. Despite Campbell's poor performance, Argentina won by 4 wickets. He also played for the East of England in 1901.

Campbell returned to England at the outbreak of the war and was commissioned first in the 17th Lancers and then the 6th (Inniskilling) Dragoons. He was reported missing on 1 December 1917. The next news of him came from a trooper in his own regiment who, in a letter, told Campbell's family how he had carried a badly wounded Lieutenant Campbell to a German dressing station where he had left him.

In late-January 1918 the news the family had been dreading finally came through, unusually from a German officer. He stated in his letter that their son, John Argentina Campbell, had succumbed to his wounds while being cared for at a German dressing station, Hospital Number 2, the day after he arrived (2 December 1917). On hearing the news one of his colleagues wrote:

> Alike at Fettes, at Cambridge, and in the Argentine, his manliness, his straightness and his modesty won the love and respect of all that came into contact with him … .

A brother officer wrote:

> from the General to the last joined recruit everyone admired, respected and loved him, and the colonel said that he was the most magnificent specimen of mankind he had ever come across.

John Argentina Campbell is commemorated at the Honnechy British Cemetery, Nord, France. Grave Reference I, A, I. His name is also commemorated at St Andrew's Presbyterian Church, Buenos Aires.

Batting and fielding averages

	Mat	Inns	NO	Runs	HS	Ave	100	50	Ct	St
First-class	1	2	0	4	4	2.00	0	0	0	0

Bowling averages

	Mat	Balls	Runs	Wkts	BBI	BBM	Ave	Econ	SR	4w	5w	10
First-class	1	-	-	-	-	-	-	-	-	-	-	-

Major Harold Gwyer Garnett CdG (Fr)
Lancashire/A. C. MacLaren's XI /Gentlemen/Argentina
2nd Bn The South Wales Borderers
Died 3 December 1917
Aged 38
Left-handed bat/Slow left-arm orthodox/Wicket-keeper

'The best player England never selected'

Harold Gwyer Garnett was born on 19 November 1879 at Aigburth, Liverpool, the son of Alexander Garnett JP and Gladwys.

Considered to be the best left-handed bat in England he made 152 first-class appearances between August 1899 and August 1914 mostly for Lancashire but he also represented AC MacLaren's XI, Gentlemen and Argentina. He made his debut for Lancashire against Australia on 28 August 1899 at Aigburth, Liverpool. He made 0 in his only innings and caught Frank Laver off the bowling of John I'Anson for 15. The match was drawn. Playing for Lancashire against Sussex, he scored 110 and 89 before going on to score centuries against both Middlesex and Leicestershire. Although he came close on several occasions he never quite made the England XI and although he travel to Australia with AC MacLaren's XI during their 1901–1902 tour he only played in 4 of their 22 matches against Victoria (x2), New South Wales, and South Australia and then didn't perform at his best.

He moved to Argentina and began work for Hopkins and Gardom Limited of Buenos Aires. While there he was involved with the building of the famous clock tower in Retiro. Originally known as the Torre de los Ingleses (Tower of the English), it was situated in the Plaza Britannica. Since the Falklands War in 1982 the clock tower has been renamed Toore Monumental and the plaza became the Plaza Fuerza Aerea Argentina. The clock tower had originally been a gift from the local British community to the city in commemoration of the centennial of the May Revolution in 1910. While in Argentina, Garnett made three first-class appearances against the MCC in February and March 1912. Argentina won one game and lost two.

Garnett returned to England in both 1911 and 1914 and began to play for Lancashire again. By this time he had become quite an outstanding wicket-keeper and was picked to represent the Gentlemen versus Players at Lord's. He made his final first class match for Lancashire against Northamptonshire on 28 August 1914 at Old Trafford, Manchester in the County Championship. He made 27 in his only innings and caught Claud Woolley off the bowling of John Sharp for 0. The match was drawn. During his first class career he made 5798 runs his highest score being 139 including 5 centuries. He also took 8 wickets for 224 runs his best figures being 2 for 18. He also made 185 catches and 18 stumpings.

He was one of the first first-class cricketers to enlist at the beginning of the war and was soon commissioned, eventually becoming a major in the 2nd Bn South Wales Borderers. He was killed in action on the Italian Front on 3 December 1917.

His body, like so many others, was never recovered and he is commemorated on the Cambrai Memorial, Louerval, Panel 5.

Batting and fielding averages

	Mat	Inns	NO	Runs	HS	Ave	100	Ct	St
First-class	152	245	22	5798	139	26.00	5	185	18

Bowling averages

	Ma	Balls	Runs	Wkts	BBI	Ave	Econ	SR	5w	10
First-class	152	334	224	8	2/18	28.00	4.02	41.7	0	0

46635 Private George Charles Lee Wilson
Canterbury
1st Bn The Canterbury Regiment (New Zealand
Expeditionary Force)
Died 14 December 1917
Aged 30
Left-handed Bat/Left-arm Slow-Medium

'Bowled balls almost impossible to follow'

George Charles Lee Wilson was born on 1 May 1887 in Christchurch Canterbury, New Zealand, the son of Samuel and Jane Wilson of Christchurch. After leaving school he was apprenticed as a carpenter.

George played his club cricket for Sydenham in the Canterbury Cricket Association. A left-hand spinner, he could take much credit for Sydenham winning the championship for the first time during the 1912–13 season when he took fifty-seven wickets at an average of 11.96. The following season his bowling didn't let up and he took a further fifty-three wickets at an average of 9.62.

He made six first-class appearances between December 1913 and March 1914, four in the Plunket Shield and two for New Zealand against Australia in New Zealand. He made his debut for Canterbury against Otago in the Plunket Shield on Christmas Day 1913 at Lancaster Park in Christchurch. He made 3 runs in his only innings and took 2 wickets for 9 runs off 8.4 overs. He also caught Robert Rutherford off the bowling of Harold Monaghan for 0. Christchurch finally came out on top by six wickets. In his second match, this time against Wellington once again at Lancaster Park, on 1 January 1914, Wilson took 4 for 76 off 25 overs in the first innings and 7 for 80 off 39.4 overs in the second. He also scored 19 not out and 16. Canterbury went on to win this time by 243 runs. His batting improved still further against Auckland in the match played on 24 January 1914 and Lancaster Park. Wilson scored 34 not out and 64 not out, as well as taking 5 for 73 off 25 overs and 6 for 117 off 33.3 overs. Once again Canterbury won, this time by 318 runs. His next match came against Southland, although this was not a first-class match, at Invercargill on 10 February 1914 when Wilson

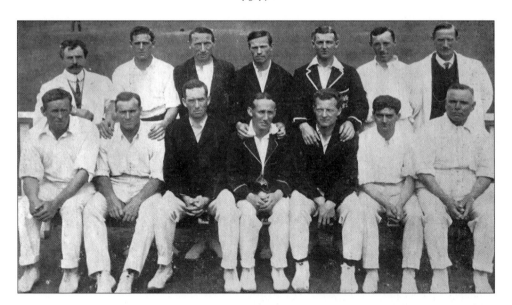

was on fire. In the first innings he took 8 for 56, and in the second he took 5 for 41 (its not known in how many overs); he also scored 28 not out; Canterbury won by 10 wickets. The final match in the Plunket Shield came against Otago Carisbrook, Dunedin on 13 February 1914. Once again there was no stopping Wilson. He took 5 for 95 off 26 overs in the first innings and 2 for 88 off 31 overs in his second, he scored 13 in his only innings. Canterbury won by an innings and 32 runs. He played in two matches for New Zealand against the visiting Australians but failed to impress or take a wicket. In the match played at Lancaster Park, Christchurch on 27 February 1914 he scored 1 and 18 and failed to take a wicket. The match became famous when Victor Trumper and Arthur Sims added 433 runs for the eighth wicket in 190 minutes. It was a world record for an eighth-wicket stand and remains so to this day. Australia finally won by an innings and 364 runs. Wilson next faced Australia on 6 March 1914 when he represented New Zealand at Carisbrook, Dunedin. Once again he failed to impress, taking no wickets and scoring 8 not out and 10; Australia won by 7 wickets. Wilson lost his place together with seven others for the next test, although it made little difference as New Zealand went down by an innings.

Wilson served in the ranks of the 1st Bn Canterbury Regiment during the war. He was killed in action on 14 December 1917 during one of the harshest winters France could ever remember.

He is commemorated in the Polygon Wood Cemetery, Grave Reference D 19.

Batting and fielding averages

	Mat	Inns	NO	Runs	HS	Ave	100	50	Ct	St
First-class	6	10	4	186	64*	31.00	0	1	1	0

Bowling averages

	Mat	Runs	Wkts	BBI	Ave	5w	10
First-class	6	716	31	7/80	23.09	4	2

Lieutenant James 'Banny' William Hugh Bannerman
Southland
2nd Bn The Otago Regiment (New Zealand Expeditionary Force)
Died 23 December 1917
Aged 30

'would rather play cricket of any sort than eat'

James William Hugh Bannerman was born on 20 May 1887 in Ophir, Otago, New Zealand. Eldest son of William and Agnes Bannerman of The Bank, Otago, he was educated at Invercargill Primary School and Southland High School, before entering Otago High School. While there he produced an underground magazine with highly revolutionary tendencies called the *Rag*. The head demanded, on pain of expulsion, the return of every copy of this 'scurrilous production', as he considered it. Bannerman collected them all up, but succeeded in keeping a copy by taking a different page from each of fifty or sixty copies. On leaving school he became a journalist on the *Southland Daily News* before taking over as editor and managing director of the *Bluff Press*.

He was a keen sportsman and excelled at both cricket and hockey. One paper described him as 'generally recognized as both an attacking batsman and a medium-fast bowler with some pace and movement'. Bannerman played for Southland on six occasions, one of them being against the visiting Australians. Although, as the opening bat, he was out for a duck in his one innings, he made up for it with his bowling and fielding and took three Australian wickets for 137 and caught W. W. Armstrong off the bowling of Groves. The match was played at Rugby Park, Invercargill, and was drawn. James' best performance was against Rangitikei when winning the Hawke Cup for Southland on 11 March 1911. He opened the batting and scored 40 while his bowling was impressive too, 11–123, and was significant in Southland's victory. Impressively, ten of his eleven wickets were clean bowled.

Bannerman made one first-class appearance for Southland against Otago on 2 April 1915 at Carisbrook, Dunedin, scoring 10 and 1 and taking 3 wickets for 84 off 21 overs. The match was drawn.

As well as being a fine sportsman and cricketer, he was also a talented writer, inherited no doubt from his famous ancestor, the Scot Robbie Burns. He wrote two important histories of cricket, *History of Otago Representative Cricket 1863–1906* (Dunedin: Dunedin Crown Printing Co.,1907) and a brochure *Early Cricket in Southland* (Invercargill: W. Smith, 1908).

In 1913 James married Louie Viva Nichol of Bluff. Being allowed leave of absence by the directors of the *Bluff Press* he took a commission in the 2nd Bn Otago Regiment on 19 June 1917 and left for France on 19 November. Shortly after arriving at the front he was killed by multiple gunshot wounds during the morning of 23 December 1917 near Polderhoek Chateau, Belgium.

He is commemorated in the Lijssenthoek Military Cemetery, Grave Reference XXVII, C. 15.

Batting and fielding averages

	Mat	Inns	NO	Runs	HS	Ave	100	50	Ct	St
First-class	1	2	0	11	10	5.50	0	0	0	0

Bowling averages

	Mat	Runs	Wkts	BBI	Ave	5w	10
First-class	1	84	3	3/84	28.00	0	0

55767 Private Walter Malcolm
Otago
3rd Bn The Otago Regiment (New Zealand Expeditionary Force)
Died 23 December 1917
Aged 23
Right-handed Bat

'Solid with his bat fast in the field'

Walter Malcolm was born on 25 December 1893 at Blenheim, Marlborough, New Zealand. A maltster by trade, he married Miss E. M. A McCoy and they resided at 6 Alfred Street, St Kilda, Dunedin.

He made one first-class appearance for Otago against Southland on 17 February 1915 at Rugby Park, Invercargill, scoring 2 and 16. Malcolm also caught the Southland opener John Doig off the bowling of Henry Siedeberg for 22. Otago won by 118 runs.

He was killed in action on 23 December 1917 and is commemorated at Poelcapelle British Cemetery, grave reference LIV. D. 10.

Batting and fielding averages

	Mat	Inns	NO	Runs	HS	Ave	100	50	Ct	St
First-class	1	2	1	18	16	18.00	0	0	1	0

Bowling averages

	Mat	Balls	Runs	Wkts	BBI	BBM	Ave	Econ	SR	4w	5w	10
First-class	1	-	-	-	-	-	-	-	-	-	-	-

1918

Second Lieutenant Leonard George Colbeck MC
Middlesex/Europeans (India)/Cambridge University
Royal Field Artillery
Died 3 January 1918
Aged 34
Right-handed Bat

'Of all these men (members of the MCC) none will be
more sincerely mourned than L G Colbeck.'

Leonard George Colbeck was born on 1 January 1884 at South Harrow, Middlesex. The younger son of Charles and Mary Colbeck, Assistant Master of Harrow School, of Standhill Cottage, Hitchin, he entered Marlborough College in 1898 as a junior scholar, becoming a senior scholar in 1899. In the cricket XI in 1902, he captained the side in 1903 and was also in the Hockey XI and represented the school at racquets. He went up to King's College Cambridge in 1903, where he was elected a Scholar, took a First in the Classics and won his Blue for cricket.

Colbeck played in 32 first-class matches between June 1905 and September 1913, seventeen University matches, ten in the County Championship, three Bombay Presidency Matches, one Gentlemen's (against the Players) and one against Australia in the British Isles. He made his debut for Cambridge University against Australia in the British Isles on 1 June 1905 at F. P. Fenner's Ground. He scored 52 not out and 8. Australia won by 169 runs. Colbeck really made his name, however, against Oxford University on 6 July 1905 at Lord's. Cambridge had already lost six wickets for 77 and their position appeared hopeless against a rampaging Oxford XI. Going in for the second time against a balance of 101, Colbeck found himself at the wicket with Harold Clark McDonnell. As Colbeck had been bowled by Nicholas Udal for 1 in the first innings, nobody expected much. That was a mistake. Over the course of eighty-five minutes Colbeck and McDonnell scored 143 runs and turned the match. While McDonnell maintained his wicket, Colbeck scored 107 before being caught by Roland Burn off the bowling of Francis Henley. During his innings, he hit thirteen 4s and was at the crease for two-and-a-quarter hours. McDonnell also managed a good knock of 60. Thanks to that innings Cambridge finally won the match by 40 runs. Colbeck's innings of 175 not out, made against W. G. Grace's XI on 4 June 1906 at Fenner's was also highly celebrated.

He made his debut for Middlesex on 14 June 1906 against Yorkshire at Lord's. Colbeck scored 2 and 30, however Yorkshire finally won by 281 runs. On 16 July 1906 he turned out for the Gentlemen against the Players at the Kennington Oval and scored 54 and 8; and caught William Quaife off the bowling of Percy May for 28, John Gunn off the bowling of May once again for 27, Thomas Hayward again off May for 10 and finally John King off the bowling of WG Grace for 88. The match was drawn. He also represented his college at hockey in 1904, 1905 and 1906 and was a member of the MCC.

On leaving University in 1907 he became a master at Rugby, remaining there until 1911 when he took up a position with the Bombay Company in India. Between August and

September 1913, Colbeck made three further first-class matches, two Bombay Presidency matches against the Hindus and the Parsees and the a Bombay Quadrangular Tournament against the Hindus. This was to be his last first class match. During his first-class career he made 1,368 runs, his highest score being 175, including three centuries and nine 50s, and made sixteen catches.

During the war he left India, returning to England, and in July 1916 took a commission in C Battery, 59th Brigade Royal Field Artillery. He was sent to France where he was soon in the thick of the fighting. A good officer, he was awarded a Military Cross for outstanding bravery. His citation read:

Second Lieutenant L. G. Colbeck Royal Field Artillery,

When in command of his battery, he handled his battery with great skill under the most trying conditions, and carried out the task allotted to him with conspicuous success.

He was invalided home in August 1917, and was pronounced unfit to go through a winter on the Western Front. He eventually persuaded the authorities to send him east to a warmer climate. While en route in HMT *Ormonde* he died of fever off the Cape of Good Hope on 3 January 1918 and was buried at sea.

When he learned of the scholar's death, Sir Walter Durnford, Provost of King's College Cambridge, wrote of him in the *Cambridge Review*:

The boy, the man, the soldier are what we love and miss; wonderful bodily gifts, high power of mind, exceptional bravery, whimsical and delightful humour were his.

He has no known grave and is commemorated on the Hollybrook Memorial, Southampton.

Batting and fielding averages

	Mat	Inns	NO	Runs	HS	Ave	100	50	Ct	St
First-class	32	60	5	1368	175*	24.87	3	9	16	0

Bowling averages

	Mat	Balls	Runs	Wkts	BBI	BBM	Ave	Econ	SR	4w	5w	10
First-class	32	-	-	-	-	-	-	-	-	-	-	-

The Reverend Harvey Staunton
Nottinghamshire
Army Chaplains Department (Chaplain 4th Class)
Died 14 January 1918
Aged 45
Right-handed Bat

'A man who excelled at everything and gave his life to God'

Harvey Staunton was born on 21 November 1870 at Staunton Hall, Nottinghamshire, the son of the Reverend Frances Staunton of Staunton Hall, Nottingham and Mrs L. A. Staunton Lees. The Staunton family had lived at Staunton Hall since the Norman conquest. Educated at the Bromsgrove School, where he was in the XI, and Selwyn College Cambridge, Harvey won his Blue in 1891, not for cricket, but for rugby union, another sport in which he excelled.

Between May 1903 and July 1905 he made 16 first-class appearances for Nottinghamshire, mostly in the County Championship, but he also played against the Gentlemen of Philadelphia and South Africa in the British Isles. He made his debut for Nottinghamshire in the County Championship on 11 May 1903 against Derbyshire at Trent Bridge, Nottingham. He scored 2 in his only innings and caught John Hulm off the bowling of Albert Hallam for 6, Nottinghamshire won by 6 wickets. He went on to play against Sussex, Leicestershire, Gloucestershire, Middlesex, Lancashire, Kent, Surrey and Yorkshire and made his final first-class appearance, like his debut, against Derbyshire at Trent Bridge on 6 July 1905, scoring 10 in his only innings he also caught Levi Wright off the bowling of Albert Hallam for 20 and John Charles Ollivierre of the bowling of John Pennington for 13, Nottinghamshire won this time by eight wickets.

During his first-class career Staunton made 456 runs including two 50s, his highest scoring being 78 against Middlesex. He made 8 catches. He also made twenty-one appearances for Nottinghamshire in the Minor Counties, as well as tuning out for the MCC.

Ordained as a curate in 1897, he served the parishes of Boxford in Berkshire, Pleasley Hill, Nottinghamshire, and Plumtree, Nottinghamshire before becoming the rector at Boughton Sulney in the same county. He was also chaplain to the Nottinghamshire County Asylum. Always interested in missionary work, he relocated to India in 1911 becoming the chaplain at Nagpur.

During the war he served in Mesopotamia as a chaplain 4th class and died of a fever at Arzizieh on 14 January 1918. He is commemorated in grave XX J 7, North Gate War Cemetery, Baghdad.

Batting and fielding averages

	Mat	Inns	NO	Runs	HS	Ave	100	50	Ct	St
First-class	16	24	0	456	78	19.00	0	2	8	0

Bowling averages

	Mat	Balls	Runs	Wkts	BBI	BBM	Ave	Econ	SR	4w	5w	10
First-class	16	54	48	0	-	-	-	5.33	-	0	0	0

Major William Robert Gregory MC
Ireland
4th (SR) Bn Connaught Rangers and Royal Flying Corps
Died 23 January 1918
Aged 36
Right-hand-Bat/Legbreak Googly

'I know that I shall meet my fate somewhere among the clouds above'

William Robert Gregory was born on 20 May 1881 at Coole Park, Gort, Galway. He was the only child of the Right Honourable Sir William Henry Gregory KCMG MP for County Galway and a former governor of Ceylon. His mother was Isabella Persse, Lady Gregory, a leading figure in the *fin de siècle* renaissance of Irish arts and culture and close friend of the poet and writer William Butler Yeats. Gregory was educated at Harrow School where he took the first classical scholarship of the year and went up to New College Oxford where he boxed lightweight for the university. Then he went on to the Slade School of Art, studied painting and became an accomplished artist and designer, illustrating books and theatres. Dublin's Abbey Theatre, in its earlier days, owed much to the beautiful sets painted and designed by Gregory, such as those for John Milllington Synge's *Deirdre of the Sorrows*, Yeats' *Shadowy Waters* and for his playwright mother's *The Image*. He also worked in the design studio of Jacques Emile Blanche in Paris. Blanche later declared that his work 'had reached the highest level of artistic and intellectual merit'. Gregory had his own exhibition of paintings in Chelsea in 1914.

He married Margaret Graham-Parry in 1907 and had a son and two daughters. A good all-round sportsman he excelled at cricket, riding, bowls and boxing, playing his club cricket for Phoenix Cricket Club and the Gentlemen of Ireland. He made one first-class appearance on 29 August 1912 at Observatory Lane, Rathmines, Dublin, turning out for Ireland against Scotland. Although he failed to score, being out for a duck in both innings, took 8 wickets for 80 runs in the first innings using leg spin, and a further wicket for 12 in the second. Scotland finally won by the narrow margin of 3 runs. Gregory's bowling performance against Scotland remains the tenth best in all matches for Ireland and the fourth best in first-class cricket for Ireland, while his bowling average of 10.22 is the second best for Ireland in first-class cricket.

He was gazetted second lieutenant into the 4th (SR) Battalion Connaught Rangers on 24 September 1915, before transferring to the Royal Flying Corps in January 1916. He became a flying officer on 19 June 1916 and joined No.40 Squadron, flying F.E.8 fighters. After several harrowing experiences the squadron was re-equipped with Nieuport XVII fighters. While flying in Nieuport A6680 he shot down and killed *Jasta II* pilot Leutnant Edouard Lubbert from Hamburg, scoring the squadron's first 'kill' in their Nieuports. He was awarded the Military Cross for bravery (*London Gazette*, 18 July 1917)

> For conspicuous gallantry and devotion to duty. On many occasions he has, at various altitudes, attacked and destroyed or driven down hostile machines, and has invariably displayed the highest courage and skill.

The French also recognized the brave pilot, awarding him the Croix d'Officer and the Legion d'Honneur for his many acts of conspicuous bravery (*London Gazette*, 14 July 1917). He was promoted to major and, in October 1917, given command of No.66 Squadron which was equipped with Sopwith Camels. The unit was transferred to the Italian front on 22 November 1917. He was shot down and killed in error near Grossa, Padua by an Italian pilot while returning from a patrol over Austrian lines on 23 January 1918. By then he had scored around eight combat victories, making him an 'ace'.

Robert's early death devastated his mother and the Irish arts community and had a terrible effect on Yeats. Yeats said that he had once asked Robert Gregory why he had joined up. Gregory's reply was 'Friendship'. Yeats went on to write four of the most moving poems to come out of the First World War. These included 'In Memory of Major Robert Gregory', which has been called the greatest elegy in the English language and compared to Milton's *Lycidas*, written almost 300 years before. Yeats described Robert Gregory as 'the epitome of manhood, excelling in all pursuits so magnificently that it was inevitable that he would be cut down in his youth'. Yeats also wrote 'Shepherd and Goatherd' and 'Reprisals'. Lady Gregory hated the latter and felt that her son was being used as a vehicle for Yeats to denounce British policy in Ireland; it was not published. In 'An Irish Airman foresees his Death' Yeats contemplates what many Irishmen thought at the time: why someone like William Gregory would risk a seemingly charmed life fighting for a cause that would benefit neither him nor his Irish countrymen.

> I know that I shall meet my fate
> Somewhere among the clouds above;
> Those that I fight I do not hate,
> Those that I guard I do not love;
> My country is Kiltartan Cross,
> My countrymen Kiltartan's poor,
> No likely end could bring them loss
> Or leave them happier than before.
> Nor law, nor duty bade me fight,
> Nor public men, nor cheering crowds,
> A lonely impulse of delight
> Drove to this tumult in the clouds;
> I balanced all, brought all to mind,
> The years to come seemed waste of breath,
> A waste of breath the years behind
> In balance with this life, this death.

He is commemorated in the Padua Main Cemetery, Italy, grave reference A. 12.

Batting and fielding averages

	Mat	Inns	NO	Runs	HS	Ave	100	50	4s	6s	Ct	St
First-class	1	2	0	0	0	0.00	0	0	0	0	0	0

Bowling averages

	Mat	Balls	Runs	Wkts	BBI	Ave	Econ	SR	5w	10
First-class	1	162	92	9	8/80	10.22	3.40	18.0	1	0

Major Reginald (Reggie) George Pridmore MC
Warwickshire
Royal Field Artillery
C Battery 240th Brigade
Died 13 March 1918
Aged 31
Right-handed Bat

'A most Gallant Sportsman and Comrade'

Reginald George Pridmore was born on 29 April 1886 in Edgbaston, Birmingham, the son of George William and Sarah Louisa Pridmore, of Coventry. Educated at the Elstow School (now closed) Bedford and Bedford Grammar School, where he was in the XI, he began training as a Stockbroker on leaving school. A first-class cricketer and hockey player, he played hockey for Coventry and represented England on nineteen occasions between 1908 and 1913. During the 1908 Olympics he represented England and was their leading goal scorer, scoring hat-tricks against both France and Scotland. He went on to score four goals in England's 8:1 victory over Ireland to take the Olympic Gold Medal. The record stood for forty-four years, until the Helsinki Olympics in 1952 when Balbir Singh Sr scored five against the Netherlands.

Between June 1909 and August 1912 Pridmore played in fourteen first-class matches for Warwickshire, thirteen of them in the County Championship and one against Australia in the British Isles. He made his debut for Warwickshire was on 3 June 1909 at Edgbaston, Birmingham when he scored 29 in his one innings. The match was drawn. He went on to play against Derbyshire, Leicestershire, Northamptonshire, Hampshire, Australia in the British Isles, Sussex, Worcestershire, Gloucestershire and Lancashire and played his final first-class match against Surrey on 15 August 1912 at Edgbaston, scoring 9 and 7 not out; the match was drawn. During his first-class career he scored 315 runs, his highest score being 49 against Derbyshire and took seven catches. He also turned out occasionally for Hertfordshire.

He took a commission in the 4th South Midland Brigade, Royal Field Artillery (TF) in September 1914 before joining 241st Brigade, Royal Field Artillery (TF) in May 1916.

Pridmore was awarded the Military Cross on the Somme in 1916 (*London Gazette*, 20 October 1916) for gallantry. His citation read:

> … during operations as Forward Observing officer. He displayed great coolness under fire, notably on one occasion when his observation post was very heavily shelled, both he and his look out man were partially buried but he carried on and sent in valuable reports.

Between August 1917 and March 1918 he was the officer commanding D Battery 241st Brigade RFA but in March 1918 he transferred to C Battery 240th Brigade RFA, then based in Italy. He was killed in action on 13 March 1918 at the Piave River, Arcade, Italy (north of Venice) and is commemorated at the Giavera British Cemetery, Arcade, grave reference Plot I Row D Grave 5. The inscription on his original wooden cross erected by his comrades read 'A most Gallant Sportsman and Comrade'.

Batting and fielding averages

	Mat	Inns	NO	Runs	HS	Ave	100	50	Ct	St
First-class	14	26	1	315	49	12.60	0	0	7	0

Bowling averages

	Mat	Balls	Runs	Wkts	BBI	BBM	Ave	Econ	SR	4w	5w	10
First-class	14	-	-	-	-	-	-	-	-	-	-	-

Major (Brevet Lieutenant Colonel) Lawrence Julius Le Fleming
Kent
2nd (Commanding 9th) Bn The East Surrey Regiment
Died 21 March 1918
Aged 38
Right-handed Bat

'So died, in the fearless performance of his duty, a gallant and accomplished soldier'

John Le Fleming was born on 3 June 1879 at Eton House, Tonbridge, Kent, the youngest of six children of the Reverend J. and Mrs Le Fleming. Educated at Tonbridge School, he was in the XI in 1896 and headed the batting with an average of 28. Deciding to make a career in the Army he was commissioned in the East Surrey Regiment and took part in the Second Boer War, being present at the Relief of Ladysmith and the Battles of Colenso and Spion Kop.

He played in 13 first-class matches between August 1897 and May 1912, 12 for Kent in the County Championship and one for the Army against the Navy. He made his debut for Kent was against Middlesex on 26 August 1897 at Lord's. He scored 40 and 2, Middlesex winning by 53 runs. He went on to play against the MCC, Lancashire, Warwickshire, Gloucestershire, Sussex, Yorkshire, Somerset, Nottinghamshire and Middlesex. He played his final first-class game for the Army against the Navy on 30 May 1912 at Lord's. He scored 11 and 24 and caught Hugh Monygomery off the bowling of Henry Baird for2. The Army won by 161 runs.

Le Fleming scored a total of 240 first-class runs, his highest score being 40 against Middlesex and made three catches; he also turned out for the Kent Second XI.

He was sent out to France with the East Surreys in October 1914 and was quickly in the thick of the fighting, being wounded in the face by a bullet during the Battle of la Bassée. After recovering, he rejoined his battalion only to be wounded again in 1915, this time in the foot at Zonnebeke. Twice Mentioned in Despatches, at the time of his death he was commanding the 9th Battalion of the East Surreys. He was killed in action on 21 March 1918, the first day of the German spring offensive. The history of the East Surrey Regiment describes his death in some detail:

the remainder of the Battalion at Vermand 'stood to' when the bombardment commenced. Shortly afterwards a shell fell among the horses of the Battalion transport, killing and wounding several of them, and wounding Captain E. L. Whiteman, the Transport Officer. Captain Whiteman succeeded in getting his transport into a place of safety, and remained at duty. At 7.30 a.m. the signallers' hut was struck, and several of them were killed or wounded. About 10 a.m. orders arrived from the 72nd Brigade that the Battalion was to move forward and occupy the high ground east of Villecholles. Lieut Colonel Le Fleming went on with a Battalion runner to reconnoitre and directed Major Clark to bring the Battalion up as quickly as possible. The Battalion was soon on the move, and presently met several artillerymen carrying the breechblocks of their guns. These men reported that the enemy was advancing along the road behind them and was not far away. Major Clark then ordered A Company (Lieut W. A. V. Waldron) to extend on both sides of the road and to move forward in the reported direction of the enemy's advance. On reaching Villecholles a position was taken up, but presently Lieut Colonel Le Fleming re-joined and ordered that one platoon of A Company should hold the road just north of the village, and that the rest of the Battalion should advance to the high ground east of it. On reaching this position every effort was made to ascertain the whereabouts of the enemy, but very little was known of it by neighbouring units. Leaving the Battalion under cover of the ridge, Lieut Colonel Le Fleming and Major Clark went forward to make a personal reconnaissance. They walked over the crest and about 200 yards down the eastern slope, when suddenly Major Clark saw some dark objects in front, and thought them to be the enemy. As he was pointing them out to his Commanding Officer heavy machine-gun fire was opened on them and Lieut Colonel Le Fleming fell, shot through the head. Major Clark threw himself down also and spoke to the Colonel, but receiving no reply looked in his face and saw that he was dead. So died, in the fearless performance of his duty, a gallant and accomplished soldier.

His body was recovered the following day due to the bravery of a runner from C Company called Private Turner who was killed later in the war. The body was brought in and carried to the dressing station at Villecholles.

Although buried with military honours and dignity, his body was unfortunately lost during the fierce fighting that continued after his death. He is commemorated on the Pozières Memorial, Panels 44 and 45.

Many people think that Fleming was the model for the colonel in Sherriff's wonderful book *Journey's End*. However, I have my doubts as Fleming didn't join the battalion until after Sherriff had left. He is described in the book as a 'decent little country squire' who had joined the Territorials and didn't feel able to stand up to the regulars of the Staff whereas Fleming was a regular.

Batting and fielding averages

	Mat	Inns	NO	Runs	HS	Ave	100	50	Ct	St
First-class	13	18	0	240	40	13.33	0	0	3	0

Bowling averages

	Mat	Balls	Runs	Wkts	BBI	BBM	Ave	Econ	SR	4w	5w	10
First-class	13	36	20	0	-	-	-	3.33	-	0	0	0

Captain Harold Augustus Hodges
Nottinghamshire
3rd Bn Monmouthshire Regiment, attd 11th Bn South
Lancashire Regiment (The Prince of Wales's Volunteers)
Died 24 March 1918
Aged 32
Not Known

'A fighter until the very end'

Harold Augustus Hodges was born on 22 January 1886 at the Priory, Mansfield, Woodhouse, Nottinghamshire, the fifth of seven sons born to William and Augusta Hodges. Educated at Roclareston School, Nottingham, after which he went to Sedbergh School, in Cumbria. He was in the rugby XV for four years, becoming captain in his last two years at the school. He was also in the cricket XI for five years, captaining the team for three years. In 1905 he went up to Trinity College Oxford and although he was in the College XI he didn't win his Blue for cricket. He did, however, get a Blue for rugby (playing against his brother who was on the Cambridge side). He went on to captain the Oxford side and play for England in two internationals against Wales on 13 January 1906, losing 3–16, and Ireland on 10 February 1906, once again on the losing side, this time by 6–16. He never played for England again. A noted French scholar after leaving Trinity he spent some time in Paris at the Sorbonne. Returning home in 1909 he became a master at Tonbridge School.

He played 3 first-class matches between August 1911 and August 1912 in the County Championship and all for Nottinghamshire (playing during the summer holidays from school). He made his debut against Derbyshire on 26 August 1911 at the Miners Welfare Ground, Blackwell. He scored 62 in his one innings, Nottinghamshire winning by 6 wickets. Hodges played his next first-class match almost a year later on 5 August 1912 against Surrey at the Kennington Oval. He scored 39 in his only innings; the match was drawn. His final first-class match was played later that month on 19 August against Middlesex at Trent Bridge. He scored 4 and 36 not out and caught Francis Mann off the bowling of Thomas Wass for 1. Once again the match was drawn. Of his 141 first-class runs, his highest score was 62 against Derbyshire. He made 1 catch.

At the outbreak of the war Hodges took a commission in the Monmouthshire Regiment and after training was sent to France in February 1915. He was soon in the thick of the fighting and was seriously wounded by a shell at Ypres in May 1915. After a brief period of convalescence back in England, he rejoined his battalion in July 1915, still with fragments of shrapnel inside him. In April 1916 he received the personal thanks of his divisional commander for preventing a serious explosion during a fire at an ammunition dump in Faceville.

During the Battle of the Somme the 3rd Battalion Monmouthshire Regiment suffered serious casualties and was all but wiped out. As a result his battalion was disbanded and he was transferred to the 1st Battalion The South Lancashire Regiment as an acting captain, his rank being confirmed in December 1916. A good and brave officer, he was Mentioned in

Despatches twice during 1917, once for carrying a wounded soldier a mile across no man's land to a first-aid post.

The gallant captain was to lose his life on 24 March 1918 during the Battle of St Quentin which had begun on 21 March. Three days later Hodges, then stationed close to Ham, was ordered to make contact with a battalion which it was believed was cut off close to a small factory on the Ham-Eppeville road. Leaving most of his men behind and taking only one junior officer with him, he moved forward towards the factory. Unfortunately, instead of finding his missing battalion, he discovered that the position had already been overrun and occupied by the Germans. Drawing his pistol he tried to hold the Germans back, giving his brother officer chance to escape. A firefight commenced in which Hodges was shot and killed. His companion, although badly wounded, managed to escape and make his way back to his own lines.

Hodges's body was later recovered and he is commemorated in Roye New British Cemetery, Somme, France, grave reference III, E.1.

Batting and fielding averages

	Mat	Inns	NO	Runs	HS	Ave	100	50	Ct	St
First-class	3	4	1	141	62	47.00	0	1	1	0

Bowling averages

	Mat	Balls	Runs	Wkts	BBI	BBM	Ave	Econ	SR	4w	5w	10
First-class	3	-	-	-	-	-	-	-	-	-	-	-

15992 Private Edward William Marvin
Transvaal
4th South African Infantry Regiment (South African Scottish)
Died 24 March 1918
Aged 39
Not known

'Born in England, served with the South Africans, died for Freedom'

Edward William Marvin was born on 7 July 1878 in St Mary's, Leicester, England, one of the six children of Edward William Marvin and Florence Sarah, née Barnard. At some point in his life he left England to settle in Johannesburg, South Africa where he met and married Cornelia Dorothy Marvin of Norwood, Johannesburg.

He played in two first-class matches for the Transvaal during the 1909 season and made his debut on 23 March 1909 in the Currie Cup against Border at the Newlands Rugby Ground, Cape Town. He scored 29 in his one innings, Transvaal winning by an innings and 12 runs. His second match was three days later against Western Province, once again in the Currie Cup. Marvin scored 18 and 0, Western Province winning by 6 runs. He also played for the Western Transvaal against the MCC during their South African tour, MCC winning by an innings and 110 runs. This was not, however, a first-class match.

During the war he enlisted in the ranks of the 4th South African Infantry Regiment and

was sent to France. He was reported missing in action on 24 March 1918 during the battle of Marrieres Wood, his death later being assumed to have taken place on that day.

Marvin's body was later recovered and he is commemorated in the Peronne Road Cemetery, Maricourt, grave reference IV. D 39.

Batting and fielding averages

	Mat	Inns	NO	Runs	HS	Ave	100	50	Ct	St
First-class	2	3	0	47	29	15.66	0	0	0	0

Bowling averages

	Mat	Balls	Runs	Wkts	BBI	BBM	Ave	Econ	SR	4w	5w	10
First-class	2	-	-	-	-	-	-	-	-	-	-	-

Captain Arthur Cyril Bateman MC
Ireland
Royal Army Medical Corps, attd 7th Bn The Queen's Own
Cameron Highlanders
Died 28 March 1918
Aged 27
Right-handed Bat

'He would never leave an injured man'

Arthur Cyril Bateman was born on 31 October 1890 at Bailieborough, County Cavan, the son of Godfrey Bateman LL.D and Frances Emily Bateman, of 28 Clarinda Park East, Kingstown, County Dublin. Educated at Portora Royal School, Enniskillen and Trinity College Dublin, he entered TCD as a medical student in 1909.

Bateman played for the Trinity First XI in 1913 in the middle order. Although not a big scorer, he was consistent and it was this consistency that got him into the Irish XI on two occasions. He made two first class appearances in July 1913 and July 1914 both for Ireland. He made his debut against Scotland on 10 July 1913 at Raeburn Place, Edinburgh. Bateman had a good game, scoring 36 and 52 and caught Robert Gardiner off the bowling of Basil Ward for 72 and John Murray (killed in action 23 September 1917) once again off the bowling of Ward once again for 29. Despite Bateman's best efforts, however, the match was drawn. His second match took place on 16 July 1914, once again against Scotland, at Observatory Lane, Rathmines, Dublin. He scored 34 and 27, Scotland going on to win by 11 runs.

He was also a prominent member of the University XV and his parents later presented the Bateman Cup in memory of their two sons, Arthur Cyril and Reginald John. This was competed for annually at Lansdowne Road towards the end of the rugby season. Unhappily, they stopped presenting the cup after the Second World War but, more recently, it was revived by the IRFU for the 2010–11 season.

Bateman was awarded his MD in 1914 and was then commissioned into the Royal Army Medical Corps (RAMC) in August 1914. Promoted to captain in 1915 he became the Medical Officer (MO) of the 7th Battalion Cameron Highlanders and was sent to France on 26 September 1917.

Bateman was awarded the MC in 1918. His citation read (*London Gazette*, 28 March 1918):

For conspicuous gallantry and devotion to duty in repeatedly going round the front line and attending to the wounded, who had been lying out in some cases for two days. Although continually exposed to hostile sniping and machine gun fire, he displayed the upmost disregard of danger.

On 28 March 1918 Arthur Bateman was wounded and taken prisoner, dying of his wounds in German hands the same day. His colonel later explained what happened in a little more detail:

Captain Bateman manfully stuck to his post until the Germans were within a few yards of him, when he started to retire along with his orderlies. Unfortunately he was hit, and fell into the hands of the enemy (and) it will be difficult for any other MO to fill his place.

His body was never recovered and he is commemorated on the Pozières Memorial, Panel 95.

Batting and fielding averages

	Mat	Inns	NO	Runs	HS	Ave	100	50	Ct	St
First-class	2	4	0	149	52	37.25	0	1	2	0

Bowling averages

	Mat	Balls	Runs	Wkts	BBI	BBM	Ave	Econ	SR	4w	5w	10
First-class	2	-	-	-	-	-	-	-	-	-	-	-

His brother, Captain Reginald John Bateman, was killed in action on 3 September 1918 while serving with the 46th Battalion Canadian Expeditionary Force Infantry. Previously Mentioned in Despatches, he was a professor of English at the University of Saskatoon and is commemorated on the Vimy memorial.

555 Corporal Arthur Edward Ochse
South Africa and Transvaal
2nd South African Infantry Regiment
Died 11 April 1918
Aged 48
Right-handed Bat

'The youngest man to make his Test debut for South Africa'

Arthur Ochse was born on 11 March 1870 at Graaff-Reinet, Cape Colony, South Africa, the son of Andrew Ochse of 5 Fame Street, Cape Town. He served as a private and later corporal with the Rand Rifles during the Second Boer War and subsequently with the Witwatersrand Rifles (formed in 1903) and the Field Intelligence Department.

Arthur Ochse made two Test appearances and three first-class appearances between March 1889 and April 1895. He was a middle-order batsman who unusually made his first-class debut in his country's very first Test match, against the English touring team. England was managed by Major R. T. Warton and the team became known as R. T. Warton's XI, captained by C. Audrey Smith. At the time these games were not recognized as Tests by England. Indeed *Wisden's Cricketers Almanac* noted that 'It was never intended, or considered

necessary, to take out a representative English team for a first trip to the Cape.' However, this view later changed and they were considered to have been test matches.

The first Test took place at St George's Park, Port Elizabeth, on 12 March 1899. Ochse scored 4 and 8, England going on to win by 8 wickets. Ochse was only 19 at the time, making him the youngest South African player ever to make his test debut. Despite his low scores he retained his place for the second test on 25 March at New Lands, Cape Town. Unfortunately, Ochse was run out for 1 in the first innings and bowled for 3 by England's slow left-arm spinner Johnny Briggs in the second. England won again by a convincing margin of an innings and 202 runs.

Ochse went on to make three first-class appearances for the Transvaal, all in the Currie Cup. Against Kimberley on 4 April 1891 at Old Wanderers, Johannesburg, he scored 45 and 99, just missing out on his century by a whisker, and took 2 wickets for 27. Despite Ochse's best efforts, Transvaal still went down by 58 runs. His second match was against Natal. This time he wasn't as successful with the bat scoring 7 and 14; but did catch John Bell-Smyth off the bowling of Charles Smith for 24. Despite this poor showing, Transvaal still won by a single wicket. He made his third and final first-class appearance against Western Province on 18 April 1895 at Albert Park, Durban. Although Ochse only managed to knock up 9 in the first innings, he scored a creditable 45 in the second. Transvaal won by 58 runs.

During the war he served with the 2nd South African Infantry Regiment and was killed in action on 11 April 1918 at Messines Ridge.

His body was never recovered or recognized and he is commemorated on the Ypres (Menin Gate) Memorial, Panels 15–16 and 16A.

Batting and fielding averages

	Mat	Inns	NO	Runs	HS	Ave	100	50	4s	6s	Ct	St
Tests	2	4	0	16	8	4.00	0	0	1	0	0	0
First-class	5	10	0	231	99	23.10	0	1			1	0

Bowling averages

	Mat	Inns	Balls	Runs	Wkts	BBI	BBM	Ave	Econ	SR	4w	5w	10
Tests	2	-	-	-	-	-	-	-	-	-	-	-	-
First-class	5		145	75	2	2/27		37.50	3.10	72.5		0	0

Captain Reginald Harry Myburgh Hands
South Africa/ Western Province
South African Heavy Artillery
Died 20 April 1918
Aged 29
Right-handed Bat

'Reggie Hands was one of the best of men'

Reginald Harry Myburgh Hands was born on 26 July 1888 in Claremont, near Capetown, South Africa, the eldest son of Sir Harry Hands KBE and his wife, the Lady Aletta Hands OBE. Educated at Diocesan College, Rondebosch, he was a bright student who won a Rhodes Scholarship and, in 1907, went up to University College Oxford to read law. He was called to the Bar in 1913.

As well as being a fine cricketer, Hands was also a first-class rugby forward, who won his Blue for rugby at Oxford and went on to play in two internationals for England against France and Scotland.

Between January 1913 and March 1914, Hands played in one Test and six first-class matches, mainly for the Western Province in the Currie Cup. He made his debut for the Western Province against the Orange Free State on 1 January 1913 at Newlands, Cape Town.

WW1. Officers of the SOUTH AFRICAN CONTINGENT'S HEAVY ARTILLERY 1915
Back Row: Lt. E.G. Farrell, Lt. J.G. Stewart, Lt. L. Edwards, Lt. L.H. Maasdorp, 2ⁿᵈ. Lt. C.P. Ward,
2ⁿᵈ. Lt. R, Levy, Lt. F. Jenvey, Lt. R.H.M. Hands, 2ⁿᵈ. Lt. S.B. Edwards, Lt. A. G. Mullins, Lt. P.N.G. Fitzpatrick, Capt. H.R. Purser,
Sitting: Capt. E.H. Tamplin, Capt. W. Bryden, Capt. W.H. Pickburn, Brev, Lt.Col. P. Peacock, Lt. Col. J.M. Rose, Major W.H. Tripp, Major C.W. Alston, Capt. Mullins (Medical Officer), Capt. E.F.C. Lane, (Union Staff).
On the ground: Lt. A.B. Crump, Lt. J.C. Reynolds (Quartermaster and Hon. Lt), Capt. A.E. Rann,
Lt. J.R. McCarthy, Lt. G.M. Bennett, Capt. C.J. Foster, 2ⁿᵈ. Lt. E.G. Ridley.

He scored 6 and 79 not out; he also made three catches, Hugh Poyntz off the bowling of Walter Mars for 23 in the first innings and again in the second innings, off the same bowler for 13, and Percy Franklin for 2.

He played in the fifth Test against England on 27 February 1914 at St George's Park, together with his brother Philip; his other brother, Kenneth, also played Test cricket against England although it was during the unofficial Test matches against the Honourable Lionel Tennyson's English team of 1924–25). Although Reginald only scored 0 and 7, Philip more than made up for this failure by scoring 83 and 49. England finally won by 10 wickets. Hands also played against Natal, Eastern Province and the MCC against whom he made his final first-class appearance on 7 March 1914 at Newlands, Cape Town. He scored 8 and 14 and caught Frank Woolley off the bowling of Charles Minnaar, (killed on 16 November 1916), for 25. During his first class career he made 289 first-class runs, his highest score being 79 against the Orange Free State. He made 7 catches.

During the war he served initially as a second lieutenant with the Imperial Light Horse in their campaign in German South West Africa. This was essentially a policing action to round up German settlers in what is modern Namibia. He transferred to 73 Siege Battery, South African Heavy Artillery and was posted to France. Promoted to lieutenant on 23 August 1915, he became a captain on 15 February 1917 and was promoted to major on 13 April 1918, although this was never confirmed.

Reginald Hands was second in command of his battery when he died of wounds on 20 April 1918 after being gassed. He is commemorated in the Boulogne Eastern Cemetery, Pas de Calais, France, grave reference VII. A. 39.

Batting and fielding averages

	Mat	Inns	NO	Runs	HS	Ave	100	50	6s	Ct	St
Tests	1	2	0	7	7	3.50	0	0	0	0	0
First-class	7	12	2	289	79*	28.90	0	2		7	0

Bowling averages

	Mat	Inns	Balls	Runs	Wkts	BBI	BBM	Ave	Econ	SR	4w	5w	10
Tests	1	-	-	-	-	-	-	-	-	-	-	-	-
First-class	7		36	22	0	-	-	-	3.66	-	0	0	0

Lieutenant Lestock Handley Adams
Cambridge University
1st Bn The Prince Consort's Own (Rifle Brigade)
Died 22 April 1918
Aged 30
Right-handed Bat

'Died side by side with the bravest in the land'

Lestock Handley Adams was born on 10 September 1887 at Ormskirk, Lancashire. The son of the Reverend H. F. S. Adams, Vicar of Holy Trinity, Red Hill, and Ethel Emma Louisa Reid, he was educated at St Lawrence College, Ramsgate, where he was captain of the First XI, and the hockey XI. He went up to Queens College Cambridge where he played a Seniors Match at the invitation of Robert Baily to face an XI created by C. E. Lucas. The match, billed as C. E. Lucas' XI versus R. E. H. Baily's XI, was played on 4 May 1908. Adams, batting last, only managed 4 in his first innings but did take three wickets for 33. He scored a further 4 in his second innings, but took no further wickets. Baily's side won by 61 runs.

Between May 1908 and June 1910 Adams played in 6 first-class matches, 5 for Cambridge University and 1 for the Gentlemen of England. He made his first class debut against Lancashire on 25 May 1908 at F. P. Fenner's Ground, Cambridge. He scored 1 and 21, Lancashire won by 171 runs. Adams went on to play against G. J. V. Weigall's XI, Kent, Sussex and the MCC, playing his final first-class match against Cambridge University for the Gentlemen of England on 27 June 1910. He scored a double duck and took 2 wickets for 95 off 19 overs in the first innings taking two further wickets in the second innings for 32 off 9 overs. Cambridge University won by 6 wickets. During his first class career Adams scored 61 runs his highest score being 21 against Lancashire. He also took 17 wickets for 531 runs, his best figures being 6 for 86. He made one catch. He also played for the Perambulators against the Etceteras, and the Winnipeg Cricket Association.

After Cambridge he moved to Winnipeg, Canada where he became a master at St John's College. While there, in 1913, he met and married Emilie Anderson d'Auquier. He was also a member of the Canadian Cadet Officer Training corps. Returning to England at the outbreak of the war, he took a commission in the Royal Fusiliers, later transferring to the 1st Battalion Rifle Brigade, being promoted to lieutenant and sent to France.

On 11 April 1918 the 1st Rifle Brigade was rushed up in buses to a position on the la Bassée Canal to stem the German breakthrough on the Lys. Over the next eleven days it was involved in severe fighting in the area around Hinges and Robecq. On 22 April, 1st Rifle Brigade, together with 1st Hampshires, took part in an attack which helped to secure the canal. During this fighting Lance Sergeant Joseph Woodall earned his Victoria Cross on the far side of the canal at la Pannerie, near Hinges, and Lieutenant Lestock Handley Adams lost his life.

He is commemorated in the le Vertannoy British Cemetery, Hinges, grave reference A. 2.

1918

Batting and fielding averages

	Mat	Inns	NO	Runs	HS	Ave	100	50	Ct	St
First-class	6	10	5	61	21*	12.20	0	0	1	0

Bowling averages

	Mat	Balls	Runs	Wkts	BBI	Ave	Econ	SR	5w	10
First-class	6	866	531	17	6/86	31.23	3.67	50.9	1	0

5876 Lance-Corporal Osborne (Ossie) Henry Douglas
Tasmania
22nd Bn Australian Imperial Force
Died 24 April 1918
Aged 38
Not Known

'the flags were lowered to half mast yesterday as a mark of respect
for the gallant soldier who gave his life for his king and Empire'

Osborne Henry Douglas was born on 14 March 1880 in Launceston, Tasmania. The son of lawyer and politician Adye Douglas, who represented Tasmania on the South Yarra Ground in 1852, and Lady Ida Douglas, of 99 High Street, Sandy Bay, Hobart. He was educated at Hutchins School, Hobart, before going up to the University of Tasmania to read law. After completing his law degree, he moved to Melbourne and bought himself into a practice with his friend Alex Proudfoot in Nhill. He became involved in Nhill civic affairs and captained its local cricket team, East Melbourne, between 1906 and 1909.

Described by *Wisden* as 'a very good left-handed defensive bat', he made 7 first-class appearances between December 1898 and March 1905, all for Tasmania, including his two matches against the MCC. He made his first class debut on 9 December 1898 against New South Wales at the Sydney Cricket Ground. He scored 3 and 39, and caught William Howell off the bowling of John Bingham for 10. New South Wales winning by a resounding innings and 487 runs. Douglas went on to play against Victoria three times and the MCC twice. He played his final first-class match on 24 March 1905, once again against New South Wales, this time at the Tasmania Cricket Association Ground, Hobart. Douglas scored 13 and 31, Tasmania winning by 68 runs. During his first-class career he amassed 299 runs, his highest score being 59 against the MCC, and made 3 catches.

During the war he served with the 22nd Battalion Australian Imperial Force, embarking for France on the *Nestor* in October 1916. Arriving in France in early 1917, he was wounded seriously in the hand in May 1917 during the Battle of Bullecourt and sent to recover in England. Promoted to lance corporal, he returned to his battalion and was killed in action near Albert on 24 April 1918.

He was initially buried in the Albert Road Cemetery, close to where he fell. However, in 1920, his mother, Lady Ida Douglas, learned that he had been exhumed and re-interred at Dernancourt Communal Cemetery. She was assured that 'This work is carried out with every measure of care and reverence and in the presence of a Chaplain.'

An obituary in the *Nhill Free Press*, on Friday 17 May 1918 stated that:

the flags were lowered to half mast yesterday as a mark of respect for the gallant soldier who gave his life for his king and Empire, and one who leaves behind a record worthy of emulation.

Osborne Douglas is commemorated in the Dernancourt Communal Cemetery Extension, grave reference X. A.

Batting and fielding averages

	Mat	Inns	NO	Runs	HS	Ave	100	50	Ct	St
First-class	7	13	0	299	59	23.00	0	1	3	0

Bowling averages

	Mat	Balls	Runs	Wkts	BBI	BBM	Ave	Econ	SR	4w	5w	10
First-class	7	-	-	-	-	-	-	-	-	-	-	-

Lieutenant William Knowles Tyldesley
Lancashire
5th Bn (attd 9th) Loyal North Lancashire Regiment
Died 26 April 1918
Aged 30
Left-handed Bat/Left-arm Medium-Fast

'One of Lancashire's greatest losses'

William Knowles Tyldesley was born on 12 August 1887 at Wigan in Lancashire. The son of James and Annie Tyldesley of Westhoughton and one of four brothers, all of whom would go on to play first-class cricket for Lancashire and one who would also make seven Test appearances. All four were taught to play by their father J. D. Tyldesley, a Westhoughton club professional. The brothers were also on the Old Trafford ground staff. Tyldesley married Edith Rosina Tyldesley of 26 Victoria Avenue, Levenshulme, Manchester.

Between June 1908 and August 1914, Tyldesley made 87 first-class appearances, mainly for Lancashire and mainly in the County Championship. He made his debut against Kent on 11 June 1908 at Old Trafford, Manchester. He scored 16 and 17 and took 1 wicket for 4 off 1 over, and made two catches, Harold Hardinge off the bowling of William Huddleston for 4 and Edward Humphreys off the bowling of Walter Brearley for 9. Kent won by 213 runs. He also played against Australia in the British Isles in 1909 and South Africa in the British Isles in 1912 and made his final first-class appearance on 28 August 1914 against Northamptonshire at Old Trafford. Tyldesley scored 92 in his only innings and took catches from William Denton off the bowling of James Heap for 36 and Sydney Smith off the bowling of William Huddleston for 39. The match was drawn. Tyldesley made 2,979 first-class runs, including 3 centuries and 12 fifties. His highest score was 152 against Derbyshire. He also took 8 wickets for 383 runs, his best figures being 2 for 0. He made 52 catches.

During the war he enlisted as a private into the ranks of the 5th Battalion Loyal North Lancashire Regiment, rising to the rank of corporal. Commissioned on 9 October 1915 into the 9th Battalion Loyal North Lancashire Regiment, he was killed in action on 26 April 1918 at Kemmel Hill during a British counter-attack.

He is commemorated at the La Clytte Military Cemetery grave reference IV. B. 37

Batting and fielding averages

	Mat	Inns	NO	Runs	HS	Ave	100	50	Ct	St
First-class	87	137	7	2979	152	22.91	3	12	52	0

Bowling averages

	Mat	Balls	Runs	Wkts	BBI	Ave	Econ	SR	5w	10
First-class	87	682	383	8	2/0	47.87	3.36	85.2	0	0

The Brothers (all of whom seemed to have died young)

Richard Knowles Tyldesley (1897–1943) made 397 first-class appearances, mainly for Lancashire, and seven tests against South Africa and Australia.

Harry Tyldesley (1893–1935) made nine first-class appearances for Lancashire and the MCC.

James Darbyshire Tyldesley (1889–1923) made 116 first-class appearances for Lancashire.

34381 Gunner Ernest Frederick Parker
Western Australia/The Rest
102 Howitzer Battery 2nd Brigade Australian Artillery
Died 2 May 1918
Aged 34
Right-handed Bat

'A brave heart and a quick wit he was loved by all'

Ernest Frederick 'Ernie' Parker was born on 5 November 1883 in Perth, Australia. The son of George and Marian Ada Parke, he was educated at the Perth High School where he played in the XI and St Peter's College, Adelaide, where he also played for the XI. Parker was a first-class all-round sportsman, excelling at both tennis and cricket. He reached the men's single final in 1909, being beaten in the final by the famous Tony Wilding 2–6, 6–1, 6–2, 6–3. However, he won the doubles final, partnering J Keane and beating Wilding and Crooks. In 1913 he took the Australian men's singles title defeating Harry Parker 2–6, 6–1, 6–2, 6–3. As well as the men's singles title he took the doubles again, this time together with Alf Hedeman defeating Harry Parker and Ray Taylor.

Between January 1906 and March 1910 Parker made thirteen first-class appearances. All but two, which he played for The Rest against Australia, were for Western Australia. He made his debut for Western Australia was on 27 January 1906 at the Western Australia Cricket Association Ground. He scored 30 and 4 and caught Cornelius Chamberlain off the bowling of William Kelly for 3. Western Australia won by 103 runs. Going on to play against New South Wales (twice), MCC, The Rest (against Australia twice), South Australia (five times), Victoria (three times), his final first-class match was against Victoria on 12 March 1910 at the Western Australia Cricket Association Ground, Perth. Parker scored 14 and 18, Victoria winning by two wickets. During his first-class career, Parker scored 883 runs including 2 centuries and 5 fifties. His highest score being 117 against Victoria. Parker made 9 catches. He also turned out for Western Australia against the MCC on 11 April 1903 the match was drawn and for Perth against the MCC on the 15 April 1903 this match was also drawn. Neither was a first class match.

During the war Parker served with 102 Howitzer Battery, 2nd Brigade, Australian Artillery embarking for the front from Melbourne on 11 May 1917 on HMAT *Ascanius* A11. He was killed by a shell on 2 May 1918. An account of his death was sent from the front to his parents who allowed a local newspaper to print it:

Parker was with his company at a place called Caestre, and Ernest and a man named McCleery, and another were sitting outside their hut having tea (that is tea in the meal sense, the exact liquid being cocoa). They did not like the cocoa, and nearby they saw somebody lighting a fire to boil a billy, so McCleery went over to see if they could get some tea. He found that he could get tea, and returned for his own, and Ernest's mugs. He had not gone many yards when a shell dropped in front of the hut, killing Ernest and some other poor chap whose name is not known. McCleery said that Parker had five wounds, any one of which was sufficiently severe to be fatal. The shell also wounded four out of five men in the hut.

He is commemorated in the le Peuplier Military Cemetery, Caestre, grave reference C. 1

Batting and fielding averages

	Mat	Inns	NO	Runs	HS	Ave	100	50	Ct	St
First-class	13	26	0	883	117	33.96	2	5	9	0

Bowling averages

	Mat	Runs	Wkts	BBI	BBM	Ave	SR	4w	5w	10
First-class	13	26	0	-	-	-	-	0	0	0

Lieutenant Frederick Hugh Geoffrey Trumble
Royal Navy
Royal Navy (HMS *Warwick*)
Died 10 May 1918
Aged 24
Right-handed Bat

'A sad end for a very fine officer'

Frederick Hugh Geoffrey Trumble was born on 9 October 1893 at Brading, Isle of Wight. The son of Frederick Hugh Geoffrey and Mrs A. C. Trumble of The Old House, Haywards Heath, Sussex, he was educated at the Royal Naval College Dartmouth, entering in September 1908 where he was in the XI, captaining it in 1910.

He made one first-class appearance for the Royal Navy against the Army on 25 June 1914 at Lord's, scoring 0 and 8 despite his poor showing the Royal Navy went on to win by 170 runs.

On leaving Dartmouth in 1912 he was commissioned as a midshipman, became an acting sub lieutenant in 1914 and lieutenant in 1917. Trumble was serving as a lieutenant on board HMS *Warwick* when it was used in a blocking operation at Ostend. *Warwick* was the flagship of Rear Admiral Sir Roger Keyes who later wrote of the incident in his memoirs:

We were just going to shove her off, when Trumble, the First Lieutenant of the Warwick, standing beside Tomkinson and me, leant over and caught hold of the muzzle of a Lewis gun, which was mounted on her side, saying 'We had better save this.' I don't know how it happened, but the gun went off and the bullet hit him in the forehead, and he dropped dead beside us.

Trumble's body was returned to England and buried with full military honours according to the *Dover Express* of 17 May 1918.

FUNERAL OF THE HEROES OF THE OSTEND RAID.

Only four bodies of those who lost their lives in the blocking up of Ostend Harbour were brought to Dover, and in two cases the bodies were sent away for burial. The funeral at Dover took place on Thursday afternoon, at St James's Cemetery, of Lieut Fred Hugh Jeffery Trumble RN and Lieut Gordon Ross RNVR. Full Naval honours were accorded, and a large number of Naval ratings followed. The interment took place close to the spot where those who lost their lives in the Zeebrugge raid were laid to rest. The Rev. F. M. Tunniclifle RN was the officiating clergyman, and at the conclusion of the service the 'Last Post' was sounded by two Royal Marine buglers.

The following mourners (Lieut Trumble) were present: Mrs Trumble (mother), Commander Bayldon (uncle), Mrs Pink (aunt), and Lieut Pink (cousin). Lieut Gordon Ross came from Canada. Floral tributes were sent by the following: From his mother (anchor); from Aunt Carrie: in loving memory, from Aunt Edie; Alan, Barbara and Gerald; to Lieut Gordon Ross RNVR, from Savage, Mickey and Bubbler: with greatest respect, from the ship's company, HMS Warwick (harp); with greatest respect from the ship's company, HMS *Warwick* (anchor); from the captain and officers of HMS *Warwick*; from Vice Admiral Roger Keyes, in endeavouring most gallantly to save others in Ostend Harbour; from Vice Admiral Roger Keyes in memory of Lieut Trumble RN, in grateful appreciation of his gallant services in action with the enemy; from Commander L. Wood Bayldon RNR; in memory of our fallen comrade from officers and men of the Dover Motor Launch Flotilla: with heartfelt sympathy, from Admiral Dampier's staff; to Lieut G. Ross RNVR, with deepest sympathy from a few friends at the Grand Hotel.

For his actions during the attack on Ostend, Trumble was Mentioned in Despatches.

Frederick Hugh Geoffrey Trumble is commemorated in the Dover (St James) Cemetery, grave reference L. V. 9. If you're passing, drop in and pay your respects to a very brave officer and cricketer.

Batting and fielding averages

	Mat	Inns	NO	Runs	HS	Ave	100	50	Ct	St
First-class	1	2	0	8	8	4.00	0	0	0	0

Bowling averages

	Mat	Balls	Runs	Wkts	BBI	BBM	Ave	Econ	SR	4w	5w	10
First-class	1	-	-	-	-	-	-	-	-	-	-	-

Captain Egerton Lowndes Wright MC
Lancashire/Oxford University
Oxfordshire and Buckinghamshire Light Infantry
Died 11 May 1918
Aged 32
Right-handed Bat/Wicket-keeper

'One of two sons lost to the war'

Egerton Lowndes Wright was born on 15 November 1885 at Adlington, Chorley, Lancashire, the second son of Henry Lowndes Wright of Burnt House, Adlington, Lancashire and Alice Maud Wright, daughter of James Eckersley. He was educated at Winchester College, together with his three brothers all of whom served in the war (one, Frank Lowndes Wright, died in 1922 as a result of wounds received in October 1914). Some years after the war their father published a memoir entitled *Four Brothers & the World War: the Private Record of their Father for his Grandchildren* (Combridges, Hove 1933). Geoffrey Wright served with the RFA earning an MC and Bar and was seriously wounded in September 1916. Philip Wright won both the DSO and the MC, also serving with the 1st Oxfordshire and Buckinghamshire LI.

Egerton Wright, better known as 'Toddy', was a senior commoner prefect while at Winchester, captain of the Commoner VI, a member of the association football team and, in 1904, partnered the Honourable C. N. Bruce in winning the Public Schools' Racquets Championship. On leaving school he went up to New College Oxford, obtaining his soccer Blue in his first year and playing against Cambridge in 1905 and 1908. He was in the University Cricket team, captained the side in 1907 and 1908 and also turned out for Lancashire. He took his degree with Honours in Classical Moderations and History and entered the firm of Wilson, Wright and Davies, solicitors, in Manchester and Preston. Egerton Wright married Miss Violet Shakespeare in 1911 and they had two children, one of whom, James Egerton Lowndes, went to Winchester.

Wright played in 37 first-class matches between May 1905 and May 1910. The majority were University matches but he also played for Lancashire in the County Championship on four occasions and against South Africa in the British Isles once (1907). He made his debut for Oxford University against the Gentlemen of England, captained by the formidable W. G. Grace, on 22 May 1905 at the University Parks, Oxford. He scored 24 and 67; Oxford University won by 50 runs. He made his final first-class appearance for Lancashire at Headingly against Yorkshire on 16 May 1910 in the County Championship. Wright scored 7 and 4, and caught Haworth Watson off the bowling of Walter Brearley for 0. The match was drawn. He also played for the MCC, E. L. Wright's XI and Oxford University Authentics.

During his first-class career Wright scored 1,638 runs, his highest score being 95 against Cambridge University. Although he never managed a first-class century he did manage 10 fifties and took one wicket for 40 as well as taking 26 catches.

At the outbreak of war he was commissioned into the Oxfordshire and Buckinghamshire Light Infantry and went to France in March 1915. He served successively as adjutant to his battalion and on the staff of a brigade, a division and a corps and, being twice Mentioned in

Despatches and receiving the Military Cross. At the end of 1916 he was appointed Brigade Major of 6 Infantry Brigade and served in that capacity till his death.

Wright was killed in action near Barly on 11 May 1918 and is commemorated in the Barly French Military Cemetery, grave reference II. A. C.

Batting and fielding averages

	Mat	Inns	NO	Runs	HS	Ave	100	50	Ct	St
First-class	37	68	2	1638	95	24.81	0	10	26	3

Bowling averages

	Mat	Balls	Runs	Wkts	BBI	Ave	Econ	SR	5w	10
First-class	37	51	40	1	1/6	40.00	4.70	51.0	0	0

Major Harold Thomas Forster DSO & Bar MC & Bar
Hampshire/MCC
Princess Charlotte of Wales's (Royal Berkshire Regiment)/
Northamptonshire Regiment
Died 29 May 1918
Aged 39
Left-handed Bat/Left-arm Slow-Medium

'One of the most remarkable men and decorated cricketers of the war'

Harry Thomas Forester was born on 14 November 1878 at St Faith, Winchester, Hampshire. The son of Brian Robert Forster and Victoria Theresa, née Read, after leaving school Forster decided to join the forces and enlisted in the ranks of the Royal Marine Light Infantry, serving between 1897 and 1899. Two years seems to have been enough with the marines and he bought himself out. However, civilian life didn't seem to suit him either and he re-enlisted into the ranks of the Royal Berkshire Regiment for a period of seven years with a further five in the reserves (subsequently he extended this to twelve). His leadership abilities were quickly recognized and he was eventually promoted to the rank of company sergeant major. He met and married Victoria Theresa Read and they had several children. After serving in Gibraltar and Ireland, he was sent to France with 1st Royal Berkshires on 13 August 1914, becoming one of the famous 'Old Contemptibles'.

He made 5 first-class appearances for Hampshire between May 1911 and August 1911, four in the County Championship and one against the MCC. He made his debut for Hampshire against the MCC on 15 May 1911 at Lords; he scored 6 and 2, but made up for his poor batting figures with his bowling. He took 5 wickets for 38 off 18.2 overs during the first innings and 4 for 54 off 27 overs in the second, he also managed to catch the MCC opener John Douglas off the bowling of John Newman for 30. Despite Forster's best efforts the MCC went on to win by 1 wicket. He also played against Derbyshire, Sussex and Kent and played his final first-class game against Gloucestershire on 10 August 1911 at the County Ground, Southampton. He failed to bat or take a wicket during the match which but did catch Arthur Roberts off the bowling of John Newman for 51. It was during this match that CB Fry scored 258 not out passing his 28000 runs in first class cricket when he reached 128. The match was drawn.

Forster scored 33 first-class runs during his career, his highest score being thirteen against Derbyshire. He also took 10 wickets for 212 runs, his best figures being 5 for 38. Hampshire wanted to buy him out of the Army but he turned down the opportunity to play professionally. He also played hockey for his battalion.

He travelled to France with his regiment at the beginning of the war and was wounded on 30 October 1914. He returned to England for a short convalescence before returning to action. Commissioned on 15 June 1915, he was posted to the 2nd Battalion Royal Berkshire

Regiment and promoted to lieutenant on 28 December. In June 1916 he was Mentioned in Despatches and, on 19 August 1916, was awarded the Military Cross for bravery. The award was backdated and referred to his time as a Company Sergeant Major. His citation read:

Coy. S./M. (now 2nd Lt.) Harold Thomas Forster, R. Berks. R.
For gallantry and devotion to duty. A very gallant warrant officer, he has maintained the same standard in the performance of his duties.

He became the battalion's adjutant on 22 October 1916 and was Mentioned in Despatches again on 25 May 1917. On 26 September 1917 he was awarded a Bar to his Military Cross and the Distinguished Service Order (both in *London Gazette*, 26 September 1916). He was again Mentioned in Despatches on 21 December 1917.

The citation for the bar to his MC read:

Lt Harold Thomas Forster MC Royal Berkshire Regiment.
For conspicuous gallantry and devotion to duty. He took over command of his battalion when his colonel had become a casualty, and led them with great skill to their objective, twice changing direction in order to avoid hostile barrage. He then made a personal reconnaissance and ascertained the position of the enemy, after which he formed a defensive flank, and was able to re-establish his line when it had been driven back by determined hostile counter-attacks. He remained perfectly cheerful throughout, showing a fine example of fearlessness and contempt for danger.

The citation for his DSO read:

Lt Harold Thomas Forster DSO MC
For conspicuous gallantry and devotion to duty during an attack. He performed invaluable work as Adjutant throughout the day, rallying and controlling the men and showing great grasp of the situation. He set a fine example of courage and resource to all.

In April 1918 he was promoted to major and transferred to the 2nd battalion Northamptonshire Regiment as second in command, later being promoted to lieutenant colonel and becoming commanding officer.

During this time he wrote several letters home and they are an interesting reflection on life at the front and the thoughts of soldiers while serving there:

My Own Darling Girl,
Just received your letter dear and was very pleased to get it.
The weather appears to have changed there as it has here.
Yes Kiddie, you must tell Gash that he cannot have the ground after Xmas as we want it ourselves, then next year we can plant nearly all of it with potatoes which should keep you going as the back garden does not appear to be any good. As you say he had a cheek but I know him. He would soon collar the lot if he had a chance.
I do hope you won't have bad weather when Percy is there, perhaps you would get him to put some winter cabbage plants in which will come in very handy to you.
I wish I could get home for a time and square up things a bit but if I do I don't want anyone else staying there. I want you and the boys all to myself. If I am lucky enough to get leave soon I expect you will be on your own, all the visitors will have gone. As we shan't be out of here till the 1st I wonder if Joe will manage to come down or not.

We have the parson to tea in the trenches too but he is a jolly fine chap.
Now my darling girl I will close, kiss the boys with all my love to my darling girl.
I remain your loving husband
Harold Forster

Another letter gives an idea of conditions at the front:

My Darling Kid,
I was looking forward to a letter today but there is no mail so we are all disappointed. Never mind perhaps we shall do better tomorrow.

It's been raining nearly all the time since I wrote yesterday and the place is awful. We had a dugout fall in on three men this morning owing to the rain but we dug them out in time. The trenches are rotten today.

We have had some more good news today so altogether we are doing grand. Our new armoured cars are doing well evidently.

Well I have no news Kiddie dear.

Kiss Vic for me.

With all my love to you.
Your loving husband
Harry

He was reported missing on 29 April 1918 at Bouleuse Ridge, near Ventelay, Marne. However, it took until 23 March 1919 before his death was presumed to have taken place on that date. Information relating to his death was later gathered by his family. One report stated that a shell exploded beneath the horse which he was riding and that he suffered injuries to his chest and face and was taken to a field dressing station before being taken to hospital. A report regarding his injuries came from a Private E. Bradwell, 2nd Northants:

Major Forster was at Details, Bouvancourt. We had to retire from there and he continually went forward to see how things were going on during the retirement. As far as I can remember it was the third day of our retirement that he went up on horseback with his groom to the front line and was wounded and was brought back on horseback by his groom. After that the Germans came on very fast and we had to retire further, so that if he is still missing he may have been captured before he could get away to safety. The place was by an aerodrome on a hillside, this side of Vezilly. His groom was very severely wounded and is in hospital.

He was awarded a Bar to his Distinguished Service Order on 16 September 1918, a few months after his death. The citation read:

Lt (A./Maj.) Harold Thomas Forster, DSO MC, R. Berkshire Regiment attd North'n R. For conspicuous gallantry and devotion to duty. He assumed command of his battalion when his colonel was killed, and by his coolness and skill extricated it from a critical situation and formed a defensive flank of the utmost importance. For three days and nights, by his pluck and energy, he set an example to his men of inestimable value under adverse conditions of continuous and heavy shellfire.

Although it took some time to find Harold Forster's grave it was finally located. He is now commemorated in the Terlincthun British Cemetery, Wimille, grave reference VII. A. C. 12.

Despite failing to receive an obituary in *Wisden* at the time (a mistake which has since been corrected) he was one of the most decorated cricketers to serve in the First World War. Mentioned in Despatches five times, he was also awarded an MC and Bar and a DSO and Bar. A remarkable and brave man indeed.

Batting and fielding averages

	Mat	Inns	NO	Runs	HS	Ave	100	50	Ct	St
First-class	5	8	3	33	13	6.60	0	0	3	0

Bowling averages

	Mat	Balls	Runs	Wkts	BBI	Ave	Econ	SR	5w	10
First-class	5	494	212	10	5/38	21.20	2.57	49.4	1	0

Major Karl Otto Siedle MC
Natal
174th Brigade, Royal Field Artillery
Died 30 May 1918
Aged 28
Not Known

'The bravest South African I ever saw'

Karl Otto Siedle was born on 26 June 1889 in Durban, Natal, South Africa. He was the son of English-born Otto and Amelia Mary Siedle, née Watson, of Durban, South Africa.

Siedle made one first-class appearance for Natal against the MCC in South Africa on 8 December 1913 at the City Oval, Pietermarizburg South Africa. He made a duck in his first and only innings and failed to take a wicket. However, he caught Albert Relf off the bowling of Joseph Cox for 10. The match was drawn.

During the war he served with the 174th Brigade Royal Field Artillery. A good and gallant officer, he was promoted to major and while serving on the Western Front earned the Military Cross for a brave and gallant act. His citation read:

T/Captain (A/Major) Karl Otto Siedle, RFA.
For conspicuous gallantry and devotion to duty while in command of his battery during a withdrawal. He remained out all day on a forward slope, directing the fire of his own and another battery with great effect on enemy troops and transport. He also sent back a great deal of the most valuable information.

(*London Gazette*, 16 September 1918).

Siedle died of wounds on 30 May 1918 in Doullens, France. He is commemorated in the Bagneux British Cemetery, Gezaincourt, grave reference III. A. 14.

His brother Jack played first-class cricket before the war, appearing in 18 tests and 123 first-class matches. He scored over 7,000 runs during his career. His sister, Perla, was a noted soprano.

Batting and fielding averages

	Mat	Inns	NO	Runs	HS	Ave	100	50	4s	6s	Ct	St
First-class	1	1	0	0	0	0.00	0	0	0	0	1	0

Bowling averages

	Mat	Balls	Runs	Wkts	BBI	BBM	Ave	Econ	SR	4w	5w	10
First-class	1	54	18	0	-	-	-	2.00	-	0	0	0

40338 Corporal Charles Bryan Tomblin
Northamptonshire
2nd Bn The Northamptonshire Regiment
Died 1 June 1918
Aged 27
Not Known

'Not long enough in this world to make the impact he should have made'

Charles Bryan Tomblin was born on 29 June 1891 at Walgrave, Brixworth, Northamptonshire, although some sources say he was born in the village of Old. He married Catherine J. Tomblin of Peachfield, Walgrave, Northamptonshire.

He made two first-class appearances for Northamptonshire, both in the County Championship. The first was on 4 June 1914 at the County Ground, Northampton against Kent when he scored 2 and 3, and caught William Fairservice off the bowling of Sydney Smith for 2, Kent winning by 227 runs. His second appearance was against Sussex on 12 June 1914 at Northampton. Tomblin scored 3 and zero, and caught the Sussex opener Herbert Wilson off the bowling of George Thompson for 5. Sussex won by 24 runs. He also played for Northamptonshire's Second XI.

Tomblin first served with the Bedfordshire Regiment as private 30527, before transferring to the Northamptonshire Regiment. He was promoted to corporal while serving with the Northamptons but was killed in action at Sissonne, France on 1 June 1918. He is commemorated in Sissonne British Cemetery, grave reference H. 15.

Batting and fielding averages

	Mat	Inns	NO	Runs	HS	Ave	100	50	Ct	St
First-class	2	4	0	8	3	2.00	0	0	2	0

Bowling averages

	Mat	Balls	Runs	Wkts	BBI	BBM	Ave	Econ	SR	4w	5w	10
First-class	2	-	-	-	-	-	-	-	-	-	-	-

Lieutenant Ellis Louis George Neville Grell
Trinidad and Tobago
2nd Bn The Prince of Wales's Own (West Yorkshire
Regiment)/27th Punjabis
Died 5 June 1918
Aged 25
Not Known

'A gentler man or more determined personality is hard to find'

Ellis Louis George Neville Grell was born on 24 December 1890 in Trinidad, the only son of Ellis Grell. He was educated at Saint Mary's College Trinidad, before being returned to England and educated at Wellington and Clifton College (1906–08). While at Clifton he was in the first XI.

Grell played in two first-class matches between September 1910 and March 1911, his debut being for Trinidad against Barbados on 26 September 1910 in the Inter-Colonial Final at Bourda, Georgetown. He didn't have a good game, scoring 1 and 8, Barbados winning by an innings and 48 runs. In his second match he was playing for the visiting MCC against Trinidad at Queen's Park Oval, Port of Spain on 10 March 1911. This time he did better, scoring 17 and 25, and catching Alfred Harragin off the bowling of John Hearne for 6. Trinidad won by 7 wickets. Grell also played for Staten Island County Cricket club.

On completing his education he emigrated to Canada and while there held a commission in the British Columbia Horse. At the outbreak of the First World War he resigned his commission and transferred to Lord Strathcona's Horse, arriving in England early in 1915. He obtained a further commission and was gazetted to the 10th, and then 1st and 2nd Battalions, West Yorkshire Regiment. Seriously wounded at Ypres in October 1916, he returned home to recover.

He never recovered fully from his wounds and was sent to India in August 1917 where he joined the Indian Army, being attached to the 27th Punjabis. He was only in India a few months when he was taken ill and died after a brief illness on 5 June 1918 at the Station Hospital, Landour.

He is commemorated in the Landour General Cemetery, Plot D, grave 52 and also on the Port of Spain Cenotaph.

Batting and fielding averages

	Mat	Inns	NO	Runs	HS	Ave	100	50	Ct	St
First-class	2	4	0	51	25	12.75	0	0	1	0

Bowling averages

	Mat	Balls	Runs	Wkts	BBI	BBM	Ave	Econ	SR	4w	5w	10
First-class	2	-	-	-	-	-	-	-	-	-	-	-

Second Lieutenant Edwin John Leat
Somerset
6th Bn The Dorsetshire Regiment
Died 8 June 1918
Aged 33
Not Known

'Was never destined to see his son'

Edwin John Leat was born on 24 April 1885 at Wellington, Somerset. He was the son of Edwin C. Leat and Mrs Leat, of 19 Tip Hill, Ottery St Mary, Devon and Winifred Emily Leat of 'Reigate', Upton Road, Slough, Buckinghamshire. Leat studied at St Luke's College, Exeter, a teacher training establishment, became a teacher and, eventually, headmaster at the Chalvey School.

Between August 1908 and August 1910 he played two first-class games for Somerset, as well as several minor county matches for Buckinghamshire. His debut match for Somerset came on 13 August 1908 against Kent in the County Championship at the County Ground, Taunton. Leat scored 11 and 1, and caught Edward Humphreys off the bowling of Ernest Robson for 149. Kent won by an innings and 114 runs. His second match was two years later, on 29 August 1910, once again at the County Ground, Taunton, and also against Kent. Leat scored 6 in his one innings and took 2 catches, Everard Radcliffe off the bowling of Frank Joy for 4, and William Rhodes, again off the bowling of Joy, for 9. The match was eventually drawn. He made seventeen appearances for Buckinghamshire in the minor counties between 1908 and 1911.

During the war Leat served as a second lieutenant with the 6th Battalion Dorsetshire Regiment and was killed in action on 8 June 1918 near Beaumont Hamel, France.

The 17th Division decided to mount a strong trench raid on the German line close to Beaumont Hamel and 6th Dorsets, together with the East Yorkshires, attacked on a 600-yard front. The Dorsets had to cross a long ravine, infamously known as Y Valley. The raid was launched at 10.05pm on 8 June 1918 after every man was issued with a tot of rum. It was all over in less than an hour and, although considered a success, the battalion lost two officers, one of whom was Edwin Leat.

His body was never recovered and he is commemorated on the Pozières Memorial, Panel 48.

Leat married, but died without ever seeing his son, who was born two months after his death.

Batting and fielding averages

	Mat	Inns	NO	Runs	HS	Ave	100	50	Ct	St
First-class	2	3	0	18	11	6.00	0	0	3	0

Bowling averages

	Mat	Balls	Runs	Wkts	BBI	BBM	Ave	Econ	SR	4w	5w	10
First-class	2	-	-	-	-	-	-	-	-	-	-	-

Major Henry Wilfred Persse MC & Bar
Hampshire
2nd Bn Royal Fusiliers (City of London Regiment)
Died 28 June 1918
Aged 32
Right-handed Bat/Right-arm Fast

'His fearless example and great skill were mainly instrumental in making good the
defence at a critical part of the line'

Henry Wilfred Persse was born on 19 September 1885 at Portswood, Southampton, Hampshire. He was the son of Lieutenant Colonel Edward Persse and Margaret, née Clerk, of 48 Westwood Road, Southampton and married Marjorie Frances Hoskyn, daughter of Mr and Mrs Hoskyn of Southampton, in July 1915.

Between May 1905 and August 1909 Persse played in 51 first-class matches for Hampshire, mostly in the County Championship. He made his debut on 8 May 1905 against Surrey at the Kennington Oval and he scored 14 not out, and 12, also taking 3 wickets for 56 off

1907

R.W.F. Jesson. C.B.Llewellyn. C.P.Mead. A.Bowell. J.Stone. J.Newman. W.Langford.
H.W.Persse. C.A.R.Hoare. E.M.Sprot. ~ ~ ~. F.H.Bacon.
M.B.Lawson

25 overs in the first innings, and 4 further wickets for 59 off 21 overs in the second. He also caught the Surrey opener, Thomas Hayward, off the bowling of Harry Baldwin for 58 and Frederick Holland off the bowling of William Langford for 28 runs. Surrey won by 30 runs. Persse played against the Australians in the British Isles on 6 June 1905 at the County Ground, Southampton scoring 24 and 23 and took 4 wickets for 174 off 41 overs. Australia won by an innings and 112 runs. His final match was against Kent on 5 August 1909 at the Saint Lawrence Ground, Canterbury. He scored 0 and 3 and took 2 wickets for 54 off 13 overs. Kent won by 10 wickets. During his career Persse scored 889 runs including three fifties, his highest score being 71. He took 127 wickets for 3,813 runs, his best figures being 6 for 64 against Leicestershire. He made 40 catches.

Persse was commissioned as a second lieutenant in the 6th Battalion Royal Fusiliers on 15 August 1914 (*London Gazette*, 29 September 1914), later transferring to the 2nd Battalion during the war. He rose to the rank of major and was second in command of his battalion. A brave man, he also went on to earn the MC (*London Gazette*, date 20 October 1916) and a Bar (*London Gazette*, 18 June 1917, page 5982). I have not been able to find the citation for the MC but the Bar was awarded for his actions in January 1916:

> Lt (Acting Captain) Henry Wilford Persse MC R. Fus. Special Reserve.
> For conspicuous gallantry and devotion to duty. As second in command he had to take over the front after midnight, a very difficult task under heavy shellfire and the line uncertain. After daylight he made a bold reconnaissance of the whole line. His fearless example and great skill were mainly instrumental in making good the defence at a critical part of the line.

Persse was wounded twice. On the second occasion the wounds proved fatal and he died near St Omer, France on 28 June 1918. He is commemorated at the Longuenesse (St Omer) Souvenir Cemetery, grave reference V. C. 7.

His brother, Edward Aubrey, was killed in action on 14 October 1918 while serving with the Royal Field Artillery, aged 37.

Batting and fielding averages

	Mat	Inns	NO	Runs	HS	Ave	100	50	Ct	St
First-class	51	84	8	889	71	11.69	0	3	40	0

Bowling averages

	Mat	Balls	Runs	Wkts	BBI	Ave	Econ	SR	5w	10
First-class	51	6993	3813	127	6/64	30.02	3.27	55.0	3	0

Major Eric Anthony Rollo Gore-Brown CdG (Fr)
Europeans (India)
Dorsetshire Regiment/2nd & 3rd King's African Rifles
Died 3 July 1918
Aged 28
Unknown

'His loss is a great personal grief to me'

Eric Anthony Rollo Gore-Brown was born on 13 June 1890 at Ryde on the Isle of Wight, the son of the Reverend R. M. Gore Browne MA and the Honourable Mrs Gore Browne, of Leckhampstead, Buckingham. He was educated at Twyford School, near Winchester, Eastam's, Southsea, Oundle and the Royal Military College Sandhurst.

Commissioned second lieutenant in the Dorsetshire Regiment in 1910, he spent some time in India with his regiment and while there made his one first-class appearance for the Europeans against the Parsees during a Bombay Presidency match on 26 August 1912 at the Deccan Gymkhana Ground, Poona. He scored 12 and 0 and took no wickets. The Parsees won by six wickets. A good all-round athlete, he also won prices for boxing and the sabre.

He was employed with the King's African Rifles from December 1913 and Advanced to captain in 1915. On 21 September 1915 he was wounded in the action at Longido in German East Africa and was carried by stretcher and mule cart seventy miles, more than halfway to Nairobi. On his recovery he assisted in the training of troops in Nairobi. He was awarded the Croix de Guerre by the French government for his good work in training troops in Nairobi and other places in East Africa.

Early in 1918 he entered German East Africa and later commanded the fort at Nhamacurra, Portuguese East Africa where, after a gallant defence lasting three days from 1 to 3 July, the garrison was overwhelmed by a large German force under von Lettow Vorbeck. Acting Lieutenant Colonel Gore-Brown had no option but to save the remnant of his force as best he could: The action was later described:

> Now only the KAR on the right held fast ... the cheering German troops raced across sugar and sisal fields ... the British found themselves all but rivetted down by cross fire ... Their commander, Major E.A.Gore-Browne, had no choice but to order a gradual withdrawal towards a wide stream in the hope of fording it and taking up stronger positions on the opposite bank. Suddenly ... the usually unflappable KAR troops became infected with the Portuguese panic. Instead of retiring in order, they swarmed into the river and tried to swim to the other side ... nearly half the force was shot dead, snapped up by crocodiles or drowned in the boiling current. Among those lost was Gore-Browne, who went under while trying to stem the rout ...

His commanding officer later wrote of him:

> His loss is a great personal grief to me, as well as to all ranks of the 3rd King's African Rifles, and will be most particularly felt in the battalion, in which he was held in great esteem by all ranks.

He is commemorated on the Mombasa British Memorial.

Batting and fielding averages

	Mat	Inns	NO	Runs	HS	Ave	100	50	Ct	St
First-class	1	2	0	12	12	6.00	0	0	0	0

Bowling averages

	Mat	Runs	Wkts	BBI	BBM	Ave	SR	4w	5w	10
First-class	1	10	0	-	-	-	-	0	0	0

His brother, Harold Rolo Gore-Brown, was killed in action on board HMS *Invincible* during the Battle of Jutland on 31 May 1916.

125760 Gunner Ernest Herbert Relf
Sussex
337 Siege Battery Royal Garrison Artillery
Died 27 July 1918
Aged 29
Right-handed Bat/Right-arm Medium Pace

Relf brothers (from
left to right): Albert,
Ernest and Robert.

'And all the brothers were valiant'

Ernest Herbert Relf was born on 19 November 1888 at Sandhurst, Berkshire, the son of
John and Ellen Sophie Relf. He became a professional cricketer and made 12 first-class
appearances for Sussex between May 1912 and August 1914, 10 in the County Championship
and two University matches. He made his debut for Sussex was on 13 May 1913 against
Lancashire at Old Trafford in Manchester. He scored 9 not out and 24. Relf also caught John
Sharp off the bowling of Joseph Vine for 134. Lancashire won by 132 runs. He also played
against Kent, Essex, Leicestershire, Somerset, Warwickshire, Hampshire, Cambridge
University and Northamptonshire, making his final first-class match on 10 August 1914,
against Leicestershire at the County Ground, Hove. He scored 0 and 23 not out and caught
Harry Whitehead off the bowling of Henry Roberts for 8; Sussex won by 221 runs. Relf
made 232 first-class runs, his highest score being 36, took 8 wickets for 212 runs, his best
figures being 2 for 24. He made five catches.

He married his longtime girlfriend May Clarence Relf, and they resided at 3 King's Road,
Reading. During the war Ernest served with 337 Siege Battery, Royal Garrison Artillery. However,
he became ill and had to be returned home. He was admitted to the 5th Northern General
Hospital, Leicestershire where despite the best efforts of the doctors he died on 27 July 1918.

Relf is commemorated in Reading Cemetery, special memorial 33. 8752. Although it is
registered as a Commonwealth War Grave, he shares it with both his mother and brother
and has a private headstone. He left his wife, May Clarence Relf, £148 4s 9d in his will. If you
live in the area, always worth a visit and perhaps a few flowers.

Batting and fielding averages

	Mat	Inns	NO	Runs	HS	Ave	100	50	Ct	St
First-class	12	23	3	232	36	11.60	0	0	5	0

Bowling averages

	Mat	Balls	Runs	Wkts	BBI	Ave	Econ	SR	5w	10
First-class	12	360	212	8	2/24	26.50	3.53	45.0	0	0

Ernest was one of three Relf brothers who played for Sussex prior to the war. His brother
Albert played over 500 times for Sussex and appeared in 13 tests for England. Robert played
for the county and scored three double centuries. The Sussex Cricket Club is erecting a
plaque to the fallen of the Great War.

540499 Second Corporal David William Jennings
Kent
Royal Engineers
20th (TF) Depot Kent Fortress
Died 6 August 1918
Aged 29
Right-handed Bat

'Despite it being one of the finest Kent batting sides anyone could remember, he still made his mark'

David William Jennings was born on 4 June 1889 at Kentish Town, London, the son of David James Jennings of 34 St Martin's Terrace, Marlborough.

He played 35 first-class matches for Kent between August 1909 and August 1914, mostly in the County Championship. He made his debut for Kent on 16 August 1909 against Surrey at the Kennington Oval. He scored 4 in his only innings but did hang on to two catches, Andrew Ducat off the bowling of Frank Woolley for 35, and William Smith, also off Woolley's bowling for 10. Kent won by 9 wickets. He also appeared for Kent against Lancashire, Yorkshire, Gloucestershire, Leicestershire, Somerset, Hampshire, Middlesex, Worcestershire, Nottinghamshire, Lord Londesborough's XI, and Essex. He made his final appearance against Worcestershire on the 20 August 1914 at the St Lawrence Ground, Canterbury. Jennings scored 3 in his only innings and caught Frederick Pearson off the bowling of Colin Blythe for 9. Kent won by an innings and 154 runs.

Jennings also played against the visiting Australians on 29 August 1912 at the St Lawrence Ground, made 6 not out in his first and only innings and caught the Australian middle-order bat Sydney Gregory off the bowling of Frank Woolley for a duck. He scored a total of 1,064 runs during his first-class career, including three centuries and four 50s. His highest score being 106. He also took 1 wicket for 80 of 95 balls and made twenty-eight catches. During a recent sale the candlesticks (Sheffield 1910, 7.5-in high) awarded to Jennings for his contribution to the 1910 Championship win were offered for sale. They were formed as three stumps, three bats and a ball. They failed to sell.

Jennings enlisted with three other Kent players, Kenneth Hutchings killed in action 3 September 1916, Colin Blythe killed in action 8 November 1917 and Charles Eric Hatfeild killed in action 21 September 1918. Jennings served with the 20th (TF) Depot Royal Engineers (Kent Fortress). While in France he was gassed and suffered shellshock.

Returning home there was little that could be done. He died in hospital in Tunbridge Wells on 6 August 1918.

He is commemorated in Marlborough Old Cemetery, grave reference 764. Worth paying your respects if your passing.

Batting and fielding averages

	Mat	Inns	NO	Runs	HS	Ave	100	50	Ct	St
First-class	35	48	4	1064	106	24.18	3	4	28	0

Bowling averages

	Mat	Balls	Runs	Wkts	BBI	Ave	Econ	SR	5w	10
First-class	35	95	80	1	1/13	80.00	5.05	95.0	0	0

Captain John Hugh Gunner
Hampshire
15th Bn The Hampshire Regiment
Died 9 August 1918
Aged 34
Right-handed Bat

'Did his best in everything he did'

John Hugh Gunner was born on 17 May 1884 at Brook House, Bishop's Waltham, Hampshire. The son of Charles Richard Gunner, who played one first class match for Hampshire in 1878, and Kate Gunner of Ridgemede, Bishop's Waltham. He was educated at Marlborough College where he was in the XI and captained the side in 1902; he was also in the Hockey XI. Gunner went up to Trinity College Oxford and, although he represented his college at cricket, he did not represent the University or get his Blue; he did get his half Blue for hockey however. He married Dorothy Gunner of South Warren Road, Bournemouth and, on leaving university, joined his father's firm, Gunner and Sons Solicitors, the fifth generation to do so.

He made 6 first-class appearances for Hampshire between July 1906 and August 1907 his debut being against the touring West Indian side on 2 July 1906 at the County Ground, Southampton. Gunner scored 32 in his only innings, Hampshire going on to win by 6 wickets. He went on to play against Somerset, Northamptonshire, Derbyshire and Leicestershire, all in the County Championship. He played his final first-class game on 12 August 1907 against Leicestershire at the County Ground, Southampton. Gunner scored 2 in his only innings. The match was drawn.

During his first-class career Gunner made 65 runs, his highest score being 32 against the West Indians, he took 4 catches. He also played for the Oxford Authentics and Hampshire Hogs, was a member of the MCC and played hockey for his county.

He joined the Hampshire Yeomanry (Carabineers), in 1904 retiring in 1914. At the beginning of the war he returned to his regiment but later transferred to the 15th Battalion The Hampshire Regiment (2nd Portsmouth). He became second in command of his battalion but was seriously wounded on 9 August 1918 at Kemmel, Belgium, after being bombed in a German trench during a raid. Gunner died of his wounds while being carried back to his own lines.

He is commemorated in the la Clytte Military Cemetery, grave reference VI. C. 7.

Batting and fielding averages

	Mat	Inns	NO	Runs	HS	Ave	100	50	Ct	St
First-class	6	9	1	65	32	8.12	0	0	4	0

Bowling averages

	Mat	Balls	Runs	Wkts	BBI	BBM	Ave	Econ	SR	4w	5w	10
First-class	6	-	-	-	-	-	-	-	-	-	-	-

He lost two brothers during the war. Sub Lieutenant Edward Geoffrey Gunner, Royal Navy, died on 26 November 1914 aged 20 whilst serving on HMS *Bulwark* and is commemorated on the Portsmouth Naval Memorial.

Captain Benjamin George Gunner MC died on 7 October 1915, aged 23, whilst serving with the 1st Battalion Northumberland Fusiliers and is buried in Brandhoek Military Cemetery, grave reference I. G. 13.

Captain Ludovic Heathcoat-Amory
Oxford University
The Royal 1st Devon Yeomanry
Royal Artillery
Died 25 August 1918
Aged 37
Right-handed Bat/Right-arm Fast

'Always a credit to himself and his country'

Ludovic Heathcoat-Amory was born on 11 May 1881 in Westminster, London, the first son of Sir John Heathcoat Heathcoat-Amory, 1st Baronet, a textile industry family from Tiverton and Henrietta Mary, née Unwin. He was educated at Eton College (Miss J. M. Evans' House) and went up to Christchurch College Oxford in 1900.

Heatcoat-Amory played in 6 first-class matches for Oxford University between June 1902 and May 1903, all University Matches. He made his debut for the university on 16 June 1902 against Surrey at University Parks, Oxford. He scored 4 and 26, took 4 wickets for 55 off 22 overs and caught Ernest Nice off the bowling of Ralph Williams for 2. Oxford University won by 2 wickets. He went on to play against the Gentlemen of England and Worcestershire and played his final first-class match against Somerset on 28 May 1903, once again at the University Parks, Oxford. He scored 5 in his only innings and the match was drawn. He made 76 first-class runs during his career, his highest score being 26 against Surrey, took 9 wickets for 165, his best figured being 4 for 55, and took 8 catches. Between 1902 and 1910 he played in the minor counties for Devon. In 1904 he undertook a tour of South Africa, India, Australia and New Zealand with his Oxford friend Edward Frederick Lindley Wood, later the 1st Earl of Halifax.

On 12 July 1911 he married Mary Stuart Bannatyne, daughter of James Fitzgerald Bannatyne. They had three children, Patrick Gerald Heathcoat-Amory, born in 1912 and killed in action at El Alamein 1942, Michael Ludovic Heathcoat-Amory, born in 1914 and killed in an aircraft accident in 1936 and Edgar Fitzgerald Heathcoat-Amory, born in 1917 and killed in Normandy in 1944.

In October 1914 he took a commission in the Royal 1st Devon Yeomanry, becoming attached to the Royal Artillery. He was promoted to lieutenant on 31 December 1914, Captain 29 August 1916 and to staff captain RA on 15 January 1917. He went to France on 14 December 1916, and served in France and Belgium. He was Mentioned in Despatches for bravery in the field but died of wounds at Bayonvillers, France on 25 August 1918.

He is commemorated in the Daours Communal Cemetery extension, grave reference plot VI row B grave 2.

Batting and fielding averages

	Mat	Inns	NO	Runs	HS	Ave	100	50	Ct	St
First-class	6	11	0	76	26	6.90	0	0	8	0

Bowling averages

	Mat	Runs	Wkts	BBI	Ave	5w	10
First-class	6	165	9	4/55	18.33	0	0

Probate was granted to his widow: £42,944.8.7d

Captain Donald Clark Johnston
Oxford University
1/8th Scottish Rifles (Cameronians)
Died 13 September 1918
Aged 23
Unknown

'A gallant gentleman'

Donald Clark Johnson was born on 2 December 1894 in Shanghai, China to John Clark and Frances E. Johnston. He was educated at Malvern School, where he played for the First XI, and Brasenose College Oxford, where he played in the trial match. He later married Ethel M. Johnston of Sellarsbrook, Monmouth.

He played two first-class matches for Oxford University during the 1914 season, making his debut on 15 June 1914 against G. J. V. Weigall's XI at the University Parks Ground, Oxford. Johnson scored 0 in his only innings, took 2 wickets for 227 off 10 overs and caught William Knowles twice, off the bowling of Orme Bristowe, for 29 in the first innings and 9 in the second. Oxford University won by an innings and 44 runs. His second first-class match was against L. G. Robinson's XI on 2 July 1914 at Old Buckenham Hall, Attleborough. He scored 6 in his only innings; the match was drawn.

He served with the 8th Scottish Rifles (Cameronians) during the war and was killed in action on 13 September 1918.

An account of Johnston's death appeared in *The 8th Scottish Rifles* by Colonel J. M. Findlay. In his contribution, Captain W. Whigham Ferguson MC records that on 30 July 1918, when he resumed command of Y Company after the attack on Beugneux, he discovered that all the officers had become casualties. However, before the next attack could take place on 1 August 1918 reinforcements were needed badly. Just two hours before zero hour, Captain Johnston and Lieutenant Hardie (who had never been in action before) arrived in the darkness and Ferguson set out the plan to them:

> I explained the position to them by the failing light of an 'orilux' electric lamp, with the aid of a map and sketches. Four hours later, when the objective was reached, it was my sad experience to find that both these officers were casualties, Captain Johnston having paid the full sacrifice, and Lieut Hardie being wounded.

The battalion's war diary records that the attack commenced at 4.15am and took place in dense fog, shell-smoke and clouds of mustard gas. Despite a stiff fight by the enemy, Hill 158 was taken.

Ferguson was wrong about Johnston being killed on 1 August 1918. He was in fact seriously wounded and died of his wounds on 13 September.

Donald Clark Johnston is commemorated in the St Sever Cemetery, Rouen, grave reference, Officers C. 5. 2.

Batting and fielding averages

	Mat	Inns	NO	Runs	HS	Ave	100	50	Ct	St
First-class	2	2	1	6	6	6.00	0	0	2	0

Bowling averages

	Mat	Balls	Runs	Wkts	BBI	Ave	Econ	SR	5w	10
First-class	2	174	71	2	2/27	35.50	2.44	87.0	0	0

Second Lieutenant Thomas Archibald Truman
Gloucestershire
Army Service Corps
Died 13 September 1918
Aged 37
Right-handed Bat

'Never forgotten always loved'

Thomas Archibald Truman was born on 29 December 1880 at Newton Abbot, Devon, the only son of Thomas and Catherine Truman. A fine athlete, he played rugby three-quarter for both Devon and Gloucestershire, club cricket for Penzance and first-class cricket for Gloucestershire. As a footballer he played for Gloucester City where he made eight appearances as a full back and inside forward between 1903 and 1904 and then again between, 1909 and 1910 scoring a single goal goal. He married Margret Truman, née Lee, of 12 Pendarvis Road, Penzance, Cornwall.

He made 4 first-class appearances for Gloucestershire between June 1910 and May 1913 with his debut being against Warwickshire on 13 June 1910 at the Spa Ground, Gloucestershire. He scored 0 in both innings and took no wickets for 1 run, Gloucestershire losing by 110 runs. He also played against Nottinghamshire and Sussex. He played his final match on 29 May 1913 against Sussex, once again at the Spa ground. On this occasion he scored 0 and 6, took 1 wicket for 10 off 5 overs and caught Herbert Chaplin off the bowling of Alfred Dipper for 26. He made 39 first-class runs with a high score of 12 against Warwickshire, took one wicket for 11 runs and made 5 catches.

In May 1917 he enlisted into the Inns of Court Officers Training Corps as private 1408 Truman and was later gazetted into the Army Service Corps, serving with the 5th Divisional Train, Heavy Transport. While serving in France he was taken ill with pneumonia and peritonitis and removed to 1st Canadian Casualty Clearing Station, near Etrun, France where he died on 13 September 1918.

He is commemorated in the Duisans British Cemetery, Etrun, grave reference VI. H. 6.

His wife never remarried and he is also commemorated on her headstone in Penzance Cemetery.

Batting and fielding averages

	Mat	Inns	NO	Runs	HS	Ave	100	50	Ct	St
First-class	4	8	2	39	12*	6.50	0	0	5	0

Bowling averages

	Mat	Balls	Runs	Wkts	BBI	Ave	Econ	SR	5w	10
First-class	4	36	11	1	1/10	11.00	1.83	36.0	0	0

Captain (Quartermaster) Charles 'Charlie' Young Adamson
Queensland
6th Bn Royal Scots Fusiliers
Died 17 September 1918
Aged 43
Left-handed Bat/Left-arm (unknown style)

'A lover of Australia, but when the bugle sound he rallied to its cause'

Charles Young Adamson was born in Neville's Cross, County Durham on 18 April 1875. The son of John Adamson of Little Grant, Wisconsin, he was educated at Durham School where, between 1891 and 1893, he was in the First XI. During this time, and later, he played for the Gentlemen of Durham, W. F. Whitwell's, Durham County (1895–96) and Durham Amateurs (1911). Between 1894 and 1914 he also represented Durham Minor Counties. On leaving school he became a hotel proprietor.

He continued to play cricket representing Durham Club and Durham City. An all-round sportsman, he played rugby for the Barbarians, Bristol and the British Isles, winning 4 caps against Australia in 1899. He scored 2 tries and 4 conversions from half back and was ever present in the series, which the Lions won 3–1. He was said to be 'The greatest half-back never selected for England'.

After the 1899 rugby tour Adamson decided to remain in Australia, settling in Brisbane. Here he played for the Valley District Cricket Club and made his one first-class match for Queensland against New South Wales on 25 November 1899 at the Brisbane Cricket Ground, Woolloongabba, Brisbane. He scored 0 and 10 and caught Frank Iredale off the bowling of William McGlinchey for 10; New South Wales won by an innings and 85 runs.

During the Second Boer War he served with the 4th (Queensland Imperial Bushmen) Contingent and went with them on 18 May 1900 to South Africa, was promoted to corporal on 1 June 1900 and quarter-master sergeant on 6 April 1901. He returned from South Africa on 5 August 1901.

During the First World War he was commissioned as a temporary quartermaster, with the honorary rank of lieutenant (*London Gazette*, 20 January 1915) into the 23rd Battalion (4th Tyneside Scottish) Northumberland Fusiliers. He transferred as a captain to the 6th Battalion, Royal Scots Fusiliers. Adamson was killed in action on 17 September 1918, during the Second Battle of Doiran, during an attack by his battalion on the Bulgarian trenches called the Tongue, the Knot and the Tassel, during which 6th Royal Scots Fusiliers suffered 50 per cent casualties.

He is commemorated in the Karasouli Military Cemetery, Salonika, grave reference No F. 1293

Batting and fielding averages

	Mat	Inns	NO	Runs	HS	Ave	100	50	Ct	St
First-class	1	2	0	10	10	5.00	0	0	1	0

Bowling averages

	Mat	Balls	Runs	Wkts	BBI	BBM	Ave	Econ	SR	4w	5w	10
First-class	1	72	67	0	-	-	-	5.58	-	0	0	0

Lieutenant Oswald Massey Samson
Oxford University/Somerset
143 Siege Battery Royal Garrison Artillery
Died 17 September 1918
Aged 37
Left-handed bat/Slow left-hand orthodox

'Mr Beaton said he deserved the VC for the way in which he behaved'

Oswald Massey Samson was born on 8 August 1881 in Taunton, Somerset, the son of C H Samson FRIBA, third and youngest son of Charles Henry Samson FRIBA of The Laurels, Taunton, and of Hillmorton Road, Rugby. He was a scholar of Cheltenham College from 1895 to 1899 and represented the First XI. On leaving school Samson went up to Hartford College Oxford as a mathematical scholar and took a double first in mathematics as well as winning the University Junior Mathematical Exhibition. In 1903 he won his Blue for cricket.

He made 49 first-class appearances between June 1900 and August 1913, 4 for Oxford University and the remainder for Somerset in the County Championship. He made his debut first-class match, when he was only 18 years old, on 14 June 1900 for Somerset against Oxford University; he scored 23 in his only innings. The match was drawn. His final first-class match came on 11 August 1913 against Sussex when he scored 16 and 0, Sussex winning by 5 runs. During his first-class career Sampson made 1,464 runs, his highest score being 105, took 5 wickets for 88 runs and made 32 catches.

Samson was appointed a master at Rugby School in September 1903 and taught the Army Class. He joined an Officer Cadet Battalion in 1916 and received his commission in the Royal Garrison Artillery in April 1917, going out to France the following autumn. He was promoted to lieutenant in June 1917.

On the morning of 17 September 1918 he was on duty at the battery about 2.00am when the enemy put down a heavy concentration of gas and high explosive. One of these shells scored a direct hit on his battery, wounding him in both legs. He was removed to the field aid post under heavy fire, but died of his wounds and gas burns shortly after reaching the dressing station.

His major later wrote:

> Mr Beaton said he deserved the VC for the way in which he behaved, smiling and talking though severely wounded. His last words were: 'I am sorry to have been so much trouble; I shall never forget what you have done for me.' I can hardly tell you how deeply the whole Battery feel your son's loss. He was a most efficient and capable Officer, and took everything in a thoroughly Sportsman like way.

He was initially buried near Driencourt. Subsequently his remains were removed and he is now commemorated in the Peronne Communal Cemetery Extension, grave reference IV. D. 9.

A Memorial Service for him was held in Rugby School Chapel on 26 September 1918. On 16 October 1918 a notice regarding his death appeared in the *Meteor* magazine (no. 628):

As a Mathematical Master of the Army Class, he was a vigourous and inspiring teacher, resourceful in ideas for breaking the monotony of a lesson, games and singing. He brought to the Town successes which often surprised itself. In amateur theatricals, and in simple games at his own house, he shared his capacity for enjoyment with his boys, and won their affection and regard. As Coach of the Young Guard, he was zealous and patient, without any inclination to suppress individuality, for he admired originality and resource in games more than conventional form. In all capacities as a teacher, he seemed able to give his pupils confidence in their own abilities by his sympathy, simplicity and unfailing good humor. He was always young and kept his friends young. With a boy's outlook on life, he had a man's judgement, which was influenced by no prejudices and no catchwords. Only those who knew him intimately can know to the full his cheerful disposition, his modesty, his unselfishness and his loyalty to his home and friends. He was buoyant and gay at all times; never put his ideas or his likings in the first place; never without good cause and unfeigned regret, refused to grant a favor asked of him.

Batting and fielding averages

	Mat	Inns	NO	Runs	HS	Ave	100	Ct	St
First-class	49	85	5	1464	105	18.30	1	32	0

Bowling averages

	Mat	Balls	Runs	Wkts	BBI	Ave	Econ	SR	5w	10
First-class	49	102	88	5	2/4	17.60	5.17	20.4	0	0

Lieutenant Archibald Newcombe Difford
Western Province/Transvaal
1st Cape Corps, South African Forces
Died 20 September 1918
Aged 35
Right-handed bat

'Not a man to ever back down'

Archibald Newcombe Difford was born on 9 April 1883 in Somerset, although some records say Cape Town, South Africa. He was the second child of four born to Abraham Difford. He married Katrina (Kate) Wilhelmina van Lier Kuys on 7 June 1913 in Cape Town, South Africa and they had two children, Mary and John.

Difford played 16 first-class matches between December 1904 and December 1911, mostly for Western Province and the Transvaal. He made his debut first-class match for the Western Province on 26 December 1904 in the Currie Cup against Eastern Province at Newlands, Cape Town. He scored 0 and 2 and caught Robert Gleeson off the bowling of Harold Carolin for 6. Western Province won by 6 wickets. He also played against the MCC, Orange Free State, Eastern Province, Transvaal, Griqualand West, Natal, Border and the Rest against Wanderers. His final match took place on 28 December 1911 for the Transvaal against The Rest, at Old Wanderers, Johannesburg. He scored 38 and 53. Transvaal won by 5 wickets. Difford made 824 first-class runs, including one century and 6 fifties, his highest score being 103 against Griqualand West. He also took 2 wickets for 32 and made 8 catches.

He was commissioned into A Company 1st Cape Corps on 18 January 1917 and was killed in action at Khan Jibeit, Palestine, on 20 September 1918. He is commemorated in the Jerusalem War Cemetery, grave reference L. 18.

Batting and fielding averages

	Mat	Inns	NO	Runs	HS	Ave	100	50	Ct	St
First-class	16	28	0	824	103	29.42	1	6	8	0

Bowling averages

	Mat	Balls	Runs	Wkts	BBI	Ave	Econ	SR	5w	10
First-class	16	54	32	2	1/13	16.00	3.55	27.0	0	0

Captain Charles Eric Hatfeild MC
Kent/Oxford University/MCC
10th Bn (Royal East Kent and Royal West Kent Yeomanry)
10 Bn The Buffs (East Kent Regiment)
Died 21 September 1918
Aged 31
Left-handed bat/Slow left-arm orthodox

'His gallantry was exceptional'

Charles Eric Hatfeild was born on 11 March 1887 at Hartsdown, Margate, Kent. The son of Captain C. T. Hatfeild, 1st King's Dragoon Guards, and Mrs M. H. S. Hatfeild of Hartsdown, Margate, he was educated at Wellington House School, Westgate-on-Sea and Eton, where he was in the XI between 1903 and 1906. In 1903, during the match against Harrow, he took 12 wickets for 91 runs and played a large part in Eton's single-innings victory against their old rival, Eton's first victory since 1893. He went up to New College Oxford, winning his Blue in 1908 and playing for the university between May 1907 and July 1909. Due largely to his batting, Oxford won the match against Cambridge in 1908 by 2 wickets, Hatfeild scoring 25 and 35.

He made 65 first-class appearances mainly for Oxford University, Kent and the MCC between May 1907 and July 1914. He made his debut against Worcestershire on 23 May 1907 at the University Parks, Oxford. He scored 1 and 4 and caught John Jackson off the bowling of John Lowe for 0 and Norman Jolly off the bowling of Humphrey Gilbert for 8.

Oxford won by 86 runs. He was selected for the MCC tour of Argentina in 1912. Hatfeild played in 3 of the 9 matches against Argentina at the Harlington Club Ground, Buenos Aires, Argentina won by 4 wickets, Beunos Aires Cricket Club, Buenos Aires, the MCC won by 210 runs and finally the Lomas Athletic Ground, Buenos Aires, the MCC won by 2 wickets. Hatfield played his final first class game for Kent against Essex on 13 July 1914 at the Nevill Ground, Tunbridge Wells. He made 18 in his one innings and took 1 wicket for 46 off 12 overs. Kent won by an innings and 117 runs. During his 65 first-class appearances Hatfield made 1,498 runs, his highest score being 74. He also took 64 wickets for 1,474 runs, his best figures being 5 for 48, and took 45 catches. He also represented the Free Foresters and G. J. V. Weigall's XI.

He attended Wye South East Agricultural College in 1910 and 1911 with a view to going into farming. He was commissioned into the 10th Royal East Kent Yeomanry in 1912 later transferring into the 10Bn East Kent Regiment (The Buffs). He served with them in Gallipoli, Egypt, Palestine and France, was Mentioned in Despatches and awarded the Military Cross for bravery in the field in 1918. His citation reads:

> For conspicuous gallantry in leading his company during the advance at Templeux-le-Guerard towards the Hindenburg Line on 18 September 1918. In spite of the fire of hostile machine guns, which repeatedly held up the advance, he got his men forward, exposing himself fearlessly. It was largely due to this officer's splendid example that the advance during the day was carried out so rapidly.

On 21 September 1918 the 10th Buffs began an advance on the Zogda trench, which was about 1,200 yards in front of their position and uphill towards Quennenmont Farm. At 5.40am the companies formed up. C and D companies formed the front line with A Company in support. The ground was very open with little cover and the Germans in front of them were well dug-in with several machine-gun positions protected by wire. The companies advanced behind a barrage which was successful enough to get them among the thick belts of wire near Zoo Trench. Here the infantry got caught up while the barrage went on. The Germans emerging from their dug-outs caught the 10th Buffs in the open and laid down an intense fire. C and D Companies could do nothing but try to find cover in shell holes. A Company was then driven back by a counter-attack. When darkness fell, the remaining Buffs managed to get back, having lost Captain Hatfield MC, Second Lieutenant Oxley and twelve men killed. Two officers and twenty-eight other ranks wounded, one officer twenty men missing.

He is commemorated in the Hargicourt Communal Cemetery Extension, grave reference C.11.

Batting and fielding averages

	Mat	Inns	NO	Runs	HS	Ave	100	Ct	St
First-class	65	101	8	1498	74	16.10	0	45	0

Bowling averages

	Mat	Runs	Wkts	BBI	Ave	5w	10
First-class	65	1475	64	5/48	23.04	2	0

His father died in 1910 and his mother went on to become Margate's first lady Mayor in 1926. She employed her dead son's batman as her chauffeur.

205113 Sergeant Charles Barnett Fleming
Derbyshire
12th Bn Tank Corps
Died 22 September 1918
Aged 31
Right-handed Bat

'A lover of all things mechanical'

Charles Barnett Fleming was born on 28 February 1887 in Derby, the fifth of nine children of Frederick Fleming a foreman pattern maker and Hannah Fleming. The family resided at 72 Bedford Street, Derby.

He made one first-class appearance for Derby against Essex on 22 August 1907 at the County Ground, Derby, scoring 2 and 3 and Essex winning by 222 runs.

Fleming served with the 12th Battalion Tank Corps and was killed in action on 22 September 1918 at Grevillers, France. He is commemorated in the Grevillers British Cemetery, grave reference XIII. D. 23.

Batting and fielding averages

	Mat	Inns	NO	Runs	HS	Ave	100	50	Ct	St
First-class	1	2	0	5	3	2.50	0	0	0	0

Bowling averages

	Mat	Balls	Runs	Wkts	BBI	BBM	Ave	Econ	SR	4w	5w	10
First-class	1	-	-	-	-	-	-	-	-	-	-	-

Lieutenant Colonel John Francis Sartorius Winnington DSO
Worcestershire
1st Bn The Worcestershire Regiment, commanding 1/4th Bn
The Northamptonshire Regiment
Died 22 September 1918
Aged 42
Right-handed Bat

'quite one in a hundred, who had done a great deal for the Northamptons.
I am very sorry indeed that he is gone'

John Francis Sartorius Winnington was born on 17 September 1876 at Charlton Kings, Gloucestershire. The son of Captain John Taylor Winnington and Rose Winnington, née Sartorius, he was commissioned as a second lieutenant into a Militia battalion of the Worcestershire Regiment on 30 January 1895, later transferring into the Regular Army. He served with the regiment during the Second Boer War in 1899–1900 and was promoted to captain in 1901.

He made one first-class appearance playing for Worcestershire against Oxford University at the University Parks on 11 June 1908. He scored 0 and 20 in Worcestershire's crushing victory by 332 runs.

On 20 July 1910 he married Joyce Mary Marriage they had two children, Susanne (1913) and Patricia Rose (1917).

He was promoted to major and served with the 1st Battalion Worcestershire Regiment during the war. He took part in the battle of Neuve Chapelle after which he was promoted to lieutenant colonel, and Mentioned in Despatches for his actions during the battle (*London Gazette*, 22 June 1915). He was also awarded the Distinguished Service Order. His citation read:

> Major John Francis Sartorius Winnington, 1st Battalion, The Worcestershire Regiment. For conspicuous gallantry and ability from 10th to 12th March, 1915, at Neuve Chapelle, when he commanded the two leading Companies in several attacks, and subsequently commanded the Battalion. Showed great foresight in correctly anticipating the desires of the Brigade Commander in regard to the advance of other Troops, at a time when Orders could not be conveyed to them. (*London Gazette* 28 April 1915)

He was invalided after the Battle of Neuve Chapelle from the effects of the strain and exposure of the three days and nights of fighting. On recovery he was posted to Gallipoli where he was once again Mentioned in Despatches for his gallant actions (*London Gazette*,

12 July 1916). Due to the intense fighting at Gallipoli, his health once again broke down and he was deemed physically unfit for further duty and returned home. It was the last time he was to serve with the Worcestershire Regiment.

He became Assistant Inspector of Recruiting in 1917 before being posted to the 1/4th Battalion Northamptonshire Regiment and being sent to Palestine with them. He died of wounds on 22 September 1918 near Kefar Kassin, Ramle, Palestine.

The Worcestershire Regiment in the Great War by Captain H. FitzM. Stacke explains his death a little more clearly:

> THE COLONEL KILLED.
> I am sorry to say Lieut Anthony, who was scout officer, was killed; whilst a stray shell, after everything was practically over, burst at Colonel Winnington's feet and injured him terribly. He lived for a couple of days but then died. He is a very great loss, as he was a first-class CO, quite one in a hundred, who had done a great deal for the Northamptons. I am very sorry indeed that he is gone.

He was Mentioned in Despatches once again for his actions with the Northamptonshire Regiment (*London Gazette*, 5 June 1919)

He is commemorated in the Ramleh War Cemetery, grave reference C. 31 and on a window in the cloisters of Worcester Cathedral.

Batting and fielding averages

	Mat	Inns	NO	Runs	HS	Ave	100	50	Ct	St
First-class	1	2	0	20	20	10.00	0	0	0	0

Bowling averages

	Mat	Balls	Runs	Wkts	BBI	BBM	Ave	Econ	SR	4w	5w	10
First-class	1	-	-	-	-	-	-	-	-	-	-	-

Captain William St Clair Grant MC
Gloucestershire
5th Bn The Queen's Own Cameron Highlanders
Died 26 September 1918
Aged 24
Right-handed bat/Medium Pace

'I never knew anyone so full of life'

William St Clair Grant was born on 8 September 1894 in Bhagalpur, Bengal, India. He was the son of William St Clair Grant, a Scottish rugby international half-back who won two caps for Scotland, both against England, in 1873 and 1874 and who died in 1896 in India. He is often confused with his son who didn't play international rugby. Grant was educated at Clifton College, Bristol, where he was in the XI and Pembroke College Cambridge, but failed to get his Blue.

He played 4 first-class matches for Gloucestershire in 1914. He made his debut against Sussex on 13 July 1914 at the Central Recreation Ground, Hastings. He scored 3 and 16, Sussex winning by 364 runs. Grant went on to play against Kent, Nottinghamshire and Yorkshire, he made his final first-class match against Yorkshire on 30 July 1914 at St George Road, Harrogate. He scored 9 and 6 and Yorkshire won by an innings and 118 runs. Of his four- first-class matches he was on the losing side for three of them, the fourth against Nottinghamshire at Trent Bridge was drawn. He made 55 first-class runs his highest score being 16 against Sussex. He made one catch.

William St Clair Grant was gazetted second lieutenant from the cadet corps into the 3rd Battalion Gloucestershire Regiment on 18 September 1914 and promoted to lieutenant on 27 September 1915, becoming a temporary captain on 28 October 1915. At some point in his career he transferred to the 5th Battalion Cameron Highlanders. He was battalion adjutant from April to July 1917, September to October 1917 and March to July 1918. In May 1918 he was awarded the Military Cross for bravery, his citation reading:

William St Clair Grant, Cam. Hldrs.
For conspicuous gallantry and devotion to duty. On two occasions he made a reconnaissance under heavy artillery barrage, bringing back a full account of the situation. He went round the line while fighting was in progress encouraging the men. The example set by him was most inspiring to all ranks in the front line.

He was further decorated in July 1918 with the Belgian Croix de Guerre.

Seriously wounded during a bombardment, Grant died in a field hospital near Passchendaele, Belgium on 26 September 1918. He is commemorated in the Gwalia Cemetery, grave reference II. G. 14.

Batting and fielding averages

	Mat	Inns	NO	Runs	HS	Ave	100	50	Ct	St
First-class	4	7	0	55	16	7.85	0	0	1	0

Bowling averages

	Mat	Balls	Runs	Wkts	BBI	BBM	Ave	Econ	SR	4w	5w	10
First-class	4	24	22	0	-	-	-	5.50	-	0	0	0

Second Lieutenant Frederick Henri Abraham
British Guiana
16th Bn The Lancashire Fusiliers
Died 2 October 1918
Aged 32
Right-handed Bat/Right-arm Medium

'exceedingly popular with both the men and officers of this regiment, and much respected in account of his character & gallantry'

Frederick Henri Abraham was born on 5 February 1888 at Soesdkke, East Bank, Demerara, British Guiana, the only son of five children. His father was Frederick Abraham, who also played first-class cricket for British Guiana, and his mother was Catherine Marie Antoinette Abraham, née July, of Georgetown, British Guiana. He was educated at Queen's College.

Abraham played ten first-class matches for British Guiana between March 1904 and January 1912. His debut was against Lord Brackley's XI at Bourda, Georgetown on 6 March 1905 when he scored 9 and zero, took one wicket for 44 runs and caught Cyril Foley off the bowling of Joseph Woods for 16. Lord Brackley's XI won by 42 runs. He went on to play against Barbados, Trinidad, W. C. Shepherd's XI and the MCC and his final first-class match was on 12 January 1912 against Trinidad at the Kensington Oval, Bridgetown in the Inter-Colonial Tournament. He scored 1 and 14 and took four wickets for 30 runs off fourteen overs. He also played for the Georgetown Cricket Club and managed his best ever bowling record against W. C. Shepherd's XI on 19 October 1909 when he took nine wickets for 82 runs. During his first-class career he made 362 runs, his best score being 64 against Barbados, took twenty-four wickets for 585, runs his best figures being four for 30, and made nine catches.

He served with the Lancashire Fusiliers during the war, being commissioned as a second lieutenant into the 16th Battalion. He was killed in action on 2 October 1918 at Joncourt, France. A letter from his commanding officer, Lieutenant Colonel Compton-Smith, gives more details regarding Abraham's death:

Dear Monsieur Rénier
Your nephew 2nd Lieut Fred Abraham was killed on October 2nd, just South of JONCOURT, RAMICOURT road about 9.15 am.

The Battalion was attacking RAMICOURT, and your nephew was in command of the left front company (D). This company was checked by machine-gun fire from the direction of WAINCOURT, and your nephew very gallantly endeavoured to bring a

Lewis gun into position to fire on the hostile machine gun. He was shot in the head while so doing, and passed away at once without pain.

He is buried just EAST of a sunken road, about 1000 meters EAST of JONCOURT. The cemetery where he lies contains about 130 graves of those who fell on the same day. The cemetery is marked by a cross on a mound, but the actual grave is only marked by a stick with a time disc bearing number 453. This number is, however, registered, and a cross with his name will be put up in due course by the British Graves Registration Commissioners.

I enclose a map on which I have marked by means of arrows the position of his grave, the place where he fell, & the position (approximately) of the machine gun which killed him. I hope this will enable you to identify the localities.

Your nephew was exceedingly popular with both the men & officers of this regiment, and much respected in account of his character & gallantry.

If there is any further assistance that I can give you in any way, I shall be most happy to do so, if you will let me know.

Yours sincerely,
Gd Compton- Smith, Lt Col.
16th Lancashire Fusiliers

He is commemorated in the Joncourt East British Cemetery, grave reference C. 16.

Batting and fielding averages

	Mat	Inns	NO	Runs	HS	Ave	100	50	Ct	St
First-class	10	18	0	362	64	20.11	0	2	9	0

Bowling averages

	Mat	Balls	Runs	Wkts	BBI	Ave	Econ	SR	5w	10
First-class	10	1148	585	24	4/30	24.37	3.05	47.8	0	0

Lieutenant Alfred Hartley
Lancashire
263 Siege Battery Royal Garrison Artillery
Died 9 October 1918
Aged 39
Right-handed Bat

'Thank God, we know he batted well in the last game of all

Alfred Hartley was born on 11 April 1879 in New Orleans, Louisiana, United States of America, the son of an English father, George, a cotton merchant, (who also played three first-class cricket matches for Lancashire) and an American mother, Alice. The census returns from 1891 to 1911 record the family living firstly in Sale (on Beaufort Road) and then in Timperley Lodge, Timperley.

Alfred's father died in 1909 and he took over the family business. He moved to London and married M. E. Hartley of 73 Holland Park, London. An outstanding sportsman, he was given three trials in for Lancashire in 1907, going on to play for the Second XI. He made 116 first-class appearances between August 1907 and May 1914, mostly for Lancashire in the County Championship. His debut was on 15 August 1907 against Middlesex at Old Trafford, Manchester in the County Championship. Hartley scored 21 and 3 but Middlesex won by an innings and 28 runs.

During his first-class career he amassed 5,049 runs, including six centuries and thirty-nine half centuries, with a high score of 234 against Somerset in 1910. He also took one wicket for 61. In 1911 he was *Wisden's* cricketer of the year. On learning of this a paper wrote of him:

> Hartley is not a batsman to draw the crowd, his methods being the reverse of striking to the eye. His style is good and his bat straight, but he does nothing to astonish those who are looking on ... He is understood to be ambitious of further distinction in the cricket field, but whether he will ever rise to Test matches remains to be seen.

A poor testimonial indeed for the cricketer of the year.

He played his final first-class match on 28 May 1914, once again in the County Championship against Essex at Old Trafford. Hartley scored 21 and 7, Essex winning by 156 runs. He also played for Lancashire's Second XI and was selected to play for the Gentlemen against the Players twice, once at Lord's and once at The Oval.

He served with 263 Siege Battery Royal Garrison Artillery during the war, firstly within the ranks before taking a commission and reaching the rank of lieutenant shortly before his battery reached France in 1918.

Alfred died of wounds received in action on 9 October 1918 at Maissemy, France and is commemorated in Vandencourt Cemetery, Maissemy, Aisne, France, grave reference III. C. 26 and on a memorial tablet in the pavilion at Old Trafford.

Batting and fielding averages

	Mat	Inns	NO	Runs	HS	Ave	100	Ct	St
First-class	116	191	9	5049	234	27.74	6	39	0

Bowling averages

	Mat	Balls	Runs	Wkts	BBI	Ave	Econ	SR	5w	10
First-class	116	75	61	1	1/39	61.00	4.88	75.0	0	0

His brother Charles Robert Hartley also played for Lancashire on over 100 occasions.

53906 Private Ernest Elgood Crawshaw
Canterbury
1st Bn The Canterbury Regiment, New Zealand
Expeditionary Force
Died 9 October 1918
Aged 29
Right-handed Bat

'Always played the game'

Ernest Elgood Crawshaw was born on 23 June 1889 in Christchurch, Canterbury, New Zealand. The son of Thomas and Louisa Crawshaw, of Christchurch, he was educated at the High School, Christchurch, where he represented the XI. On leaving school he became a public accountant and married Mrs Elsie Lorriane Gunn of 28 Papanui Road, Christchurch in 1915.

He played in eight first-class matches for Canterbury between December 1907 and April 1914. His debut was against Auckland on 14 December 1907 at the Hagley Oval, Christchurch; he made 3 and zero and took two wickets for 74 off 19.4 overs. Auckland

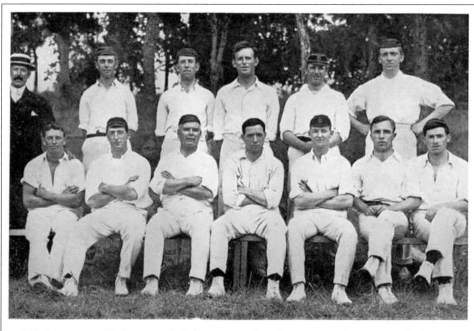

J. N. Fowke.   H. B. Lusk.   E. R. Caygill.   J. H. Bennett.   A. Sims.   T. Carlton.
D. M. Sandman.   W. Carlton.   C. Boxshall.   D. Reese.   W. R. Patrick.   E. E. Crawshaw.   A. Norman.
(*Captain*)

won by an innings and 135 runs. He went on to play against Otago (three times), Wellington (three times) and Auckland (twice). His final first-class match was on 10 April 1914 for D. Reese's Canterbury XI against Wellington at the Basin Reserve, Wellington. He scored 12 and 5 and took one wicket for 27 off five overs; Wellington won by 117 runs. Crawshaw scored a total of 73 runs, with his highest score being 26 Auckland, took thirteen wickets for 382, his best figures being two for 20, and eleven catches.

During the war he enlisted in the ranks of the 1st Battalion Canterbury Regiment and travelled as part of D Company 36th Reinforcements to France, sailing from Wellington on the *Balmoral Castle* on 2 May 1918. He was killed in action on 9 October 1918 at le Cateau, France. He is commemorated at the Naves Communal Cemetery Extension, Nord, France, grave reference IV. E. 10.

Batting and fielding averages

	Mat	Inns	NO	Runs	HS	Ave	100	50	Ct	St
First-class	8	16	3	73	26	5.61	0	0	11	0

Bowling averages

	Mat	Runs	Wkts	BBI	Ave	5w	10
First-class	8	382	13	2/20	29.38	0	0

Lieutenant Colonel William Oliver Matless Mosse
Europeans (India)
Royal Munster Fusiliers
Died 10 October 1918
Aged 58
Not Known

'After a lifetime of service, died a few weeks short of the end'

William Oliver Matless Mosse was born on 3 March 1860 in Kingston, Jamaica to Charles Benjamin Mosse (1830–1912) and Olivia Spry Ramos (1838–1860). He was the second son of this marriage and it would appear his mother died either at or shortly after his birth. Charles Benjamin Mosse remarried and went on to have four more children and to become The Honourable Charles Benjamin Mosse CB CMG, Surgeon General of Jamaica, who travelled extensively.

Originally commissioned into the West Cork Artillery in March 1879 as a second lieutenant Mosse later joined the Indian Army, serving with the 114th Mahrattas. He became a lieutenant in October 1891, a major in 1900 and lieutenant colonel in 1904. He also found time to marry Ellen Eliza Grimsdale on 15 August 1890 at St Margaret's, Uxbridge. They had three children, Charles, Kathleen, and Doris, two of whom, and probably all three, were born in India. After Mosse retired from the Army the family returned to England, settling in Hurstpierpoint in Sussex.

He played in one first-class match for the Europeans against Hindus in the final of the Bombay Triangular Tournament played at the Gymkhana Ground, Bombay on 21 September 1908. He scored 27 and zero and took one wicket for 19, the Europeans winning by 119 runs.

Between 15 August 1917 and his death on 10 October 1918, he served with the 1st Garrison Battalion Royal Munster Fusiliers. His son, Lieutenant Charles Oliver Robins Mosse (1891–1965), wrote an interesting account, now held in the Imperial War Museum, about the reaction of people in London the day war was declared:

> Things getting more exciting daily. Peter came back with a complete sequence of 'special' editions of *The Star, Evening News*, etc. and the house is littered with them. The town is all excited about German and French mobilization and the war between Russia and Austria. The general feeling is violently anti-German but around Trafalgar Square there were several people dishing out printed pamphlets headed 'Reasons why England must not go to war'.
>
> In the evening [we] went to a play called 'Eliza comes to stay' at a theatre on the Strand. The noise of newsboys and shouts of the crowd made it impossible to fix one's attention on the play. At about 11pm terrific bursts of cheering could be heard from the street outside, echoing and resounding from Trafalgar Square to Westminster and Buckingham Palace. We left the theatre as did everybody I think and walked down to Buckingham Palace through considerable crowds. At the palace there was a crowd of several thousand collected in the hopes of hearing the King speak from the balcony; the cheering was such as I have never heard before nor expect to hear again. It was known that war had been declared against Germany.
>
> We returned home at about 12.30; our party was split up in the crowds and we had no small difficulty in getting back; the shouting continued in the streets and the crowds did not disperse till early morning. One of the most memorable nights in history.
>
> (Diary of Lieutenant Charles Mosse, 120th Rajputana Infantry, 3–4 August 1914)

Colonel Mosse died together with his wife on 10 October 1918 when the RMS *Leinster*, was sunk by a German U-boat *UB-123* just outside Dublin Bay. Of the seventy-seven crew and 694 passengers, 501 died. Many were military personnel, including many nurses. Proportionately, this was the worst loss of life ever in British waters.

Mosse's body, together with that of his wife, was among those recovered and he is commemorated in Grangegorman Military Cemetery, Dublin, grave reference CE, Officers, 20.

Batting and fielding averages

	Mat	Inns	NO	Runs	HS	Ave	100	50	Ct	St
First-class	1	2	0	27	27	13.50	0	0	1	0

Bowling averages

	Mat	Runs	Wkts	BBI	Ave	5w	10
First-class	1	31	1	1/19	31.00	0	0

Lieutenant Gordon Charles White
South Africa/Transvaal
1st Cape Corps, South African Infantry
Died 17 October 1918
Aged 36
Right-handed Bat/Legbreak

'I've never seen a loss more sadly mourned'

Gordon Charles White was born on 5 February 1882 at Port St John's, Cape Province, South Africa. He married Iris Maisie Ann Bateman and they had two children, Beverley and Jane.

White was one of South Africa's most celebrated cricketers and played his domestic cricket for the Transvaal. He appeared in seventeen tests, making ninety-seven first-class matches in all. During a distinguished career he scored 872 test runs, including two centuries and four fifties, with a high score of 147 against England on 10 March 1906. He also made 3,740 first-class runs, including four centuries and seventeen fifties, his highest score being 162, and took nine test wickets for 301 runs and fifteen first-class wickets for 310. White was a member of the South African teams that toured England in 1904, when he scored 937 first-class runs including 115 against Nottinghamshire, although didn't play in a Test. He toured England with the South Africans again in 1907, this time playing in three Tests although he only made 15 runs. However, he did manage to score 162 against Gloucestershire at Bristol. He also played in five Tests during the 1912 Triangular Tournament in England, a competition played between Australia, England and South Africa, the only Test-playing nations at the time.

His first-class debut was for Transvaal against Griqualand on 6 April 1903 in the Currie Cup, where he scored 2 in his only innings at St George's Park, Port Elizabeth; Transvaal won by 216 runs. Although not the best of starts, he made up for this during his second first-class match against Eastern Province played on 8 April 1903, once again at St George's Park and once again in the Currie Cup, scoring 54 not out. Transvaal won by ten wickets.

White's Test debut for South Africa was against England on 2 January 1906 at Old Wanderers, Johannesburg and he made 8 and 81 and took two wickets for 13, South Africa winning by one wicket. He played his final Test on 12 August 1912, once again against England, this time at the Kennington Oval and made 4 and 1. England won by ten wickets. He made fourteen appearances against England and three against Australia and turned out for the Reef against the MCC.

He received a commission into the 1st Cape Corps, South African Infantry during the First World War, serving with another celebrated South African cricketer, Archibald Newcombe Difford who was killed in action on 20 September 1918. Although later promoted to captain, he refused to accept the promotion considering that other and better men had been passed over and retained the rank of lieutenant. He served at Morogoro during the South African Campaign where he was wounded, returning to South Africa on board HM Hospital Ship *Oxfordshire* in July 1917. Posted to Egypt in March 1918, he joined 160 Brigade, took part in the Battle of Megiddo and was wounded during a bayonet charge at Khan Jibeit close to Jerusalem on 20 September 1918. He was evacuated to 47th Stationary Hospital in Gaza, Palestine where he died on 17 October 1918. The regimental diary mentioned his loss:

> On October 17th news was received of the death that day from wounds in hospital at Gaza of Lieutenant Gordon White. He was expected to recover, but suddenly collapsed. He was a most popular officer and his demise was a very great grief to all ranks.

He is commemorated in the Gaza War Cemetery, grave reference XXVII. D. I.

Batting and fielding averages

	Mat	Inns	NO	Runs	HS	Ave	100	50	6s	Ct	St
Tests	17	31	2	872	147	30.06	2	4	4	10	0
First-class	97	152	17	3740	162*	27.70	4	17		46	0

Bowling averages

	Mat	Inns	Balls	Runs	Wkts	BBI	BBM	Ave	Econ	SR	4w	5w	10
Tests	17	14	498	301	9	4/47	4/47	33.44	3.62	55.3	1	0	0
First-class	97		5323	3109	155	7/33		20.05	3.50	34.3		8	2

Lieutenant George William Edendale Whitehead
Kent
Royal Field Artillery/Royal Flying Corps
Died 17 October 1918
Aged 23
Right-handed Bat/Legbreak Googly

'George Whitehead was a perfect flower of the public schools'

George William Edendale Whitehead was born on 27 August 1895 in Bromley, Kent. The son of Sir George Hugh Whitehead, 2nd Baronet, and Gertrude Grace Whitehead, née Ashcroft, of Wilmington Hall, Dartford, Kent, and The Shrubbery, Oxford, he was educated at Clifton College, Bristol, where he played in the First XI for four years, being captain in both 1913 and 1914. Following the tradition of big-hitting cricketers from Clifton, he made a remarkable 259 not out against Liverpool in 1912 and played three times at Lord's for Public Schools against the MCC. In 1914 he was given a trial for Kent. While at school he was described as being 'the perfect flower of the public schools'. He was 'as happy with a good book as when he was scoring centuries' and so modest that 'strangers sometimes failed to realise his worth'.

George Whitehead made two first-class appearances for Kent in 1914, the first on the 24 August 1914, in the County Championship, against Warwickshire at the Bat and Ball Ground, Gravesend. He scored 5 and 1, and caught Ernest Field twice, once off the bowling of Alfred Freeman for 1, and Frank Woolley for 24. Kent won by 99 runs. His second appearance was on 27 August 1914, once again in the County Championship against Middlesex at Lord's. Whitehead scored 4 and 2, and caught Elias Hendren off the bowling of Colin Blythe, Middlesex winning by 298 runs.

Although he was due to attend Trinity College Oxford, he chose instead to continue his education at the Royal Military Academy Woolwich and on 28 July 1915 was commissioned in the Royal Artillery, and sent to the front five weeks later on 3 September 1915. He took part in the Battle of Loos, writing home and describing his experiences:

Dear Father and Mother

I'm perfectly all right and safe as they don't know our position. We are just off a main road, so we got a few stray shells aimed at it last night, but no one was hurt. A few stray bullets came over too: they must have been very wild shots as we are a long way out of effective rifle range.

I hear this morning that we are to fire no more and that the DAC have no more ammunition for us. I don't know what can be up, if they have made a mess of things on the way or what.

There isn't a strike on, is there? If only we had all the ammunition I'm certain we'd go right on. Perhaps it will turn up this afternoon, then we shall be all right. I don't think many fellows would strike if they saw the Infantry coming back from the trenches after an attack. I've only passed a few wounded and none of the gassed, as

I'm usually with the guns or the OP but even those who come out don't look fit for much. Poor devils! Fancy knowing twelve hours before-hand when you are going to charge. Do you remember what I was like before the Rugby match last year and that was only a game?

I spent all this morning laying wire. We laid it rather well I thought, not a bit of it touching the ground until we reached the communication trenches, then of course we had to tie it down. It took four hours. I then reached the OP to find that we had just been told we were not to fire next day. Sic vos non vobis [*Thus do you, but not for yourselves*]. I don't mind that though, but we thought at first we were going back to do a month's training. Tin soldiering is worse than anything I know on earth.

The following year 1916 Whitehead took part in the Battle of the Somme. He wrote home again:

Our present position is just behind an old Hun trench in which we live. There are a lot of splendid dug-outs further up the trench 30 or 40 feet deep, but unfortunately the Hun left none behind him in the part we occupy. We have had three dug-outs dug down to about 20 feet, in which some of the men sleep and one is used for a telephone dug-out. I'm sleeping in one end of that now. I started at the bottom of the trench under the open sky when it was fine. Then when it looked like rain I moved to a little communication-trench from one of the gun-pits to the main trench. It had boards and corrugated iron over it, but a couple of nights ago we had some pretty heavy rain and I woke to find myself lying in a pool of water, my blankets wet through, the sides of the trench falling in and threatening to bury me and my bed and clothes. I'm sorry I didn't sleep in my clothes as I should have kept my things moderately dry, but I didn't and the trench fell in over my bags and my coat. I lost all my studs too, so at present, nobody having a spare one, I am wearing a 'British Warm' all day with the collar turned up.

October 20th 1916

In 1917 he wrote home once again describing conditions and talking about his attempts to join the Royal Flying Corps:

No one who hasn't been out can realise what it is like to sit in a trench from which you can't move and be shelled for hours with heavy stuff.... . then to walk home through hundreds of corpses in all stages of decomposition, to a dug-out a foot deep in water, and remember the Gunners are generally in action for a couple of months at a time. If I get into the RFC I shall try to become a pilot.... . The danger of spills is almost always due to over-confidence and carelessness, which is a very good reason why I shouldn't come to grief, if you think of it. Can you ever remember me trying to hit just because I had made fifty, or because I had hit a couple of fours unless there was no need for my side to make more runs? Well, I don't see myself doing unnecessary 'stunts' ... but we'll talk it over next weekend perhaps.

He got his wish and became a pilot with the Royal Flying Corps (from April 1918 Royal Air Force), serving with No. 53 Squadron flying R.E. 8s. He was shot down and killed by ground fire together with his observer, Second Lieutenant Reginald Hopkin Hill Griffiths MC at 7.50am on 17 October 1918 near Lauwe while artillery spotting. The mayor of Lauwe later wrote to Whitehead's father describing what happened:

Final Wicket

My Dear Sir,

Lauwe, December 28th 1918

On Thursday October 17th, at nine o'clock in the morning an English aeroplane appeared flying very low and carrying two persons, Lieutenant Whitehead and Lieutenant Griffiths. Your son raised himself in the machine, and with a flag in his hand, amid the cheers of the population, proclaimed our happy deliverance.

The aeroplane flew over the town repeatedly, always saluted by the inhabitants, until when flying near the Railway Station, which is twenty-five minutes walk from the centre of the town, it was fired at by German machine-guns. Flying at a low height it was hit by bullets which, alas, wounded your son and his observer. The machine made a steep dive and the lifeless bodies of your brave men were borne into a room in our hospital. They were buried the next day in the Military Cemetery by a party of English soldiers.

He is commemorated in the Harlebeke New British Cemetery in Belgium, grave reference I. D. 14. George Whitehead and Reginald Griffiths lie side by side.

His brother, James, played a single first-class match for the MCC in 1912.

Bating and fielding averages

	Mat	Inns	NO	Runs	HS	Ave	100	50	Ct	St
First-class	2	4	0	12	5	3.00	0	0	3	0

Bowling averages

	Mat	Balls	Runs	Wkts	BBI	BBM	Ave	Econ	SR	4w	5w	10
First-class	2	-	-	-	-	-	-	-	-	-	-	-

Lieutenant Colonel Arthur Houssemayne du Boulay DSO
Kent/Gloucestershire
Royal Engineers
AQMG Third Army, GHQ Royal Engineers.
Died 25 October 1918
Aged 38
Right-handed Bat/Right-arm Medium Pace.

'A big hitter in every sense of the word'

Arthur Houssemayne du Boulay was born on 18 June 1880 at 10 Medway Villas, New Brompton, Chatham, Kent, the eldest son of twelve children born to Colonel Woodforde George du Boulay and Rose du Boulay, née Hawkins. Educated at Cheltenham College, where he was in the XI in 1895, 1896 and 1897, captaining the side in 1897, he entered the Royal Military Academy Woolwich on leaving school. On 21 September 1909 he married Blanche Laura Hornung at Roffey and they had three children, Neville, Angela and Suzanne. The family resided at 3 West Halkin Street, Belgrave Square, London.

Du Boulay made nine first-class appearances between June 1899 and May 1910, all but two in the County Championship, five for Kent, three Gloucestershire and one for the MCC. His debut for Kent was against Somerset on 19 June 1899 in the County Championship at the Recreation Ground, Bath where he scored 49 not out in his first innings and, oddly, 49 not out in his second. He also took one wicket for 43 off fifteen overs; the match was drawn. His first appearance for Gloucestershire was on 24 August 1908 against Surrey in the County Championship, played at Ashley Down Ground, Bristol. He scored 21 in his only innings and Gloucestershire won by ten wickets.

He went on to play against Nottinghamshire, Middlesex, Lancashire, the visiting Australians, Gloucestershire and Sussex and played his final first-class match on 4 May 1910 for the MCC against Nottinghamshire at Lord's. He scored 18 in his only innings. The match was drawn.

Du Boulay made 303 first-class runs, his highest score being 58 against Nottinghamshire, took three wickets for 177, his best figures being one for 4 and made two catches. His final first-class match was for the MCC against Nottinghamshire on 4 May 1910 at Lord's and he scored 18 in his only innings. The match was drawn. He also played for The Royal Military Academy Woolwich, the Royal Engineers and represented the Army against the Navy in 1908, 1909 and 1910. A big-hitting batsman, he scored a remarkable 402 not out for the School of Military Engineering against the Royal Marines at Chatham.

Commissioned as a second lieutenant from the Gentlemen Cadets, Royal Military Academy Woolwich, into the Royal Engineers on 22 November 1899 du Boulay was promoted to lieutenant on 22 November 1902 and served in the Second Boer War in 1902, taking part in operations in the Transvaal, Orange River Colony and Cape Colony. He was promoted to captain on 4 December 1908 and was an assistant instructor at the School of Military Engineering between 1905 and 1908.

During the war du Boulay was promoted to major (18 August 1916) and then brevet lieutenant colonel (1 June 1917) and was appointed Deputy Assistant Adjutant and Quartermaster General. He was awarded the Distinguished Service Order (*London Gazette*, 3 June 1918) and was Mentioned in Despatches on five occasions as well as receiving the Order of Agricultural Merit (France), Officer of the Order of Leopold II with Palm (Belgium) and the Croix De Guerre (Belgium).

Arthur du Boulay died of illness at the 46th Casualty Clearing Station and 6th Stationary Hospital on 25th October 1918.

He is commemorated in the Fillievres British Cemetery, grave reference A. 36.

His brother, Second Lieutenant Hubert Lionel Houssemayne du Boulay, 3rd Battalion, attached to 1st Battalion Wiltshire Regiment was killed in action on 3 September 1916 and is commemorated on the Thiepval Memorial, France, Pier and Face 13 A.

His brother-in-law, John Peter Hornung MC, was killed in 1916.

Batting and fielding averages

	Mat	Inns	NO	Runs	HS	Ave	100	Ct	St
First-class	9	14	3	303	58	27.54	0	2	0

Bowling averages

	Mat	Balls	Runs	Wkts	BBI	Ave	Econ	SR	5w	10
First-class	9	264	177	3	1/4	59.00	4.02	88.0	0	0

Captain Hugh Jones MC
Gloucestershire
13th Bn The Gloucestershire Regiment
Died 10 November 1918
Aged 29
Not Known

The last first-class cricketer to die during the war

Hugh Jones was born on 21 December 1888 at Nass House, Lydney, Gloucestershire.

He made one first-class appearance for Gloucestershire against Worcestershire in a County Championship match on 6 July 1914 at the County Ground, Worcester. He scored 11 and zero and dropped an easy catch; the match was drawn due to rain. He served with the 13th Battalion Gloucestershire Regiment during the war, earning the Military Cross for bravery in 1916, (*London Gazette*, 23 October 1916):

Temp. Captain Hugh Jones, Gloucestershire Regiment.
For conspicuous gallantry during operations. While clearing trenches with his company after an attack, the enemy opened a heavy bombardment. He displayed the greatest courage whilst standing in the open under shellfire for two hours assisting his men to get into safety. Later he went by himself, under heavy shellfire, and fetched stretchers for his wounded.

He was wounded twice and, exhausted from his wounds and years of front line fighting, was sent home to recover, arriving on 2 November 1918. He died at the Fort Pitt Military Hospital in Chatham, of pneumonia following influenza on 10 November 1918, the final day of the war. Hugh Jones is commemorated in Lydney (St Mary) Churchyard, Gloucestershire, south of the church, on the main path.

Batting and fielding averages

	Mat	Inns	NO	Runs	HS	Ave	100	50	Ct	St
First-class	1	2	0	11	11	5.50	0	0	0	0

Bowling averages

	Mat	Balls	Runs	Wkts	BBI	BBM	Ave	Econ	SR	4w	5w	10
First-class	1	-	-	-	-	-	-	-	-	-	-	-

Major Reginald (Reggie) Oscar Schwarz MC
South Africa-Middlesex-Transvaal
6th King's Royal Rifle Corps, attd HQ, 1st Echelon
Died 18 November 1918
Aged 43
Right-handed Bat/Right-arm-medium, Right-arm off break

'He possessed the most supreme modesty and self-effacement'

Reginald Oscar Schwarz was born on 4 May 1875 in Lee, London. The son of Robert George Schwarz, a merchant from Bagshot in Surrey, he was educated at St Paul's School, London before going up to Christchurch College Cambridge in 1893. Although he failed to win his Blue for cricket he did win it for rugby, another sport in which he excelled, taking part in the Varsity match in 1893. He went on to represent England in three rugby union internationals against Scotland (1899), Wales and Ireland (1901). At club level, Schwarz played for Richmond, Middlesex and the Barbarians. After leaving university he became a member of the Stock Exchange (1911) and a partner in the firm of Parsons and Henderson.

Although an outstanding rugby player, it was as a cricketer that he was to find fame. Between May 1901 and July 1914 he made 125 first-class appearances including twenty Tests, playing his debut first-class match for Webbe's XI against Oxford University at the University Parks on 16 May 1901. He scored 7 and 35, took two wickets for 17 and caught Edward Dillion off the bowling of Foster Cunliffe for 8 and Richard More off the bowling of Cunliffe, again, for 22. A. J. Webbe's XI won by 168 runs. His final match was on 2 July 1914, playing for the L. G. Robinson's XI, at Old Buckingham Hall, Attleborough. He scored 8 and 3 not out and took one wicket for 75. The match was drawn. In between, he played first-class matches for the MCC, Middlesex, B. J. T. Bosanquet's XI and H. D. J. Leveson-Gower's XI.

In 1902 Schwarz emigrated to South Africa, working for Sir Abe Bailey, the well-known diamond dealer as his personal secretary. He continued playing first-class cricket, making his South African debut for the Transvaal on 6 April 1903 against Griqualand West at St George's Park, Port Elizabeth and scoring 12 not out. Transvaal won by 216 runs. He also represented South Africa in twenty Tests, helping to put South African cricket on the world map. His debut Test was against England on 2 January 1906 at Old Wanderers, Johannesburg. He scored 5 and 2 and took three wickets for 72 off twenty-one overs and made two catches, Frederick Flane off the bowling of George Faulkner for 1 and Ernest Hayes off the bowling of Sibley Snooke for 3. South Africa won by one wicket.

He made 374 Test runs, his highest score being 61, took fifty-five wickets for 1,417 runs. He also took eighteen wickets. Having learned to bowl a Googly from Bosanquet, he topped the South African bowling averages in 1904 and 1907. He was named *Wisden* cricketer of the year in 1908. Schwarz retired from regular play after the 1912 season, though he appeared thrice more for L. G. Robinson's XI over the next two seasons.

In August 1914 Schwarz served in German South West Africa and was Mentioned in Despatches . After Africa, he joined the 6th Battalion King's Royal Rifle Corps, joining the unit in France in January 1916. By 11 November 1918 Schwarz had been wounded twice, became a major and been given a staff job. He was awarded the Military Cross in the New Year's Honours list of 1917 (*London Gazette*, 1 January 1917).

Taken ill the day after the Armistice, and exhausted from years of fighting, Schwarz died of influenza on 18 November 1918. He is commemorated in the Étaples Military Cemetery, grave reference XLV, A. 4.

He played in a total of 125 first-class matches

Batting and fielding averages

	Mat	Inns	NO	Runs	HS	Ave	100	50	6s	Ct	St
Tests	20	35	8	374	61	13.85	0	1	1	18	0
First-class	125	192	24	3798	102	22.60	1	20		107	0

Bowling averages

	Mat	Inns	Balls	Runs	Wkts	BBI	BBM	Ave	Econ	SR	4w	5w	10
Tests	20	31	2639	1417	55	6/47	7/89	25.76	3.22	47.9	4	2	0
First-class	125		13553	7000	398	8/55		17.58	3.09	34.0		25	3

Lieutenant-Colonel Herbert Walter Green DSO
Europeans (India)
The Buffs (East Kent Regiment), attd 1st Bn The Queen's
(Royal West Surrey Regiment)
31 December 1918
Aged 40
Wicket-keeper

'A workman that needed not to be ashamed'

Herbert Walter Green was born on 2 April 1878 at Watford, Hertfordshire, England. The son of Walter James and Maria Jane Green of 13 Queen's Rd, Tunbridge Wells, he was educated at Charterhouse and was in the XI in 1896. Going up to Exeter College Oxford, he not only represented his college but also the Band of Brothers and Oxford Authentics XI.

Green received a university commission into The Buffs (East Kent Regiment) in 1900, shortly after leaving Exeter College. Like so much of the British Army, he served in India and played one first-class match for the Europeans (India). This was a Bombay Presidency Match against Parsees at Poona on 21 September 1903 at The Deccan Gymkhana Ground, Poona, in which Green scored 5 and 8 and caught both R. E. Modi off the bowling of Bruce Manson (killed in action on 4 November 1914) for 17 and B. Machhliwala off the bowling of Manson, once again for 7. The Parsees won by an innings and 6 runs.

When war broke out Green found himself serving in Nigeria with the West African Force. In 1916 he was posted to France where he commanded a battalion of the Essex Regiment, followed by the Buffs, serving with them on the Somme. He was promoted to acting brigadier general commanding 10 Infantry Brigade and was awarded the DSO (*London Gazette*, 18 January 1917), 'For gallant and distinguished service in the field'.

In October 1918 he commanded the 1st Battalion of the Queen's and was seriously wounded at Landrecies on 7 November 1918. He died on 31 December 1918 at No. 8 General Hospital at Rouen following surgery.

He is commemorated in the St Sever Cemetery Extension, Rouen, grave reference S. V. L. 13.

Batting and fielding averages

	Mat	Inns	NO	Runs	HS	Ave	100	50	Ct	St
First-class	1	2	0	13	8	6.50	0	0	2	0

Bowling averages

	Mat	Balls	Runs	Wkts	BBI	BBM	Ave	Econ	SR	4w	5w	10
First-class	1	-	-	-	-	-	-	-	-	-	-	-

Other Cricket Clubs Played For

FREE FORESTERS CRICKET CLUB

English amateur Cricket Club. Foresters were established in 1856 by the Rev. William Kirkpatrick, rector of Sutton Coldfield (In 1847 he had also set up the Sutton Coldfield Cricket Club), for players from the Midland Counties of England. It has no home ground and is a 'wandering' club. The name came from popularity of archery at Rectory Park before cricket was played there. Their first match was played against the Pilgrims of the Dee, on 20 July 1856 at Rectory Park, Sutton Coldfield. From 1912 their matches against both Oxford and Cambridge had first-class status. This practice stopped in 1968.

The team colours which were adopted in 1858 are crimson, green and white. Their badge consists of two capital Fs wrapped in a Hastings knot with the motto 'United though Untied'. Which basically means that Foresters are free to play for other clubs, and even play against Free Foresters.

I ZINGARI

I Zingari (also known as IZ, or The Gypsies) was established on 4 July 1845 by a group of Old Harrovians during a dinner party at the Blenheim Hotel on London's Bond Street. It has therefore become one of the oldest cricket clubs still playing and turns out about twenty times a year. I Zingari is a 'wandering' club, without a home ground. Uniquely for an amateur club, Wisden reported on all its matches between 1867 and 1905. The principles of the club were to foster the spirit of amateur cricket and the rules of the club were famously idiosyncratic (The Entrance fee be nothing and the Annual Subscription do not exceed the Entrance, to keep your promise, keep your temper and keep your wicket up.). William Boland, a barrister at law, was appointed the Perpetual President, and remains in that post even though dead. As a result, the leader of the club is termed the 'Governor'.

The club colours are black, red and gold, symbolizing the motto 'out of darkness, through fire, into light'.

BUTTERFLIES CRICKET CLUB

The Butterflies Cricket Club was founded in 1862 by Arthur Wilson and A.G.Guillemard, Rugbeians who had not won their first XI colors. They played their first match on 26 June 1863 against Forest School at Walthamstow. In 1864 membership was extended to young men who had been educated at Charterhouse, Eton, Harrow, Westminster, and Winchester. This has remained the situation ever since. In 1865 the Butterflies played the Paris club in France. This was the first visit by any English team. The club grew and by 1872 there were 212 members. The 1883 England test team that returned home from Australia with the ashes contained no fewer than six Butterflies. Thirteen Butterflies have been captain of England, including Sir Pelham Warner and Douglas Jardine. The club still plays around 30 fixtures a year.

INCOGNITI CRICKET CLUB

Incogniti cricket club was founded in 1861 and is the third oldest 'wandering' (without its own home ground) cricket club after I Zingari (1845) and Free Foresters (1856)

The club was founded after a match at Lords on 25 May 1861, when a scratch team captained by Charles Brune defeated the XYZ club.

The club's colours are purple, black and gold, and its club motto *Incogniti Incognitis* 'unknown only to the unknown' appears on the club's roll of honour on the first landing of the staircase in the pavilion at Lord's.

Passed distinguished member have included Arthur Conan Doyle, Reggie Schwarz and Douglas Jardine.

MARYLEBONE CRICKET CLUB (MCC)

The MCC is based at Lords Cricket Ground, St John's Wood, London. It was formerly the worldwide governing body of cricket. Marylebone Cricket Club was founded in 1787, although can trace its ancestry to the early 18th century (or earlier) when it was called 'The Nobleman's', 'The Cricket Club' or the 'Gentlemen's Club'. Thomas Lord, a professional bowler at the Whites Conduit (part of a popular sporting club based at the Star and Garter on Pall Mall) acquired the ground as a more private venue for players. 'The Gentleman's Club' then began to call themselves 'the Mary-le-bone-club'.

From the beginning of the twentieth century, the MCC organized the England cricket team and, outside of Test Matches the touring England team officially played as 'MCC' up to and including the 1976/77 tour of Australia. The club colours are scarlet and gold.

EUROPEANS (INDIA)

The Europeans cricket team was an Indian first-class cricket team which took part in the annual Bombay tournament. The team was founded by members of the European community in Bombay and played their cricket at the Bombay Gymkhana. The Europeans were involved in the Bombay tournament from its very beginnings in 1877. The Europeans accepted a challenge from the Parsees cricket team to take part in a two day match. At this time, the competition was known as the Presidency Match. They played first-class matches from 1892 to 1948.

There was also a European team composed of European cricketers from the Madras Presidency who played in the Madras Presidency Matches.

GENTLEMEN vs PLAYERS

This was a first-class match between teams consisting of amateurs (the Gentlemen) and professionals (the Players). The difference between the two was really defined by English class structure that was apparent during both the 19th and 20th centuries. The Players were basically working-class wage-earners who made their living from cricket. The Gentlemen were members of the middle and upper classes, who had learned to play the game on their public school cricket fields

The first match was played in 1806, with a second match the same year. However due to the Napoleonic wars it was not played again until 1819. After this it was played on an annual basis until with changes in society it was abolished by the MCC in 1963 when all first-class cricketers became professional. A total of 274 Gentlemen vs Players matches were played between 1806 and 1962. The Players won 125 games and the Gentlemen 68. There were also 80 draws and one tie.

H. D. G. LEVESON-GOWER'S XI

Sir Henry Dudley Gresham Leveson Gower (Shrimp) (8 May 1873 – 1 February 1954) played first class cricket for Oxford University and Surrey. He also captained the English Test Team. Leveson Gower became an England Test selector in 1909, and was chairman of selectors in 1924 and from 1927 to 1930. He was knighted for his services to cricket in 1953. Touring Test teams would play annually against H. D. G. Leveson-Gower's XI.

THE GENTLEMEN OF PHILADELPHIA

The Gentlemen of Philadelphia was a team that represented Philadelphia, Pennsylvania, in first-class cricket between 1878 and 1913. Even though the USA had played the very first international match against Canada in 1844, after that date the game in America began to decline. This decline was made worse by the rise in popularity of baseball. However the decline that was taking place in the rest of the country wasn't taking place in Philadelphia and cricket remained popular until the outbreak of World War One. Philadelphia produced a first class team that rivaled many others in the rest of the cricketing world. The team was made up of players from the four major cricket clubs in Philadelphia: Germantown, Merion Belmont and Philadelphia. Players from smaller clubs, such as Tioga and Moorestown and local colleges, such as Haverford and Penn also played for the Philadelphians. Over its 35 years, the team played in 88 first-class cricket matches. Of those they won 29, lost 45 and drew 13 with one game being abandoned.

Cricketers by Team

TEST CRICKETERS (12)

Major William Booth	(England/Yorkshire)
Kenneth Lotherington Hutchings	(England/Kent)
Leonard James Moon	(England/Cambridge/Middlesex)
Colin Blythe	(England/Kent)
Fred Cook	(South Africa/Easter Province)
Reginald Hands	(South Africa/Western Province)
Bill Lundie	(SA/Eastern Province/Transvaal/Western Province)
Claude Newberry	(South Africa/Transvaal)
Arthur Edward Ochse	(South Africa/Transvaal)
Reggie Shwarz	(South Africa/Middlesex/Transvaal)
Gordon White	(South Africa/Transvaal)
Tibby Cotter	(Australia/New South Wales)

HAMPSHIRE (23)

Evelyn Ridley Bradford	14 Sept 14
Arthur Maitland Byng (Jamaica)	14 Sept 14
John Thomas Gregory	27 Oct 14
Geoffrey Percy Robert Toynbee	15 Nov 14
George Amelius Crawshay Sandeman	26 April 15
Bernard Maynard Lucas Brodhurst	27 April 15
Kenneth Herbert Clayton Woodroffe (**Camb Univ/Sussex**)	9 May 15
Gordon Belcher	15 May 15
James Frederick Sutcliffe	14 July 15
Cecil Howard Palmer (**Worcestershire**)	26 July 15
Maxmillian David Francis Wood (**European India**)	22 Aug 15
Arthur Jaques	27 Sept 15
Francis Hugh Bacon	21 Oct 15
Alexander Gordon Cowie (**Cambridge University**)	7 April 16
Cecil Halliday Abercrombie	31 May 16
Alban Charles Phidias Arnold (**Cambridge University**)	7 July 16
Herbert James Rogers	12 Oct 16
Charles Henry Yaldren	23 Oct 16
Robert Wilfred Fairey Jesson	22 Feb 16
Cecil Herbert Bodington	11 April 17
Harold Thomas Forster	29 May 18
Henry Wilfred Persse	28 June 18
John Hugh Gunner	9 Aug 18

GLOUCESTETRSHIRE (18)

Wilfred Methven Brownlee	12 Oct 14
William Stanley Yalland	23 Oct 14
John Nathaniel Williams (**Hawke's Bay**)	25 April 15
Edmund Marsden	26 May 15
Claude Lysaght Mackay	7 June 15
Ronald Turner	15 Aug 15
Theodore Humphry Fowler	17 Aug 15
Burnet George James	26 Sept 15
Francis Bernard Roberts (**Cambridge Univ**)	8 Feb 16
Oswald Eric Wreford-Brown	7 July 16

John William Washington Nason (**Camb Univ**)	26 Dec 16
Ernest Ewart Gladstone Alderwick	26 Aug 17
Donald Lacy Priestley	30 Oct 17
Hugo Francis Wemyss Charteris	23 April 16
Thomas Archibald Truman	13 Sept 18
William St Clair Grant	26 Sept 18
Arthur Houssemayne Du Boulay (Kent)	25 Oct 18
Hugh Jones	10 Nov 18

MIDDLESEX (17)

Bernard Charles Gordon Lennox	10 Nov 14
Wilfred Stanley Bird (Oxford University)	9 May 15
Guy Greville Napier (MCC, **Europeans (India), Cambridge University**)	25 Sept 15
John Wyndham Hamilton McCulloch	21 Oct 15
Sholto Douglas	28 Jan 16
Harry Broderick Chinnery (Surrey)	28 May 16
Cecil Argo Gold	3 July 16
Foster Hugh Egerton Cunliffe (**Oxford University**)	10 July 16
William Manstead Benton	17 Aug 17
John Henry Sneyd Hunt	16 Sept 16
Leonard James Moon (**England, Cambridge Univ**)	23 Nov 16
Maurice Edward Coxhead (**Oxford University**)	3 May 17
Richard Percy Lewis (**Oxford University**)	7 Sept 17
Alan Ivo Steel	8 Oct 17
Clifford Allen Saville	8 Nov 17
Leonard George Colbeck (**Europeans (India), Cambridge University**)	3 Jan 18
Reginald Oscar Schwarz (South Africa, Transvaal)	18 Nov 18

SOMERSET (13)

Harold Edwin Hippisley	23 Oct 14
Ralph Escott Hancock	29 Oct 14
Hervey Robert Charles Tudway	18 Nov 14
Charles Gerrard Deane	14 Dec 14
Percy D'Aguilar Banks	26 April 15
Frederick Cecil Banes-Walker	9 May 15
Hubert Frederic Garrett	4 June 15
Frederick Percy Hardy	9 March 16
Leonard Cecil Leicester Sutton	3 June 16
John Alexander Hellard	1 July 16
Ernest Shorrocks	20 July 16
Edwin John Leat	8 June 18
Oswald Massey Samson (**Oxford University**)	17 Sept 18

WORCESTERSHIRE (10)

Arnold Stearns Nesbitt	7 Nov 14
Frederick Bonham Burr	12 March 15
John Edmund Valentine Isaac	9 May 15
Cecil Howard Palmer (**Hampshire**)	26 July 15
Bernard Philip Nevile	11 Feb 16
Harold Godfrey Bache (**Cambridge University**)	15 Feb 16
William Beaumont Burns	7 July 16
Arthur Whitmore Isaac	7 July 16
Christopher George Arthur Collier	25 Aug 16
John Francis Sartorius Winnington	22 Sept 18

Final Wicket

KENT (8)

Kenneth Lotherington Hutchings (**England**)	3 Sept 16
Ernest Herbert Simpson	2 Oct 17
Colin Blythe (**England**)	8 Nov 17
Lawrence Julius Le Fleming	21 March 18
David William Jennings	6 Aug 18
Charles Eric Hatfeild (**Oxford University**)	21 Sept 18
Charles Eric Edendale Whitehead	17 Oct 18
Arthur Houssemayne Du Boulay (**Gloucestershire**)	25 Oct 18

SUSSEX (8)

Arthur Horace Lang (**Cambridge University**)	25 Jan 15
Kenneth Herbert Clayton Woodroffe (**Cambridge University and Hampshire**)	9 May 15
Geoffrey Charles Walter Dowling	30 July 15
Bernard Henry Holloway	27 Sept 15
George Lumley Whatford	22 Nov 15
Charles Denis Fisher (**Oxford University**)	31 May 16
John William Washington Nason (**Cambridge University-Gloucestershire**)	26 Dec 16
Ernest Herbert Relf	27 July 18

SURREY (7)

Esme Fairfax Chinnery	18 Jan 15
Wilfred John Hutton Curwen (**Oxford University**)	9 May 15
Alan Marshal (**Queensland**)	23 July 15
Harry Broderick Chinnery	28 May 16
Francis Bertram Myers	15 Sept 16
Henry George Blacklidge	23 May 17
John Edward Raphael (**Oxford and London County**)	11 June 17

WARWICKSHIRE (7)

William Hugh Holbech (**MCC**)	1 Nov 14
Norman Kingsley Street	10 Aug 15
Alexander Basil Crawford (**Nottinghamshire**)	10 May 16
Percy Jeeves	22 July 16
Samuel Harold Bates	28 Aug 16
Harold James Goodwin (**Cambridge University**)	24 April 17
Reginald George Pridmore	13 March 18

NOTTINGHAMSHIRE (6)

Ralph Eustace Hemingway	15 Oct 15
Alexander Basil Crawford (**Warwickshire**)	10 May 16
William Riley	9 Aug 17
Charles Pepper	13 Sept 17
Harvey Staunton	14 Jan 18
Harold Augustus Hodges	24 March 18

DERBYSHIRE (6)

Frank Miller Bingham	22 May 15
Charles Neil Newcombe	27 Dec 15
Arthur Marsden	31 July 16
Geoffrey Laird Jackson (**Oxford University**)	9 April 17
Guy Denis Wilson	30 Nov 17
Charles Barnett Fleming	22 Sept 18

ESSEX (6)

Geoffrey Boisselier Davies (**Cambridge University**)	26 Sept 15
Frank Street	7 July 16

Henry David Keigwin (**Scotland**) — 20 Sept 16
Edward Charles Coleman — 2 April 17
Ralf Hubert Robinson — 23 Aug 17
James Valiant — 28 Oct 17

LANCASHIRE (5)
John Asquith Atkinson Nelson — 12 Aug 17
Harold Gwyer Garnett (**AC MacLaren's XI /Gentleman/ Argentina**) — 3 Dec 17
William Knowles Tyldesley — 26 April 18
Egerton Lowndes Wright (**Oxford University**) — 11 May 18
Alfred Hartley — 9 Oct 18

LEICESTERSHIRE (3)
Harold Wright (**MCC**) — 14 Sept 15
Arthur Edward Davis — 4 Nov 16
William Ward Odell (**London County**) — 4 Oct 17

NORTHAMPTONSHIRE (3)
James Henry Aloysius Ryan (**Ireland**) — 25 Sept 15
Sydney Thomas Askham — 21 Aug 16
Charles Bryan Tomblin — 1 June 18

YORKSHIRE (2)
Major William Booth (**England**) — 1 July 16
Fairfax Gill — 1 Nov 17

OXFORD UNIVERSITY (25)
Mark Kincaid Mackenzie — 25 Sept 14
Frederick Harding Turner — 10 Jan 15
Ronald Owen Lagden — 3 March 15
George King Molineux (**Gentleman of England**) — 5 May 15
Wilfred Stanley Bird (**Middlesex**) — 9 May 15
Wilfred John Hutton Curwen (**Surrey**) — 9 May 15
Douglas Robert Brandt — 6 July 15
Geoffrey Dayrell Wood — 13 Oct 15
Frank Noel Tuff — 5 Nov 15
Charles Dennis Fisher (**Sussex**) — 31 May 16
Foster Hugh Egerton Cunliffe (**Middlesex**) — 10 July 16
George Bruce Gilroy — 15 July 16
William Gerald Knox Boswell — 28 July 16
Richard Percy Lewis (**Middlesex**) — 7 Sept 17
George Bruce Gilroy — 15 July 16
Edward Alfred Shaw — 7 Oct 16
Arthur Franklin Willmer — 20 Sept 16
Charles Frearson Younger (**Scotland**) — 21 March 17
Geoffrey Laird Jackson (**Derbyshire**) — 9 April 17
Maurice Edward Coxhead (**Middlesex**) — 3 May 17
Egerton Lowndes Wright (**Lancashire**) — 11 May 18
Ludovic Heathcoat-Amory — 25 Aug 18
Donald Clark Johnston — 13 Sept 18
Oswald Massey Samson (**Somerset**) — 17 Sept 18
Charles Eric Hatfeild (**Kent**) — 21 Sept 18

CAMBRIDGE UNIVERSITY (20)
Archer Windsor Clive — 25-Aug-14
Eustace Crawley — 2 Nov 14

Arthur Horace Lang (**Sussex**)   25 Jan 15
Charles Howard Eyre   25 Sept 15
Geoffrey Boisseller Davies (**Essex**)   26 Sept 15
Eric Frank Penn   18 Oct 15
Francis Bernard Roberts (**Glous**)   8 Feb 16
Harold Godfrey Bache (**Worcestershire**)   15 Feb 16
Alexander Gordon Cowie (**Hampshire**)   7 April 16
Gerald Howard Smith   29 March 16
Alban Charles Phidias Arnold (**Hampshire**)   7 July 16
Edward Stone Phillips   8th May 15
Geoffrey William Van Der Hopley   12 May 15
Kenneth Herbert Clayton Woodroffe (**Hampshire/Sussex**)   13 May 15
Cyril Stanley Rattigan   13 Nov 16
John William Washington Nason (**Gloucs/Sussex**)   26 Dec 16
Harold James Goodwin (**Warwickshire**)   24 April 17
Edward Hedley Cuthbertson   24 July 17
Logie Colin Leggatt   31 July 17
Lestock Handley Adams   22 April 18

MCC (13)

Payne Gallwey (**Army**)   14 Sept 14
Gerald Ernest Francis Ward   30th Oct 14
George Arthur Murray Docker   17 Nov 14
Edmund Peel Thomson   21 Dec 14
William Mackworth Parker (**Army**)   30 July 15
Leslie William Davidson   3 Aug 15
Harold Wright (**Leicestershire**)   14 Sept 15
Attwood Alfred Torrens   8 Dec 16

ARMY (4)

William Thomas Payne-Gallwey (**MCC**)   14 Sept 14
Walter Evelyn Parke   13 Oct 14
Hugh Montagu Butterworth (**Oxford University**)   25 Sept 15
George Henry Neale   28 Sept 15
Joseph Williams   10 July 16
Brian Danvers Butler   18 Aug 16
Charles George Edgar Farmer   18 Aug 16
Charles Ernest Higginbotham (**SA Army**)   11 March 15
William Mackworth Parker (**MCC**)   11 March 15
Meredith Magniac (**South African Army**)   25 April 17

ROYAL NAVY (2)

John Matthew Murray   31 May 16
Frederick Hugh Geoffrey Trumble   10 May 18

EUROPEAN (INDIA) (21)

William Miles Kington   20 Oct 14
Henry Lawrence Anderson   29 Oct 14
Steuart Ronald Gordon   31 Oct 14
Bruce Edward Alexander Manson   3/4 Nov 14
William George Sydney Cadogan   12 Nov 14
De Courcy Ireland   28 Jan 15
Francis Whitechurch Townend   29 March 15
Henry Louis Rosher   14 April 15
Eustace Frederick Rutter   13 May 15

Francis Hunt Gould	6 June 15
Maxmillian David Francis Wood (**Hampshire**)	21 Aug 15
Arthur Corbett Edwards (**Orange Free State**)	25/26 Sept 15
Guy Greville Napier (**Middlesex, Cambridge University, MCC, Gentlemen vs Players**)	25 Sept 15
Kenelm Rees McCloughin (**Free Foresters, RD Robinson's XI, Army**)	26 Sept 15
Edward Campion	25 Feb 16
William Drysdale	29 Sept 16
Percy Macclesfield Heath	14 July 17
Leonard George Colbeck (**Middlesex /Cambridge University**)	3 Jan 18
Eric Anthony Rollo Gore-Brown	3 July 18
William Oliver Matless Mosse	10 Oct 18
Herbert Walter Green	31 Dec 18

IRELAND (5)

James Henry Aloysius Ryan (**Northamptonshire**)	25 Sept 15
Francis Henry Browning	26 April 16
George Frederick Macnamara	17 Aug 16
William Robert Gregory	23 Jan 18
Arthur Cyril Bateman	28 March 18

SCOTLAND (7)

James Elliot Balfour-Melville	25 Sept 15
David Kennedy	1 July 16
William Greive	18 July 16
Henry David Keigwin (**Essex**)	20 Sept 16
Walter Greive	1 April 17
William Grant Spruell Stuart	23 April 17
John Congreve Murray	23 Sept 17

NEW ZEALAND (17)

Anthony Frederick Wilding (**Canterbury**)	9 May 15
Alan Wallace (**Auckland**)	10 May 15
Hugh Latimer Tuke (**Hawk's Bay**)	7 June 15
Tomas Marshall Percy Grace (**Wellington**)	8 Aug 15
Albert Ernest Pratt (**Auckland**)	19 July 16
Andrew Moncrieff Given (**Otago**)	19 July 16
Frank Dredge (**Wellington**)	22 Aug 16
Rupert George Hickmott (**Canterbury**)	16 Sept 16
John Nathaniel Williams (**Hawk's Bay/Glouc**)	25 April 15
Roland George Blinko (**Hawke's Bay**)	6 Jan 17
Gilbert Howe (**Wellington**)	10 Jan 17
James Gordon Kinvig (**Wellington**)	1 July 17
Vivian Claude Kavanagh (**Auckland**)	9 Aug 17
Thomas James Bryden (**Otago**)	12 Oct 17
James William Hugh Bannermann (**Southland**)	23 Dec 17
Walter Malcolm (**Otago**)	23 Dec 17
Robert William Barry (**Canterbury**)	3 Dec 15

AUSTRALIA (16)

Charles James Backman (**South Australia**)	25/29 April 15
Alan Marshal (**Queensland/Surrey**)	23 July 15
Matthew Stanley McKenzie (**Tasmania**)	8 Dec 15
Frank Leslie Lugton (**Victoria**)	29 July 16
Edward Lionel Austin Butler (**Tasmania**)	23 Aug 16

William Keith Eltham (**Tasmania**)	31 Dec 16
Laurence Frank Gatenby (**Tasmania**)	14 Jan 17
George Augustus Poeppel (**Queensland**)	2 Feb 17
Norman Frank Callaway (**New South Wales**)	3 May 17
Hubert George Selwyn-Smith (**Queensland**)	7 June 17
Frederick Bisset Collins (**Victoria**)	4 Oct 17
Richard Angwin Rail (**Western Province**)	9 Oct 17
Gother Robert Carlisle Clarke (**New South Wales**)	12 Oct 17
Albert 'Tibby' Cotter (**Australia/New South Wales**)	31 Oct 17
Osborne Henry Douglas (**Tasmania**)	24 April 18
Ernest Frederick Parker (**Western Australia**)	2 May 18
Charles Young Adamson (**Queensland**)	17 Sept 18

SOUTH AFRICA (23)

Norman Seraphio Hobson (**Eastern Province**)	25 Nov 14
Charles Reginald Handfield (**Transvaal**)	6 May 15
John Edmund Valentine Isaac (**OFS, Worcestershire**)	9 May 15
Frederick James Cook (**South Africa, Easter Province**)	30 Nov 15
William Henry de Rockstro Malraison (**Transvaal**)	31 May 16
Garnet Edwin Driver (**Griqualand West**)	7 Sept 16
Claude Ludovic Hickman Mulcahy (**Natal**)	11 July 16
Donald Eric Carlsson (**Transvaal**)	14 July 16
Claude Newberry (**South Africa, Transvaal**)	1 Aug 16
Charles William Rorich Minnaar (**Western Province**)	16 Nov 16
James Stewart Swallow (**Border**)	17 Nov 16
Donald Mcintosh Sinclair (**Transvaal**)	11/13 July 16
William Eric Carlsson (**Western Province**)	14 July 16
Henry Bernard Stricker (**Transvaal**)	15 Feb 17
Richard Stanley Worsley (**Orange Free State**)	4 May 17
Eric Balfour Lundie (**South Africa-Eastern Province-Transvaal-Western Province**)	12 Sept 17
Edward William Marvin (**Transvaal**)	24 March 18
Arthur Edward Ochse (**South Africa and Transvaal**)	11 April 18
Reginald Harry Myburgh Hands (**South Africa/Western Province**)	20 April 18
Karl Otto Siedle (**Natal**)	30 May 18
Archibald Newcombe Difford (**Transvaal, Western Province**)	20 Sept 18
Gordon Charles White (**South Africa/Transvaal**)	17 Oct 18
Reginald Oscar Schwarz (**South Africa-Middlesex-Transvaal**)	18 Nov 18

OTHER SIDES (16)

Leonard Slater (**Gentlemen of the South**)	14 Sept 14
Arthur Maitland Byng (**Jamaica/Hampshire**)	14 Sept 14
Rowland Raw (**Gentleman of England**)	7 Aug 15
Wilfred Francis Reay (**Gentlemen of England**)	8 Oct 15
Joseph Edward Lynch (**Gentlemen of Ireland**)	25 Sept 15
William Magee Crozier (**Dublin University**)	1 July 16
Gilbert Sackville (**Lord Sheffield's XI, Earl de la Warr's XI**)	16 Dec 15
Francis Stuart Wilson (**Jamaica**)	24 May 15
Herbert Packer Bailey (**Barbados**)	31 July 17
Harry Ernest Charles Biedermann (**Argentina**)	10 Aug 17
William Ward Odell (**Leicestershire/London County**)	4 Oct 17
Theodore Arthur Tapp (**London County**)	21 Oct 17
John Argentina Campbell (**Argentina**)	2 Dec 17
Harold Gwyer Garnett (**Lancashire/AC MacLaren's XI /Gentleman v. Players**)	3 Dec 17
Ellis Louis George Neville Grell (**Trinidad and Tobago**)	5 June 18
Frederick Henri Abraham (**British Guiana**)	2 Oct 18